W9-AVY-775

Praise for Destinations

"The explanations, whether of grammatical principles, the modes, or the theory and practice of reading, writing, and thinking, are clear, straightforward, and easy to understand without being condescending. . . . The writing samples and exercises are thought-provoking, engaging, and appropriate to the level of the students, both where they are in their writing ability and where they need to be."

—*Sandra Barnhill Stephenson*, South Plains College

"[*Destinations* will be] of great value to students and teachers alike . . . This book is the best I've seen for sound rhetorical grounding and ample, on-the-spot, meaningful workbook exercises."

—*Julie Ann Mix*, Wayne State University

"I've told everyone in our department about this book! I think it's a very comprehensive text; I also find it appropriate for this level. I think it is far superior to other books currently available."

—*Susan R. Spence*, University of Texas at El Paso

"This text draws upon the latest research in collaborative, interactive learning to encourage students who are most timid about their writing to become more confident. . . . It is creative and interesting and encourages students to be the same by asking critical questions."

—*Janet M. Wallet-Ortiz*, Western New Mexico University

"[*Destinations*] is a solid text that would be an excellent choice for developmental students. It covers every aspect of teaching basic writing."

—*Ray Foster*, Scottsdale Community College

"[*Destinations*] has some of the best models that I have seen in a text for this level."

—*Margo L. Eden-Camann*, Georgia Perimeter College/Clarkston

"I cannot say enough about the reading selections and how the exercises are built around the readings. [*Destinations*] is a workbook that really provides students with space to *work* and exercises that transfer integration into application and, hopefully, mastery of skills."

—*Dornell L. Woolford*, Wor-Wic Community College

"The readings are interesting and of high caliber. This book takes the writing process very seriously."

—*Melissa Matters*, Southern California Bible College and Seminary

"[*Destinations*] does more with visuals and photos as a way to engage the student and start him or her off on the writing process than any other book I've seen."

—*Teresa Kozek*, Housatonic Community College

"[*Destinations*] has a character of its own that is fresh and useful."

—*Donald Brotherton*, DeVry University

Copyright © 2007, The McGraw-Hill Companies, Inc. All rights reserved.

For our students at HFCC
Also for Geoff, Scott, Lisa,
David, and Tiziana

To access premium
content in
www.mhhe.com/destinations
Please use the
following code:
G8JR-Y9P7-TTEH-9487-THW4

DESTINATIONS

UPDATE EDITION

An Integrated Approach to Writing Paragraphs and Essays

Richard E. Bailey

Henry Ford Community College

Linda Denstaedt

Oakland Writing Project

Boston   Burr Ridge, IL   Dubuque, IA   Madison, WI   New York   San Francisco   St. Louis
Bangkok   Bogotá   Caracas   Kuala Lumpur   Lisbon   London   Madrid   Mexico City
Milan   Montreal   New Delhi   Santiago   Seoul   Singapore   Sydney   Taipei   Toronto

The McGraw·Hill Companies

Higher Education

Published by McGraw-Hill, an imprint of The McGraw-Hill Companies, Inc., 1221 Avenue of the Americas, New York, NY 10020. Copyright © 2007 by The McGraw-Hill Companies, Inc. All rights reserved. No part of this publication may be reproduced or distributed in any form or by any means, or stored in a database or retrieval system, without the prior written consent of The McGraw-Hill Companies, Inc., including, but not limited to, any network or other electronic storage or transmission, or broadcast for distance learning.

Some ancillaries, including electronic and print components, may not be available to customers outside the United States.

This book is printed on acid-free paper.

1 2 3 4 5 6 7 8 9 0 QWD/QWD 0 9 8 7 6

Student Edition ISBN-13: 978-0-07-340714-2
ISBN-10: 0-07-340714-3

Instructor's Edition ISBN-13: 978-0-07-329222-9
ISBN-10: 0-07-329222-2

Editor-in-chief: *Emily Barrosse*
Publisher: *Lisa Moore*
Sponsoring editor: *John Kindler*
Editorial assistant: *Jesse Hassenger*
Marketing manager: *Lori DeShazo*
Media producer: *Alexander Rohrs*
Media project manager: *Marc Mattson*
Production supervisor: *Tandra Jorgensen*
Project manager: *Christina Gimlin*
Manuscript editor: *Andrea McCarrick*
Design manager: *Cassandra Chu*
Cover designer: *Yvo Riezebos*
Interior designer: *Glenda King*
Art editor: *Katherine McNab*
Manager, photo research: *Brian J. Pecko*

Composition: *10/12 Sabon by ICC*
Printing: *45# Scholarly Matte, Quebecor Dubuque*

Cover photo: © Redseal/Digitalvision

The credits section for this book begins on page C-1 and is considered an extension of the copyright page.

Library of Congress Cataloging-in-Publication Data

Bailey, Richard E., 1952–
    Destinations : an integrated approach to writing paragraphs and essays / Richard E. Bailey, Linda Denstaedt.
        p.   cm.
    Includes index.
    ISBN-13: 978-0-07-340714-2
    ISBN-10: 0-07-340714-3 (alk. paper)
    1. English language—Paragraphs—Problems, exercises, etc.   2. English language—Rhetoric—Problems, exercises, etc.   3. Report writing—Problems, exercises, etc.   4. College readers.   I. Denstaedt, Linda.   II. Title.

PE1439.B29   2004
808'.042—dc22
                                                                    2004060951

www.mhhe.com

Contents

Copyright © 2007, The McGraw-Hill Companies, Inc. All rights reserved.

Copyright © 2007, The McGraw-Hill Companies, Inc. All rights reserved.

PART THREE   INTEGRATING PATTERNS: SPECIAL ASSIGNMENTS 213

CHAPTER 14 THE ARGUMENTATIVE ESSAY 285

PART FOUR   A TOOL KIT   323

CHAPTER 15 BUILDING VOCABULARY 324

Copyright © 2007, The McGraw-Hill Companies, Inc. All rights reserved.

**PART FIVE   READING AND THINKING CRITICALLY:
                TEXTS AND VISUALS   457**

Copyright © 2007, The McGraw-Hill Companies, Inc. All rights reserved.

About the Authors

RICHARD E. BAILEY has taught English at Henry Ford Community College since 1976. He has directed a number of interdisciplinary curriculum development projects, with funding from the National Endowment for the Humanities and the National Science Foundation. In recognition of that work Rick was recognized as an Outstanding Educator of the Year at Michigan's Trends in Occupational Education conference and, for collaborative projects, with the 2001 Millennium Team Award given by Michigan's Liberal Arts Network for Development. Past president of the Community College Humanities Association, he has published three books for middle school language arts educators (Frank Shaffer Publications, 1993, 1994, 1995) and a creative writing book, *The Creative Writer's Craft: Lessons in Poetry, Fiction, and Drama,* for high school and community college level students (National Textbook Company, 1998). Each summer he directs the Cranbrook Writers' Guild Conference for promising poets and fiction writers in Michigan. In addition to book-length publications, he has published poems, short stories, and freelance articles in popular magazines and journals.

LINDA DENSTAEDT is currently the co-director of the Oakland Writing Project (University of Michigan), an affiliate of the National Writing Project. She works as an educational consultant, conducting workshops for writing teachers, coaching teachers of disadvantaged students, and facilitating writing retreats for educators. She is a member of Michigan Classroom Discourse Group, focusing on discourse analysis and ethnographic, action research on writing and student engagement. Linda co-authored *The Creative Writer's Craft: Lessons in Poetry, Fiction, and Drama* for National Textbook–McGraw-Hill and five other texts on writing, grammar and reading comprehension for Instructional Fair. A National Board Certified Teacher, Linda designed and implemented the Communication Arts Center (CAC) at Clarkston High School, a writing center to develop student writers and staff expertise in literacy and writing across the curriculum. Her work was featured in *Publishing with Students: A Comprehensive Guide* by Chris Weber (Heinemann) and selected by Michigan Education Association for a television commercial series, *Public Schools Work,* that showcases innovative programs. Michigan Council of Teachers of English recognized her as Creative Writing Teacher of the Year in 1996. She is a frequent presenter at state, regional, and national conferences.

Preface to the Instructor

"One's destination is never a place but rather a new way of looking at things."

—*Henry Miller*

WRITING: PART OF THE JOURNEY

One of our primary goals in teaching writing is to change the way our students look at writing. Far too often, students come to the first day of class thinking of the course as something simply to "get through," something without any real connection to what goes on outside the classroom—either in their lives, in other courses, or in their jobs. The strategies we devised to change their minds helped inspire and shape *Destinations,* a textbook that explores how college writing—specifically writing paragraphs and essays—can enhance students' lives and help them achieve their goals.

Destinations attempts to keep students focused on the big picture and to help them become active, "real-life" writers by offering an integrated approach to composition. In an integrated approach, reading is treated as a prelude to speech, speech as a prelude to composition, and composition as a prelude to further speech and further refinement of thinking. In an integrated classroom, reading, speaking, listening, thinking, and writing activities all assist students in developing as writers. Even as the text breaks writing down into helpful stages, parts, and patterns, it emphasizes that writing is a fully integrated process. Each leg of the journey is important, but in the end, the steps are all connected.

FOUR KEY FEATURES THAT DISTINGUISH *DESTINATIONS* FROM OTHER WRITING TEXTS

- **Integrated Coverage of Process and Skills.** *Destinations* takes students through the **writing process** in each chapter, not just once in a chapter on process. Prewriting, drafting, and revising are taught in a **decision-making model** based on **self-assessment** and **peer feedback,** and they feature **real student walk-throughs.** Editing is taught in context in each writing process chapter, stressing its crucial importance as a step in effective communication. **"Editing Focus"** sections help students see how avoiding comma splices or aiming for sentence variety works in real papers, not just in isolation; for more detailed coverage, these sections are cross-referenced with the **Tool Kit** (handbook) section of the text.

- **Integrated Paragraph-to-Essay Instruction.** *Destinations* devotes special attention to the transition between writing paragraphs and essays. **"Going to the Next Level"** sections in assignment chapters show students how to take the skills they have mastered in writing and developing paragraphs and apply them in larger, more complex assignments. Connections between the reasons we write and the patterns we choose to write in are explained and emphasized, and assignment chapters also devote time to the discussion, illustration, and recognition (in professional and student writing) of **mixing patterns.**

Copyright © 2007, The McGraw-Hill Companies, Inc. All rights reserved.

- **Integrated Approaches to Writing and Language Learning.** *Destinations* emphasizes that learning to write is not simply ticking off boxes next to a list of skills; it's not divorced from the other ways in which we use language every day; and it's not something that we do only in classrooms, as an expression of our "student" selves. Writing relates in essential ways to reading, speaking, and thinking, and it has everything to do with who we are outside of the classroom walls. **A wide variety of exercises,** as well as **Destinations Boxes,** help students use thinking, reading, writing, and speaking skills throughout the process—and draw connections between them.

- **Integrated Practice and Models.** Because students learn best by doing, we've kept blocks of explanatory text to a minimum. Instead, each chapter provides abundant opportunities—**8 to 30+ exercises per chapter**—for writing practice. These exercises go far beyond the "skill-and-drill" basics, allowing students to engage with tasks and processes while learning about them. There are also ample opportunities to learn by example. Each chapter offers **examples of successful student writing,** as well as **student work that may need improvement and reworking;** exercises related to these models provide opportunities for individual students or small groups to apply their critical reading and assessment skills. These selections were chosen from an extensive database of actual student models, and the related activities and analysis stem from years of classroom research. Additional exercises and samples are available in the Tool Kit, the Instructor's Manual, and the online support materials.

DESTINATIONS ALSO OFFERS . . .

- **47 Professional Readings, 12 Black and White Photographs.** Throughout the text, and most specifically in Chapter 21, professional readings and visuals deal with a variety of topics of interest to student writers. Selections range in length and difficulty so students can prepare for the challenging reading and thinking work ahead of them in more advanced college courses. Chapter 21 also includes a **section on "reading" and analyzing visuals.**

- **Chapter Maps and Destinations Boxes.** The **Chapter Map** that opens each chapter (with the exception of those in the Tool Kit) serves as a quick guide to its contents. Each chapter also features a **Destinations Box,** which highlights some specific ways students can apply the skills and processes from that chapter to their personal lives, in the classroom, and on the job. For instance, the Destinations Box for Chapter Nine—Definition—emphasizes the importance of defining words and ideas when discussing a movie with friends, limiting your point in a paper, or explaining a policy to coworkers and customers.

- **Integrated Technology.** (OLC) appears in the margins of the book to let students know they can go online to www.mhhe.com/destinations for more help or further practice with related topics. See "Online Learning Center" under "Supplements" for more details.

- **Integrated Writer's Workout Prompts.** In this updated edition of *Destinations,* we've added icons throughout the text, alerting students and instructors to additional exercises available on *Writer's Workout,* a powerful online learning resource that helps students improve their writing skills. *Writer's Workout* includes diagnostic quizzes; interactive mini-lessons covering grammar, sentence structure, punctuation, and essay writing; excerpts from professional writers; and more.

A USER'S MAP

- **Part One: An Introduction to College Writing** presents a strategies-based overview of the demands of college writing and reading, with a variety of exercises that span all elements of language learning. Students will address questions of purpose and audience, learn the basics of the writing process, and determine their own writing goals.

- **Part Two: Structuring College Writing** walks students through six commonly used patterns of paragraph development—illustration and example, narration, process, cause and effect, comparison/contrast, and definition. Students have a chance to take their writing to "the next level" and expand their paragraph ideas into full-length essay assignments. In each chapter, a walkthrough of sample student writing includes a special editing focus, illustrating in-context use of grammar and sentence skills.

- **Part Three: Integrating Patterns: Special Assignments** gives students the chance to practice common reading-thinking-writing processes that include writing with research (from finding and using sources to avoiding plagiarism), preparing for the essay exam, and mastering expository writing. It also includes a chapter (and assignments) on writing effective arguments.

- **Part Four: A Tool Kit** is a valuable resource and workbook for grammar review, strategy development, or practice in specific skills, including (but not limited to) vocabulary development, sentence basics, sentence variety, punctuation and grammar, and critical reading and thinking strategies. We know instructors often feel strongly—one way or the other—about grammar's place in the writing classroom, and this part of the book is flexible; it could be part of your syllabus or serve as an out-of-class reference/practice book for students.

- **Part Five: Reading and Thinking Critically: Texts and Visuals** features a number of readings and visuals for students to respond to and discuss as they learn to enhance textual and visual literacy. This section of the text focuses largely on critical reading and thinking strategies. Apparatus will prompt students to read interactively, and to craft responses before, during, and after reading a selection, to deepen their understanding and appreciation of the text.

SUPPLEMENTS TO ACCOMPANY *DESTINATIONS*

For the Student

- **Online Learning Center at www.mhhe.com/destinations.** This resource-rich Web site that accompanies *Destinations* is powered by Catalyst, McGraw-Hill's premier online tool for writing and research. Students will find over 3,000 grammar and usage exercises, Bibliomaker software that helps them format source information in one of five documentation styles, an online source evaluation tutorial, and much, much more. **OLC** appears in the margins of the book to let students know they can go online to www.mhhe.com/destinations for more help or further practice with related topics.

- **A number of helpful dictionaries, thesauri, and other reference tools** are available inexpensively when packaged with this text:
  - Random House Webster's College Dictionary (0-07-240011-0)
  - Merriam-Webster Paperback Dictionary (0-07-310067-6)

Copyright © 2007, The McGraw-Hill Companies, Inc. All rights reserved.

- Merriam-Webster Student Notebook Dictionary (0-07-299091-0)
- Merriam-Webster Paperback Thesaurus (0-07-310067-6)
- Merriam-Webster Notebook Thesaurus (0-07-310068-4)
- Merriam-Webster Vocabulary Builder (0-07-310069-2)
- Merriam-Webster Collegiate Dictionary/Thesaurus CD-ROM (0-07-310070-6)

For the Instructor

- **Annotated Instructor's Edition of *Destinations*** (ISBN 0-07-249992-3). This version of *Destinations* is the same as the student text, but it also includes answers to all exercises, as well as teaching tips in the margins.
- **Instructor's Manual to accompany *Destinations*.** Available to instructors online at www.mhhe.com/destinations, this guide features sample syllabi and clasroom strategies from the book's authors. NOTE: Instructors will need a password, which can be obtained from their local McGraw-Hill representative, or simply by contacting us at english@mcgraw-hill.com.
- **PageOut.** McGraw-Hill's PageOut service, free to adopters of McGraw-Hill texts, is available to help you get your course up and running online in a matter of hours. Additional information about the service is available at http://www.pageout.net.
- **Partners in Teaching: Teaching Basic Writing Listserv (www.mhhe.com/tbw).** Moderated by Laura Gray-Rosendale of Northern Arizona University and offered by McGraw-Hill as a service to the developmental composition community, this listserv brings together senior members of the college community with newer members—junior faculty, adjuncts, and teaching assistants— through an online newsletter and accompanying discussion group to address issues of pedagogy, both in theory and practice.

ACKNOWLEDGMENTS

Destinations benefited from the vision and efforts of many people. We would like to thank the McGraw-Hill staff, especially Sarah Touborg, who helped with the initial drafts, and Alexis Walker, whose wisdom and expertise helped us give focus and shape to this book. Thank you also to Judith Stanford for her contributions to the Update Edition. In addition, Anne Stameshkin, Andrea McCarrick, and Christina Gimlin, members of the editorial and production team, were essential to the realization of this project. We would also like to thank Jesse Hassenger, Cassandra Chu, Marty Granahan, Joshua Feldman, Todd A. Kimmelman, and Chris Narozny.

Many of our peers generously reviewed the manuscript in various stages and offered advice that refined our work. We would like to express our gratitude to:

Bob Bennett, North Idaho College
Joseph Booker, Palo Alto College
Richard Brodesky, Pima Community College
Donald Brotherton, DeVry University
Sandra Barnhill, South Plains College
Irene Clark, California State University, Northridge
Maureen Connolly, Joliet Junior College
Jennifer Costello Brezina, College of the Canyons
Tamera Davis, Pratt Community College

Copyright © 2007, The McGraw-Hill Companies, Inc. All rights reserved.

Patricia Dungan, Austin Community College

Margo Eden-Camann, Georgia Perimeter College, Clarkston

Ray Foster, Scottsdale Community College

Phyllis Gowdy, Tidewater Community College

Nikka Harris, Rochester Community and Technical College

Robin Ikegami, Sacramento City College

Edis Kittrell, Montana State University

Teresa Kozek, Housatonic Community College

Melissa Matters, Southern California Bible College and Seminary

Adrienne Mews, Lane Community College

Judy Mitchell, Oklahoma State University, Oklahoma City

Julie Ann Mix, Wayne State University

Maureen Morley, Cuyahoga Community College

Beth Penney, Monterey Peninsula College

Rachel Schaffer, Montana State University—Billings

Sandra Tate Solis, Northwest Vista College

Susan Spence, University of Texas, El Paso

Karen Taylor, Genesee Community College

Ted Wadley, Georgia Perimeter College

Janet Wallet-Ortiz, Western New Mexico University

Teresa Ward, Butte College

Dornell Woolford, Wor-Wic Community College

Jeff Wylie, Maysville Community College

Finally, we thank our colleagues for their support and advice, especially Laura Mahler.

We hope that you and your students enjoy using *Destinations*. If you'd like to send us feedback—and we warmly encourage you to do so—please email us at english@mcgraw-hill.com. May this text, and the courses in which it is used, help students make connections between the lives they live, the lives they are preparing for, and an exciting range of destinations.

PART ONE

An Introduction to College Writing

1 Meeting the Demands of College Writing

Take out a piece of paper and a pen. In college your writing will often begin like this, with an assignment. Assignments have a purpose. In some cases, you will write simply to explore ideas and make connections between one idea and another or between classroom learning and the real world. More often you will write to convey information or to demonstrate what you know about course content. Finally, you will sometimes write to persuade, to change your reader's mind, and possibly to motivate her to act. More often than not, the reader of your writing will be a teacher, instructor, or professor who provides you with a subject.

How you write will also be a factor in the writing context. The form of your writing will vary, from journal entry to summary, from paragraph to essay, from short-answer and essay test to report and term paper.

IN THIS CHAPTER: A PREVIEW

Purpose and Form in Writing

Writing Content and Focus

Critical Reading and Thinking

- Four Strategies to Read and Think Critically
- Reading with a Pen
- Drawing Inferences

Setting Goals and Becoming a Reflective Student

- Reflective Writing

PURPOSE AND FORM IN WRITING

WW The Writing Process

In the following exercises you will explore why you write and how purpose, form, subject, and reader all affect the writing process.

EXERCISE 1.1

Circle the purpose that best relates to the various forms of writing you know. Indicate your subjects and readers. Some forms of writing may have more than one purpose. The first row has been filled in as a model.

Copyright © 2007, The McGraw-Hill Companies, Inc. All rights reserved.

EXERCISE 1.1 continued

A. thinking on paper (explore your thoughts, ideas, feelings, and beliefs)

B. conveying information (share what you know and what you have learned)

C. persuading your reader (change your reader's mind, motivate him to do something)

Purpose	Form	Subject	Reader
Ⓐ B C	shopping list	*things needed at the store*	*me*
A B C	diary		
A B C	e-mail		
A B C	notes to family members		
A B C	letters		
A B C	writing in the workplace		

EXERCISE 1.2

Circle the purpose that best relates to forms of writing in college. Indicate possible subjects and readers. Some forms of writing will have more than one purpose. The first row has been filled in as a model.

A. thinking on paper (explore your thoughts, ideas, feelings, and beliefs)

B. conveying information (share what you know and what you have learned)

C. persuading your reader (change your reader's mind, motivate him to do something)

Purpose	Form	Subject	Reader
Ⓐ B C	journal entry	*personal writing, class notes or assignments, reactions to readings, notes on reading*	*me, professors*
A B C	summary		
A B C	paragraph		
A B C	essay		
A B C	short-answer test		
A B C	essay test		
A B C	lab report		
A B C	term paper		

EXERCISE 1.3

Review your responses in Exercises 1.1 and 1.2 and write short answers to the following questions. Explain your thinking.

1. What is the most common purpose in your personal writing?

2. What is the most common purpose in your college writing to this point?

3. What is the biggest difference between personal and college writing?

4. In what forms of writing are spelling and grammatical correctness most important?

WRITING CONTENT AND FOCUS

The focus of your writing will vary according to your purpose for writing. In assignments asking you to think on paper (journal writing, for example), the focus is on the writer and subject. You don't need to worry too much about the reader's reaction. The writing isn't for an audience. It's for you. In assignments asking you to convey information, the focus is on the subject and the reader. You show your reader, often a professor, that you know what you're talking about. In assignments asking you to argue and persuade, the focus is on the writer, the subject, and the reader. There is a subject—for example, Should the legal drinking age be lowered? There is an audience—a reader who is not convinced it's a good idea. And along with the evidence you present, there is your personal knowledge of the subject that influences the reader's thinking.

FOCUS ON:		
Writer (I)	Subject (It)	Reader (You/We)
emotion, feeling, belief, and opinion	information and explanation	persuasion, motivation, and action

*The focus of this entry is on the **writer** and his experience, thoughts, and beliefs. Therefore, the writer doesn't seem worried about a reader.*

The use of "I" is acceptable in this form of writing.

Spelling and grammatical correctness are not big issues because this writing isn't for an audience.

*The focus in this assignment is on the **subject,** explaining the test process. The writer tries to answer questions the reader might have about the workplace.*

In this type of assignment, the writer does not talk about herself or her feelings, opinions, or beliefs. The writer avoids using "I" for this reason.

Spelling and grammatical correctness are very important here.

*The focus of this message is on the **reader.** The writer tries to persuade her teacher to go easy on her because her kids are sick.*

"I" is appropriate in this form of writing. The writer has to talk about herself. She wants to express her feeling of regret for and provide a rational explanation for not turning in her work. Sick kids and trying to catch up are her subjects.

Spelling and grammatical correctness are somewhat less important in an e-mail, but if the writer wanted to impress her teacher, she might edit her message more carefully.

Copyright © 2007, The McGraw-Hill Companies, Inc. All rights reserved.

A. Unedited Student Journal Entry

PURPOSE: thinking on paper (explore your thoughts, ideas, feelings, and beliefs)

Whats so great about drinking? I don't get enjoyment, pleasure, or satisfaction from it. It seems like everyone my age is drinking just to get drunk and stupid. People drink to be more social and or to enhance life. Life would be boring without alcohol right? Not in my opinon. I like to talk to and aproach people, I can act goofy and stupid, and I can enjoy myself. People have found it hard to believe that I don't enjoy drinking. I suppose it is odd, considering most eighteen year olds pass the weekends with getting hammered and wasted at parties. Ive been there and done that. Ive had a good time too. People get hurt physically and mentally when drinking. People will say things they don't mean or do things they wouldn't do when they were sober. I imagine this is another reason why so many people do drink: A temporary solution to life's problems.

B. A Report on a Workplace Visit for a Technical Physics Class

PURPOSE: conveying information (share what you know and what you have learned)

This facility was doing tests on truck frames, with the goal of making trucks lighter by reducing the mass of the frame. The manufacturer needs to be sure the truck frame is strong enough to be safe in normal operation. A number of tests were devised to obtain data. Technicians outfitted a vehicle with instrumentation and took it to an appropriate site so data could be collected and recorded. Test situations included travel over rough terrain, ordinary highway mileage, and sudden shocks such as those caused by potholes. After data were recorded, the vehicle was then returned to the test facility, where the recorded data were, in effect, played over and over. In a few weeks' time, the vehicle was subjected to a lifetime of road wear. Engineers analyzed the results.

C. An Unedited e-mail Message from a Student to Her Teacher

PURPOSE: persuading your reader (change your reader's mind, motivate him to do something)

FROM: sadsoul22@omni.com
    DATE: Sun, 13 Oct 2002 19:44:29 EDT
    SUBJECT: Your 2B
    TO: Professor Safer

Sorry i didn't turn in my essay! i'll take care of it, as soon as i can. the past week has been tough, my kids have a serious case of ear infection and the flu for two weeks now, so it has been pretty challenging for me. and on top of that we left to canada friday and i just got back two hours ago. I'm done with my most of the work and i'm working as hard as i can. so sorry for the delay. is tomorrow ok?
    Sue

Destinations: Going Places with College Writing

Getting to Know Yourself

Most of us have feelings, beliefs, or ideas that we rarely think about or question. Maybe you love to sing. Perhaps you think the government needs to do more about the environment. When someone asks us to write about these thoughts in an organized way, we are given the chance to explore *why* we feel or think something—and how we can best express it. More often than not, we are a little surprised by what we discover. Writing is actually a great way to find out more about yourself—challenging at first for many of us but worth the effort.

The "Write" Audience

Whenever you write, ask yourself who your reader is. Just as you shift gears when you stop talking to a friend outside of class and address a teacher instead, you need to adjust how you write, what you choose to say, and the words you use, when you write for different readers. Depending on your audience and the context in which you find yourself, you might be a student, a friend, a granddaughter, and a coworker all in one day. If you write a paper for an instructor and then email a friend, you are writing to two very different readers. If you go on to write a letter to a prospective employer, you are addressing yet another reader. Being sensitive to your tone and language, professionally and personally, will help you earn trust and respect in all of your relationships.

Get Ahead: Moving towards Successful Writing

Knowing what you want to say (subject and focus), why you're saying it (purpose), how you will say it (form), and who you're saying it to (reader/audience) will give you a head start on any writing project. Taking the time to reflect on and explore your ideas will make the writing process less frustrating and the end result more successful. Becoming a successful writer in college will help prepare you for almost any career. Within most chapters, **Destinations boxes** like this one will show you how the skills learned in that chapter can help you get ahead in the classroom, the working world, and your personal life.

EXERCISE 1.4

Read the following passages. Circle the form of writing that best describes each passage. Select the primary purpose of the passage. Then indicate the focus of the passage.

All right, I could tell rock was getting way too popular. All my friends who used to dog it are forming their own bands. They are even changing their appearances. Kids who always had short hair are coming out with "college hair". Kids who used to be straight home dogs are dying their hair and sporting chained wallets. Kids who used to sell drugs are looking to become rock stars as there next source of income. Every weekend now someone is asking me who's playing and at what bar. It's out of hand. People are infactuated with it. "Hey man, didn't you play guitar back in the Day? Lets' start a band." No thanks. There is just way too much hype. It dosen't make any sense why people decide to try and get famous with the same thing everyone else is trying to get famous with. The odds of wining decline just a little bit. Girls are the funniest. A friend I know is in a band he is convinced they don't even like this hardcore bandwagon. They just follow the crowd.

Form: report   journal   essay   letter

Purpose:

  thinking on paper (explore your thoughts, ideas, feelings, and beliefs)
  conveying information (share what you know and what you have learned)
  persuading your reader (change your reader's mind, motivate him to do something)

Focus:

Writer (I)	emotion, feeling, belief, and opinion
Subject (It)	information and explanation
Reader (You/We)	persuasion, motivation, and action

Vehicle 33 arrived at the scene of the accident at 2:25 p.m. Scene was the Southwest corner of Canfield and Beck. Two car collision. Driver of one car, middle aged male, was unconscious, breathing 25 bpm, bleeding from the mouth. Trauma to the head and face. Situation called for airway management. C-collar was applied. Patient was boarded, oxygen administered high flow, transported by ALS. Driver of the other car, 18 yr old female, was sitting on the curb, responsive. Quick survey indicated possible fracture of ulna, right arm; lacerations. Fracture was splinted. Patient was stable when transported to emergency.

Form: report   journal   essay   letter

Purpose:

  thinking on paper (explore your thoughts, ideas, feelings, and beliefs)
  conveying information (share what you know and what you have learned)
  persuading your reader (change your reader's mind, motivate him to do something)

Focus:

Writer (I)	emotion, feeling, belief, and opinion
Subject (It)	information and explanation
Reader (You/We)	persuasion, motivation, and action

  I worked on your campaign last year in the Cleveland area. Your stance on water quality and Ohio's participation in the Great Lake Alliance was very important to me. In fact, that issue sold me on your candidacy.

  For that reason, I urge you to alter your stated position on future funding for the EPA. I know you are a member of the committee that will recommend funding, and I know you are a man of conscience and vision. The EPA has been an important factor in the cleanup of Lake Erie. Cutting its funding and its ability to regulate industry along the water's edge will have long-term and I fear *negative* effects on one of Ohio's greatest natural resources.

Form: report   journal   essay   letter

Purpose:

  thinking on paper (explore your thoughts, ideas, feelings, and beliefs)
  conveying information (share what you know and what you have learned)
  persuading your reader (change your reader's mind, motivate him to do something)

Copyright © 2007. The McGraw-Hill Companies, Inc. All rights reserved.

EXERCISE 1.4 continued

Focus:

Writer (I)	emotion, feeling, belief, and opinion
Subject (It)	information and explanation
Reader (You/We)	persuasion, motivation, and action

In Walter E. Williams's article "Making a Case for Corporal Punishment," Williams expresses his opinion on this controversial subject. He states that the old-fashioned way of whipping misbehaved children produces more civilized young people. Parents today do not discipline their kids the way they used to. Children in today's society are hostile and disrespectful toward adults. Williams believes that whipping these children, as a form of punishment, would make them as respectful as the children of yesterday. By disciplining children, parents and other figures of authority would have more control over the children of today.

Form: report   journal   essay   letter

Purpose:

thinking on paper (explore your thoughts, ideas, feelings, and beliefs)
conveying information (share what you know and what you have learned)
persuading your reader (change your reader's mind, motivate him to do something)

Focus:

Writer (I)	emotion, feeling, belief, and opinion
Subject (It)	information and explanation
Reader (You/We)	persuasion, motivation, and action

EXERCISE 1.5

Now review the writing you do at home, at work, and at school. List three to five examples of writing you do. Fill in detail about the writing context: form, purpose, focus, subject, and reader. The first row has been provided as a model.

Form	Purpose	Focus	Subject	Reader
shopping list	*thinking on paper—remind myself to get things at hardware*	*subject*	*items needed to finish a job*	*me*

Copyright © 2007, The McGraw-Hill Companies, Inc. All rights reserved.

EXERCISE 1.5 continued

Form	Purpose	Focus	Subject	Reader

CRITICAL READING AND THINKING

Because of the volume of reading required in college, your academic survival will depend on being a critical reader. You will identify a purpose for reading, apply strategies to help you read effectively, and monitor your comprehension. Further, you will analyze decisions writers make to create and format a text that communicates with a reader.

Four Strategies to Read and Think Critically

Four strategies will help you develop your critical reading and thinking skills. Consciously apply these strategies before, during, and after you read materials for your classes, as well as essays written by your peers. Learning to be a critical reader and thinker will also help you become a critical writer.

1. Make personal connections.
2. Determine important information and ideas.
3. Ask questions to focus and clarify meaning.
4. Draw inferences by identifying connections between parts of the text.

Reading with a Pen

Critical reading and thinking are active. Critical readers go beyond just reading the words. They pay attention to their understanding as they read. Reading with a pen is an excellent way to read critically. Critical readers circle, underline, highlight, and make notes in the margin as they read. They use the four strategies of critical reading to monitor their understanding and to ensure they grasp the author's purpose and meaning. Often multiple readings are necessary to thoroughly understand what you have read. Get in the habit of reading and rereading.

EXERCISE 1.6

As you read the excerpt below, place a *P* in the margin and write a word or two about the personal connection you make with the reading. Underline one or two sentences that seem important. In the margin, write a word or two explaining why you think

EXERCISE 1.6 continued

P—my father always says "it don't."

these sentences are important. As you read, write a question in the margin that you would like the writer to answer. The first marginal note has been provided as a model.

READING: from "Mother Tongue," by Amy Tan

Lately, I've been giving more thought to the kind of English my mother speaks. Like others, I have described it to people as "broken" or "fractured" English. But I wince when I say that. It has always bothered me that I can think of no way to describe it other than "broken," as if it were damaged and needed to be fixed, as if it lacked a certain wholeness and soundness. I've heard other terms used, "limited English," for example. But they seem just as bad, as if everything is limited, including the people's perceptions of the limited English speaker.

I know this for a fact, because when I was growing up, my mother's "limited" English limited *my* perception of her. I was ashamed of her English. I believed that her English reflected the quality of what she had to say. That is, because she expressed them imperfectly her thoughts were imperfect. And I had plenty of empirical evidence to support me: the fact that people in department stores, at banks, and at restaurants did not take her seriously, did not give her good service, pretended not to understand her, or even acted as if they did not hear her.

My mother has long realized the limitations of her English as well. When I was fifteen, she used to have me call people on the phone to pretend I was she. In this guise, I was forced to ask for information or even to complain and yell at people who had been rude to her. One time it was a call to her stockbroker in New York. She had cashed out her small portfolio and it just so happened we were going to go to New York the next week, our very first trip outside California. I had to get on the phone and say in an adolescent voice that was not very convincing, "This is Mrs. Tan."

And my mother was standing in the back whispering loudly, "Why he didn't send me check, already two weeks late. So mad he lie to me, losing me money."

And then I said in perfect English, "Yes, I'm getting rather concerned. You had agreed to send the check two weeks ago, but it hasn't arrived."

Drawing Inferences

When you draw an inference, you "read between the lines." That is, you see something the writer is saying indirectly, without coming right out and saying it. The inferences you draw are based on actual statements the writer makes. You might, for example, infer that Tan was ashamed of her mother. She doesn't say *exactly* that. She says she was ashamed of her mother's limited English and that she perceived her mother as "limited." Does that mean she was ashamed of her mother? It is a matter of interpretation, of inference.

EXERCISE 1.7

Circle the form of writing that best describes the passage from Amy Tan's essay, "Mother Tongue." Place a check mark next to the primary purpose and focus of the passage.

Form: report   journal   essay   letter

EXERCISE 1.7 continued

Purpose:

thinking on paper (explore your thoughts, ideas, feelings, and beliefs)
conveying information (share what you know and what you have learned)
persuading your reader (change your reader's mind, motivate him to do something)

Focus:

Writer (I)	emotion, feeling, belief, and opinion
Subject (It)	information and explanation
Reader (You/We)	persuasion, motivation, and action

WW Putting Yourself on a Schedule

SETTING GOALS AND BECOMING A REFLECTIVE STUDENT

Your improvement as a writer will depend on your awareness of strengths and weaknesses in your writing. To monitor your progress, develop the habit of keeping track of the skills you need to improve. Set goals and reflect on your work. Doing so will help you become a better writer and a more effective student.

Reflective Writing

Reflective writing helps you examine your attitudes, confusions, and achievements.

1. Keep a journal to capture the personal experience of learning to write. Reread your journal regularly. Journaling enables you to see trends that might help you solve a writing problem or identify a successful strategy.
2. Keep track of your instructor's remarks on your papers. Using the tally grids in Chapters 18, 19, and 20, record the type and number of errors you make. Use the exercises in those chapters to learn what the errors are and how to correct them.

EXERCISE 1.8

Answer the following questions to explore your previous writing experience and to help set goals for improvement.

1. What kinds of papers do you like to write?

2. Who taught you to write your first successful paper? What was the subject? What made the paper good?

3. What kinds of papers do you dislike writing?

4. Describe one assignment in particular that was very difficult for you.

Copyright © 2007, The McGraw-Hill Companies, Inc. All rights reserved.

EXERCISE 1.9

Apply what you have learned in this chapter to analyze what you described in Exercise 1.8 as writing assignments you liked and disliked.

The Writing Context					
	Form	Purpose	Focus	Subject	Reader
Writing assignment you liked					
Writing assignment you disliked					

1. What do you like about writing and believe you do well?

2. According to your analysis in these exercises, what do you need to work on to be more effective as a college writer?

2 *The Writing Process*

I use a three-step approach to writing papers: read the assignment, type the paper, turn it in. If this sentence describes your approach to writing, it will be a big shift to think of writing as a process. Why change? First, a process approach allows writers to relax. They know that the beginnings of a good piece of writing are a long way from the finished product. In fact, the first words on the page might never appear in a final draft. Second, they know from the outset that writing will take time and energy. Third, they have strategies to approach the decisions all writers have to make. The writing process is rarely a neat step-by-step process. However, you may find this process model helpful.

IN THIS CHAPTER: A PREVIEW

The Writing Process

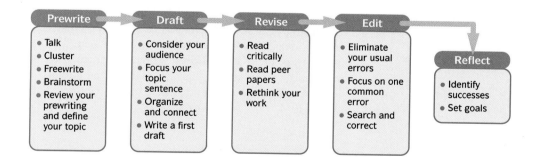

Prewrite	Draft	Revise	Edit	Reflect
• Talk • Cluster • Freewrite • Brainstorm • Review your prewriting and define your topic	• Consider your audience • Focus your topic sentence • Organize and connect • Write a first draft	• Read critically • Read peer papers • Rethink your work	• Eliminate your usual errors • Focus on one common error • Search and correct	• Identify successes • Set goals

Follow a Student through the Writing Process

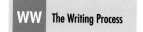
WW The Writing Process

THE WRITING PROCESS

Prewrite: Reduce Your Fear of the Blank Page

How do I get started? All writers begin by facing the blank page; therefore, a positive approach sets the tone for the rest of the work. Prewriting generates thinking and ideas on a topic. It is only the first step in the writing process.

Copyright © 2007, The McGraw-Hill Companies, Inc. All rights reserved.

Talk

Talk, one strategy for prewriting, is relaxed and temporary. It does not require you to make a commitment the same way writing does. As you talk to someone about your topic, you explore your thinking and respond to the listener, who helps you by adding ideas or personal experiences that develop your topic further.

EXERCISE 2.1

Have a conversation with another student to prepare for the writing that will follow. Briefly describe a childhood leisure activity, something you especially enjoyed. You might talk about a sport, picnics with your family, going to a relative's house, drawing at the kitchen table, or going to the park.

- Take turns talking for ten minutes.
- Begin discussing the childhood leisure activity of your choice, but allow the conversation to remind you of other activities.
- As you recall events, include facts, details, examples, and the exact words you used or heard.

EXERCISE 2.2

Write for five to ten minutes about your conversation with your classmate. Begin by writing a sentence that introduces your topic. Review the following list of sentences that might introduce the topic of drawing at the kitchen table. Then write a similar sentence to introduce your topic.

- My love of art began with a box of crayons and a coloring book.
- If you want to create artists, burn coloring books.
- Crayons, scissors, glue, and paper make hours of fun and memories.

Cluster

Clustering is a second prewriting strategy. Clustering systematically searches for related ideas. It helps a writer picture a subject. This is an effective strategy because it connects ideas and allows writers to trace their thinking. Each time you add new links to the chain, you are making the subject smaller and more specific, or you are imagining a new idea that might contain a whole set of more specific ideas within it.

EXERCISE 2.3

Use the following clustering diagram as a model to generate possible topics. Examine the photograph "Boy Fishing" to further prompt your thinking on the topic of childhood. As you look at it, think about how this photograph connects to you. What does it remind you of? What view of childhood does it suggest to you?

- Draw your own diagram on a piece of paper.
- Place the first word that comes to mind in an oval marked "Begin Here."
- Add additional lines and ovals as you extend your thinking.
- Push for at least four or five topic chains. Be flexible and open to new thinking.

EXERCISE 2.3 continued

"Boy Fishing"

Copyright © 2007, The McGraw-Hill Companies, Inc. All rights reserved.

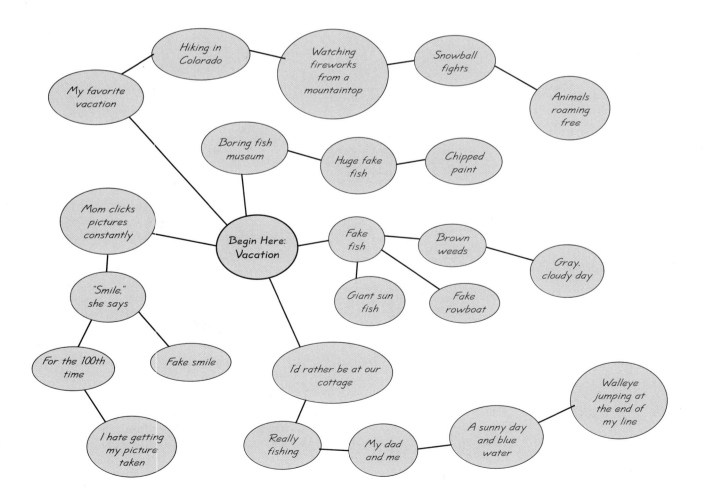

Freewrite

A third prewriting strategy is freewriting. The key to freewriting is staying loose and informal. Keep your hand moving. When you talk, you don't stop to correct your grammar. Instead, you allow lapses in grammar and thinking to exist without correction. Freewriting is the same. The writer does not worry about spelling and grammar because freewriting is not for an audience. Freewriting is just for you. It enables you to recall forgotten memories, uncover ideas that have personal value, and understand attitudes in a new or deeper way.

EXERCISE 2.4

Examine the photograph "The Breakfast Table" to prompt your thinking on childhood. Freewrite for five to ten minutes without stopping. Allow your thinking and writing to wander. As you do so, you may discover memories or ideas that surprise you. Allow these discoveries to emerge.

- Be messy. Don't edit your grammar or spelling.
- Be playful. Avoid logical stories. Change subjects, looking for new directions to follow.
- Be open to words, feelings, and memories. Then explore what comes to mind.

"The Breakfast Table"

Brainstorm

Brainstorming is a fourth prewriting strategy. It can be as simple as randomly listing ideas on a topic. It can also be organized, using strategies to go deeper into a topic. More is better in brainstorming.

Copyright © 2007, The McGraw-Hill Companies, Inc. All rights reserved.

EXERCISE 2.5

Brainstorm a list of childhood memories. Use the following lists as models for brainstorming on your own.

- Random listing: begin by listing as many possible topics about childhood that you can imagine.
- Piggybacking: review your random list and find three categories to explore and go deeper into.

Random Listing			
flashlight tag	reading groups	Spiderman comics	Halloween
boy scouts	my first fish	soccer games	food fights
raking leaves	Taffy, my dog	making Christmas cookies	pick-up baseball
mowing lawns	lemonade stands	hating dance lessons	Billy moving away
my secret ring	the Santa lie	sharing a bedroom	my first bike

Piggybacking		
Firsts	**Holiday Traditions**	**Jobs**
• fish • fishing pole that broke the first time I used it • girlfriend—Lucy in 6th grade who was a foot taller than me • two-wheel bike • time I broke a window playing ball • time I got caught soaping windows on Halloween	• making Christmas cookies—cornflake wreaths and gingerbread people • cutting out pumpkins—I got to dig out the insides and draw the faces • going Christmas caroling at the retirement home • going to Grandma's on Christmas Eve	• lemonade stand with my friend Billy who drank up all the lemonade • raking leaves in the neighborhood • mowing the Peterson's lawn—my first business • taking out the garbage and discovering maggots in the trash can

Review Your Prewriting and Define Your Topic

Prewriting is only the beginning. It is not a first draft. Before you begin drafting, take a few minutes and review your prewriting. You have just generated many feelings, memories, and ideas about childhood. Now it is time to reread what you generated and define your topic.

EXERCISE 2.6

Define the topic you will write about. In the following table, list the possible topics you generated. A couple topics have been provided as models.

- Give the topic a name that summarizes it.
- Indicate which prewriting strategy you used to discover this topic.
- Then use the questions that follow to select the topic you will use.

EXERCISE 2.6 continued

Possible Topics	Prewriting Strategy
my dog Taffy	*freewriting*
we grow up too fast	*clustering*

- Which one interests you most?

- Which one generated the strongest feelings in you?

- Which one generated the most specific examples or reasons?

- Which one seems most clearly organized in your mind?

EXERCISE 2.7

Writers select the prewriting strategy that is most effective for them and best suited to the form and purpose of their writing. Some writers may even use two strategies to explore a topic. Review your prewriting work and answer the following questions below to determine which strategy was most effective for you.

1. Which strategy was easiest for you to use? Why?

2. Which strategy generated the deepest thinking? Why?

3. Which activity provided the most interesting topic? Why?

4. Which strategy would you like to use again? Why?

Draft

What do I want to say? Who will read this paragraph? What form is appropriate? Drafting organizes prewriting into a readable text. Remember, you will write multiple drafts of a paper. Your job in the first draft is to identify the main point, organize the prewriting into a logical structure, and shape it to meet a reader's expectations. These expectations are vital when you are writing for a grade or a job.

Consider Your Audience

1. Who will read this paragraph and what do they expect?
2. How much do they know about my topic?

EXERCISE 2.8

Reread your list of possible topics from Exercise 2.5. Then reread your prewriting to gather all the memories, feelings, and ideas you had about this topic. You may want to do additional brainstorming, freewriting, clustering, or talking about it.

- Write a sentence that states the point you want a reader to understand.
- Select five to seven details, examples, or reasons that will explain your point to a reader who does not know you.
- Select two or three of the most convincing details, examples, or reasons.

Do this for two possible topics.

EXAMPLE:

Topic: *We Grow Up Too Fast*

Sentence: *At ten, I wanted to be twenty, and that wish made me act too grown up and lose out on the silly fun of being young.*

Details, examples, or reasons: (check the most convincing):

I got interested in boys way before my girlfriends. I guess you could say I was boy crazy.

I wore makeup, and my mom let me wear makeup when I was in sixth grade.

All I could think about was getting married.

I tried to hang out with older girls who were doing older stuff. They hung out at the mall and called boys on the phone.

I quit playing with dolls or riding my bike. I had to be cool all the time.

I read Glamour *magazine and wanted to be a model.*

I wanted my hair and clothes to look like the models in the magazines.

1. Topic:

Sentence:

Details, examples, or reasons: (check the most convincing):

Copyright © 2007, The McGraw-Hill Companies, Inc. All rights reserved.

EXERCISE 2.8 continued

2. Topic:

Sentence:

Details, examples, or reasons: (check the most convincing):

Focus Your Topic Sentence

Focus is essential, and it begins with your topic sentence. The topic sentences states the purpose of a paragraph, and it is often the first sentence of a paragraph. Think about your purpose. You have a subject and something to say. So your topic sentence will focus these two things: subject and point. Develop this 1 (subject) + 1 (point) approach. Getting that sentence focused will also focus the paragraph. Take a few minutes to step back and analyze your first sentence. Are you specific enough?

First Draft

<u>Vacations in a cramped car and equally small tent</u> created an <u>unbreakable family bond</u>.
            (subject)   *(point)*

Focusing Questions

Which vacation?
Which location led to more bonding: the car or the tent?
What kinds of bonds were formed?
What occurred that caused the bonding?

Second Draft

                1   +   1
<u>Two brothers and a dog in a pup tent</u> create <u>laughter and a bond of love.</u>
         (subject)   *(point)*

EXERCISE 2.9

Write a topic sentence that states the subject and your point.

Organize and Connect

Organization and connections announce a relationship between the details, examples, and reasons. Ask yourself the following questions:

- Can a reader follow my thinking?
- Do I create a relationship between the facts, details, examples, and reasons?
- Did I insert transitions to create a logical order and connect the details, examples, and reasons?

Copyright © 2007, The McGraw-Hill Companies, Inc. All rights reserved.

EXERCISE 2.10

Select one of the topics you examined in Exercise 2.8. Using the key details, examples, and reasons, create an order for a paragraph. Try these common orders:

EXAMPLE:

Topic: *Babysitting Horror Story*

List	Time—Chronological Order	Order of Importance
I was afraid of dogs.	Mrs. Meyer put the dogs out so I wouldn't be afraid of them.	I was foolish and babysat for 3 kids under 5 and two smart dogs that know how to jump and loved chasing cats. I should never have said yes.
I was babysitting three kids: all under five years old.	The kids went down for a nap. I flipped on the television and relaxed.	
There were two big Weimaraners in the yard.	A neighbor called in a panic. The two Weimaraners were chasing her cats.	Mrs. Meyer put the dogs out so I wouldn't be afraid of them.
Their favorite activity was jumping the fence and chasing the cats in the neighborhood.	I called my house. No one was home. I got a neighbor to watch the kids while I chased the dogs.	The kids went down for a nap. I flipped on the television and relaxed.
The dogs figured out a way to leap on the car and jump the fence.	I had to fight my fear to leash the dogs and drag them back to the house.	A neighbor called in a panic. The two Weimaraners were chasing her cats.
		I had to fight my fear to leash the dogs and drag them back to the house.

Topic:

List	Time—Chronological Order	Order of Importance

EXERCISE 2.11

Review your responses to Exercise 2.10. Select the transitional words from the following table that seem most appropriate for the paragraph you plan to write.

List	Time—Chronological Order	Order of Importance
first	before	most important
in addition	after	least important
another	next to	as well as
finally	behind	equally important

Write a First Draft

EXERCISE 2.12

Write a first draft. Begin with a sentence that states your point.

Revise

Will a reader feel what I felt or understand what I understood about my topic? How can I get an A? Communication is the goal of writing, whether you are interested in creating a feeling or understanding for your readers or whether your goal is to get a good grade. It is a good idea to now step back from your writing. A draft is your beginning, but there is more to do before your work is finished. Experienced writers often say the end product is not at all what they thought they would write when they began. Revision means rethinking. Give yourself time to do this important step.

Read Critically

Reading published writers critically will help you to improve your writing. Their work can serve as models for you if you can look closely at what they are doing and try it in your writing. Read with comparison in mind. Ask these questions:

- How does the writer present information?
- What does the writer do that I admire?
- How does the writer solve a problem that I have in my writing?
- Is there a technique in the professional model that I can try?

EXERCISE 2.13

Read the following paragraph three times, following the instructions that follow it.

READING: from "Growing Up Game," by Brenda Peterson

This hunting trip was the first time I remember eating game as a conscious act. My father and Buddy Earl shot a big doe and she lay with me in the back of the tarp-draped station wagon all the way home. It was not the smell I minded, it was the glazed great, dark eyes and the way that head flopped around crazily on what I knew was once a graceful neck. I found myself petting this doe, murmuring all those graces we'd been taught long ago as children. Thank you for the sacrifice, thank you for letting us be like you so that we can grow up strong as game. But there was an uneasiness in me that night as I bounced along in the back of the car with the deer.

Destinations: Charting Your Course with the Writing Process

The Prewriting Process: Thinking Through Ideas

You may be surprised by how much you know about even the least likely-sounding topic you find yourself assigned to write about. Freewriting in your journal, brainstorming alone or with others, or just talking ideas through with a professor or a friend will help you discover what you know now, what you want to know, and what your feelings on the subject are. When you sit down to write your paper, you won't be starting from scratch. That alone will make your first draft more successful.

Revise and Get Organized

Successfully revising a paper is a lot like reviewing your wardrobe. What works? What doesn't? Can you get that jacket tailored to fit better, or should you just chuck it? Are those ripped jeans you've been wearing for the last few years still OK, or do they give people the wrong impression of you? Do you have the basics—black pants, white shirts—that you need? When revising a paper, you need to ask yourself similar questions: What's working? What isn't? Can a certain passage be altered to be more persuasive, or should you just take it out? Is the colloquial language you use appropriate, or should you substitute more formal language? Is the basic structure of the paper sound? Do you have the right evidence (quantity and quality) to support your point? It takes work, planning, and a careful eye to revise your paper, as well as the willingness to rethink your ideas and conclusions based on the new information and insights you will inevitably come across during the course of the writing process.

From Good Editing to Getting the Job

When applying for a job, be sure to carefully edit your resume and cover letter. Potential employers will view errors in your application as signs of bad writing or carelessness. Incorrect grammar and spelling will detract from (or even contradict) the message you are trying to send about your capability, passion, and talents. A potential employer has good reason to be picky in this area; in the workplace, the ability to express yourself clearly reflects not only on you but also on your employer. Good editing will give you a better shot at getting—and keeping—a job.

EXERCISE 2.13 continued

1. **First reading:**   Read without a pen or pencil. Simply try to understand the author's subject and purpose. Then, in a sentence or two, write your view of the author's purpose.

2. **Second reading:**   Underline two sentences that express Peterson's subject and purpose. Circle the details that support or explain her purpose as you read the rest of the paragraph.

3. **Third reading:**   Place a checkmark in the margin next to a sentence or two that you admire. Look for sentences that do any of the following:
   - present information in an interesting way
   - use a technique that you would like to try
   - solve a problem that you have in your writing

4. **Rethinking after a close reading:**   In a sentence or two, write your view of the author's purpose.

Read Peer Papers

A real audience tells you if your writing says what you think it says. In a response group, you are both a writer and a reader. You bring your writing for review, and you read peer work. Response groups work most effectively when readers avoid focusing on the writing's problems or fixing it. Instead, the most effective groups discuss the writing's strengths as well as weaknesses.

Copyright © 2007, The McGraw-Hill Companies, Inc. All rights reserved.

EXERCISE 2.14

Take a step back at this stage of the writing process, and form a response group.

- Form a group with three or four members of your class.
- Carefully read the box "Creating Powerful Response Groups" to clarify your job as writer and reader in a group.
- Take turns sharing your writing and listening to the group respond to your work.
- As a reader, talk specifically about the writing.
- As a writer, jot down remarks your readers make that will help you when you revise your paper.

Creating Powerful Response Groups

As a Writer	As a Reader
1. Distribute copies of your work to group members.	1. Identify the point or purpose of the paragraph or essay.
2. After you read your work aloud, listen quietly and take notes as the group members talk.	2. Identify the topic sentence and key words that state the purpose. Does it grab your interest?
3. At the end of the group, ask for clarifications, additional advice, or expansion ideas.	3. Discuss key details, examples, or reasons. Notice the details or examples that grab your interest. Are they connected?
4. Thank the group for their comments.	4. Notice places where the writing is confusing, inconsistent, or underdeveloped.
5. Collect the copies so you can use their notes or comments for your revision.	5. Identify the conclusion. What does the writer emphasize in the conclusion?

Rethink Your Work

Experienced writers make significant changes in their writing when they revise. They know the exploratory sentences they started with may not be as focused and meaningful as those that come after careful consideration of meaning and purpose. As you revise, read critically. Look for evidence that you have achieved your purpose. Identify what you do well and where your papers are weak. Listen to the views of other readers. Ask these questions:

- Do I keep a reader's interest?
- Were my readers confused? What can I do to reduce their confusions?
- Can I try something new? What do professional writers do that I could try? What do other writers in my class do that I could try?

As you revise, rethink. Be open to adding, cutting, or reorganizing your writing. If you need to leave something behind, that means your thinking and writing has probably become more focused.

Revising Strategy 1: Add

Add details, examples, and explanations that answer questions raised by your readers. It's not too late to add completely new content at this point. Where connections are lacking, add sentences that elaborate or relate one part of your paper to another.

Revising Strategy 2: Cut

Cut details, examples, and explanation that your readers did not understand or that did not seem sufficiently connected to the rest of the writing. Don't be afraid to cut deeply. Save your early draft. If you need to, you can always put something back in the essay. Cutting and adding, however, often help you see your writing in a new light.

Revising Strategy 3: Reorganize

Reorganize your work so that it looks, feels, and reads differently. Consider the best placement for sentences; sometimes what you write at the end of a paragraph or paper works better at the beginning. Consider starting with impact and arranging your examples in order of importance, using the most significant example first. Reorganizing forces you to think differently about your subject.

EXERCISE 2.15

Review the peer feedback and your self-assessment. Determine which revising strategy will help you clarify your meaning and purpose. Add, cut, and reorganize to revise your paragraph.

Edit

I am terrible with grammar, isn't there a quick way to edit? Too often, students simply scan their papers before turning them in for a grade. This reading and rereading differs little from the reading they do when they draft their papers. If an error finds them, they correct it, but they are not searching for errors. Good editing is a focused, systematic search for problems. To edit effectively, you need to anticipate the errors you make, search for those errors, and correct them.

Eliminate Your Usual Errors

Are my sentences clear and complete? Am I consistent with my verb tense or pronoun usage? Do I tend to use too many or too few commas? Do I write run-on sentences? These are just a few of the common grammatical problems of college writers. Know the consistent grammatical problems that you have.

This is easier than it sounds. You may already know, for example, that your spelling is weak. When your professors return work to you, they will alert you to errors that appear in your paper. Keep a tally of errors you make in the grids provided in Chapters 18, 19, and 20. When error patterns become apparent to you, anticipate the occurrence of these errors in your papers. The following editing strategies may also help.

Editing Strategy 1: Use a Checklist

Your professors may provide you with an editing checklist for papers; in the meantime use the following universal checklist to begin.

WW Spelling

EDITING CHECKLIST
Words
I removed unnecessary contractions.
I removed informal language.
I checked my capitalization.
I corrected all spelling errors by consulting a dictionary, a peer editor, or my computer spell-check, being sure to look for words my computer spell-check missed.

Copyright © 2007, The McGraw-Hill Companies, Inc. All rights reserved.

Sentences

I checked all my end marks.

I use complete sentences with subjects and verbs.

I control my sentences so their meaning is clear.

I removed inappropriate sentence fragments.

Paragraphs

I indented each new paragraph.

EXERCISE 2.16

Use the preceding checklist to review your paragraph.

Focus on One Common Error

Read your work carefully with a single error in mind. The most common editing errors are covered in Chapters 18, 19, and 20. Use the lessons and activities there to solve these common problems.

Editing Strategy 2: Eliminate One Error at a Time

Read your paper several times using the following guidelines. Concentrate on one error at a time.

- Read each sentence individually or read backwards, from the last sentence to the first, see each sentence in isolation. Making sure that each sentence is complete, clear, and concise will focus your editing search.
- Look for spots that signal a consistent error. If you know you have trouble with punctuation, look at those sentences that might require commas, semi-colons, colons, or apostrophes.

Search and Correct

Editing is not easy. People tend to overlook errors; they automatically self-correct as they read. Therefore, employ search strategies that help you edit strategically.

Editing Strategy 3: Read Your Work Aloud

Use one of the following approaches:

- Read aloud slowly. Listen and look closely at each word. Watch out for missing words, words missed by spell-check, and confusing language.
- Read aloud with feeling. If you have difficulty reading certain spots with emotional emphasis, you may find places where the meaning has broken down. Often those spots also have spelling or grammatical errors.

Editing Strategy 4: Highlight Signal Words

Highlight words that signal punctuation. For example, highlight all the coordinating conjunctions and then use the rules for items in a series or compound sentences to determine the need for commas (see Chapter 16).

 Spelling

Editing Strategy 5: Use Computer Aids—Spell-Checks and Grammar-Checks

Your computer has a grammar-check that alerts you to confusing or grammatically incorrect sentences. Do not ignore it. Use it as an aid. If the computer questions your sentences, you should too. However, like spell-check, grammar-check can be

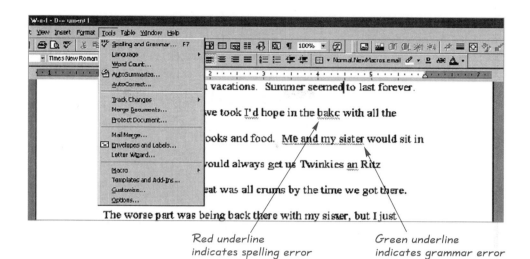

Red underline
indicates spelling error

Green underline
indicates grammar error

unreliable. To the computer, "I'd hope in the back" is just as correct as "I'd hop in the back." It takes a human reader to know the difference and to select the correct word and spelling. Computer aids do not replace careful proofreading and knowing how to make good decisions about grammar.

Editing Strategy 6: Use Proofreading Pals

Proofread your paper with someone with an objective eye. Tell this person about the errors you are inclined to make. To the best of your ability, explain to this reader what the errors are and how to correct them. By explaining your errors, you will develop the ability to identify them as well. Read your paper aloud, or ask your proofreading pal to do so, and search for your errors. Proofreading works best with two sets of eyes.

Editing Strategy 7: Double-Check Your Work

If you are writing for college, reread your assignment. Check for specific directions that define length, content, typing format, or other requirements. Taking time for this final double-check can save you from making a simple mistake that might affect your grade. If you are writing for your job, be sure you know what your boss's expectations are before you turn in your work.

This is also a good time to make an appointment with your professor or your boss to confirm that you have done the job correctly. These people will admire you for asking before you submit your work, so do not hesitate to ask them to clarify their expectations.

EXERCISE 2.17

Use at least two editing strategies to produce a final edited draft of your paragraph.

Reflect: Build Confidence

How have I changed as a writer? Writing experiences (whether in college, work, or personal life) offer unique challenges, but as you face these challenges you grow. Reflection is an important but often overlooked step in the writing process. By stopping and identifying something you have achieved, you gain confidence. Confident writers know they have strategies that can be applied to any writing experience.

Copyright © 2007, The McGraw-Hill Companies, Inc. All rights reserved.

Identify Successes

Remember what you do well and what you enjoy. Becoming a good writer involves realizing and using your strengths.

EXERCISE 2.18

Take a few minutes to reflect on your successes. Write one or two sentences that explain two things you have learned from this chapter and how you successfully applied them to your writing. Use a specific example from your work to support your thinking.

Set Goals

As you move forward, set realistic goals. Use your successes to identify a change in your writing. Become aware of breakthroughs in your skills and use of strategies. Strive to create additional breakthroughs. Remember that small achievements add up to large gains.

EXERCISE 2.19

Now that you have examined your successes, determine what challenges you face. Rate yourself using the following scale—5 indicates a task that you consider a challenge most of the time, and 1 indicates a task for which you have the required skills and strategies.

Stages	Strategies and Skills	5	4	3	2	1
Prewrite	1. I prewrite to explore my ideas and think deeper about a topic.	—	—	—	—	—
Draft	2. I focus my paragraphs with a clear purpose.	—	—	—	—	—
	3. I organize my ideas and make connections.	—	—	—	—	—
	4. I insert details, examples, and reasons to explain my thinking.	—	—	—	—	—
Revise	5. I read critically to identify and use the successful techniques of other writers.	—	—	—	—	—
	6. I identify the strengths and weaknesses in my papers.	—	—	—	—	—
	7. I apply specific revision strategies to my papers.	—	—	—	—	—
	8. I am flexible and willing to make changes in my writing.	—	—	—	—	—
Edit	9. I employ all or some of the following editing strategies:	—	—	—	—	—
	▪ use a checklist	—	—	—	—	—
	▪ eliminate one error at a time	—	—	—	—	—
	▪ read my work aloud	—	—	—	—	—
	▪ highlight signal words	—	—	—	—	—
	▪ use spell-check or grammar-check on my computer	—	—	—	—	—
	▪ use a proofreading pal	—	—	—	—	—
	▪ double-check the assignment and expectations	—	—	—	—	—

Copyright © 2007, The McGraw-Hill Companies, Inc. All rights reserved.

EXERCISE 2.20

Finish the following sentences in order to explore your learning experience and to set goals.

1. My attitude toward writing is

2. I still need to work on

FOLLOW A STUDENT THROUGH THE WRITING PROCESS

STUDENT MODEL

Christina's Unedited Freewrite

I could talk with my family and friends forever; I love to communicate with as many people as I can. My major is communication so obviously I can communicate. But when it comes to giving a speech my face becomes red, my voice begins to quiver and crack. Me standup in front of people and tell a speech, no way! I become extremely nervous I feel my heart pounding out of my chest. I feel I can't take a breath while my face is rushing with blood. I took speech classes before and it never helps. My eyes are always focused on the paper, I can't give eye contact, and I don't know what to do. Last semester I gave a speech in my history class and I went through all the symptoms one can go through. I also gave a speech in my Spanish class and I couldn't maintain eye contact. What is it about giving speeches that I cant over come? If the teacher decides to ask me a question or read what I wrote sitting down I'm fine. But once I have to stand in front of the class that's when everything crumbles. I realized that I must overcome my fear and anxiety, so began to volunteer speeches. They keep getting worse. My speech teacher said I have to be confident. I think I'm very confident I just can't do a speech in front of the class without becoming nervous. Then I thought to myself, maybe I need to be extremely confident in what I'm talking about. I began to do extensive research on all my speech and almost memorize the whole speech. Still I get nervous. What I began doing is writing very little on my note cards therefore forcing myself to keep eye contact. What I found myself doing is finding a focal point and fix my eyesight on it. Which is a little better, at least the students and the teacher could see my face and not just the top of my forehead.

continued

Christina's Drafting Decisions

Focus

My fear of giving speeches destroys any speech I give. Now I'm more afraid of the fear than giving speeches.

Details

- But once I have to stand in front of the class, that's when everything crumbles.
- But when it comes to giving a speech my face becomes red, my voice begins to quiver and crack. I become extremely nervous. I feel my heart pounding out of my chest. I feel I can't take a breath while my face is rushing with blood.
- My eyes are always focused on the paper, I can't give eye contact, and I don't know what to do.

Organize

- My body goes crazy and takes over until I just crumble in front of the room.
- There is this series of fear symptoms that overcome me.
- I'm sure I'm a victim of revenge because I make fun of other speakers to relieve my embarrassment.

Connect

Show how my fear creates problems that I can't stop and how trying to overcome the fear creates more problems that don't help. Use chronological order transitions: first, then, after the other symptoms start.

Christina's Draft Expansion

Adjusting Focus

My body goes crazy and takes over until I just crumble in front of the room.

There is this series of fear symptoms that overcome me.

~~I'm sure I'm a victim of revenge because I make fun of other speakers to relieve my embarrassment.~~

Adding Detail

But when it comes to giving a speech my face becomes red, my voice begins to quiver and crack. I become extremely nervous [Add: I fiddle with the corners of my paper and rock back and forth. Then I start talking faster and faster and lower and lower until I can barely be heard.] I feel my heart pounding out of my chest. I feel I can't take a breath while my face is rushing with blood. I took speech classes before and it never helps. My eyes are always focused on the paper, I can't give eye contact, and I don't know what to do.

Using Chronological Order to Make Connections

<u>Whenever</u> I give a speech, I know that fear is right around the corner.

<u>At first</u>, my face just turns red, but I can feel my cheeks burning, and I know the rest will begin soon.

<u>Then</u> my voice starts to quiver and crack. I sound like a teen-ager going through puberty.

<u>That's when</u> I know I'm not hiding my fear. Everyone knows I'm scared. So I start fiddling with the corners of my paper, and I rock back and forth.

The only thing I can think of is getting done, so I start talking faster and faster.

<u>At this point</u>, my eyes are glued to the paper, and I'm reading faster and faster. I can't make eye contact, or I know I'll never finish.

<u>By the end</u> of the speech, no one can hear me because I'm speaking in a low whisper.

Christina's First Draft

Me stand up and give a speech? No way. I know that fear is right around the corner. First, I can feel my cheeks burning, and I know they're a very bright red. That's when I start to get really, really scared, and so my voice starts to quiver and crack. I sound like a teen-ager going through puberty. I lose eye contact and focus on a spot in the back of the room to hide my growing fear, but usually, I start fiddling with the corners of my paper. When that happens, I know I can't stop it, and I rock back and forth. The rocking is a dead give-away. The only thing I can think of is getting done, so I start talking faster and faster. People can't really understand me, and I know that I should be pronouncing the words better. At this point, my eyes are glued to the paper, and I'm reading faster and faster and faster. I can't make eye contact, or I know I'll never finish. By the end of the spech no one can hear me because I'm speaking in a low whisper.

Christina's Second Draft

My first thought when I give a speech is, no way. I know that fear is right around the corner. ~~First, I can feel my cheeks burning, and I know they're a very bright red.~~ <u>The first sign of fear is burning cheeks, and I know this first symptom starts a whole series of symptoms that I cannot stop.</u> ~~That's when I start to get really, really scared, so~~ <u>Next</u> my voice starts to quiver and crack I sound like a teen-ager going through puberty. ~~I lose eye contact amd~~ <u>Then</u> I focus on a spot in the back of the room ~~to hide my growing fear, but usually~~ <u>and lose eye contact.</u> <u>That's when</u> I start fiddling with the corners of my paper. ~~When that happens I know I can't stop it, and~~ <u>Shortly after the fiddlling begins</u> I rock back and forth. The rocking is a dead giveaway <u>that I'm out of control.</u> The only thing I can

continued

Copyright © 2007, The McGraw-Hill Companies, Inc. All rights reserved.

think of is getting done so I start talking faster and faster and people can't really understand me and I know that I should be pronouncing the words better. At this point <u>I can't make eye contact, or I know I'll never finish so</u> my eyes are glued to the paper. ~~and I'm reading faster and faster and faster. I can't make eye contact, or I know I'll never finish.~~ By the end of the speech no one can hear me because I'm speaking in a low whisper. <u>Actually, this uncontrollable craziness has become more frightening than speaking.</u>

Christina's Third Draft with Editing Marks

¶ My first thought when I give a speech is. ~~no way~~. I know ~~that~~ fear is *(have to)* *(No way!)* right around the corner. The first sign of fear is burning cheeks ~~and I know~~ *they are bright red, and I know* this first symptom starts a whole series ~~of symptoms~~ that I cannot stop. Next, my voice starts to quiver and crack. I sound like a ~~teen-ager~~ *teenager* going through puberty. Then, I focus on a spot in the back of the room ~~and lose~~ *losing* eye contact. ~~That's when I start fiddling~~ *After that, I fiddle* with the corners of my paper. Shortly after the fiddling begins, I rock back and forth. ~~The rocking is a dead giveaway that I'm out of control. The only thing I can think of is getting done so I start talking~~ *I just want to get done, so I talk* faster ~~and faster and people can't really understand me and I know that I should be pronouncing the words better.~~ At this point, ~~I can't make eye contact, or I know I'll never finish so~~ my eyes are glued to the paper, *and eye contact is completely gone.* By the end of the speech ~~no one can hear me because I'm~~ *I am* speaking in a low whisper. Actually, this uncontrollable craziness ~~has become~~ *is* more frightening than speaking.

Christina's Final Edited Paragraph

My first thought when I have to give a speech is, No way! I know fear is right around the corner. The first sign of fear is burning cheeks. I know they are bright red, and I know this first symptom starts a whole series that I cannot stop. Next, my voice starts to quiver and crack. I sound like a teenager going through puberty. Then, I focus on a spot in the back of the room, losing eye contact. After that, I fiddle with the corners of my paper. Shortly after the fiddling begins, I rock back and forth. I just want to get done, so I talk faster. At this point, my eyes are glued to the paper and eye contact is completely gone. By the end of the speech, I am speaking in a low whisper. Actually, this uncontrollable craziness is more frightening than speaking.

Christina's Reflection

The most important thing I learned was focusing my paper before I start. Often I just go with what I get and don't stop to see if I have enough examples to explain it. Then I have to twist the examples to fit. This time, I focused before I started and actually changed my paper.

Stages	Strategies and Skills	5	4	3	2	1
Prewrite	1. I prewrite to explore my ideas and think deeper about a topic.	__	__	X	__	__
Draft	2. I focus my paragraphs with a clear purpose.	__	__	__	__	X
	3. I organize my ideas and make connections.	__	__	__	X	__
	4. I insert details, examples, and reasons to explain my thinking.	__	__	__	__	__
Revise	5. I read critically to identify and use the successful techniques of other writers.	__	__	X	__	__
	6. I identify the strengths and weaknesses in my papers.	__	__	X	__	__
	7. I apply specific revision strategies to my papers.	__	__	__	X	__
	8. I am flexible and willing to make changes in my writing.	__	__	__	__	X
Edit	9. I employ all or some of the following editing strategies:					
	▪ use a checklist	__	__	__	__	__
	▪ eliminate one error at a time	__	__	__	X	__
	▪ read my work aloud	__	__	__	X	__
	▪ highlight signal words	__	__	__	X	__
	▪ use spell-check or grammar-check on my computer	__	__	__	__	__
	▪ use a proofreading pal	__	__	__	__	__
	▪ double-check the assignment and expectations	__	__	__	__	__

1. *My attitude toward writing is changing a little bit. Because this paragraph turned out so good, I think I will be more willing to make changes in my next paper.*

2. *I still need to work on identifying strengths and weaknesses. I hated to do that before because I thought I'd only see weaknesses. Now I think I have strengths too.*

Copyright © 2007, The McGraw-Hill Companies, Inc. All rights reserved.

3 *Paragraph and Essay Structure*

So what am I supposed to say? And what's this paper supposed to look like? When you go for a job interview, you need to say the right things and dress properly. The same is true when you turn in writing for your college classes. It has to look right and say the right things. Readers of college writing have very definite expectations about the form and content of your writing. They expect you to organize and develop your ideas in paragraphs and essays.

IN THIS CHAPTER: A PREVIEW

Paragraph Form

- The Topic Sentence
- Paragraph Structure: Deductive and Inductive Order
- Paragraph Content

Essay Form

- The Thesis Statement
- Introductions and Conclusions
- Essay Content

Further Exploration

PARAGRAPH FORM

Think of the paragraph as a container of information. Readers of college writing are accustomed to a container with specific dimensions. The number of sentences in a paragraph may range from three to fifteen sentences or more. The first line of the paragraph is indented. Indentation is a visual cue to your reader that you have started a new paragraph. In the following figure, the writer of essay A knows how a paragraph written for college should look.

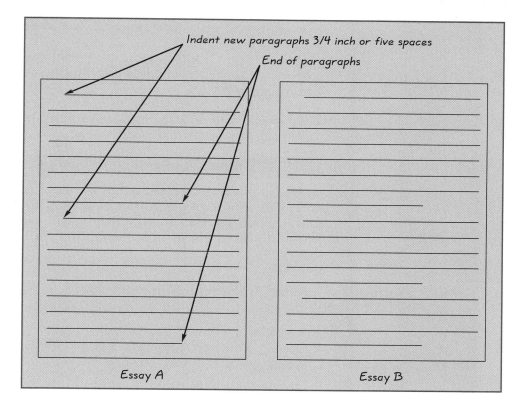

Essay A   Essay B

EXERCISE 3.1

Compare the two essays illustrated above. List the possible problems with the form of essay B.

1.

2.

The Topic Sentence

A good topic sentence directs the reader's attention to a specific focus. To formulate an effective topic sentence, develop the habit of asking yourself, What exactly am I saying about my topic?

> **Vague:** Championship wrestling is really cool.

"Really cool" doesn't direct the reader's attention to anything specific about championship wrestling.

$$1 \quad + \quad 1$$

> **Focused:** Championship wrestling has continuous action, which makes it very entertaining.

"Continuous action" focuses the reader's attention on a specific dimension of wrestling.

> **Too Specific:** Last week I lost two pounds.

Copyright © 2007, The McGraw-Hill Companies, Inc. All rights reserved.

This sentence states a fact. It does not really focus the reader's attention on a subject.

$$1 \quad\quad\quad + \quad\quad\quad 1$$

Focused: <u>Losing weight</u> is possible only when a person makes <u>hard choices many times a day.</u>

"Losing weight" is the subject; "hard choices many times a day" focuses the reader's attention on a specific dimension of the subject.

EXERCISE 3.2

Read the following topic sentences. Place a *V* for vague next to those topic sentences that are not adequately focused. Place an *S* next to topic sentences that are too specific. Place an *F* for focused next to those topic sentences that direct the reader's attention to a specific focus on the topic. Circle the terms that establish the focus.

EXAMPLE:

Bubble gum comes in different shapes. *V*

1. When I think of marriage, I want someone with that certain something.
2. Some people start smoking due to peer pressure.
3. Saturday morning television is designed to sell small children a lot of worthless junk.
4. Computers are the wave of the future.
5. Everything I know about cars I know because of my older sisters.
6. Organized sports teach kids about discipline and time management.
7. I like to lie under a shade tree on a warm summer day and take a long nap.
8. What we call "flu" is a virus.
9. Gardening is one of my favorite pastimes.
10. Women: can't live with them, can't live without them.

EXERCISE 3.3

For each of the following topics, write a topic sentence that has a 1 + 1 structure. Underline the terms that direct the reader's attention to a specific focus on the topic.

EXAMPLE:

$$1 \quad\quad\quad + \quad\quad\quad 1$$

<u>My brother has a special pair of shoes</u> for each of <u>his hobbies.</u>

1. Swimming
2. Textbooks
3. Musical instruments
4. Household chores
5. Old age
6. Insects
7. Bottled water
8. Mountains
9. Jewelry
10. Math

Paragraph Structure: Deductive and Inductive Order

It is common to place the topic sentence at the beginning of a paragraph. Doing so sends a clear message to the reader: *this is what I am talking about in this paragraph.* However, there are times when it makes sense to place the topic sentence at the end of a paragraph. When you begin with your supporting details, you "hook" your reader and create interest in your topic. When it comes at the end of a paragraph, your topic sentence states the main idea as a conclusion.

Deductive Order	Inductive Order
• begins with a topic sentence • follows with supporting details • ends with a concluding sentence that "sums up"	• begins with specific detail • follows with additional supporting details • ends with a topic sentence stating the main idea of the paragraph
Advantage: the reader immediately knows the point of the paragraph.	*Advantage: specific detail makes the reader want to keep reading.*

DEDUCTIVE ORDER

Topic: math

Focus: uses in everyday life

Supporting details (examples)

Concluding sentence

People use math all the time in daily life. When a person goes shopping, she adds up the prices of her items before she gets to the checkout line to avoid overspending. At least once a month, people have to balance their checking accounts. Sometimes a consumer will have to figure out loan terms (when buying a new car, for example) and which approaches to financing the purchase will be most economical. In my own case, when I work at the family store all summer, I balance a cash box every day. Monthly I write out a budget and mail checks to pay bills. I rarely use a calculator for these routine chores, and I believe my mind is sharper for it.

INDUCTIVE ORDER

Topic: flu, grand-mother visiting, learning to crochet

Supporting details (narrative)

Focus: a "woman thing" I just don't get

When I was thirteen years old, I came down with the flu. I was stuck in the house for a week. My grandmother came to visit me to see how I was feeling. She had a crazy idea that she would teach me how to crochet. She thought that it might help pass time. Well, bless her heart, she tried. She brought me yards of pretty blue yarn and two knitting needles. My mom and grandma sat on the couch with me, trying to explain the concept of "knit one, pearl two." It just didn't work. I practiced and practiced. The most that I could come up with was an odd-shaped potholder. My grandmother and my mother gave me the impression any woman could knit. They had me convinced that I would have an afghan in no time. They were right, if you want to call an odd-shaped potholder an afghan. Every once in a while, I pick up my mom's needles and give it a try. Those horrible memories come back. I remember: I can't do this, and furthermore, I don't like it. Knitting is one of those "woman things" I just don't get.

Copyright © 2007, The McGraw-Hill Companies, Inc. All rights reserved.

EXERCISE 3.4

Find the sentence that works best as a topic sentence for each of the following lists. Then arrange the sentences into a paragraph. Write the paragraph on a piece of paper, eliminating any sentences that do not relate to the focus of the paragraph. Use inductive order in one of the paragraphs.

EXAMPLE:

1. He puts a lot of thought into the art he gets.
2. The first time I looked in the mirror and saw a thirty-something mom looking back at me, I thought of getting a tattoo.
3. His tattoos are a collection of significant and meaningful things in his life.
4. He is able to display his devotion on his skin for all to see.
5. Skeptics who do not understand another's love for living art have to look at the fan of body art.
6. By understanding his tattoos, you begin to understand him.
7. The fan of body art has sentimental feelings about tattoos.

   Deductive order: 5, 7, 1, 3, 4, 6. Eliminate 2.

1. Late fees are ridiculous.
2. But if you pay with a credit card, you have to pay later, which can be a hassle.
3. Credit cards just aren't for everyone.
4. If you're not careful, it can take forever to pay off a bill.
5. Credit cards can be a big hassle.
6. Not all businesses take credit cards, like fast food places.
7. Some people end up using them for petty things like gas and food, and before they know it they owe more money than they ever imagined.
8. The interest rates can go through the roof.
9. Sometimes the card gets bent or scratched, and it won't work.
10. There can be problems if you get behind on your bill.
11. There's nothing more to pay.
12. When you buy things with cash, on the other hand, it's a done deal.
13. That can be a hassle, but it's when it works that the real trouble starts.

1. You get together often for pizza parties with your teammates and your coaches.
2. A good soccer player controls the ball with his head up high and his eyes on the field, not on the ball.
3. In high school, soccer games are two forty-minute periods.
4. It is a lot of work to stay ahead in the game.
5. There's a lot of practice involved in learning to dribble down the field.
6. Soccer is a lot of fun on and off the field.
7. Soccer players need endurance to stay ahead in the game.
8. It is definitely a game of coordination, body position, and skill.
9. The main skill is running back and forth down the field, trying to maneuver around opponents and still having the soccer ball under control.

EXERCISE 3.4 continued

10. Spending lots of time together both on and off the field improves performance as a team.
11. Sometimes a defenseman will not get a break until halftime comes, and then it is back on the field for the second half.
12. What makes it fun are the friendships.
13. You meet a lot of nice guys.
14. The challenge makes it fun.

1. She was new to the area.
2. For example, all of the kids who learned their times tables 1 through 12 got to go to Showbiz Pizza.
3. Cleaning her cage had its downfalls.
4. Her name was Scarlett.
5. I learned a great deal and had a blast doing it.
6. I learned all of my times tables that year.
7. What I remember best is that we had a guinea pig in our class.
8. I was one of the winners.
9. I was selected to take care of her at home over the Christmas holiday.
10. Mrs. Kress was creative and full of life.
11. I will never forget my fourth-grade teacher, Mrs. Kress.
12. She was orange and brown in color, with long hair.
13. The smell was terrible.
14. They were actually edible.
15. She always held contests.
16. We had a great time in class that year.
17. We made donuts in class once.

Paragraph Content

A paragraph explores a clearly focused topic in a number of related sentences. The main idea is stated in your **topic sentence**. Sentences following the topic sentence explore and explain the main idea. They provide **supporting details** that relate directly to the specific **focus** of the paragraph. Supporting details come in a variety of forms, such as examples, facts, and stories. The type of support you provide in your paragraph depends on your **purpose** for writing. A **conclusion sentence** restates the main idea of the paragraph or directs the reader's attention to content in the next paragraph.

PURPOSE
• explore your thoughts, ideas, feelings, and beliefs
• share what you know and what you have learned
• change your reader's mind, motivate him to do something

Copyright © 2007. The McGraw-Hill Companies, Inc. All rights reserved.

EXAMPLES:

STUDENT MODEL

Topic: *tanning booths*

People go to tanning booths for a variety reasons. Some people start going to tanning booths at a young age, in high school, for example. They say they like the way they look when they have a nice tan. They spend a lot of time and money keeping themselves tan. They can't just go once in a while. They have to go all the time, or their tan will fade. Look isn't the only reason. Some individuals go right before vacation to get some color. That way when they get to the beach, their tan is already started, and nature can then take over. Finally, there are those people who are simply addicted to tanning. Some women go so often that their skin gets discolored and blotchy. They know they should take a break, but they don't listen. Their skin is already wrinkled, and sometimes these women are still quite young. It's just important to them that they look tan year-round. Going to a tanning booth once in a while, maybe before a vacation, might be acceptable, but compulsive tanning is just plain dangerous.

Supporting details:

they like the way it looks

they're going on vacation

they want to be tan year-round

habit-forming

Conclusion sentence

Focus: reasons people go to tanning booths

Type of supporting detail: (examples), facts, story

Purpose: A. explore your thoughts, ideas, feelings, and beliefs
 (B) share what you know and what you have learned
 C. change your reader's mind, motivate him to do something

Topic: *fish in a person's diet*

There are many advantages to increasing the amount of fish in a person's daily diet. Fish is easier to digest than red meat, so benefits to the digestive system are likely. Seafood contains little or no fat. Consequently, people in cultures with high contents of fish in their diet have a lower incidence of obesity. Then again, those fats found in fish actually have a positive effect on the consumer's health. For example, fish have oils that lower an individual's cholesterol. Research shows that the omega-3 fatty acids found in fish benefit the heart and vascular systems. There may even be favorable effects on those suffering from autism, Alzheimer's disease, and attention deficit disorder. Pilot studies have been done to incorporate fish oils into a variety of foods. Imagine, fish oil in your ice cream. How tasty. That may be where the food industry is going. Researchers claim that people who eat fish live longer.

Supporting details:

easy to digest

low fat

good fat

effects of good fat

more good fats live longer

Conclusion sentence

Focus: advantages of fish in one's daily diet

Type of supporting detail: examples, (facts,) story

Purpose: A. explore your thoughts, ideas, feelings, and beliefs
 (B) share what you know and what you have learned
 C. change your reader's mind, motivate him to do something

Topic: *video games*

Video games can be educational in a positive way. The first time I saw a video game, I knew I had to play. I was around four years old. Some of my relatives were playing "Super Mario Brothers" for the Nintendo

Supporting details: *story*

Entertainment System (NES) at my grandparent's house. I didn't play that day, but I knew I would. Soon after, when I got that NES on Christmas, I was a happy boy. I sat and played games all day, every day. As often as I could, I would go to Hollywood Video and rent a new game. Once, when I was four, I rented a role-playing game (RPG). It required a whole lot of reading. That wasn't something I could do too well, but I had fun anyway. In fact, that game inspired me to start learning to read. The first words I can remember figuring out were "continue" and "game over." Knowing the difference between those words helped a lot. I also learned a little math from remembering my high scores. I've been playing video games ever since I got that NES. I'd like to think that I learn a little something from every new game that I play. It may not be that important, but I learn something.

Conclusion sentence

Focus: educational value of video games

Type of supporting detail: examples, facts, (story)

Purpose: A. explore your thoughts, ideas, feelings, and beliefs
B. share what you know and what you have learned
(C.) change your reader's mind, motivate him to do something

EXERCISE 3.5

For each paragraph, identify the words in the topic sentence that describe the focus of the paragraph. Then indicate the type of supporting detail and the writer's purpose.

Motorcycles have always terrified me. My ex-boyfriend had a motorcycle. I was afraid every time he would ride it. I knew he took risks and didn't care if anything horrible happened to him. That made the feeling in my stomach worse. I only rode with him four times. Every time I got on that motorcycle I felt like I was putting my life in danger. I did not like feeling that way. After I graduated from high school, my friend Rob went out and bought a motorcycle. He offered to take me for a ride. I put a helmet on and tried to enjoy the ride. I didn't know if he was a good driver or not. He had taught himself how to ride his motorcycle, and he hadn't been riding for much more than a week. At first I thought I was going to fall off the bike. Then I scraped my leg when he got too close to a parked car. After a few minutes, I was ready to be dropped off. That is the last time I got on a motorcycle.

Focus:

Type of supporting detail: examples, facts, story

Purpose: A. explore your thoughts, ideas, feelings, and beliefs
B. share what you know and what you have learned
C. change your reader's mind, motivate him to do something

So what exactly is the attraction of Las Vegas? The bright lights and casinos entice a person to come right in and try her luck. The moment a person enters a casino, she leaves the hot, dry desert air in exchange for the wonderful aroma of nicotine-stained walls and cheap (but free) booze. A slot machine bell announces an occasional winner. There are no clocks to remind her of the time she is wasting

Copyright © 2007, The McGraw-Hill Companies, Inc. All rights reserved.

Destinations: Shifting Gears from Paragraph to Essay

Be Specific: It's in the Details

"I'll have the personal stuffed crust pan pizza with extra cheese, ham, and pineapple." "One Venti Double Non-Fat Caramel Latte, please." When you place an order, you don't normally say simply "pizza" or "coffee"—you need to be specific to get what you want from the person taking your order. Similarly, when developing an essay, you need to be specific in order to get the response you want from your reader. Vague, unsupported statements—like vague orders—won't make your point.

Introducing . . .

Whether you are preparing an oral presentation or writing an essay, nothing hooks an audience like a great first sentence, and nothing wins them over like a strong introduction. Whether structured deductively (stating your point right away) or inductively (laying out your evidence first), the introduction is the first thing your audience will hear or read, so it needs to establish purpose and direction *and* be interesting. Keep in mind that you don't have to write your introduction first. In fact, the best opening paragraphs are often written (and are always revised) after a solid draft of the paper has been completed.

Paragraph-to-Essay on the Job

In the working world, you'll often need to carry a project through from idea to completed project. Here are some examples:

- An assistant at a non-profit is given his boss's vague notes from a meeting and asked to write a grant letter. He might ask his boss some questions and do additional research to make sure the information in the letter is accurate, the arguments for giving money are persuasive, and the tone is confident.

- A high school principal writes a brief proposal about how to raise test scores in her school; if the board approves her plan, she will have to follow that proposal to see that the initiatives and programs proposed are created and carried through.

The journey from idea to completion can seem daunting at first, but the final product is usually highly rewarding—in the classroom or on the job.

EXERCISE 3.5 continued

while losing her hard-earned money. No way! If she feels like it, there are great shows to be seen. Some of the nation's most famous stars entertain nightly in the casinos of Las Vegas. If she gets tired, she can simply go upstairs to her half-price room. If she gets hungry, she can eat like royalty from a variety of food stations located throughout the casino. Nothing can compare with the atmosphere of Vegas!

Focus:

Type of supporting detail: examples, facts, story

Purpose: A. explore your thoughts, ideas, feelings, and beliefs
B. share what you know and what you have learned
C. change your reader's mind, motivate him to do something

Charles Williams of El Cajon, California, was charged with two counts of murder and twenty-six other felony charges. The fifteen-year-old shot and killed two classmates, injuring thirteen others at Santana High School on March 5th of 2001. Due to the horrific nature of the crime, he will be charged as an adult. In Pontiac, Michigan, an eleven-year-old boy shot and killed a stranger outside a party store. Because of his history of violent behavior, there was a dispute over whether he should be tried as an adult. He was found guilty under juvenile charges and sentenced to a facility till the age of twenty-one. Alexander Bedford of South

EXERCISE 3.5 continued

Florida will be tried as an adult on first-degree murder charges. Fourteen-year-old Bedford confessed to stabbing his mother to death, after she asked him to "fetch an extension cord and prepare for a whipping." If convicted, he could face life in prison. These are a few of the many cases in which juveniles committed violent offenses and suffered the consequences of adult sentencing.

Focus:

Type of supporting detail: examples, facts, story

Purpose: A. explore your thoughts, ideas, feelings, and beliefs
 B. share what you know and what you have learned
 C. change your reader's mind, motivate him to do something

ESSAY FORM

Your writing in college will often take the form of an *essay*. The essay is a multi-paragraph form. It may consist of only four or five paragraphs. It has a clear introduction, body, and conclusion.

Introduction Paragraph

- captures the reader's interest
- establishes the importance of your topic
- clearly defines the focus of the essay in a **thesis statement**

Body Paragraphs

- explore topics related to the thesis, stated in the **topic sentence**
- provide supporting details
- connect with other paragraphs in the essay with the repetition of key terms

Conclusion

- retrieves important ideas or details related earlier in the paper
- points to important actions or insights
- appeals to the reader

The Thesis Statement

The thesis statement expresses the main point or points of an essay. Like the topic sentence, the thesis statement provides the reader with a sense of orientation, with

Thesis Statement

Topic Sentence	Thesis Statement
One thing that makes baseball challenging is the rules involved in the game.	Because of the complex rules of the game, baseball is often a game of strategy and drama.
A convenient way to get to know another culture is to visit restaurants and enjoy the food of that culture.	Food, music, and holiday celebrations all provide an insight into what makes one culture different from another.
Nonindigenous organisms have changed the ecology of the Great Lakes.	Such factors as nonindigenous organisms, changing weather patterns, and industrial pollution have had negative effects on the ecology of the Great Lakes.

Copyright © 2007, The McGraw-Hill Companies, Inc. All rights reserved.

the idea that there is a plan behind the writing. But the thesis statement promises more than the topic sentence: it makes a promise to the reader that the essay will explore specific ideas in a focused, organized manner.

EXERCISE 3.6

Read the following thesis statements. Place a *V* next to those that are vague. Next to those that seem focused, jot down two or three questions the writer promises to explore in the body of the essay.

EXAMPLE:

> I'm terrified of flying. *V*
>
> **Focused:** Because of my terrible fear of flying, I have a special ritual both before and while I fly to minimize anxiety.

Questions the writer promises to answer:

    A. *Why am I so afraid of flying?*
    B. *What is my "before-flying" ritual?*
    C. *What is my in-air ritual that minimizes anxiety?*

1. A good hobby can develop a person's concentration and have other important benefits.
   A. What is the hobby?
   B. What are some types of hobbies?
   C. What are the important benefits?

2. Since Saturday morning television is designed to sell small children a lot of worthless junk, parents need to monitor what their kids watch.
   A. What should kids be watching?
   B. How should parents monitor their kids?
   C. What is the worthless junk?

3. Older siblings either make life easier or a living hell for their brothers and sisters.
   A. What do they do to make it hell?
   B. Why do they do it?
   C. How do your siblings make you feel?

4. Hockey is the greatest sport on earth.
   A. Why?
   B. When did it start?
   C. Who are the best players?

5. Advances in technology are visible in a number of new films coming out of Hollywood.

6. Digital photography enables the amateur photographer to do a variety of things that were once the skills of only highly trained professionals.

EXERCISE 3.6 continued

7. The cougar is an endangered species in Florida.

8. The price of gold has not changed in the past two years.

9. Even though the Olympics is supposed to emphasize fair play and pure-competition, the events are almost always influenced by world politics.

10. California is the most populous state in the union.

EXERCISE 3.7

For each of the following topics, write a focused thesis statement that makes a promise to the reader. In the spaced provide below each topic, write two or three questions the thesis promises to answer.

EXAMPLE:

Household chores—Sharing household chores makes lighter work and gives family members a chance to bond.
A. *What household chores can't be shared?*
B. *Which ones can be shared and how is work made lighter?*
C. *How does bonding occur?*

1. Reading

2. Old age

Copyright © 2007, The McGraw-Hill Companies, Inc. All rights reserved.

EXERCISE 3.7 continued

3. Insects

4. Bottled water

5. Math

| WW | Introductory Paragraph |

| WW | Writing Effective Leads for Feature Articles |

Introductions and Conclusions

The beginning and end of an essay have special functions. Introductions grab the reader's attention and set the tone of the essay. They also establish the importance of the topic and focus the essay with a thesis statement. Conclusions, on the other hand, help the reader see how the individual parts of the essay add up to something. *What was I supposed to understand? What am I supposed to do?* These are questions a conclusion should answer.

There are many ways to introduce and conclude a piece of writing, depending on the form and the reader.

Introduction	Form	Conclusion
Instead of writing "In this paper I'm going to tell you about . . ."		*Instead of writing "In conclusion" or "In summary . . ."*
• tell a story • cite examples • present statistics	Essay	• review an important detail • tell a related story
• define key terms • state the divisions of your topic	Essay test	• assert connections between key ideas • discuss consequences
• state the purpose of your report	Report	• present the results of the investigation or activity
• summarize a reading to define a problem • cite examples to dramatize a problem	Term paper	• propose solutions to the problem • present a quote to help the reader think beyond the scope of the paper.

Essay Content

The content of your essay is organized according to the questions you promise to answer for your reader. During the writing process, you will see that the following ways of structuring your ideas will come in handy. Structuring your ideas helps you explore and organize what you know.

Structure	Description
Illustration and example	Explores ideas in greater degrees of specificity
Narrative and description	Examines an incident or experience, focusing on specific place, time, people, events, and outcome
Process	Explains a procedure by describing steps involved, props and equipment used, people involved
Cause and effect	Explores "symptoms" of a problem, prior conditions or reasons, solutions to or consequences of the problem
Comparison and contrast	Examines similarities and differences in point-by-point or block organization
Definition	Specifies meaning of terms or important ideas: component parts, function or purpose, origins, illustrations

EXAMPLE:

Vocal Teacher's Nightmare

Music artists. They make it look so easy. Don't they? They sing and sing, hit after hit, platinum record after platinum record. I can't sing. I hear songs on the radio, and I want to sing along. I open my mouth expecting to let out harmonious tunes that will make birds chirp and babies smile. Instead I blurt out foreign, off-tune notes that make birds flee and babies cry. I have back up singers in the form of dogs, howling from everywhere in hearing distance. <u>I can do somethings well; singing is not one of them.</u>

It is hard for me to remember when I first became aware of my not-so-dazzling singing ability. <u>I can, however, recall about seven months ago when I last attempted singing.</u> I could tell it wasn't going to be good from the start. My friends wanted to do some karaoke. I figured I would sit there very quietly, listening and watching my friends like Court or Dave, who could sing well. Things looked good. My friends were having fun singing, and I was going unnoticed. Unfortunately, all good things must come to an end. I was spotted. Becca turned and looked at me. Grinning, she said it was my turn to sing. I tried to get out of it, but my friends were persistent. There was no way out, so I gave up and picked a song. "Summer of 69" was my choice. The words appeared on the TV, and I started to sing. By the time the first line rolled off my tongue, my friends were in hysterics. I must have missed every correct note in that song.

<u>Singing is a lot harder than it looks.</u> There isn't a lot behind it, but everything has to be done precisely. You have to breathe well and have strong lungs. This shouldn't be a problem for me since I've been playing hockey all my life and my lungs have good endurance. Secondly, you must have finely tuned vocal cords. You would think that you would have this covered. After all you have been using your voice all your life. Puberty gave you some trouble, but you're back on your feet and in control of your voice. Wrong. You have to hit the high notes, and make the low notes sound good. Your singing has to be the right pitch, tone, and loudness, and you have to coordinate it perfectly to the music.

Don't judge me by my singing. <u>It's not like I do everything bad.</u> I am a good hockey player. I have been playing since I was three years old and love it. I am good at golf. I

Copyright © 2007, The McGraw-Hill Companies, Inc. All rights reserved.

Intro

Thesis statement
Topic sentence
Body paragraph

Narrative

Topic sentence
Body paragraph

Process

Topic sentence
Body paragraph

Examples

have only been playing for four years now, but I am getting better every time I play. I listen well too. A lot of friends come and talk to me often for help. I'll listen to what they say, actually paying attention, and try my best to help them. So I guess I am not a lost cause in the talent pool. I have talents to offset my flaws.

Conclusion

The only way I can ever become a good singer is to take a vocal class. I would need a trained professional; she would need ear plugs. If after hearing my atrocious voice she was still willing to teach me, I think I would be able to catch on. At least to the point where I'd survive my next karaoke attempt. I had a singing class once in the third grade, but what can they really teach you at that age? I was probably a bad singer then too. My teacher was really nice, encouraging me to sing. I had to; I was being graded on it. Looking back, I really didn't like that class.

EXERCISE 3.8

Read the following essay and underline the thesis statement and topic sentences. Write short responses to the discussion questions that follow and identify the purpose of the essay.

In newspaper headlines, we read of children shooting children with guns, they found in their own homes. "We thought it wasn't loaded," say grief-stricken kids. People want guns in their homes for protection. However, research shows that the person most likely to shoot you or a family member probably lives in your house. Simply put, guns kept in the home for self-protection are more often used to kill somebody you know than to kill in self-defense.

Throughout my childhood, there were guns in our home. My dad was a police officer. He had several revolvers he used for work and several rifles he used for hunting. From the time we were little, my dad took every precaution to prevent his kids from accidentally stumbling upon his guns. Unloaded guns were stored in one room; bullets were hidden in another. He taught us that guns were not toys. I always assumed other cops took the same precautions with their kids. For the most part, all of them did. For all of us, guns were simply a part of our lives, whether hidden away in a closet, hanging from our dad's belt, or proudly displayed in a cabinet. None of us kids thought our parents needed to be protected from the guns kept in our homes.

When I was in middle school, I learned a lesson about the dangers of guns in the home. Dennis was my dad's partner at work. More importantly, he was one of my dad's best friends from childhood. When they weren't working, my dad and Dennis were hanging out together. Our families made up one big family. One summer day my mom got the call from the police commander. He asked her to find dad and get him over to Dennis's house. Dennis was dead. He had shot himself in the head with his police revolver. His wife had found him dead in their bedroom.

Having guns in the home can provide a person with a sense of control and safety, but there are also consequences for having loaded guns in the home. Kids take out their parents' guns and shoot each other by accident. Spouses hear "intruders" in their home and shoot family members by accident. In fact, according to "Guns in the Home," "A gun is used for protection in fewer than two percent of home invasion crimes." Then there is suicide. As my father's friend shows, reaching for a gun and pulling the trigger takes a second, but the consequences can last a lifetime.

EXERCISE 3.8 continued

I've often wondered if Dennis would still be here today, enjoying his kids and grandkids, if a gun had not been so accessible to him. Would a few extra minutes have given him the chance to reach out to another person and maybe find a better solution to the problems he was facing? Odds are that when one uses a gun to solve the problem, the consequences are going to be deadly permanent.

1. What promises does the writer make to the reader in the thesis statement of this essay?

2. Why does the writer talk about her personal experience?

3. What is the purpose of the essay?

4. Can you suggest an effective title for the essay?

5. Circle the purpose that best reflects your view of the essay.
   A. explore your thoughts, ideas, feelings, and beliefs
   B. share what you know and what you have learned
   C. change your reader's mind, motivate him to do something

FURTHER EXPLORATION

1. Review the "Essay Content" section in this chapter. Then go to Chapter 21 and read one of the essays. What is the writer's purpose? How does the writer structure his or her ideas in the essay?

2. Select an article from a magazine you enjoy reading and analyze it. Determine the writer's purpose and approaches to structuring his or her ideas.

3. List the kinds of writing you have done so far in college and the kinds of writing you will do in the classes you are enrolled in this semester. For each kind of writing, indicate the length (paragraph or essay) and purpose.

4. Talk to students who are enrolled in a career program that interests you. Find out what kind of writing they have had to do, including its length (paragraph or essay) and purpose.

Copyright © 2007, The McGraw-Hill Companies, Inc. All rights reserved.

PART TWO

Patterns of Thinking and Writing

4 *Illustration and Example*

Evidence—give me evidence. This might be the number one request of college teachers. College writing requires that you make claims and provide evidence to support your claims. Examples and illustrations are common forms of evidence that are always available to you. You use examples and illustrations to support your claim that

- computers in the classroom have positive effects
- some teen mothers do an admirable job of raising their children
- carpooling can have both advantages and disadvantages

Paragraphs constructed with illustrations provide convincing evidence. To develop their ideas, writers use either an extended example or several related examples. The example captures the reader's attention and explains at the same time.

IN THIS CHAPTER: A PREVIEW

Illustration-and-Example Thinking

- Elements of Illustration
- Whole-to-Part Analysis
- Related Examples
- Extended Examples

A Process Approach to Writing the Illustration-and-Example Paragraph

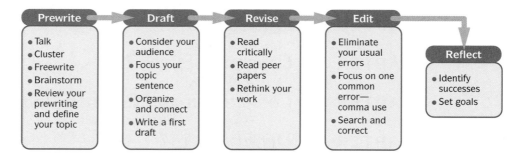

Prewrite	Draft	Revise	Edit	Reflect
• Talk • Cluster • Freewrite • Brainstorm • Review your prewriting and define your topic	• Consider your audience • Focus your topic sentence • Organize and connect • Write a first draft	• Read critically • Read peer papers • Rethink your work	• Eliminate your usual errors • Focus on one common error—comma use • Search and correct	• Identify successes • Set goals

Student Sample of the Writing Process

WW Annie Dillard

ILLUSTRATION-AND-EXAMPLE THINKING

You use examples in every aspect of your life. When you tell friends about your busy weekend, you use specifics to convince them you are exhausted. You worked eight hours at the laundry folding shirts and unbuttoning buttons, wrote a three-page essay on poverty in the 1920s, and studied angles and formulas for a math test. On top of all this, you made a buffet dinner for twenty aunts, uncles, and cousins for your mother's fiftieth birthday. As a college writer, you will use examples to illustrate a topic or explain a concept.

Elements of Illustration

Point	Example	Fact or Detail	Impact
What is crucial to understand?	What will clearly illustrate the point?	What specific facts or details are appropriate to explain the example?	How does this affect people or events?

READING: from "America's Gambling Craze," by James Popkin with Katia Hetter

Impact

Example 1

Example 2

Example 3

Example 4

Fact

Example 5

Facts

Point

Example 6

Impact

Example 7

Fact

Today the Bible Belt might as well be renamed the Black-jack Belt, with floating and land-based casinos throughout Mississippi and Louisiana and plans for more in Florida, Texas, Alabama, and Arkansas. Meanwhile, the Midwest is overrun with slot hogs, none of the porcine variety. Iowa, Illinois, and Indiana have a number of floating casinos, and a land-based casino is scheduled to open in mid-May just outside Detroit, in Windsor, Ontario. Low-stakes casinos attract visitors to old mining towns in Colorado and South Dakota, and Indian tribes operate 225 casinos and high-stakes bingo halls nation-wide. Add church bingo, card rooms, sports wagering, dog and horse racing, and jai alai to the mix and it becomes clear why Americans legally wagered $300 billion in 1992—a 1,800 percent increase over 1976.

What's the deal? Not long ago, Americans held gambling in nearly the same esteem as heroin dealing and applauded when ax-wielding police paid a visit to the corner dice room. But moral outrage has become as outmoded as a penny slot machine. In 1955, for example, baseball commissioner Ford Frick considered wagering so corrupt he prohibited major leaguers from overnighting in Las Vegas. Last year, by contrast, Americans for the first time made more trips to casinos than they did to Major League ballparks—some 92 million trips, according to one study.

DISCUSSION QUESTIONS

1. How does the list of examples support Popkin and Hetter's point?

2. What kinds of facts do Popkin and Hetter use to strengthen their examples?

Copyright © 2007, The McGraw-Hill Companies, Inc. All rights reserved.

3. Why do Popkin and Hetter state their point so late in the paragraph?

Whole-to-Part Analysis

Illustration-and-example thinking can be aided by analyzing the parts of a topic. This analysis involves identifying specific details and seeing the relationship of parts to a whole. Often this work reveals crucial understandings that are essential to making a claim.

EXERCISE 4.1

For each of the following items, cite a topic. Identify more and more specific parts of each topic. Try to go to three degrees of specificity. Then identify a claim you might make from your analysis.

EXAMPLE:

sport ⟶ *football* ⟶ *quarterback* ⟶ *passing game* ⟶ *interception*

Point: *A quarterback can save a game, but he can also be the primary cause for losing.*

1. modes of transportation ⟶

   Point:

2. college classes ⟶

   Point:

3. summer jobs ⟶

   Point:

4. common illnesses ⟶

   Point:

5. friendship ⟶

   Point:

Related Examples

Examples build support. They help convince readers to adopt your point of view. While writers vary the number of examples they use, they are careful to connect them. Sometimes writers connect similar examples; sometimes they connect contrasting examples.

Similar Examples—from "America's Gambling Craze," by James Popkin with Katia Hetter

1. Today the Bible Belt might as well be renamed the Black-jack Belt, with <u>floating and land-based casinos</u> throughout Mississippi and Louisiana and plans for more in Florida, Texas, Alabama, and Arkansas.

2. <u>Meanwhile</u>, the Midwest is overrun with slot hogs, none of the porcine variety. Iowa, Illinois, and Indiana have a number of <u>floating casinos</u>, and a <u>land-based casino</u> is scheduled to open in mid-May just outside Detroit, in Windsor, Ontario.

Contrasting Examples—from "America's Gambling Craze," by James Popkin with Katia Hetter

1. In 1955, <u>for example</u>, baseball commissioner Ford Frick considered wagering so corrupt he prohibited major leaguers from overnighting in Las Vegas.

2. Last year, <u>by contrast</u>, Americans for the first time made more trips to casinos than they did to Major League ballparks—some 92 million trips, according to one study.

EXERCISE 4.2

Identify related examples for each of the following topic sentences.

- List personal examples or factual examples from newspapers, magazines, or books.
- Review your list to determine which three or four examples would make the most convincing connections.
- Cross out the examples that do not fit.
- Identify the relationship between the related examples.
- Determine if your examples are similar or contrasting.

EXAMPLE:

Point: Dieting can be a maze of confusion.

A. *On the Atkins or the Suzanne Sommers diets, dieters totally avoid some foods while they eat lots of fat and protein.*

B. *Then there are diets where people take pills to kill their appetite, but they eat anything they want.*

C. ~~*I know someone who finally just gave up and had her stomach stapled.*~~

D. *Some diets, like Weight Watchers, are highly controlled and have group support systems. The person who wants to lose weight joins a club and attends regular meetings; in such cases, the individual often has to buy special products the club markets, like milkshakes and complete meals.*

E. *Short, intense diets, like the three-day juice diet, the flush your kidneys diet, and the cabbage soup diet enable a person to lose up to ten pounds fast.*

Connection: *Diets teach contradictory lessons on what a person can and cannot eat.*

Relationship: *contrasting examples*

Copyright © 2007, The McGraw-Hill Companies, Inc. All rights reserved.

EXERCISE 4.2 continued

1. Point: The credit card trap begins with the offer to buy now and pay later.

Connection:

Relationship:

2. Point: Asking for help is difficult, but it can be the best way to solve a problem.

Connection:

Relationship:

3. Point: A good friend is a person you can trust.

Connection:

Relationship:

Copyright © 2007, The McGraw-Hill Companies, Inc. All rights reserved.

EXERCISE 4.2 continued

4. Point: Good study habits are the key to success in college.

Connection:

Relationship:

5. Point: Video games are an addictive waste of time.

Connection:

Relationship:

EXERCISE 4.3

Provide two similar examples and one contrasting example for each of the following topic sentences. Use personal examples or examples from newspapers, magazines, or books. Notice how the connecting terms "signal" similarity and difference.

EXAMPLE:

I have a number of people to look to as role models.

For example, my father has provided me with a really good work ethic.

Likewise, my mother has taught me to listen carefully and think before speaking.

In contrast, my friend Dean sometimes leads me in the wrong direction.

1. The "chick-flick" is a myth because it seems that Hollywood's prime market is men.

EXERCISE 4.3 continued

For example,

Likewise,

In contrast,

2. What's the best family car? The answer isn't easy.
   For example,

Likewise,

In contrast,

3. Athletes serve as role models for the world.
   For example,

Likewise,

In contrast,

Extended Examples

Facts and details make examples interesting and convincing. They are the heart of illustration-and-example thinking. Six basic questions will help you elaborate and extend your examples. A single extended example can support a claim.

Who?	What?	Where?	When?	Why?	How?

EXERCISE 4.4

For the following items, identify an example that agrees or disagrees with the claim. Extend your thinking by exploring three or four of the preceding questions to focus and elaborate on a single example. Freewrite the answer to the questions by citing specific facts or details.

EXAMPLE:

Claim: Birthdays hold the richest memories.

One example: *my twelfth birthday*

Extend your thinking:
   WHAT: I got a mountain bike.
   WHERE: I rode it to Connie's house.
   WHAT: It was blue and silver with a black seat.

Copyright © 2007. The McGraw-Hill Companies, Inc. All rights reserved.

EXERCISE 4.4 continued

I will never forget my twelfth birthday. I got a mountain bike and a pair of nylons. The bike was a blue and silver Huffy three-speed with a black seat and thin black tires. It had a bell on the handlebars. My dad joked that the bell was to warn people that I was loose and on the roads. Plus, a water-bottle carrier was attached to the frame. But I also got my first pair of nylons. I quickly put the nylons on, and then I jumped on the bike and rode straight to Connie's house to show her. She raced out of her house and met me on the sidewalk. She got her bike, and we rode around the neighborhood showing our friends. Just before I left for home, I remembered my other gift, but the nylons were filled with runs. I guess I wasn't ready to be a lady at twelve.

1. Money is the best gift.

   One example:

   Extend your thinking:

2. Babysitting is a tough job.

   One example:

   Extend your thinking:

3. Technology is essential to daily living.
   One example:
   Extend your thinking:

4. A movie is a perfect date.
   One example:
   Extend your thinking:

Copyright © 2007, The McGraw-Hill Companies, Inc. All rights reserved.

EXERCISE 4.4 continued

5. The boss makes or breaks a job.

One example:

Extend your thinking:

A PROCESS APPROACH TO WRITING THE ILLUSTRATION-AND-EXAMPLE PARAGRAPH

The illustration-and-example paragraph connects specific detail to an idea. Once that connection is made, however, the writer's job is to provide a detailed explanation. Sometimes writers choose to develop a single example—an extended example—in an entire paragraph. Or they may choose to present multiple examples, each with its detailed explanation. To practice connecting specific details to an idea, write an illustration-and-example paragraph, using either an extended example or multiple examples. Following are some suggested topics for your illustration-and-example paragraph.

Specific Topics	General Topics
The advantages of organized sports in school	Events that had an impact on you
	• family events
The disadvantages of organized sports in school	• work events
	• school events
The difficulties of being a kid today	
The advantages of being married (or being single)	People that had an impact on you
	• role models
Strategies for saving money	• teachers
Strategies for getting good grades	• someone always in trouble
Strategies for getting fired	• parents or grandparents
Approaches for staying thin or gaining weight	• sisters, brothers, or other relatives
	• neighbors
Ways to find and keep a babysitter	• a boss
Planning a perfect vacation (or party)	A topic of your own choice

ELEMENTS OF ILLUSTRATION

Point	Example	Fact or Detail	Impact
What is crucial to understand?	What will clearly illustrate the point?	What specific facts or details are appropriate to explain the example?	How does this affect people or events?

STUDENT MODEL

Point

Example 1

Impact

Example 2

Impact

Point Restated

Sometimes the most unlikely people can become friends. One unlikely friend was Fran, the team captain. She was a really nice girl, and she always got her way with our coach, which irritated me at first. Later I realized that having a friend who could manipulate people always worked in my favor. She had the gift of gab and could usually change our coach's mind, telling her we tried our best, the other team was taller and stronger, or the referees were prejudiced. Often this worked, and we didn't have to do laps. Her abilities worked off the court as well. So I liked hanging out with her even though I didn't like her at first. She taught me how to talk to people in a straight and honest way. The other unlikely friend was Monica, the team troublemaker. She was always yelled at for doing dumb things like not looking and getting smacked in the head, bringing food onto the court, or arriving late to practice. Coach made her run laps, but she also really liked Monica because she never talked disrespectfully to anyone. That's probably why Monica and I stayed friends after volleyball was over. We took biology and math classes together. She helped me study for tests and taught me how to be organized. Plus, Monica kept me laughing all the time. Even unlikely people have qualities that build good friendships.

PREWRITE

- Talk
- Cluster
- Freewrite
- Brainstorm
- Review your prewriting and define your topic

Select one or more of the following prewriting strategies to explore a topic and develop your ideas for an illustration-and-example paragraph.

Talk

EXERCISE 4.5

Present your topic to two or three peers. Take turns talking. If you are talking about a topic your peers are acquainted with, try to use your specific examples to explain what makes your understanding of this topic different and unique. When it's your turn to listen, take note of the examples you hear, their meaning, and the questions you have about your peers' topics. When it is relevant, ask questions that pertain to who, where, what, when, why, and how.

Cluster

EXERCISE 4.6

Use the following clustering diagram to develop a topic. If you know the point you want to make, begin there. Then explore the examples, facts, and details that support your point. Eventually determine the impact of these examples on other people. However, if you know the examples but are unsure about your point or the impact, begin there.

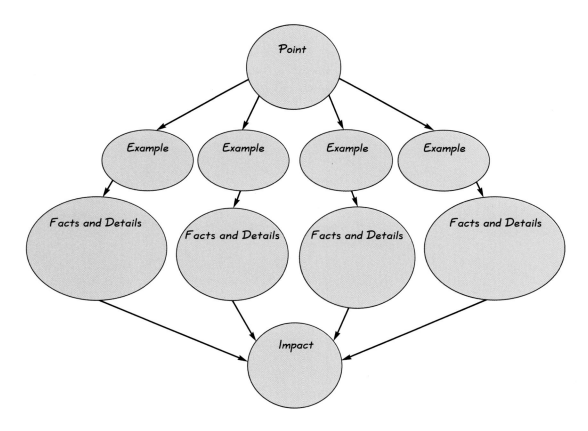

Freewrite

EXERCISE 4.7

Write as much as you can in five minutes about the topic that interests you. As you write, keep in mind the need to cite examples to develop your ideas. When you think of an example, try to explore it within at least three or four sentences that add detail.

Copyright © 2007, The McGraw-Hill Companies, Inc. All rights reserved.

Brainstorm

EXERCISE 4.8

Review the list of topics on page 61. Select three topics and practice developing multiple examples for each one. Jot down at least four related examples. Write a topic sentence that connects the examples to a clearly defined point you would make if writing a paragraph on the topic.

EXAMPLE:

Topic: *Fast foods*

Examples:

McDonald's Big Mac and fries combo with an apple pie

Burger King Whopper with cheese

Wendy's baked potato with broccoli and cheddar

Kentucky Fried Chicken extra-crispy chicken strips and barbecue sauce

Point: *Every fast-food chain specializes in hot food in minutes.*

Impact: *Fast-food chains offer a diet for the terminally overweight.*

1. Topic:

Examples:

Point:

Impact:

2. Topic:

Examples:

Point:

Impact:

3. Topic:

Examples:

Destinations: Taking Shortcuts and Scenic Routes with Illustration and Example

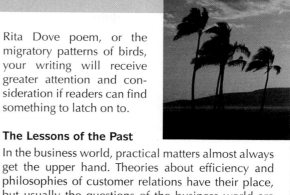

For Example . . .

One of the first rules of good communication is to be specific. General statements—e.g., My brother is annoying; my boss is the greatest—might convey the speaker's main idea, but they do not have much impact on the listener. Real communicative power comes in the form of specific examples: My brother refuses to take phone messages for me, he teases me relentlessly about my taste in clothes, and he sold my CD collection; my boss mentors me, pays me well, and she gave me her tickets to the baseball game tonight. These examples give the listener a real idea of just how annoying or great these people are. Specific examples and illustrations provide weight and strength to any point you may make. Use them often.

Drawing Your Reader In

While logic is the foundation of all academic writing (your points need to make sense in order not to be dismissed), the strongest piece of writing is more than simply logical. Your work also needs to be *engaging*. The surest way to draw your reader into your piece is through the use of examples and illustrations which, in addition to providing the basic evidence for your writing, can also evoke laughter, sympathy, anger, and fear in your audience. Whether you choose to focus on a battle in the Vietnam War, an interpretation of a Rita Dove poem, or the migratory patterns of birds, your writing will receive greater attention and consideration if readers can find something to latch on to.

The Lessons of the Past

In the business world, practical matters almost always get the upper hand. Theories about efficiency and philosophies of customer relations have their place, but usually the questions of the business world are more mundane: How many boxes can we get to Cleveland by Thursday? What are Anna's job responsibilities? How much will it cost to develop a new product, and how much revenue will it bring in? The tangible and the calculable are the primary concerns in nearly every non-academic field you might work in. Hence, in a business setting, your ability to draw effectively on real world events and facts by employing examples and illustrations is essential. If you want to convince your boss to take a risk on a new product, for example, you will probably need to demonstrate how similar products have fared in the past or how many paying customers would be interested. The more specifically you can support your claims, the more seriously your ideas will be taken.

EXERCISE 4.8 continued

Point:

Impact:

Review Your Prewriting and Define Your Topic

EXERCISE 4.9

Use the following questions to review your prewriting and select a topic for an illustration-and-example paragraph.

- Which one is the most interesting and generated the strongest examples?
- Which one can be supported with specific facts and details?
- Which one had the most significant impact on you or other people?
- Which one helped you discover something new or interesting about yourself or the subject you selected?

Copyright © 2007, The McGraw-Hill Companies, Inc. All rights reserved.

DRAFT

- Consider your audience
- Focus your topic sentence
- Organize and connect
- Write a first draft

Write a draft that organizes your prewriting into a single paragraph. This first draft will establish the subject and state the point of your illustration-and-example paragraph.

Consider Your Audience

EXERCISE 4.10

Now that you have selected a topic, consider who will read your paragraph. Use the following questions to consider how to convey your point to your audience.

- Why is this topic important to your audience?
- What special meaning does this topic have for you? Why do you want your audience to understand this meaning?
- Will your audience agree or disagree with your thinking? Will you be asking them to think about a subject in a new way?

Return to the exercises on illustration-and-example thinking in this chapter and decide which way of thinking about your topic will help you connect best with your audience.

Focus Your Topic Sentence

Topic sentences announce the subject and the point of a paragraph. An effective illustration-and-example paragraph is dependent on identifying one of the following: the point or the impact. Use a 1 (subject) + 1 (point or impact) approach to strengthen your topic sentences.

EXERCISE 4.11

In each of the following topic sentences, underline the words expressing the subject of the paragraph. Then indicate the point or impact, which will most likely be developed with examples.

EXAMPLE:

$$1 \qquad + \qquad 1$$
A <u>young person</u> can acquire <u>a conscientious work ethic</u>.

1. Careful use of the learning lab enables a student to approach a skill from many different directions.

2. The high divorce rate suggests teen marriages are doomed.

3. Choosing friends poorly is the best way a person can get on the wrong side of a parent.

4. Recent movies demonstrate the amazing achievements of computer-generated special effects.

5. Interviewing skills may be more important than job skills.

Organize and Connect

Paragraphs that use illustration-and-example thinking are often organized by listing the examples. These paragraphs use three common transitional approaches: time, place, or enumeration. Following is a list of the most common illustration-and-example transition words and phrases.

ILLUSTRATION-AND-EXAMPLE TRANSITION WORDS AND PHRASES

The transition phrases you use will be determined by your subject matter. However, the general categories below offer useful forms of transition and connecting terms.

Time	Place	Enumeration/Order
As a kid	In elementary school	First
During adolescence	In middle school	Second
As an adult	In high school	Third
In the morning	Here at home	Initially
Most afternoons	At work	Next
In the evening	Near the front of the restaurant	Finally
At the beginning of my shift	All around the dining room	On the one hand
After a few hours	Back in the kitchen	On the other hand
Toward closing time		Then again
Occasionally		
Once in a while		

EXERCISE 4.12:

Read the following paragraph. Underline words or phrases the writer uses to make transitions from one example to the next.

Teachers and parents always promote reading, but the end result of loving books is becoming a bookworm. Unfortunately, the bookworms I knew in school did not seem happy. In fourth grade, for example, there was a kid named Scott Hoff. He just looked stiff and angry; he wore ties, and his hair was always carefully combed. He was very studious and had a way of sneering when he talked to other kids. He rarely smiled or laughed. He read during recess probably because no one wanted to play with him. In middle school, Jackie Ritter was an amazing math student. She looked lonely and weighted down; she wore long plaid skirts and heavy sweaters and carried a book bag that would break your back. She sat near the front of the room and always had her work done. When she finished, she opened a book and read. She always got As, but she never got any dates. In high school, yet another bookworm I knew was Dave Falconer. He was good in math too. He already knew he wanted to be an engineer, and he was one of the first kids to understand and start working with data processing. He read technical books all the time. He had a great future ahead of him, but he never seemed to have fun during high school. All three of these kids were noticeably different from other kids. Reading seemed to help them be smart, but it didn't help them have happy lives.

Copyright © 2007, The McGraw-Hill Companies, Inc. All rights reserved.

Write a First Draft

EXERCISE 4.13

Draft a single paragraph and use the checklist as a guide.

_____ Review your prewriting to clarify your purpose and what you want your audience to understand.

_____ Use the 1+1 approach in your topic sentence.

_____ Insert transitions to connect ideas and details.

> ## REVISE
> - Read critically
> - Read peer papers
> - Rethink your work

Begin revising by asking yourself these questions: Will an audience understand my purpose? Is there sufficient detail? Are my ideas connected and is my purpose clearly defined?

Read Critically

EXERCISE 4.14

Examine the following paragraph. Underline the topic sentence and circle transition words or phrases. Then answer the questions that follow.

My old granny is an interesting character. She loves to play the lottery, especially the Big Game. She has a system that she thinks brings her good luck. She always buys tickets at the Draper Party Mart two days before the drawing. She puts the tickets in the same white envelope and tucks them in the same zipper pocket in her purse. On the day of the drawing, we watch television together and check her numbers. Together we select the numbers for the next week. Although Granny loses most of the time, she won one hundred dollars once. Occasionally she wins five dollars. However, she spends all her winnings to buy more tickets. Right now she really needs a new coffee maker, a new dress, or a warmer coat. These days, she says she is old and old things suit her just fine. After all, she is hooked. Betting on the lottery doesn't make much sense when you think about it.

Focus

1. Is the paragraph's subject clear? Will the reader feel the impact of the examples?

Detail

2. Are the examples strong enough to convince the reader?

Copyright © 2007, The McGraw-Hill Companies, Inc. All rights reserved.

EXERCISE 4.14 continued

3. Are there sufficient facts and details for each example?

Connections

4. Does the writer present the examples in an order that is effective? Does anything seem out of order or irrelevant?

5. Is the order made clear by connecting words?

Taking a Critical View

6. What are the strengths and weaknesses of the paragraph?

Strengths	Weaknesses

7. What will improve this paragraph?

Read Peer Papers

EXERCISE 4.15

Form a group of three or four students and take turns reading and discussing your paragraphs. Use the questions from Exercise 4.14 to identify each paragraph's strengths and weaknesses. Offer suggestions for a revision plan.

Rethink Your Work

Effective writers learn to control their subject. They can provide detail on an example in two or three sentences, or if it is necessary, they can elaborate on a single example and build a whole paragraph around it. In such a paragraph, the writer makes use of an extended example. Here the writer from Exercise 4.12 explores his subject with an extended example.

STUDENT MODEL

Student Sample

Bookworms have always seemed antisocial to me, but at one time, I actually knew a person who made being a bookworm seem attractive. My tenth-grade English teacher was the best example of a bookworm I've ever known. Her name was Miss Ackerman. She was small and wore huge skirts she seemed to swim in; her stick legs barely showed at the bottom of her skirts. She even acted like a bookworm, beginning the class in September by explaining rules of courtesy. She even showed girls the proper way to sit in their chairs so they were ladylike. In her class, we read _The Great Gatsby_, and she told us to read with pencils, to underline sentences and whole paragraphs in our books, and to write notes in the margin. That was supposed to make us love reading. In that class, we discussed literature, and she asked us to find passages we really loved. She explained that loving a book helped her remember it, and she recited her favorite passages from memory. She was probably the smartest person I ever knew. She must have been a bookworm her whole life. In her class, being a bookworm almost seemed like a good thing to be.

EXERCISE 4.16

Review your draft, and look for an idea or detail that could be expanded into an extended example. Think about what the extended example enables you to say _in addition to_ or _in contrast to_ what you already said in your paragraph. Add facts and details to extend one example. You may choose to write a new paragraph that contains a single extended example.

EDIT

- Eliminate your usual errors
- Focus on one common error— comma use
- Search and correct

Prepare to turn your paragraph in for a grade. Make sure you are not repeating errors you usually make. Then look for new errors that may distract your reader from the purpose and meaning of your writing.

Eliminate Your Usual Errors

EXERCISE 4.17

Turn to the grids in Chapters 18, 19, and 20 where you have been keeping track of the errors you make. List those errors in the spaces provided below. Then proofread your paper and correct the errors you find.

_____   _____   _____

_____   _____   _____

WW Commas

Focus on One Common Error—Comma Use

The comma signals a pause at various points in the sentence. These pauses indicate places where parts of the sentence come together. It is common to pause in a list or series.

Items in a Series

Her attitude, her poise, and her ability to make music are wonderful.

Learning to ski presents one hazard after another. It is tough enough to stand up on skis. You also have to learn to go up a hill on a towrope, snowplow to slow yourself down, and stop at the bottom.

Being a hostess sounds like a cake job, but it isn't. People are always wanting something you can't give them. They want a booth instead of a table, a table farther away from the smoking section, or an empty table for eight so they don't have to wait.

Watch also for pauses at the beginning and in the middle of a sentence.

Pause before the Main Part of a Sentence

When I was a little girl, my father used to work for the gas company.

This part of the sentence introduces the main idea.

This part of the sentence expresses the main idea.

As the crooks were breaking into the house, the alarm went off.

Once they got back outside, the cops were waiting for them.

Pause in the Middle of a Sentence (between two complete sentences)

No friends could come over or call, and I could not leave the house or make any phone calls.

two complete sentences

It was getting late, so everyone on the beach that night decided to go home.

A friend of the family was passing by, and he saw my transgression.

EXERCISE 4.18

Insert commas as needed below for items in a series and pauses at the beginning and in the middle of sentences. Some sentences may be correct as written.

1. I love taking family vacations to our cottage. I get to talk with my mom fish with my dad and water-ski with my brother.

2. My friend Michelle hates crazy drives. She has discovered that honking flapping your arms and screaming obscenities will not stop them.

3. If a boy gets into a fight nine times out of ten it is because he's a jealous boyfriend.

4. If you move in with a friend because you want more freedom you might be surprised by the rules you give yourself: for example, keep the kitchen clean by

Copyright © 2007, The McGraw-Hill Companies, Inc. All rights reserved.

EXERCISE 4.18 continued

doing the dishes immediately after meals take out the trash when the bag is full pick up your clothes to keep your room clean or do your laundry every weekend.

5. At the end of the story the boy died and the migrant worker wished that he could be someone's father again.

6. The clock controls my life. I roll over at 5:30 a.m. trying to ignore it choke down breakfast trying to beat it and rush from class to class being a slave to it.

7. The patient's condition grew worse and the nurses had to help him with things he no longer could do for himself.

8. I worked at headquarters while learning the top operations of the company. They taught me to do financial documents for new clients spreadsheets for long-term clients and year-end reports for IRS.

9. Toward the evening after a long and peaceful dinner we have to get the kids ready for bed.

10. He has to make sure he has all the money for the bank every month or they will take his car away.

Search and Correct

EXERCISE 4.19

Double-check your grammar. Read your paragraph for a single error—comma use.

EXERCISE 4.20

Double-check your spelling. Computer spell-checks make mistakes. Therefore, it is essential that you proofread your paper before turning it in for a grade. Focus your close reading on typographical errors.

EXERCISE 4.21

Find a proofreading pal. After you have double-checked your paper, exchange papers with that student and proofread each other's work. Find out what errors your classmate would like you to search for. Using your list from Exercise 4.17, tell your classmate what errors you are inclined to make.

REFLECT
- Identify successes
- Set goals

Each time you write, you build skills and strategies. The last step in the writing process is to reflect and recognize what you did well and what you learned.

Identify Successes

EXERCISE 4.22

Take a few minutes to reflect on your successes. Write one or two sentences that explain two things you have learned from this chapter and how you successfully applied them to your writing. Use a specific example from your work to support your thinking.

Set Goals

EXERCISE 4.23

Now that you have examined your successes, determine what challenges you face. Rate yourself using the following scale—5 indicates a task that you consider a challenge most of the time, and 1 indicates a task for which you have the required skills and strategies.

Steps	Strategies and Skills	5	4	3	2	1
Prewrite	1. I prewrite to explore my ideas and think deeper about a topic.	—	—	—	—	—
Draft	2. I focus my paragraphs with topic sentences.	—	—	—	—	—
	3. I organize my ideas and make connections.	—	—	—	—	—
Revise	4. I read critically to identify and use the successful techniques of other writers.	—	—	—	—	—
	5. I identify the strengths and weaknesses in my papers.	—	—	—	—	—
	6. I apply specific revision strategies to my papers.	—	—	—	—	—
Edit	7. I employ all or some of the following editing strategies:					
	▪ apply rules to use commas correctly	—	—	—	—	—
	▪ use spell-check on my computer	—	—	—	—	—
	▪ read a printed copy of my paragraph aloud to check for spelling errors and typographical errors	—	—	—	—	—

EXERCISE 4.24

Finish the following sentences in order to explore your learning experience and to set goals.

1. My attitude toward writing is

2. I still need to work on

Copyright © 2007, The McGraw-Hill Companies, Inc. All rights reserved.

STUDENT SAMPLE OF THE WRITING PROCESS

STUDENT MODEL

Theresa's Brainstorming

1. Topic: *history*
   Examples:
   > *Centuries and centuries of events*
   >
   > *Memorize facts, places, wars, dates, and names*
   >
   > *Multiple-choice and fill-in-the-blank tests*

   Point: *History is not my favorite subject. In fact, it might be my most hated.*

   Impact: *I forget everything I learned the minute I walk out the door.*

2. Topic: *my first job*
   Examples:
   > *Christmas gift wrapper at $2.25 an hour*
   >
   > *Long lines of impatient shoppers*
   >
   > *Paper cuts and boxes too big or too small*
   >
   > *No breaks and 30-minute lunches*
   >
   > *Babies crying and toddlers running around unattended*

   Point: *Working with the public is an eye-opening experience.*

   Impact: *I want to go to college to get a decent job so I don't have to wait on people.*

3. Topic: *child rearing*
   Examples:
   > *My mother is all about her children.*
   >
   > *She is a worrier and is always helping me and my brother and sisters.*
   >
   > *She is very religious and wanted us all to go to church.*
   >
   > *She doesn't work. She stays home and takes care of her family.*
   >
   > *She was always there when I got up in the morning, when I came home from school, and when I went to bed at night.*

   Point: *My mother was a helpful and involved mother.*

   Impact: *I really love my mother.*

Theresa's Unedited Freewrite

My mother is a very helpful person. She is always there when you need something. She is an Italian, whose mother actually came from Italy. She loves to play cards, also family gatherings. She is always happy when the whole family is together. She likes to do family movie nights and not go out. Instead we rent a movie and pop popcorn. She likes to rent a comedy so we all laugh together. That's probably because she is a worrier. My mother always worries about me, my brother, and two sisters. She hopes that we will succeed in life. She always thinks that she is sick. I think it is just her imagination. It's probably because she is alone. She never leaves the house. I always feel bad about this. I kind of wish she could find something to do. All she does is sit at home and watch TV. She hardly talks to her friends anymore. She does talk to her sister. My mother loves angels. She has been collecting them for years. We all buy her these angels. She is in a fan club and everything. She will sit there and watch QVC and wait for them to come on TV. She orders everything she sees on there. From the statues, to pictures, even little miniatures. One thing that reminds me of my mother is a deck of cards. My mother and I used to play cards together all the time. Rummy was our game. We would play in the middle of the night. Like midnight until about two in the morning.

Theresa's Unedited First Draft

Family is the focus of my mothers life. She is always happy when the whole family is together. Not just holidays and birthdays. She likes to do family movie nights. Instead of going out, we rent a movie and pop popcorn. She likes to rent a comedy so we all laugh together. She also likes to play games. After dinner, we do the dishes and play a game. She especially likes to play cards. Rummy was our game. She loved the competition, so we argue over who was cheating because we both would cheat. It was like a war between us. I think cheating and getting away with it was more important than winning the game. We would play until two o'clock in the morning.

Theresa's Revised Draft

My mother taught me the value of family fun. Family is the focus of my mothers life. She is always happy and works hard to keep the whole family together. Not just holidays and birthdays. We make time for family fun during the week. One of her favorite family events is movie night. She likes to do family movie nights. Instead of going out, we rent a movie and pop popcorn. Even though we are a lot older and a lot bigger, we all climb onto the sofa and eat out of the same huge bowl filled with buttered popcorn. She likes to always rent a comedy so we all laugh together. Another family fun event is game night. She also likes to play games. After dinner, we do the dishes and pull out the games. play a game. She especially likes to play cards. Rummy is our favorite was our game. We laugh a lot more than we win because everyone cheats. She loved the competition, so we argue over who is was cheating because we both would cheat. It was like a war between us. I think cheating and getting away with cheatingit was more important than winning the game. So I have gotten really good at looking innocent. Sometimes we would play until two o'clock in the morning. Family

continued

Copyright © 2007, The McGraw-Hill Companies, Inc. All rights reserved.

fun nights taught me how important a family is and how special my mother is as well.

Theresa's Editing

My mother taught me the value of family fun. ~~Family is the focus of my mothers life~~. She ~~is always happy when~~ works hard to keep the whole family together,⌃ ~~Not~~ *, on more than* just holidays and birthdays. We make time for family fun during the week. One of her favorite family events is movie night. ~~She likes to do family movie nights~~. Instead of going out, we rent a movie and pop popcorn. Even though we are a lot older and a lot bigger, we all climb onto the sofa and eat out of the same huge bowl filled with buttered popcorn. She ~~likes to~~ always rent⌃*s* a comedy so we all laugh together. Another family fun event is game night. ~~She also likes to play games~~. After dinner, we do the dishes and pull out the games. ~~play a game~~. She especially likes to play cards. Rummy is our favorite ~~was our~~ game. We laugh a lot more than we win because everyone cheats. She loved*s* the competition, so we argue over who is ~~was~~ cheating ~~because we both would cheat. It was like a war between us. I think cheating and~~ *G*etting away with cheating~~it was~~ *is* more important than winning the game. So I ~~have gotten~~ *am* really good at looking innocent. Sometimes we ~~would~~ play until two o'clock in the morning. Family fun nights taught me how important family is and how special my mother is as well.

Theresa's Final Edited Paragraph

My mother taught me the value of family fun. She works hard to keep the whole family together, on more than just holidays and birthdays. We make time for family fun during the week. One of her favorite family events is movie night. Instead of going out, we rent a movie and pop popcorn. Even though we are a lot older and a lot bigger, we all climb onto the sofa and eat out of the same huge bowl filled with buttered popcorn. She always rents a comedy so we all laugh together. Another family fun event is game night. After dinner, we do the dishes and pull out the games. She especially likes to play cards. Rummy is our favorite game. We laugh a lot more than we win because everyone cheats. She loves the competition, so we argue over who is cheating. Getting away with cheating is more important than winning the game. So I am really good at looking innocent. Sometimes we play until two o'clock in the morning. Family fun nights taught me how important family is and how special my mother is as well.

Theresa's Reflection

Steps	Strategies and Skills	5	4	3	2	1
Prewrite	1. I prewrite to explore my ideas and think deeper about a topic.	—	—	—	X	—
Draft	2. I focus my paragraphs with topic sentences.	—	—	—	X	—
	3. I organize my ideas and make connections.	—	—	—	X	—
Revise	4. I read critically to identify and use the successful techniques of other writers.	—	X	—	—	—
	5. I identify the strengths and weaknesses in my papers.	—	—	X	—	—
	6. I apply specific revision strategies to my papers.	—	—	—	X	—
Edit	7. I employ all or some of the following editing strategies:					
	▪ apply rules to use commas correctly	—	—	—	—	X
	▪ use spell-check on my computer	—	—	—	—	X
	▪ read a printed copy of my paragraph aloud to check for spelling errors and typographical errors	X	—	—	—	—

1. **My attitude toward writing is** *improving now that I have all these steps to follow. Before I just wrote something down and then typed it. The only bad part is that it takes so long.*

2. **I still need to work on** *getting help or ideas from other people. I don't really use other student writing or even the models we study in class to help me out much. I don't like changing my work.*

Copyright © 2007, The McGraw-Hill Companies, Inc. All rights reserved.

5 *Narrative and Description*

So what happened? To provide a detailed answer to this question, you tell a story, which is often called a **narration,** or **narrative.** Narratives tell the story of an action. Next to conversation, narration is probably what you do most often when you talk. You tell your friends what happened at the concert on Friday night. You tell your boss how you handled that difficult customer. You tell your parents how the car door happened to get dented at the mall. In college writing, you will use narrative for a variety of reasons:

- to explain what you did in the science lab
- to relate a field experience to classroom content
- to connect a personal experience to the theme of a story or poem
- to justify an opinion on a social issue

To use narrative effectively, you must be observant and present relevant details to your audience in a logical order. **Description** is essential to a story. It communicates facts and feelings and explains or illustrates your main idea. Unlike narration, which is active, description is static: it provides the sensory details that create the picture of the setting, persons, or objects in a story. Your narrative gains power as your control the descriptive detail.

IN THIS CHAPTER: A PREVIEW

Narrative Thinking

- Elements of Narrative
- Narrative Analysis
- Narrative as Proof
- Description as Picture
- Description as Main Idea

A Process Approach to Writing the Narrative Paragraph

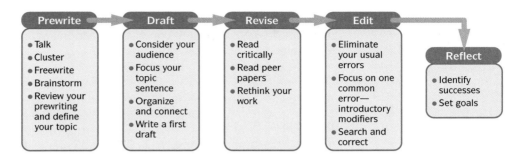

NARRATIVE THINKING

WW Louis Gates Jr.

Narrative takes your audience to the scene by introducing important people and showing them in action. Good narratives also make a point. After all, you tell a story for a reason.

Elements of Narrative

Scene	Actors	Actions	Outcome
Where and when does the narration take place?	Who is involved and critical to the action?	What are the crucial events?	How does the narrative end?

Point

Actor

Scene

Other actors

Actions

Outcome

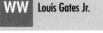

READING: from *Fabrication*, by Susan Neville

   My neighbors create their home at every moment, which involves both making things and tearing things down. Last week the husband was up in a sweet gum tree with a chain saw, balancing on a heavy branch and sawing off the limbs at the tip. Whack! Thud! The screech of the chain saw came close to his own powerful leg. His three children squealed, and the seven white dogs and the wind and the pile of leaves and bark were everywhere. Whack! Thud! A gathering of boys around the basketball hoop played and watched, and the sun set all orange and green and shined on the chain saw's metal teeth. When he got the thing de-limbed, he cut right through the trunk until the whole tree fell. Then in two seconds he cut through the trunk of a dogwood, and it was down too. My neighbor stood there like Paul Bunyan. The kids carried limbs taller than they were out to the street to be carted away with the next day's trash. In a matter of seconds, he and his wife decided not to have the stump ground up, as they had originally planned to do. Instead, they would build an octagonal bench around it and scoop out the center to grow geraniums.

DISCUSSION QUESTIONS

1. Neville returns to the point of the paragraph at the end when she explains the outcome. Why is this approach effective?

Copyright © 2007, The McGraw-Hill Companies, Inc. All rights reserved.

2. What do the details about the actions of the other actors add to the story?

3. What does Neville do to compact the actions of a whole day into a single paragraph?

Narrative Analysis

The stories you write will be most effective if you include all the elements of narrative. Reading is good practice for identifying the key elements of narrative.

EXERCISE 5.1

Read the following student samples and identify the components of the narrative. In the tables that follow each sample, list the details and write a phrase or sentence that states the point of the story.

It happened on a Thursday in August 2001, around 5:00 a.m. My boyfriend Derrick had just arrived in downtown Detroit, where he works for the *Detroit News and Free Press* in the Lafayette Building. He works eight hours a day and parks his truck, a dark blue four-wheel-drive Chevy Suburban, in the same spot every day, about walking distance from the company. He really loves that truck. But now it was gone; someone had stolen it. He laughed. Not a funny ha-ha laugh but a laugh of disbelief. He walked back to work, called me, and told me what happened. At first I didn't believe him. I left work and went home to call the police. Now all we could do was wait. The police said they would call when they recovered the vehicle. At 9:30, after eight hours, the phone rang. They had found the truck on the east side, and there was only minimal damage. The steering column was destroyed; so was the passenger lock. We were so happy to hear the news. After we went to pick it up, we bought a Club, the kind that protects the entire steering column. It won't be so easy to steal if a thief ever tries it again.

Scene	Actors	Actions	Outcome
Where and when does the narration take place?	Who is involved and critical to the action?	What are the crucial events?	How does the narrative end?

Point of the Story:

Copyright © 2007, The McGraw-Hill Companies, Inc. All rights reserved.

EXERCISE 5.1 continued

Every fourth of July my family and I have a big barbecue. Everyone brings a dish, and my father cooks four or five slabs of ribs. Each year we have it at someone else's house. This year we had it at my sister's house. She broke her knee and was having a hard time getting around. So we all thought it would be easier for her if she didn't have to travel. It so happens my uncle Mark had just gotten engaged to a girl he met on the Internet. He showed up by himself and said she would be along a little later. About an hour later, Mark, my dad, my brother-in-law Stan, and I were on the front porch. When we saw her drive up, my dad said, "What is that on the side of her car?" It was the handle and hose of the gas pump. She drove off with the whole thing and didn't even know. It was the funniest thing I ever saw. We all laughed for hours. Kim was very embarrassed, but we made her feel like she was part of the family. So she didn't feel that bad, although we did take pictures and still tell everyone the story. That is just what happens in a big family. If you do something funny, everyone hears about it.

Scene	Actors	Actions	Outcome
Where and when does the narration take place?	Who is involved and critical to the action?	What are the crucial events?	How does the narrative end?

Point of the Story:

Kids these days may be rude, but I was no angel when I was a kid. The worst trouble I ever got into was in May of 1998. I had just turned fifteen years old. One evening, my friends and I were in my older brother's room. I was looking under his bed, and I found a BB gun. My friend Moe said, "Let's go to my house and bring the gun." So I grabbed the gun and we left. We got a block away from my house, and Moe shot at an old lady's window. We ran. We got about five blocks away from my house, and two cop cars came at us. They just came right out of nowhere. One cop got out of the car and said, "Put your hands in the air." Then he said, "Whoever has the gun, step forward." When I stepped forward, he told me to put my hands on the car. He took the gun and made my friends and me get in the car. Then he took all of us home. My dad was really mad. He made me pay for the window, and I was grounded for two weeks.

EXERCISE 5.1 continued

Scene	Actors	Actions	Outcome
Where and when does the narration take place?	Who is involved and critical to the action?	What are the crucial events?	How does the narrative end?

Point of the Story:

Narrative as Proof

You will often use narrative to **support a point** or **prove a claim.** Writing a narrative requires that you look closely at your experiences and the experiences of people you know. For instance, imagine you want to make the claim "Technology does not necessarily make life easier." To prove this assertion, you might tell a story about a computer failure in the restaurant where you work or the time your brother's cell phone spontaneously called Botswana and he was stuck with a huge bill.

EXERCISE 5.2

Connect experiences and events in your life to assertions that seem to be true. Use the four components of a narrative to outline a story you could tell that relates to each of the following topic sentences.

EXAMPLE:

Sometimes just a little extra effort can make all the difference in the world.

SCENE: *Breckenridge, Colorado. The construction site, "The Gold Camp," where I worked as a laborer for Fisher Plumbing.*

ACTORS: *Kenny, the owner; Bill, the foreman; the other laborers on the job.*

ACTIONS: *(1) I'm ordered to do a difficult job. (2) I spend a long afternoon digging underneath a footing. (3) Kenny tells Bill to get the backhoe.*

OUTCOME: *I impressed the owner by not giving up on a really hard job. As a result, he liked my attitude and gave me a chance to do some better jobs.*

1. Money spent quickly is not always spent wisely.

   SCENE:

   ACTORS:

   ACTIONS:

Copyright © 2007, The McGraw-Hill Companies, Inc. All rights reserved.

EXERCISE 5.2 continued

OUTCOME:

2. Making mistakes is an essential part of learning.

SCENE:

ACTORS:

ACTIONS:

OUTCOME:

3. In times of crisis, people show their true colors.

SCENE:

ACTORS:

ACTIONS:

OUTCOME:

Description as Picture

Description communicates the main idea or impression you are communicating to the reader. By describing the setting, people, and objects in your story, you will establish context and create an emotional response that enhances your point. Close observation is the first key to communicating a main impression. Selecting the essential descriptive details is the second key. Too much description, and the point is lost in the details. Too little description, and the point is not clear enough.

EXERCISE 5.3

Rely on your senses to describe places. Sight is the most often used sense, but by combining many of the senses—along with your imagination—your description will have a multidimensional impact. Form a group to brainstorm sensory descriptions of the photograph on page 85. Describe the place. Imagine the people. Be specific.

- Use all the senses.
- State color, size, and shape.
- Make comparisons, explaining what something or someone is like or similar to.

EXAMPLE:

Place—athletic event—football stadium—high school homecoming game—halftime show—crowning of the queen—it is pouring rain

Sight	Sound	Touch	Smell	Taste
• *the queen holds her long white dress up to avoid puddles in the muddy field*	• *trumpets blare the school song*	• *rain drips off your hair and rolls down your face*	• *buttery popcorn*	• *soggy popcorn tastes like wet cardboard*
• *the king carries a multicolored golf umbrella*	• *your friend loudly sings off-key*	• *a cold breeze causes you to shiver*	• *grilled hot dogs and Polish sausage*	• *mustard and onions on your hot dog*
• *cheerleaders stand in an arch at the top of the field*	• *the crowd claps and cheers as the announcer talks*	• *your cup of hot chocolate warms your hands*	• *my date's wet wool coat smells like a dog*	• *sweet, syrupy chocolate*
• *they shake their pompons as the queen and king enter the field*	• *thunder claps louder than the crowd*	• *the hot chocolate burns the tip of your tongue*		
• *my date's mascara is running down her cheeks*	• *the speaker crackles*			
	• *the announcer reads the names, ages, and interests of the homecoming court*			
	• *the announcer says Joneston instead of Johnston*			

EXERCISE 5.3 continued

Place
Roof of a building—view of the city—graffiti painted on the asphalt—a couple's special spot

Sight	Sound	Touch	Smell	Taste

Copyright © 2007, The McGraw-Hill Companies, Inc. All rights reserved.

EXERCISE 5.3 continued

People
Cassie—Nic—the friend or friends who painted the message on her spot

Sight	Sound	Touch	Smell	Taste

WW Modifiers

Description and Main Idea

Don't overdo description. Selecting specific details to create a main impression is essential to good description. Often less is more with description. Several well-chosen details will be more effective than a long list.

EXERCISE 5.4

Review your brainstorming in Exercise 5.3 and select the essential descriptive details.

- Select one—a place, person, or thing.
- State the main impression you want to communicate to your reader.
- List five to seven details that will make that impression.

EXAMPLE:

Place: *Rainy football game—halftime*
Main impression: *It was a miserable night. I don't know why I stayed.*

Sight	Sound	Touch	Smell	Taste
• my date's mascara is running down her cheeks	• thunder claps louder than the crowd	• rain drips off your hair and rolls down your face • a cold breeze causes you to shiver	• my date's wet wool coat smells like a dog	• soggy popcorn tastes like wet cardboard

A PROCESS APPROACH TO WRITING THE NARRATIVE PARAGRAPH

To get the hang of writing narratives, practice writing a single paragraph. In this section, you will use a process approach to write a single paragraph that narrates a story and proves a claim. Following are some suggested topics for your narrative paragraph.

Specific Topics	General Topics
Getting help in school	Personal narratives
Getting blamed when you were innocent	• childhood memories
Being a good employee	• family
Being surprised or tricked	• favorite or important people
Being disappointed or frightened	Important lessons learned
Going on a trip or vacation	• at home
Making a commitment	• at school
Winning or losing	• at work
Facing sadness or loss	Historical or current events
Facing trouble with neighbors or friends	• of personal significance
	• to illustrate a point about the world
	A narrative of your choice

ELEMENTS OF NARRATIVE

Scene	Actors	Actions	Outcome
Where and when does the narration take place?	Who is involved and critical to the action?	What are the crucial events?	How does the narrative end?

STUDENT MODEL

Student Sample

Outcome

Scene and actors

Actions

Other actor

Actions

Other actor

Getting beaten by a cheater is no way to lose. In high school, I was an all-state-caliber tennis player. I was playing one of the best players in the state in a high school tournament. I was playing right near my best, hitting winners on seemingly every ball I touched. If there is such a thing as "in the zone," I was in it. Soon the kid started to call some of my shots out that were clearly inbounds. He threw his racket and swore and did all these things that would easily get him penalties or defaulted during a normal match. However, this kid got nothing. Worse than that, his coach stood there watching and never said or did a thing, as if to say they didn't respect me at all. It threw me off my game, and I couldn't concentrate. I started to put balls out of bounds. My hands were sweating, and I couldn't grip the racket. Plus, my coach just stood there watching. I felt alone on the court. On that day nobody would have beaten me, but I let a cheater win.

Copyright © 2007, The McGraw-Hill Companies, Inc. All rights reserved.

PREWRITE

- Talk
- Cluster
- Freewrite
- Brainstorm
- Review your prewriting and define your topic

Select one or more of the following prewriting strategies to explore a topic and develop ideas for a narrative paragraph.

Talk

EXERCISE 5.5

Turn to your neighbor in class or find another interested listener. Tell this person a story from your past that relates to one of the topics. Then listen to your neighbor's story.

Cluster

EXERCISE 5.6

Select a topic. Use the following clustering diagram to explore the details of the story you could tell. These details will also help you discover the point you want to make as you tell this story. Keep in mind the important elements of narrative (scene, actors, actions, and outcome) as you work.

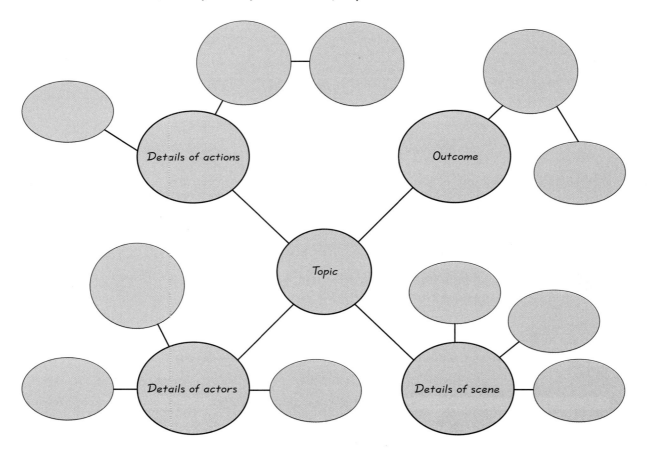

Freewrite

Copyright © 2007, The McGraw-Hill Companies, Inc. All rights reserved.

EXERCISE 5.7

Explore your topic by freewriting. Focus on the aspects of narrative listed below. Try to write as much as you can in response to each question. Do not worry about saying too much. You can cut back on the detail in the drafting stage of the process.

- Where were you when this incident happened?
- When did it happen? What happened immediately before? What happened afterward?
- Who was involved? (Consider both people who were actually there and people who were not there.)
- What specific events or actions occurred?
- What was the outcome?
- What meaning did the incident have for you?

Brainstorm

EXERCISE 5.8

Select a topic by making a series of lists.

- List the possible stories you might tell.
- List the key elements of the story: scene, actors, actions, and outcome.
- List the descriptive details, using all five senses.

Review Your Prewriting and Define Your Topic

Prewriting is only a beginning. It is not a first draft. Whether oral or written, it helps you see that you have many stories to tell and that some stories are more interesting and richer in detail than others. It is now time to review your prewriting work and define your topic so that you can write a first draft.

EXERCISE 5.9

Consider the following questions to determine the topic you will write about.

- Which topic struck you as most interesting?
- Which one generated the most material?
- Which one did your peers respond best to?
- Which one seems to provide the most promising story for the assignment?

Fill in the following table to summarize the details of your narrative. Use this summary to state a claim or the point of your story.

EXERCISE 5.9 continued

Scene	Actors	Actions	Outcome
Where and when does the narration take place?	Who is involved and critical to the action?	What are the crucial events?	How does the narrative end?

Claim or Point of the Story:

DRAFT

- Consider your audience
- Focus your topic sentence
- Organize and connect
- Write a first draft

Write a draft that organizes your prewriting into a single paragraph. This first draft will establish the subject and state the point of your narrative paragraph.

Consider Your Audience

EXERCISE 5.10

Now that you have selected a topic, consider who will read your paragraph. Use the following questions to consider how to convey your point to an audience.

- Why is this topic important to your audience?
- What special meaning does this topic have for you? Why do you want your audience to understand this meaning?
- Will your audience agree or disagree with your thinking? Will you be asking them to think about your subject in a new way?

Return to the exercises on narrative thinking in this chapter and decide which way of thinking about your topic will help you connect best with your audience.

Focus Your Topic Sentence

Writers build narrative topic sentences by combining two key elements: some reference to the story and the point that they hope to make with it. The reference to the story is established with words that identify one of the narrative components: the

Destinations: Revealing the World through Narration

Once Upon a Time . . .

Is there any phrase in the English language more arresting than "once upon a time"? We've all heard it a thousand times, but it still evokes a simple-hearted enthusiasm in us, an anticipation of what's to come. It seems that in almost any context and at any age, we enjoy hearing stories. We read stories by great (and maybe not so great) writers, we go to the movies to watch stories unfold on the big screen, we tell friends stories of memorable moments, and we share the stories of our day with loved ones. Mastering the skills of narration will benefit you in contexts far removed from the academic. Wherever you are and whatever you are doing, it is always nice (and useful!) to be able to tell a good story.

The Story of the Essay

There are many ways to structure an essay, but perhaps the most interesting, at least from a reader's point of view, is narrative. Try to think of your essay as a story: Who (or what) are the main "characters"? What kinds of things does your reader need to know about them in order for them to seem convincing? What happens to them? What kind of conclusion is the essay building toward? If you think of writing an essay as telling a story, you are likely to be better engaged as you write and, consequently, your writing will be more energetic and lively. The next time you sit down to write about a physics lab, think about the ways in which you can transform your piece of writing into more than just a recitation of facts; try to fit those facts into a coherent narrative.

The Story of Your Life

Like everyone else, people in the business world are interested in stories. Keep this in mind as you put together your resume—try to think of it as a "story of your working life." Following proper formatting guidelines, shape your resume so that it presents a snapshot of your career and of you as a person. Similarly, in a job interview, don't restrict yourself to short "yes" and "no" answers, but rather, treat the interview as an opportunity to reveal something about yourself. Remember, your interviewer is looking for someone that he or she wants to see five days a week. Don't be afraid to make yourself seem as interesting and captivating as you really are.

scene, the actors, the actions, or the outcome. Developing this 1 (story) + 1 (point) approach will strengthen your topic sentences.

EXERCISE 5.11

Underline and label the two key elements in the following topic sentences.

EXAMPLE:

$$\underbrace{\text{The first day of my computer applications class,}}_{\text{story}} \text{I made an } \underbrace{\text{amazing discovery.}}_{\text{point}}$$

1. Until they came to move in with us, I never really appreciated my grandparents.

2. The night my neighbor's burglar alarm went off, I did something really foolish and lived to tell about it.

3. Last year my mother was able to lose weight and actually keep it off.

4. Sometimes help in school comes from fellow students rather than teachers.

5. Believe it or not, having nosy neighbors can be a lifesaver.

Copyright © 2007, The McGraw-Hill Companies, Inc. All rights reserved.

Organize and Connect

Narratives often use specific references to time to organize and connect the ideas and details in the paragraph. Following is a list of the most common narrative transitions.

NARRATIVE TRANSITIONS		
before	after	meanwhile
while	as	when
later	earlier	then
eventually	subsequently	during
next	now	finally

EXERCISE 5.12

Underline all narrative transitions in the following paragraph.

Sometimes things just don't turn out the way you expect. I used to get in trouble in school all the time on the playground at recess. There were two kids who were the bullies of the playground. They were big, but I could run faster. Whenever I saw them, I got really close to them and started talking trash. When they tried to chase me, I would run away laughing. This happened almost every day. One day they had my friend Sam and me cornered in a part of the school that was bricked in. "Remember all those names you called us and then you ran away?" they said. "Try running from us now." We just answered, "What are you going to do about the name calling?" They said that they were going to beat us up. My friend Sam and I were like, *Bring it*. They tried to beat us up, but we came through. We beat them up pretty bad. By now there was a whole audience of kids. When it was over, the lunch lady grabbed us, and we had to stay in at lunch for the next two weeks. We also got in trouble with our parents. Eventually, Sam and I became friends with the bullies. We got in all that trouble for nothing.

Write a First Draft

EXERCISE 5.13

Draft a single paragraph and use the checklist as a guide.

_____ Review your prewriting to clarify your purpose and what you want your audience to understand.

_____ Use the 1 + 1 approach in your topic sentence.

_____ Insert supporting details to explain the process.

_____ Insert transitions to connect ideas and details.

REVISE

- Read critically
- Read peer papers
- Rethink your work

Begin revising by asking yourself these questions:

Will an audience understand my purpose? Is there sufficient detail?

Are my ideas connected and is my purpose clearly defined?

Read Critically

To establish a critical view of your own writing, read critically other students' writing.

EXERCISE 5.14

Examine the following paragraph. Underline the topic sentence and circle transition words or phrases. Then answer the questions that follow.

Punishment in my house was always immediate and usually fit the crime. One evening we had just finished dinner, when I decided to go to my friend Chris's house. I ignored my mother's request to help with the dishes and pretended I didn't hear her calling my name. I didn't tell anyone where I was going. It was only down the street, so I figured that there was no harm in it. I was seven or eight at the time. As I started walking down the street, I heard someone call my name in a real angry tone. It was my dad. His face was all red. He said to me, "Get inside the house. We have to talk." I went home, sat down at the kitchen table, and waited for him to come back in the house. He sat down across from me and said, "You left the house without telling your mother and me where you went and without asking if you could go. Plus you ignored your mother's request to help with the dishes." He sat there for several minutes, his palm flat on the kitchen table, without saying a word. Finally, after what seemed to be an eternity, he grounded me for the weekend and made me go up to my room to think about what I had done.

Focus

1. Is the paragraph's subject clear? Does the writer clearly state the purpose of the narrative?

Detail

2. Is there sensory description that creates a picture?

3. Is the description focused to express the main idea of the narrative?

Connections

4. Does the writer present the narrative in an order that is effective? Does anything seem out of order or irrelevant?

Copyright © 2007, The McGraw-Hill Companies, Inc. All rights reserved.

EXERCISE 5.14 continued

5. Is the order made clear by connecting words?

Taking a Critical View

6. What are the strengths and weaknesses of the paragraph?

Strengths	Weaknesses

7. What will improve this paragraph?

Read Peer Papers

EXERCISE 5.15

Form a group of three or four students and take turns reading and discussing your paragraphs. Use the questions from Exercise 5.14 to identify each paragraph's strengths and weaknesses. Offer suggestions for a revision plan.

Rethink Your Work

In most first-draft narratives, there are a number of points that beg, "Say more! Say more!" Expanding on these points will help you explore your ideas more fully and help your reader better understand what you are saying. This is the place to add description. Often this kind of expansion means adding new content and/or making new connections.

EXERCISE 5.16

Read the following student paragraph and notice the undeveloped points, which have been flagged for you. Talk with a classmate about the sensory description this student might insert to say more, create a main impression, or add emotional impact.

FLAG 1: What specific actions showed that you were best friends?

FLAG 2: Did you already have doubts about her?

I recently learned a lesson about trust; unfortunately, it was a negative lesson. There was a girl I went to high school with. Her name was Mary Miller. I thought that was really strange since my first name was Mary and my mother's maiden name was Miller. She was in many of my classes, so soon we got to know each other better and became best friends. We later found out that she lived right behind me. Because she didn't have a license, I drove her to school every day and to marching band practice. One day she left her purse in my car, so me trusting her I gave her my keys and said to go get it. I figured that she would give me my keys back in band class. Well, she ended up taking my car for the day. I figured she did but kept telling myself she wouldn't do that. Band class came around and Mary was

Copyright © 2007, The McGraw-Hill Companies, Inc. All rights reserved.

EXERCISE 5.16 continued

FLAG 3: *How do you define a trustworthy friend? Do you have other friends that are trustworthy?*

not there. I even had a friend look for my car in the parking lot when she had to walk over to a different school. She told me it wasn't there. When she finally came back to give me my keys she totally denied even taking the car. She wouldn't even look me in the face as she handed them back to me. It really hurt to see that someone I thought of as such a good friend could do something like that. Later we started talking again but I was very cautious as to how much I could trust her.

EXERCISE 5.17

Review your paragraph and flag three details that could be expanded to add meaning to your paper. Write the sentence or phrase in the space provided below. Then elaborate, adding at least two sentences to provide more detail. Finally, reflect on how this work affects your paragraph.

1. Detail 1:

Elaboration:

2. Detail 2:

Elaboration:

3. Detail 3:

Elaboration:

4. In what way will your paper be improved by adding this detail? What will your reader understand better?

EDIT

- Eliminate your usual errors
- Focus on one common error—introductory modifiers
- Search and correct

Prepare to turn your paragraph in for a grade. Make sure you are not repeating errors you usually make. Then look for new errors that may distract your reader from the purpose and meaning of your writing.

Eliminate Your Usual Errors

EXERCISE 5.18

Turn to the grids in Chapters 18, 19, and 20 where you have been keeping track of the errors you make. List those errors in the space provided below. Then proofread your paper and correct the errors you find.

_____   _____   _____

_____   _____   _____

Focus on One Common Error—Introductory Modifiers

I'm terrible with commas. I just don't know where to put them. Chances are if you make errors in grammar, spelling, or punctuation, you will see a pattern. Knowing that you have a problem is the first step to repairing it.

Introductory modifiers begin a sentence, and they are frequently used in narrative writing. They set the scene, stating time or location, and explain or describe the action in the sentence. Introductory modifiers are set off from the rest of the sentence with a comma.

Introductory Prepositional Phrases

Use a comma after an introductory prepositional phrase.

> *By the end of the game, I wanted to kick the referee off the court.*
>   2 prepositional phrases

> *In 2002, I saw my first Broadway play.*

1 prepositional phrase

Introductory Subordinate Clauses

Use a comma after an introductory subordinate clause.

> *Although I learned to type quickly, I couldn't figure out computers to save myself.*
>   subordinate clause

EXERCISE 5.19

Insert commas in the following sentences. State the reason you inserted a comma.

1. In five minutes or less my uncle can eat two Big Macs, a super-sized fries, and a large shake.

2. Before I went to college I worked as a salesperson at the mall, and I learned that selling is the hardest game in town.

3. In our own way we all saw the value of kindness.

4. While my sister was tossing dirty dishes into the oven and cupboards I was throwing beer bottles out the back window.

5. Throughout my middle school years I learned that teachers were as willing to laugh at me as my friends.

EXERCISE 5.20

Read your paragraph for a single error—comma usage with introductory modifiers. Use the following steps to develop awareness so that you can eventually apply these rules independently.

- Check the first word of every sentence.
- Highlight the first word if it is a preposition or a subordinate conjunction. These words potentially signal comma usage. (The following box contains a list of some of these words.)
- Review the sentence and insert or delete punctuation.

Highlight	Words That Commonly Signal Introductory Modifiers
prepositions	about, above, across, after, against, along, around, at, before, behind, below, beneath, beside, by, down, during, for, from, in, of, on, over, through, throughout, under, with, without
subordinate conjunctions	after, although, before, if, since, though, until, when, while

Search and Correct

EXERCISE 5.21

Double-check your grammar. Read your paragraph for a single error—introductory modifiers. Add commas as needed.

EXERCISE 5.22

Double-check your spelling. Computer spell-checks make mistakes. Therefore, it is essential that you proofread your paper before turning it in for a grade. Focus your close reading on typographical errors.

EXERCISE 5.23

Find a proofreading pal. After you have double-checked your paper, exchange papers with that student and proofread each other's work. Find out what errors your classmate would like you to search for. Using your list from Exercise 5.18, tell your classmate what errors you are inclined to make.

REFLECT
- Identify successes
- Set goals

Each time you write, you build skills and strategies. The last step in the writing process is to reflect and recognize what you did well and what you learned.

Copyright © 2007, The McGraw-Hill Companies, Inc. All rights reserved.

Identify Successes

EXERCISE 5.24

Take a few minutes to reflect on your successes. Write one or two sentences that explain two things you have learned from this chapter and how you successfully applied them to your writing. Use a specific example from your work to support your thinking.

Set Goals

EXERCISE 5.25

Now that you have examined your successes, determine what challenges you face. Rate yourself using the following scale—5 indicates a task that you consider a challenge most of the time, and 1 indicates a task for which you have the required skills and strategies.

Steps	Strategies and Skills	5	4	3	2	1
Prewrite	1. I prewrite to explore my ideas and think deeper about a topic.	—	—	—	—	—
Draft	2. I focus my paragraphs with topic sentences.	—	—	—	—	—
	3. I organize my ideas and make connections.	—	—	—	—	—
Revise	4. I read critically to identify and use the successful techniques of other writers.	—	—	—	—	—
	5. I identify the strengths and weaknesses in my papers.	—	—	—	—	—
	6. I apply specific revision strategies to my papers.	—	—	—	—	—
Edit	7. I employ all or some of the following editing strategies:	—	—	—	—	—
	▪ apply rules regarding punctuation of introductory modifiers	—	—	—	—	—
	▪ use spell-check on my computer	—	—	—	—	—
	▪ read a printed copy of my paragraph aloud to check for spelling errors and typographical errors	—	—	—	—	—

EXERCISE 5.26

Finish the following sentences in order to explore your learning experience and to set goals.

1. My attitude toward writing is

2. I still need to work on

STUDENT SAMPLE OF THE WRITING PROCESS

STUDENT MODEL

Sarina's Clustering

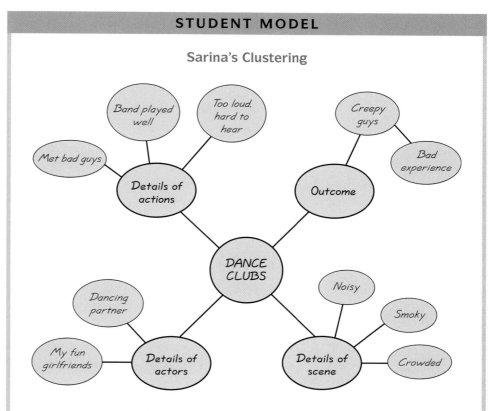

Sarina's Unedited Focused Freewrite

Saturday I went to a club with some friends, the place was packed and so noisy you couldn't hear anything. Their were no cute guys, or if there were they had girlfriends. The other guys were jerks. It was fun on the dance floor dancing with my friends, but some guy came over and started dancing with me, that was OK until he grabbed my waist and tried to pull me close. I love to dance, but I hate it when strangers touch me. Luckily I left the floor and he did not follow me. The club got more and more crowded and smoky. The air was so bad. I couldn't really breath. Even though I like hiphop, and I like my friends and dancing, I really had a bad time.

Sarina's Unedited First Draft

I learned something about myself just the other night. I went to a club with some friends. It was a Saturday night, and the place was packed with people. I love hiphop music, but the noise totally killed it. You could hardly hear anything the music it was so loud. To make matters worse, all the cute guys had their girlfriends with them. The few single guys there all seemed

continued

Copyright © 2007, The McGraw-Hill Companies, Inc. All rights reserved.

to have attitude problems. The only time I had fun was when I was on the dance floor dancing with my girlfriends. Even that was short lived. Some guy came over, and he started dancing with me. I enjoyed myself. It was actually fun until he put his hands on my waist and tried to pull me close. I love to dance, but I hate even the smallest physical contact with a stranger. I quickly walked off the floor. Luckily he got the point and did not follow me. As the evening went on the place got more crowded and very smoky. The air was so bad it was hardly possible to breathe. That is when I realized that maybe nightclubs and I just do not get along.

Sarina's Unedited Revision

Saturday night was my last night at the bar. Nightclubs and I just don't get along. I went to a club with some friends. It was a Saturday night, and the place was packed with people. The music and the crowd was loud. I love hiphop music, but the noise totally killed it. You could hardly hear anything. After fifteen minutes of head splitting noise I decided to check out the available men. To make matters worse, all the cute guys had girlfriends hanging all over them. The few single guys seemed to have attitude problems. After fifteen more minutes my friends and I decided to dance. We were having a blast out on the dance floor. But even that was short lived. A tall, blond athletic looking guy came over, and he started dancing with me. I enjoyed myself. It was actually fun until he put his hands on my waist and tried to pull me close. I love to dance, but I hate even the smallest physical contact with a stranger. After all he was just a sweaty stranger not some guy I really knew. I quickly walked off the floor. Luckily he got the point and did not follow me. As the evening went on the place got more crowded and very smoky. There wasn't anywhere to stand, and the dance floor was too crowded to move around. The air was so bad it was hardly possible to breathe. That is when I realized that I love a good band, dancing and friends, but bars are just not for me anymore.

Sarina's Editing

Saturday night was my last night at the bar. Nightclubs and I just ~~don't~~ *do not* get along. I went to a club with some friends. ~~It was a Saturday night, and~~ the place was packed with people. *and we had a hard time finding a table.* The music *was loud,* and the crowd was loud. I love hiphop music, but the noise totally killed it. You could hardly hear anything. After fifteen minutes of head splitting noise I *switched my attention to checking for* ~~decided to check out the~~

available men. To make matters worse, all the cute guys had girlfriends

hanging all over them. The few single guys seemed to have attitude

problems. After fifteen more minutes my friends and I decided to dance. the night away *We*

were having a blast out on the dance floor. But even that was short-lived.

A tall blond athletic-looking guy came over and he started dancing with

At first, having *me. I ~~enjoyed myself. It~~ was actually fun until he put his hands on my waist*

and tried to pull me close. I love to dance, but I hate even the smallest

all *physical contact with a stranger. After all he was ~~just a~~ sweaty ~~stranger~~*

~~not some guy I really knew.~~ I quickly walked off the floor. Luckily he got the

point and did not follow me. As the evening went on the place got more

crowded and very smoky. There wasn't anywhere to stand, and the dance

floor was too crowded to move around. The air was so bad it was hardly

possible to breathe. That is when I realized that I love a good band, dancing,

and friends, but bars are just not for me anymore.

SARINA'S FINAL EDITED PARAGRAPH

Saturday night was my last night at the bar. Nightclubs and I just do not get along. I went to a club with some friends. The place was packed with people, and we had a hard time finding a table. The music was loud, and the crowd was loud. I love hiphop music, but the noise totally killed it. You could hardly hear anything. After fifteen minutes of head-splitting noise, I switched my attention to checking for available men. To make matters worse, all the cute guys had girlfriends hanging all over them. The few single guys seemed to have attitude problems. After fifteen more minutes, my friends and I decided to dance the night away. We were having a blast out on the dance floor. But, even that was short-lived. A tall, blond, athletic-looking guy came over and started dancing with me. At first, I was actually having fun, until he put his hands on my waist and tried to pull me close. I love to dance, but I hate even the smallest physical contact with a stranger. After all, he was all sweaty. I quickly walked off the floor. Luckily, he got the point and did not follow me. As the evening went on, the place got more crowded and very smoky. There wasn't anywhere to stand, and the dance floor was too crowded to move around. The air was so bad it was hardly possible to breathe. That is when I realized that I love a good band, dancing, and friends, but bars are just not for me anymore.

continued

Copyright © 2007, The McGraw-Hill Companies, Inc. All rights reserved.

Sarina's Reflection

Stages	Strategies and Skills	5	4	3	2	1
Prewrite	1. I prewrite to explore my ideas and think deeper about a topic.	—	—	—	—	X
Draft	2. I focus my paragraphs with topic sentences.	—	—	—	—	X
	3. I organize my ideas and make connections.	—	—	—	—	X
Revise	4. I read critically to identify and use the successful techniques of other writers.	—	—	—	—	X
	5. I identify the strengths and weaknesses in my papers.	—	—	—	—	X
	6. I apply specific revision strategies to my papers.	—	—	—	—	X
Edit	7. I employ all or some of the following editing strategies:					
	▪ apply rules regarding punctuation of introductory modifiers	—	—	—	—	X
	▪ use spell-check on my computer	X	—	—	—	—
	▪ read a printed copy of my paragraph aloud to check for spelling errors and typographical errors	—	—	—	—	X

1. My attitude toward writing is *improving now that I have a few strategies. I liked that idea to underline a specific word. With the list of prepositions, it was easy to find them. I also used the list of connecting words to insert prepositions so that my paragraph fit together better.*

2. I still need to work on *description and details. I have a hard time deciding what is important and what is not. I also use just visual details. Although I did put in the detail about the guy being sweaty.*

6 *Process*

So how does this thing work? In your college classes, you will be called upon to read, think, and write exact descriptions of a variety of processes. Processes are dynamic. They involve beginnings and endings, progression and change, causes and effects. For this reason, processes are the focus of study in many academic areas. For example:

- How does the process of cell division occur?
- How do you determine the circumference of a circle?
- What series of events led to the War of 1812?
- How did Roosevelt's policies in the 1930s begin a process of recovery from the Great Depression?

Describing processes requires careful observation. It also requires you to identify and analyze the materials, sequence the steps involved, and explain the effects.

IN THIS CHAPTER: A PREVIEW

Process Thinking

- Elements of Process
- Time and Importance
- Process Analysis
- The Key Detail

A Process Approach to Writing the Process Paragraph

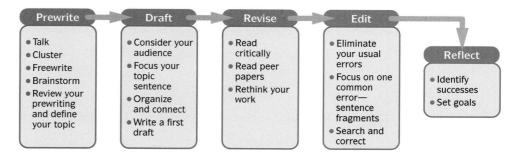

Prewrite	Draft	Revise	Edit	Reflect
• Talk • Cluster • Freewrite • Brainstorm • Review your prewriting and define your topic	• Consider your audience • Focus your topic sentence • Organize and connect • Write a first draft	• Read critically • Read peer papers • Rethink your work	• Eliminate your usual errors • Focus on one common error— sentence fragments • Search and correct	• Identify successes • Set goals

Student Sample of the Writing Process

Copyright © 2007, The McGraw-Hill Companies, Inc. All rights reserved.

WW David Lidsky

PROCESS THINKING

Like narrative, process is organized by time: first this happens, next this, and finally this. In process analysis, you dissect a complex task and examine what makes it work. Writing about a process can help you both understand it and communicate that understanding to others. The skill you develop in analyzing processes will also help you in everyday life. Once you understand how a process works, you can improve on it by making it more economical and more logical.

Elements of Process

Subject	Materials and Steps	Order	People and Impact
Why is it crucial to understand this process?	What are the essential materials and steps?	What order is appropriate to explain the process—time or importance?	How does the process affect the people involved or the work accomplished?

People and impact

Subject

Materials, steps, and order explained

People

Order and steps performed

READING: from "Polly Wanna PhD?" by Mark Caldwell

It's not just what the parrots say that makes them seem eerily human; it's the level of intelligence they easily demonstrate. Consider Griffin's [a parrot] performance on a test Pepperberg [a researcher] devised to see whether the birds could use a mirror image of an object to manipulate it. Children don't typically master that skill until they're 3 years old. In the experiment, a nut is concealed underneath the lid of a box. The nut is attached to a wire that runs up through a slit in the lid and connects to a paper clip for the parrot to yank. The slit branches out into three tracks, each of which ends in a hole through which the nut can be pulled. The trick is that two of the three slits are blocked by obstructions that can only be seen by looking in a mirror that reflects a backward view of what's inside the box. Most humans who try to solve the puzzle are baffled, but Griffin, watching intently from his perch on the lab counter, will demand to be brought over, peer into the mirror for perhaps half a second, triumphantly zip the nut down the right track, jerk it up through the opening, and grab it.

DISCUSSION QUESTIONS

1. What order does Caldwell use to explain the steps in the process?
2. What order does Caldwell use to describe Griffin's performance of the process?
3. What is Caldwell helping the reader understand about the intelligence of parrots?

Subject

Materials, steps, and order

READING: from "Leave-Taking," by Bailey White

Every summer I take a three-week vacation up north. I look forward to it all year. About a week before I leave, I start getting ready. I pack my bag, I buy a box of raisins to eat on the train, and I get down all the good books I haven't had time to read all year. I mow the lawns around the house. I clean out the freezer. I weed the

Copyright © 2007, The McGraw-Hill Companies, Inc. All rights reserved.

People and impact

garden. I wash my dog. I put everything in its place. I make Mama sit out in the yard for a day while I mop all the floors in the house. I even launder the curtains and the slipcovers on the furniture. I prepare little packages of food for Mama to eat while I'm gone, mostly bean and rice and grain dishes. I've been on a year-long campaign to reform her bad eating habits. Finally there's only one day before I leave. And that's when the horrible pangs of homesickness begin. I walk around the neat and tidy rooms of my house and smell the fresh-bleached fabrics and the Murphy Oil Soap and look out the gleaming windows over the beautiful lawn that still retains the mower stripes. "I don't want to leave," I cry.

People and impact

DISCUSSION QUESTIONS

1. What order does White use to explain her process of leaving for vacation?

2. Is this the same order you would use or recommend using to leave for vacation?

3. What is White helping the reader understand about her process of leaving?

Time and Importance

Process thinking involves steps. These steps can be organized chronologically (first, second, third) or in order of importance (saving the most important for last).

EXERCISE 6.1

The following processes are organized by time. Reorganize them according to importance, with the most important step listed last. Then briefly explain your reasons for deciding which step is most important.

EXAMPLE:

Planning a surprise party

Chronological Order	Order of Importance
Pick a date	*Assemble guest list*
Assemble guest list	*Send invitations*
Send invitations	*Arrive in time for the surprise*
Keep a secret	*Arrange food and entertainment*
Hold guests to secrecy	*Get guests to site on time*
Arrange food and entertainment	*Create a diversion*
Create a diversion	*Act as if nothing is happening*
Get guests to site on time	*Pick a date*
Act as if nothing is happening	*Hold guests to secrecy*
Arrive in time for the surprise	*Keep a secret*

Reasons: *If the host and guests can't keep a secret, there will be no surprise.*

1. Raking leaves

Chronological Order	Order of Importance
Cut the grass as short as possible	
Wait for dry weather	
Get rakes and bags	
Pick up sticks	
Rake leaves	
Bag leaves	
Take leaves to the road for pickup	

Reasons:

2. Buying a pair of shoes

Chronological Order	Order of Importance
Decide what style you want	
Go to the store	
Shop around	
Try the shoes on	
See if you like the look	
Make sure they're comfortable	
Look for the right price	
Buy them	

Reasons:

3. Doing laundry

Chronological Order	Order of Importance
Separate colors	
Select wash cycle	
Measure detergent	
Dry	
Iron	
Fold	
Put things away	

Reasons:

EXERCISE 6.1 continued

4. Creating a budget

Chronological Order	Order of Importance
Identify income per month	
List living and entertainment expenses	
List payments for revolving credit	
List due dates for each bill	
Compare income and expenses	
Identify required expenses and nonessential expenses	
Design payment schedule, personal allowance, and savings plan	
Identify areas to cut back or adjust	

Reasons:

EXERCISE 6.2

The following processes are organized by importance. Reorganize them according to time.

1. Writing a resume

Order of Importance	Chronological Order
Organize work experiences in reverse chronological order	
List education in reverse chronological order	
Check for consistent use of verbs	
Remove work experience that is unrelated to job or insignificant	
Make it readable, using bullets and indentations consistently	
Study sample resumes	
List previous work experience	
Determine job objective	
List accomplishments	
Edit the resume carefully	

2. Finding a part-time job

Order of Importance	Chronological Order
Determine if the business offers an employee discount	
Gather personal and work references	
Make a quick reference sheet of application information—social security number, driver's license number, etc.	

Copyright © 2007, The McGraw-Hill Companies, Inc. All rights reserved.

EXERCISE 6.2 continued

Order of Importance	Chronological Order
Have a resume ready in case it is needed	
Bring a pen	
Dress appropriately	
List places you want to work	

3. Finding resources for a paper in the library

Order of Importance	Chronological Order
Find books or articles that include your topic but are not the focus	
Look at the bibliographies of helpful books for other possible references	
Determine if you have enough information	
Discard books and articles that are not helpful	
Reconsider your topic to match the information	
Determine what information is available and most helpful	
Sort by relevance	
Read each resource and earmark pages with helpful information	
Search for books and articles on your topic	

4. Quitting a bad habit

Order of Importance	Chronological Order
Talk to friends to gain support	
Use positive reinforcement	
Read about positive and negative reinforcement	
Ask people who already quit for advice	
Study methods to aid quitting	
Select a method to aid quitting	
Avoid places and activities linked to the bad habit	
Quit the habit	

Process Analysis

Analysis involves taking a process apart. It may also involve organizing and grouping primary and secondary steps.

EXERCISE 6.3

Analyze the following processes. Break each process into a series of three primary steps. For each primary step, add two or three secondary steps.

EXAMPLE:

Explaining how tetanus attacks the body

Step 1: bacteria gets into body
- *a person gets a cut, burn, or insect bite*
- *contact made with the bacteria in soil or dirty object*
- *body cannot fight bacteria due to low antibodies*

Step 2: bacteria attacks body
- *bacteria multiplies and forms a toxin*
- *toxin attacks nerve fibers*
- *toxin moves toward spinal cord*
- *toxin disrupts nervous system functioning*
- *head and neck muscles become rigid*

Step 3: body shows signs of tetanus
- *lockjaw*
- *a rigid smirk, raised eyebrows, and wrinkled forehead*
- *spasms triggered by a sudden noise, movement, cough, or even a full bladder*

1. Reporting an accident at work

2. Choosing a vacation site

Copyright © 2007, The McGraw-Hill Companies, Inc. All rights reserved.

3. Learning to use new computer software

4. Selecting a boyfriend or girlfriend

5. Learning to use a new planner

The Key Detail

Processes run smoothly (or poorly) because of where they occur, who helps (or doesn't help), and the quality of the materials involved. Process thinking becomes critical thinking when observers notice key details involved in the process and can explain why they are essential details.

EXERCISE 6.4

Review the steps in the processes you analyzed in Exercise 6.3. Dig deeper into each process to explain the essential details associated with the process.

- List and explain how people, places, and materials affect the process.
- Select a key detail that makes a critical difference in the success of the process and explain why it is crucial.

EXAMPLE:

Explaining how tetanus attacks the body

PEOPLE: *To avoid tetanus, the person involved is you. You have to get regular tetanus shots and boosters to build antibodies that eliminate the threat of getting tetanus.*

PLACE: *You can get tetanus wherever germs live. However, working in dirty environments or getting cuts or abrasions can increase your exposure to tetanus bacteria. These bacteria are everywhere. They come from the feces of animals and live in the soil. So any location can be a tetanus time bomb.*

MATERIALS: *Most people can reduce their risk of contracting tetanus by getting a tetanus shot and regular booster shots and by washing wounds immediately to reduce possible infection.*

KEY DETAIL: *Knowing the process of getting tetanus is more important than knowing the process of the disease as it attacks the body. It is also good to know the signs when tetanus has progressed to its most destructive stage. The spasms can be confused for seizures, but if someone knows the combination of lockjaw, a rigid smirk, raised eyebrows, and a wrinkled forehead, then they can seek immediate medical attention.*

1. Reporting an accident at work

PEOPLE:

Copyright © 2007, The McGraw-Hill Companies, Inc. All rights reserved.

EXERCISE 6.4 continued

PLACE:

MATERIALS:

KEY DETAIL:

2. Choosing a vacation site
PEOPLE:

PLACE:

MATERIALS:

KEY DETAIL:

3. Learning to use new computer software
PEOPLE:

PLACE:

MATERIALS:

KEY DETAIL:

4. Selecting a boyfriend or girlfriend
PEOPLE:

PLACE:

Copyright © 2007, The McGraw-Hill Companies, Inc. All rights reserved.

EXERCISE 6.4 continued

MATERIALS:

KEY DETAIL:

5. Learning to use a new planner

PEOPLE:

PLACE:

MATERIALS:

KEY DETAIL:

A Process Approach to Writing the Process Paragraph

A process paragraph should do more than merely explain how to do something. It should reflect the writer's critical thinking. In choosing a topic for your process paragraph, you should draw on something you know well—or something you'd like to know well and have time to investigate. In writing your paragraph, you will explain the steps in a process in such a way that the reader will benefit from your experience and special knowledge of the process. Following are some suggested topics for your process paragraph.

Specific Topics	General Topics
Searching for information on the Internet	Daily process
Getting registered for college classes	• from childhood memories
Taking out a loan	• at home
Handling a customer complaint at work	• at school
Getting a tan at a tanning booth	• at work
Buying a used car	• for pleasure or hobbies
Explaining the causes of a war or historical event	Difficult or confusing process
Explaining the process of a disease	• you struggle to perform
Training a pet	• you have mastered
Explaining how something was discovered	How an event occurred
	• historical process
	• scientific process
	A process of your choice

ELEMENTS OF PROCESS

Subject	Materials and Steps	Order	People and Impact
Why is it crucial to understand this process?	What are the essential materials and steps?	What order is appropriate to explain the process—time or importance?	How does the process affect the people involved or the work accomplished?

STUDENT MODEL

Student Sample

Subject

First steps in process

Materials

Second series of steps

Third step

Last step

Impact

Preparing for a weekend trip is a complex process, but it is worth the effort. I have learned the hard way to prepare carefully. Packing is my first job. When I pack, I bring fewer clothes so that I have room to bring my own towels, soap, shampoo, and toiletries. My boyfriend's stepmom always runs out of clean towels and toiletry items. She prefers working in her garden to cleaning the house or making dinners or even shopping. When our bags are packed, I double-check that all the doors and windows are locked, and I turn off all but one light. We were broken into once, so I am especially careful about locks. Plus, I leave the bedroom light on since that is the typical place that people might sit up and read or be watching television. Also, I leave the radio on so it sounds like someone's home. Then I feed the turtles, Speedy and Scaredy, and our four fish. One is an Oscar. I make sure he has enough to eat because one time I forgot to feed the fish, and a couple died. I do not want to lose my expensive fish. Once we are on our way, we stop to fill up the van with gas, buy pop, and get snacks. With all the preparations done, I can enjoy the quiet ride and peaceful scenery.

PREWRITE

- Talk
- Cluster
- Freewrite
- Brainstorm
- Review your prewriting and define your topic

Select one or more of the following prewriting strategies to explore a topic and develop ideas for a process paragraph.

Talk

EXERCISE 6.5

Take turns presenting your topic to two or three peers. Explain the steps, materials, or people that make this process effective.

Copyright © 2007, The McGraw-Hill Companies, Inc. All rights reserved.

EXERCISE 6.5 continued

- As you talk, explain your attitude toward the process and which step is most demanding, interesting, pleasant, or unpleasant to you.
- As you listen, ask questions if the process is unclear or incompletely described.

Cluster

Clustering can help you identify the essential details of your topic, as well as identify their relationships.

EXERCISE 6.6

Use the following clustering diagram to explore the essential elements of your process: the subject, the materials and steps, the order, and the people and impact.

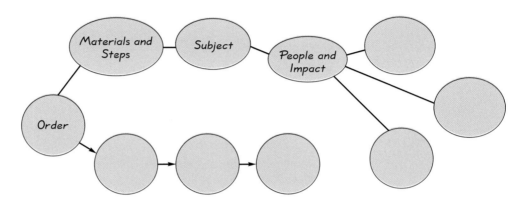

Freewrite

EXERCISE 6.7

Write for ten to fifteen minutes about a process.
    As you write, think about

- the subject—Why is it crucial to understand this process?
- the materials and steps—What are the essential materials and steps?
- the order—What order is appropriate to explain the process—time or importance? Use transition words, such as *first, second, third,* or *first, then, next,* and *finally.* These connecting words help you create a chronological order and help the reader see the process in a coherent light.
- the people and impact—How does the process affect the people involved or the work accomplished?

After freewriting, answer the following questions:

1. Which step is most important?

2. Why is this step key to the process?

Brainstorm

EXERCISE 6.8

Divide a sheet of paper into halves by drawing a vertical line down the center. On the left side of your paper, list as many steps and details as you can that relate to your process. Once you have completed the list, evaluate whether you have given enough information. Write questions on the right side of your paper that reflect what a reader might want to know about those details. Then go deeper and brainstorm the answers to those questions.

EXAMPLE:

Getting Ready for School	
Steps in the Process	**Questions the Reader Might Have**
• *Wake up*	*What time?*
• *Take shower*	*Are you alone? Do you share a*
• *Shave*	*bathroom?*
• *Brush teeth*	
• *Check in book bag to see if I'm missing anything*	
• *See what I'm going to wear*	*How fashion-conscious are you?*
• *Change my mind at least twice before I dress*	
• *Put on deodorant*	
• *Fix hair*	
• *Check car to see if I need gas*	
• *Eat a bowl of cereal*	*How much time has passed since*
• *See if I need anything from the store*	*waking up?*
• *Find a good parking spot near door of the building where my class is*	*Is parking ever a problem?*
• *Park car at the back of the lot*	
• *Drink the rest of my coffee*	*Do you procrastinate in the car, or are*
• *Smoke a cigarette*	*you in a big hurry?*
• *Check my book bag to make sure I have everything I need*	*Why do you check your bag twice?*
• *Rush to class*	*Are you always rushing?*

Review Your Prewriting and Define Your Topic

EXERCISE 6.9

Not all processes make good process papers. Use the following questions to review your prewriting and select a topic for a process paragraph.

- Which topic is most interesting and generated the most detail?
- Which one had a significant impact on you or other people?
- Which one helped you discover something new or interesting about yourself or the subject you selected?

Destinations: The Journey by Process

Thinking in Terms of a Process

Some tasks can be done in a moment, without much thought. It doesn't take a lot of preparation and concentration to tie your shoes, make a sandwich, or fill the car with gas. But other tasks are more complicated, and the important ones usually require a great deal of thought and effort: How, for example, does one graduate from college? Or maintain a successful relationship? Or find the right job? Tasks like these require you to think in terms of a process. If large goals are broken down into a series of smaller steps, they become far more manageable. For instance, graduating from college cannot be accomplished in a single night's studying but requires a series of very small accomplishments achieved over four years—quizzes taken, readings done, classes attended. By turning your attention to the immediate task at hand, you can trust that, at the end of the process, the master goal will be more easily and effectively fulfilled.

The Essay as a Process

While this book has shown you that some writing is organized within the process model, it is also true that writing any essay—in any discipline and in any model—is a process. If you feel dizzy when trying to imagine how you're going to get from an empty white sheet of paper to a great grade on a finished product, try breaking the whole thing down into manageable steps: brainstorming, freewriting, or even chatting with friends in order to figure out what you want to write about; homing in on your topic and roughing out a thesis; writing a first, very rough, draft; redrafting and rewriting; editing for typos and spelling; and finally—finally!—handing in your finished essay. If, instead of allowing yourself to be daunted by the process of writing, you think of it as a series of steps you know how to do, you should be able to face up to any assignment—and fulfill it admirably.

Big Goals, Small Steps

Your first day on the job is never easy. In addition to adjusting to a new work environment, new co-workers, and quite possibly a new city, you need to learn, on a very basic level, *how to do your job!* The change from rookie to reliable veteran will not happen overnight. It is a step-by-step process through which you will gradually learn what your colleagues know—terminology, computer programs, the basics of how your new company operates. Then you will begin to acquire more complex skills and, eventually, become knowledgeable about your position and field. By concentrating on learning one new task at a time—and discovering how multitasking itself is a process—you can become a dependable and successful employee.

DRAFT

- Consider your audience
- Focus your topic sentence
- Organize and Connect
- Write a first draft

Write a draft that organizes your prewriting into a single paragraph. This first draft will establish the subject and state the point of your process paragraph.

Consider Your Audience

EXERCISE 6.10

Now that you have selected a topic, consider who will read your paragraph. Use the following questions to consider how to convey your point to an audience.

- Why is this topic important to your audience?
- What special meaning does this topic have for you? Why do you want your audience to understand this meaning?

Copyright © 2007, The McGraw-Hill Companies, Inc. All rights reserved.

EXERCISE 6.10 continued

- Will your audience agree or disagree with your thinking? Will you be asking them to think about your subject in a new way?
- Return to the exercises on process thinking in this chapter and decide which way of thinking about your topic will help you connect best with your audience.

Focus Your Topic Sentence

Topic sentences announce the subject and the point of a paragraph. An effective process paragraph is dependent on identifying one of the following: the key detail or the impact of the process. Use a 1 (subject) + 1 (key detail or impact) approach to strengthen your topic sentence.

EXERCISE 6.11

Underline and label the key elements in each topic sentence.

EXAMPLES:

1   +   1

<u>Fixing the brakes on your car</u> is easy as long as you have <u>the right tools</u>.
subject   *impact*

1   +   1

Choose a <u>public place</u> to make <u>breaking up with your boyfriend</u> easy.
key detail   *subject*

1. A bad best man can completely ruin a wedding.

2. Imagination is the key to designing high-tech clothing

3. Voting is the last step in navigating a maze of issues, facts, and propaganda.

4. Ruining your credit is easily done in an afternoon at the local merchandise outlet.

5. Pulling water from the soil is the key to effective photosynthesis and growth.

Organize and Connect

Processes are defined by time or order. Writers use specific transition words to separate and connect the steps. Following is a list of the most common process transitions.

PROCESS TRANSITIONS				
Time			**Order**	
before	first	to begin	initially	in preparation
during	second	then	once	as the process continues
after	third	finally	further	to complete the process
		ultimately		

EXERCISE 6.12

Review the following student sample, which successfully uses a combination of time and order process transitions. Underline all the process transitions in the following paragraph.

Copyright © 2007, The McGraw-Hill Companies, Inc. All rights reserved.

EXERCISE 6.12 continued

People say that you can tell a lot about a person by their shoes. I say that you can tell a lot about a person by how clean his car is. A clean car says I am proud and feel good about myself. One of my favorite things to do is wash my car. I use a thoughtful process. First, I wash my wheels to remove the brake dust. You have to get down on your hands and knees, so you want dry pavement. I use Black Magic Wheel Cleaner. I spray it on the wheels, wait a few minutes, and then scrub them with a toothbrush. After the wheels are clean, I wash the body of the car. I scrub the roof first. That way I don't have to worry about dirt dripping on a part I have already washed. After the roof, I clean the windows and slowly make my way down the car. Around the wheel wells and lower portions of the body, just behind the wheels, I pay very close attention. Dirt gets kicked up from the wheels and is hard to get off the paint. Once I've washed the whole car, I dry it slowly. I watch for cracks in the door and hard-to-reach places. I want to make sure there is no water anywhere. If water were left, it would lead to rust. To complete the process, I go for a drive. A good cleaning prolongs the life of the car, but it also promotes a good self-image.

Write a First Draft

EXERCISE 6.13

Draft a single paragraph and use the following checklist as a guide.

_____ Review your prewriting to clarify your purpose and what you want your audience to understand.

_____ Use the 1+1 approach in your topic sentence.

_____ Insert supporting details to explain the process.

_____ Insert transitions to connect ideas and details.

REVISE
- Read critically
- Read peer papers
- Rethink your work

Begin revising by asking yourself these questions: Will an audience understand my purpose? Is there sufficient detail? Are my ideas connected and is my purpose clearly defined?

Read Critically

To establish a critical view of your own writing, read critically the writing of other student writers.

EXERCISE 6.14

Examine the following paragraph. Underline the topic sentence and circle transition words or phrases. Then answer the questions that follow.

Starting to smoke is very simple, too simple. Before you even pick up your first cigarette, the process has begun, and you are probably hooked. Maybe your folks or a relative smokes. It looks grown-up. Cigarette companies lure you in with advertising of beautiful people doing fun activities. Movies show smoking as being in control. So you sneak a cigarette, thinking they won't miss one. When you light

EXERCISE 6.14 continued

up you choke, but you tell yourself it is because you are inexperienced. You just have to get used to it. You watch how your parents smoke so you can learn the trick of inhaling. So when a friend offers you a cigarette, you take it, thinking you look beautiful. You don't listen to people who tell you how addicted you will get or the harmful side effects. You ignore the ads against smoking. Eventually you buy a pack of your own. You practice inhaling until you don't choke. You start hanging out with people who smoke so that you can smoke together. By the time that you have learned how to flick the cigarette like a tough guy, you are addicted.

Focus

1. Is the paragraph's subject clear? Will a reader understand the impact of the process?

Detail

2. Are there sufficient details about the place, people, and materials involved in the process?

3. Are there key details or steps in the process?

Connections

4. Does the writer present details in an order that is effective? Does anything seem out of order or irrelevant?

5. Is the order made clear by connecting words?

Taking a Critical View

6. What are the strengths and weaknesses of the paragraph?

Strengths	Weaknesses

7. What will improve this paragraph?

Read Peer Papers

EXERCISE 6.15

Form a group of three or four students and take turns reading and discussing your paragraphs. Use the questions from Exercise 6.14 to identify each paragraph's strengths and weaknesses. Offer suggestions for a revision plan.

Rethink Your Work

The best way to hook a reader is to emphasize the key detail. To do that, you must identify what is interesting and what is essential. Sometimes interesting details do not support the purpose of a paragraph. To clarify and strengthen your point, cut interesting but nonessential details and examples, and add details that emphasize the essential information.

Copyright © 2007, The McGraw-Hill Companies, Inc. All rights reserved.

EXERCISE 6.16

Read the following student paragraph and notice the details in the process. Talk with a classmate about the organization of the paragraph and determine the key detail. Compose questions you would ask the writer to explain the process more completely.

My morning ritual is the same every day, and in some ways it is very frustrating. When I have school, I have to do a lot of things before I leave the house. The first thing I do is work out. I have to do that before I go because it gives me a lot of energy to start my day. After I work out, I feel motivated to do other things. When I'm done working out, I take a shower and put make up on. I fix my hair and get dressed, and then I'm ready to leave. The last thing I do before I go is look for a ride since I have no car. It can take a long time, and if I'm already late to begin with, the stress level rises. When I find one, I grab my things and then leave the house.

EXERCISE 6.17

Review your paragraph and make revisions.

- Identify your point and the impact of the process.
- Identify and organize the key steps and details that illustrate your point and explain the impact.
- Emphasize the steps and details by adding background and reasons.
- Cut nonessential steps and details.

EDIT

- Eliminate your usual errors
- Focus on one common error— sentence fragments
- Search and correct

Prepare to turn your paragraph in for a grade. Make sure you are not repeating errors you usually make. Then look for new errors that may distract your reader from the purpose and meaning of your writing.

Eliminate Your Usual Errors

EXERCISE 6.18

Turn to the grids in Chapters 18, 19, and 20 where you have been keeping track of the errors you make. List those errors in the space provided below. Then proofread your paper and correct the errors you find.

_____   _____   _____

_____   _____   _____

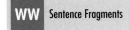

Focus on One Common Error—Sentence Fragments

In their haste to get ideas down, college writers often use end punctuation by mistake, resulting in a sentence fragment. A fragment is an incomplete thought. It occurs because the writer has used a period where a comma—or no punctuation—is preferable. The fragment has a faulty relationship with another sentence.

EXERCISE 6.18 continued

Phrase Fragments

Fragment after a complete sentence: There are many chores that I have to do around our house. <u>Like dusting, vacuuming, cleaning the bathrooms, etc.</u>

Corrected: There are many chores that I have to do around our house, like dusting, vacuuming, cleaning the bathrooms, etc.

Fragment before a complete sentence: The chore that sticks out very clearly in my mind is one that my whole family participated in, the opening of our swimming pool. <u>Every summer, no particular day, but always in June.</u> I would have to get up early, go outside, and help start the all-day chore.

Corrected: The chore that sticks out very clearly in my mind is one that my whole family participated in, the opening of our swimming pool. Every summer, no particular day, but always in June, I would have to get up early, go outside, and help start the all-day chore.

Subordinate-Clause Fragments

Fragment after a complete sentence: We realized that we had very little in common. <u>When we began to talk about what he liked to do and what I liked to do.</u>

Corrected: We realized that we had very little in common when we began to talk about what he liked to do and what I liked to do.

Fragment before a complete sentence: <u>According to Ira Berkow of the *New York Times,* who reported on the death of a freshmen football player.</u> Football is a killer of young men.

Corrected: According to Ira Berkow of the *New York Times,* who reported on the death of a freshman football player, football is a killer of young men.

EXERCISE 6.19

Underline the fragments in the following sentences. Correct the punctuation as needed. Feel free to rewrite the sentences to make them complete.

1. After working in day care for a while, I really learned to keep an eye on little kids and what they have in their mouths. Also especially to help an infant who looked like he or she was in distress.

2. The on-campus feeling you get, walking to class and interacting with other students. The computer doesn't replace that.

3. My sister and I were so hungry we couldn't stand it. Once we got to the little hole in the wall restaurant. We gave the waiter our order, and he took forever to bring our food.

4. As you walked up the driveway, you'd see two fully grown pine trees on the right. A few feet behind them sat a wooden bench swing. Large enough to seat four people.

Copyright © 2007, The McGraw-Hill Companies, Inc. All rights reserved.

EXERCISE 6.19 continued

5. I have always wanted to order a new car. Throughout my years of living at home with my parents. They would drag me and my brother into a new car showroom.

6. My dropping out of school hit my parents hard. My mom was worse than my dad. I remember hearing her cry at night. And the look on her face when she stared at me later. It was filled with disgust and lost hope

7. I have been told I am not a quitter but a fighter. A personal trait that people really admire. I try to be that way, not just look that way.

8. If I had a choice to take medicine and there was nothing else for me to do. I would take the medicine at whatever cost. That's how I was brought up.

9. I had a great time as a kid. There were many things I did to pass the time. Everything from playing video games, to riding bikes, to playing sports.

10. There are two forms of friends. Your true friends and your associates. The ones you depend on and the ones you don't. A true friend is most likely to be a person you've known for years. A person who knows many things about you. If they tell you things, you keep it a secret. Nothing they say would ever change your outlook on them.

Search and Correct

EXERCISE 6.20

Double-check your grammar. Read your paragraph for a single error—sentence fragments.

EXERCISE 6.21

Double-check your spelling. Computer spell-checks make mistakes. Therefore, it is essential that you proofread your paper before turning it in for a grade. Focus your close reading on typographical errors.

EXERCISE 6.22

Find a Proofreading Pal. After you have double-checked your paper, exchange papers with that student and proofread each other's work. Find out what errors your classmate would like you to search for. Using your list from Exercise 6.18, tell your classmate what errors you are inclined to make.

REFLECT
- Identify successes
- Set goals

Each time you write, you build skills and strategies. The last step in the writing process is to reflect and recognize what you did well and what you learned.

Identify Successes

EXERCISE 6.23

Take a few minutes to reflect on your successes. Write one or two sentences that explain two things you have learned from this chapter and how you successfully applied them to your writing. Use a specific example from your work to support your thinking.

Set Goals

EXERCISE 6.24

Now that you have examined your successes, determine what challenges you face. Rate yourself using the following scale—5 indicates a task that you consider a challenge most of the time, and 1 indicates a task for which you have the required skills and strategies.

Steps	Strategies and Skills	5	4	3	2	1
Prewrite	1. I prewrite to explore my ideas and think deeper about a topic.	—	—	—	—	—
Draft	2. I focus my paragraphs with topic sentences.	—	—	—	—	—
	3. I organize my ideas and make connections.	—	—	—	—	—
Revise	4. I read critically to identify and use the successful techniques of other writers.	—	—	—	—	—
	5. I identify the strengths and weaknesses in my papers.	—	—	—	—	—
	6. I apply specific revision strategies to my papers.	—	—	—	—	—
Edit	7. I employ all or some of the following editing strategies:					
	▪ apply rules to correct sentence fragments	—	—	—	—	—
	▪ use spell-check on my computer	—	—	—	—	—
	▪ read a printed copy of my paragraph aloud to check for spelling errors and typographical errors	—	—	—	—	—

EXERCISE 6.25

Finish the following sentences in order to explore your learning experience and to set goals.

1. My attitude toward writing is

2. I still need to work on

STUDENT SAMPLE OF THE WRITING PROCESS

STUDENT MODEL

Kinesha's Clustering

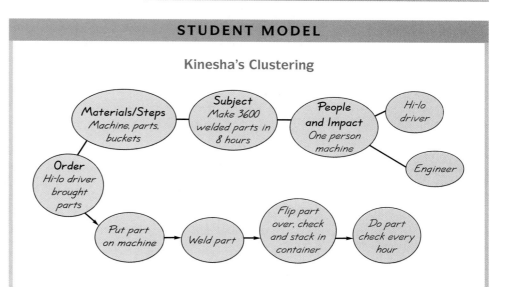

Kinesha's Unedited Freewrite

I worked first shift during my first few months at a welding plant. I was on about every machin in back welding. I liked this because I was constently doing something new. I especially liked working on lines, because I got to work with other people. Since I was the new girl I got stuck on the machine that nobody wanted. It was a stationary spot welding fender machine. It was a one-person machine. The hi-lo driver would bring me a container that had 500 parts. I'd stack the parts. I'd grab a part with one hand, and put it on a fixture. Next I'd hold down two buttons, and a rod would shoot out and the nut would go into place on the fender. The press part on the machine would weld the nut on. Then I'd grab it flip it in a metal container. Sounds fun, doesn't it? After I put 200 in a container I'd tag the container and keep on going until I got 3600, the production was 450 an hour. Plus, every hour throughout my shift I'd go do a part check which was just running a screw through the nut. If the part was bent. I had to stop the process and get an engineer to reset the machine, I couldn't leave until I made my daily production number.

Kinesha's Prewriting Questions: Which step is most important? Why is this step key to the process?

The key step is checking the quality of the nut. If the nut wasn't any good, I had to stop and start all over again. Then I had to toss an hour of work. I learned to work fast and efficiently at a job I hated. Just doing the job and not paying attention to how good a job you're doing doesn't get the job done. You have to be paying attention. Every night I had to make my quota.

continued

Copyright © 2007, The McGraw-Hill Companies, Inc. All rights reserved.

I could do it in 8 hours, or I could do it in 6 hours. They didn't care. But they did care that the job was done right. I learned to do both, but first I had to deal with my attitude. I hated the repetition and boredom.

Kinesha's Unedited First Draft

A motivated attitude is tough but key to surviving a repetitive job on the line. I learned this the hard way working first shift. I worked in back welding from 5:00am-1:30pm. I worked a stationary spot welding fender machine. It was a one-person machine in the back of the shop. All by myself. The hi-lo driver would bring me a container that had 500 parts. To set up the job, I would stack the parts on a slanted bench and they would roll off if I wasn't careful. Then I'd start the machine. First, I would grab a part with one hand and put it on a fixture a thing that had a screw sticking out. Next I would hold down two buttons a red one and a green one, and a rod would shoot out very quickly with a nut on it. The nut would go into place on the fender. The press part on the machine would weld the nut on. Then I would grab it flip it in a metal container. After I put 200 in a container I would tag the container. In addition, every hour throughout my shift I would go do a part check which was just running a screw through the nut. If the part was not bent and the screw went through easily then the part was good. If the part was bent, I had to stop the process and get an engineer to reset the machine or get new nuts and I had to toss the bad nuts and start again. I was expected to stay focused and do 450 parts an hour times 8 hours. I couldn't leave until I made my daily production number of 3600. That meant I had to stay focused and alert the whole time at a very boring job. I had no one to talk to. It was just the machine and me. Sounds fun, doesn't it? I hated it.

Kinesha's Revised Draft

A motivated attitude is tough but key to surviving a repetitive job on the line. I learned this the hard way working first shift. I worked in back welding from 5:00am-1:30pm working a stationary spot welding fender machine. The job was filled with tedious details. To set up the job, I would stack the parts on a slanted bench and they would roll off if I wasn't careful. Then I'd start the machine. First, I would grab a part with one hand and put it on a fixture a thing that had a screw sticking out. Next I would hold down two buttons, a red one and a green one and a rod would shoot out very quickly with a nut on it. Then I would grab it flip it in a metal container. After I put 200 in a container, I would tag the container. In addition every hour throughout my shift I would go do a part check If the part was bent I had to stop the process and get an engineer to reset the machine or get new nuts and I had to toss the bad nuts and start again.

I was expected to stay focused and do 450 parts an hour times 8 hours which equals 3600 parts. That meant I had to stay focused and alert the whole time with no one to talk to. I knew I'd never survive or get a better job in the plant until I learned to manage this process effectively.

Kinesha's Editing

A motivated attitude is tough but key to surviving a repetitive job on the line. I learned this the hard way working first shift. I worked in back welding from 5:00 ~~am~~ 1: 30 ~~pm~~ *(a.m.)* *(p.m. I)* ~~working~~ *(ed on)* a stationary spot welding fender machine. The job was filled with tedious details. To set up the job, I would stack the parts on a slanted bench, and they would roll off if I ~~wasn't~~ *(were not)* careful. Then I'd *(would)* start the machine. First, I would grab a part with one hand and put it on a fixture, a thing that had a screw sticking out. Next, I would hold down two buttons, a red one and a green one, and a rod would shoot out very quickly with a nut on it. Then I would grab ~~it~~ *(the part)* flip *(and)* it in a metal container. After I put 200 in a container, I would tag the container. In addition, *(I was required to do a part check every hour.)* ~~every hour throughout my shift I would go do a part check~~ If the part was bent, I had to stop, ~~the process and~~ get an engineer to reset the machine, ~~or get new nuts and I had to~~ toss the bad nuts, and start again. I was expected to stay focused and do 450 parts an hour ~~times~~ *(for eight)* 8 hours, which equals 3600 parts. ~~That meant~~ I had to stay focused and alert the whole time with no one to talk to. I knew I'd never survive or get a better job in the plant until I learned to manage this process effectively.

Kinesha's Final Edited Paragraph

A motivated attitude is tough but key to surviving a repetitive job on the line. I learned this the hard way working first shift. I worked in back welding from 5:00 a.m. to 1:30 p.m. I worked on a stationary spot welding fender machine. The job was filled with tedious details. To set up the job, I would stack the parts on a slanted bench, and they would roll off if I were not careful. Then I would start the machine. First, I would grab a part with one hand and put it on a fixture, a thing that had a screw sticking out. Next, I would hold down two buttons, a red one and a green one, and a rod would shoot out very quickly with a nut on it. Then I would grab the part and flip it in a metal container. After I put 200 in a container, I would tag the container. In addition, I was required to do a part check every hour. If the part was

continued

Copyright © 2007, The McGraw-Hill Companies, Inc. All rights reserved.

bent, I had to stop, get an engineer to reset the machine, toss the bad nuts, and start again. I was expected to stay focused and do 450 parts an hour for eight hours, which equals 3600 parts. I had to stay focused and alert the whole time with no one to talk to. I knew I'd never survive or get a better job in the plant until I learned to manage this process effectively.

Kinesha's Reflection

Stages	Strategies and Skills	5	4	3	2	1
Prewrite	1. I prewrite to explore my ideas and think deeper about a topic.			X		
Draft	2. I focus my paragraphs with topic sentences.					X
	3. I organize my ideas and make connections.					X
Revise	4. I read critically to identify and use the successful techniques of other writers.				X	
	5. I identify the strengths and weaknesses in my papers.				X	
	6. I apply specific revision strategies to my papers.				X	
Edit	7. I employ all or some of the following editing strategies:					
	▪ apply rules to correct sentence fragments				X	
	▪ use spell-check on my computer				X	
	▪ read a printed copy of my paragraph aloud to check for spelling errors and typographical errors				X	

1. My attitude toward writing is *pretty positive. I like to write. I especially like adding detail. The hard part is deciding what detail to cut. I can always think of more to say. I pretty much depend on spell-check and keep correcting my work whenever I see that squiggly red line.*

2. I still need to work on *cutting. I tend to write long sentences and ignore punctuation. I write like I talk. I go on and on without stopping or slowing down. The good thing is that I don't have a lot of sentence fragments. The bad thing is that I have a lot of sentences without commas.*

7 *Cause and Effect*

*B*ut *why? How did all this come about?* In the normal course of events, you ask yourself this question all the time. Trying to understand why things happen is part of everyday life. College courses introduce you to systematic, rational ways of understanding the world:

- How were mountains formed?
- What effects do solar winds have on satellite communications?
- In what part of the brain does attention deficit disorder originate?
- What's happening to our weather, and why?

These questions and the search for satisfactory answers make use of cause-and-effect thinking. This search involves analysis, one of the most important critical-thinking activities across the college curriculum.

IN THIS CHAPTER: A PREVIEW

Cause-and-Effect Thinking

- Elements of Cause and Effect
- Causes, Effects, and Time
- Primary Causes and Conditions
- Reasons as Causes

A Process Approach to Writing the Cause-and-Effect Paragraph

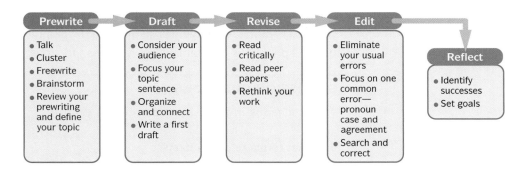

Prewrite	Draft	Revise	Edit	Reflect
• Talk • Cluster • Freewrite • Brainstorm • Review your prewriting and define your topic	• Consider your audience • Focus your topic sentence • Organize and connect • Write a first draft	• Read critically • Read peer papers • Rethink your work	• Eliminate your usual errors • Focus on one common error—pronoun case and agreement • Search and correct	• Identify successes • Set goals

Student Sample of the Writing Process

Copyright © 2007, The McGraw-Hill Companies, Inc. All rights reserved.

Going to the Next Level: Multiple-Paragraph Papers

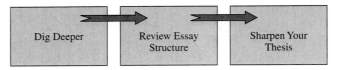

| Dig Deeper | Review Essay Structure | Sharpen Your Thesis |

CAUSE-AND-EFFECT THINKING

WW Maya Angelou

Cause-and-effect analysis begins with a situation or problem: Your car won't start. Somebody other than you gets a raise at work. You are not working up to your potential in school. Your doctor tells you that your cholesterol is high. These situations have causes; they also have consequences. Time is a factor in cause-and-effect thinking. Effects follow causes. But then, effects themselves can also have consequences. In cause-and-effect thinking, one thing leads to another.

Elements of Cause and Effect

Problem	Cause	Effect
What is the problem? When did it appear? What symptoms tell you that a problem exists?	What happened before you became aware of the problem? What conditions contributed to it?	What happened after the problem arose? What changes occurred as a result of this problem?

READING: from "Born to Bicker," by Laurence Steinberg

Problem

Cause

Effects

Cause

Problem

My own studies point to early adolescence—the years from ten to thirteen—as a period of special strain between parents and children. But more intriguing, perhaps, is that these studies reveal that puberty plays a central role in triggering parent-adolescent conflict. Specifically, as youngsters develop toward physical maturity, bickering and squabbling with parents increase. If puberty comes early, so does the arguing and bickering; if it is late, the period of heightened tension is delayed. Although many other aspects of adolescent behavior reflect the intertwined influences of biological and social factors, this aspect seems to be directly connected to the biological event of puberty; something about normal physical maturing sets off parent-adolescent fighting. It's no surprise that they argue about overflowing trash cans, trails of dirty laundry, and blaring stereos. But why should teenagers going through puberty fight with their parents more often than youngsters of the same age whose physical development is slower? More to the point, if puberty is inevitable, does this mean that parent-child conflict is, too?

DISCUSSION QUESTIONS

1. What terms in this paragraph refer to causes?

2. What terms refer to effects?

3. Are "overflowing trash cans, trails of dirty laundry, and blaring stereos" a cause or effect?

4. Judging from the words this writer uses, what do you assume his professional background is?

Causes, Effects, and Time

Think about the timing of causes and effects. Causes most often precede the problem, and effects tend to occur after the problem has arisen.

EXERCISE 7.1

Identify the problem in each of the following situations. Then indicate what comes before and what comes after to identify cause and effect.

EXAMPLE:

squabbling and bickering increases / onset of puberty / strain between parents and children

(situation)

onset of puberty ⟶ *strain between parents and children* ⟶ *squabbling and bickering*

(cause)   (problem)   (effect)

1. poor concentration and missed assignments / late nights out with friends / low grades

2. loss of refrigeration and spoiled food / intestinal disorder / power outage

3. disability and death / fatty diet / clogged arteries

4. increased smog and air pollution / CO_2 emissions / respiratory illness

5. significant weight loss / improved self-image / exercise and self-control

Primary Causes and Conditions

Careful analysis often reveals a complex set of circumstances explaining why something happens. There is often a primary cause that triggers an effect or a chain of effects. In addition, there are often existing conditions that make it possible for the problem to occur. Without this primary cause or existing conditions, the problem would not occur.

EXERCISE 7.2

Use a flowchart to analyze the following problems. Begin with the conditions, followed by the primary cause and subsequent effect. Write a sentence or two to explain your reasoning for choosing each primary cause.

EXAMPLE:

Effect: car accident

slippery roads / poor visibility / excessive speed / failure to stop in time

Copyright © 2007, The McGraw-Hill Companies, Inc. All rights reserved.

EXERCISE 7.2 continued

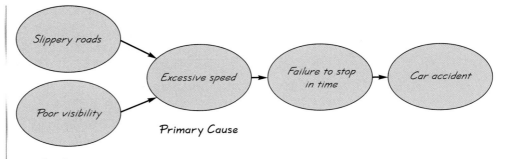

Conditions

Reasoning: *Road conditions were bad, but excessive speed was the primary cause. The driver had control over his speed. He couldn't have dried the roads or made the fog go away, but he could have driven more slowly. His speed was the main cause of the accident.*

1. Effect: a mouthful of cavities

   infrequent trips to the dentist / high-sugar foods such as soda and candy / failure to brush daily / drinking water without fluoride

2. Effect: winning the football game

   passing game / strong defensive line / best quarterback in the league / opponents' injuries

3. Effect: singing well

   natural ability / voice lessons / listening to a lot of music / singing in a choir regularly

4. Effect: landing a good job

   training and education / a vacancy in the XZY Corporation / preparing responses to interview questions / proper dress

5. Effect: losing weight

   maintaining discipline / eating less / exercising more / avoiding fast food

Reasons as Causes

Writers justify opinions and points of view by presenting and explaining reasons. Reasons can be causes of actions. For example, the Declaration of Independence states the reasons for the colonies' desire to be independent from England. Indeed, those reasons are presented as a "just cause."

EXERCISE 7.3

Briefly outline possible reasons for the following actions.

EXAMPLE:

Carpool
> Reason 1: save money
> Reason 2: ecologically responsible (less pollution)
> Reason 3: more free time to study and/or socialize

1. Exercise daily
   Reason 1
   Reason 2
   Reason 3

2. Continue living at home
   Reason 1
   Reason 2
   Reason 3

3. Meet and get to know people from other ethnic backgrounds
   Reason 1
   Reason 2
   Reason 3

4. Avoid alcohol
   Reason 1
   Reason 2
   Reason 3

5. Buy a home computer
   Reason 1
   Reason 2
   Reason 3

A PROCESS APPROACH TO WRITING THE CAUSE-AND-EFFECT PARAGRAPH

The cause-and-effect paragraph presents a problem or describes a situation and then explores causes that come before or effects that follow. Writers provide explanation and analysis so the reader can fully understand the meaning of the causes and effects. Following are some suggested topics for your cause-and-effect paragraph.

Copyright © 2007, The McGraw-Hill Companies, Inc. All rights reserved.

Specific Topics	General Topics
A computer application you struggle to understand	Personal life
The performance of your sound system	• relationships
A recipe or food that just doesn't taste right	• goals
Finding time for a hobby or pastime	• problem solving
Your parents give you too much responsibility	School life
Your parent, spouse, or significant other doesn't trust you	• social challenges
A friend doesn't pay you money he owes you	• academic challenges
A tricky communication problem with a teacher or boss	• personal motivation
Why you can't lose (or gain) weight	Work life
A problem associated with being a person your age or with your background	• conflict
	• challenges
Your problem with reading, math, or speaking in front of groups	• time management

ELEMENTS OF CAUSE AND EFFECT

Problem	Cause	Effect
What is the problem? When did it appear? What symptoms tell you that a problem exists?	What happened before you became aware of the problem? What conditions contributed to it?	What happened after the problem arose? What changes occurred as a result of this problem?

STUDENT MODEL

Student Sample

Problem

Cause 1

Cause 2

Effect

The main reason my sister and I quarrel is our upbringing. When we were children, our parents taught my sister and me to be independent thinkers. We learned at a young age how to solve our problems, on our own! While I strongly believe this is a skill every child needs, it can be detrimental if taken to the extreme. This is something I tend to do under certain circumstances, especially those circumstances that make me look "weak" in front of my sister. That's another reason we quarrel. I always felt I needed to be the "strong one," always ready to help my sister out of her next catastrophe. But what I didn't learn to do as a child was to let my sister be there for me as well. Unfortunately, the lesson we both learned as children has hindered our ability to support each other now, as adults. Those times when we could benefit from each other's support the most, we often turn away from each other, and the long silent treatment begins again.

Copyright © 2007, The McGraw-Hill Companies, Inc. All rights reserved.

PREWRITE

- Talk
- Cluster
- Freewrite
- Brainstorm
- Review your prewriting and define your topic

Select one or more of the following
prewriting strategies to explore a topic and develop ideas
for a cause-and-effect paragraph.

Talk

EXERCISE 7.4

Talk to one or two other students who chose the same topic you did. Discuss the causes and effects that are important to you. Once each person has shared his or her ideas on the topic, write down what you learned. Use the following questions to guide additional writing:

- On what points did you agree with your peers?
- On what points did you disagree?
- Which of your ideas did your peers find important?
- Which of their ideas did you find important?

Cluster

EXERCISE 7.5

Use clustering to explore a topic that interests you. The following diagrams will help you focus your thinking on causes and effects. After clustering, review your thinking and determine the possible content for your paragraph.

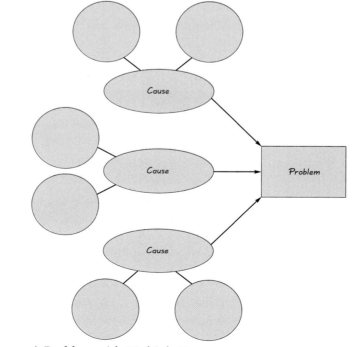

A Problem with Multiple Causes

EXERCISE 7.5 continued

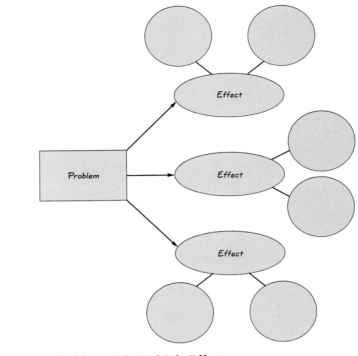

A Problem with Multiple Effects

Freewrite

EXERCISE 7.6

Use the following questions to focus your freewriting. Write for ten to twenty minutes to get started.

- When did you become aware of this situation or problem?
- What steps did you take to determine the cause of the problem?
- What are the causes and who is responsible for them?

Brainstorm

EXERCISE 7.7

Review your prewriting exercises and list everything you discovered in the process. If new ideas and details come to mind, add those to your list.

Review Your Prewriting and Define Your Topic

EXERCISE 7.8

Use the following questions to review your prewriting and define your topic for a cause-and-effect paragraph.

- Which topic is most interesting and generated the most detail?
- Which topic had a significant impact on you or other people?
- Which one helped you discover something new or interesting about yourself or the subject you selected?

Copyright © 2007, The McGraw-Hill Companies, Inc. All rights reserved.

> **DRAFT**
> - Consider your audience
> - Focus your topic sentence
> - Organize and connect
> - Write a first draft

Write a draft that organizes your prewriting into a single paragraph. The first draft will establish the subject and state the point of your cause-and-effect paragraph.

Consider Your Audience

EXERCISE 7.9

Reread your prewriting to examine all your ideas about your topic. To size up your audience's knowledge of your subject, consider the following dimensions of your topic.

- Why is this topic important to your audience?
- What special meaning does this topic have for you? Why do you want your audience to understand this meaning?
- Will your audience agree or disagree with your thinking? Will you be asking them to think about your subject in a new way?
- Return to the exercises on cause-and-effect thinking in this chapter and decide which way of thinking about your topic will help you connect best with your audience.

Focus Your Topic Sentence

EXERCISE 7.10

Underline the key terms in each of the following topic sentences. Then indicate whether the paragraph will focus on causes or effects.

EXAMPLE:

<u>Smoking changes a person's life</u> in a number of <u>small but important ways</u>.

    (cause)   (effects)

Focus: *effects*

1. All sorts of mischief can come from leaving kids home alone after school.
   Focus:

2. I was forced to quit my latest job for a number of reasons.
   Focus:

3. People in my community have made a number of changes in their way of life as a result of drought conditions.
   Focus:

EXERCISE 7.10 continued

4. Having braces on your teeth completely alters how you relate to members of the opposite sex.

Focus:

5. There are many reasons carpooling can be a good idea.

Focus:

Organize and Connect

EXERCISE 7.11

Using the following outline as a model, make a rough outline for your cause-and-effect paragraph. Write your topic sentence and list the causes or effects you wish to discuss.

EXAMPLE:

Topic sentence: A major problem at work is the backup of people in front of the cash register.

    I. *Some customers take too long*

      A. *Mrs. Peters*

        1. *Always has pennies*

        2. *Forgets her glasses*

        3. *Wants to talk*

      B. *The grass cutters*

        1. *Arrive at lunch time*

        2. *Bunch up in the aisle and tell jokes*

  II. *Credit card purchases take longer than cash*

III. *Owner's attempt to be a "full-service" store*

        1. *Requires lots of shelves*

        2. *Creates cramped aisles and limited walking space*

        3. *Makes the store look cluttered*

  IV. *At high-traffic times, management should open more registers*

EXERCISE 7.12

Look over the following lists of transitions commonly used in cause-and-effect writing. Then read the paragraph that follows. Underline the topic sentence in the paragraph and then identify the causes of violence the author cites. Finally, from the lists of transitions, choose those that would make sense in the paragraph and indicate in the margin where you would insert them.

Cause-and-Effect Transitions		
accordingly	consequently	since
although	if . . . so	then
as a result	in fact	therefore

EXERCISE 7.12 continued

Transitions for Listing Causes as Reasons		
First Reason	**Second Reason**	**Third Reason**
one reason	another	finally
most important	in addition	also
major reason	likewise	furthermore
primary reason	similarly	moreover
for instance	specifically	most important

Violence has become the answer to many teenagers' frustrations in life. Everywhere you look, whether on television or in the newspaper, young people are turning to violence to solve their problems. The introduction to violence starts when they are very small. Television shows everything from guns to blood and death. Media glamorizes the violent behaviors of the shows. Teens relate to these dramas and feel violence is the way to end their depression. An important cause is a lack of a good family structure. Those teens lacking love and family structure, which are so important for becoming an adjusted individual, often get into trouble. They all too often take out their troubles through violent actions. Violence may be seen as a cry for help, a way to get attention for some adolescents. Teens see that the only time they are noticed is when they become violent, hurt others, or cause trouble. Sometimes, however, they are simply scared or confused and do not know how to properly express or release those emotions. Then violence like so many other times becomes the vent in which they release steam.

Causes:

Write a First Draft

EXERCISE 7.13

Use the following checklist as a guide to draft your cause-and-effect paragraph.

_____ Review your prewriting to clarify your purpose and what you want your audience to understand.

_____ Insert details to explain causes or effects you discuss.

_____ Use the 1 + 1 approach in your topic sentence.

_____ Insert transitions to connect ideas and details.

REVISE

- Read critically
- Read peer papers
- Rethink your work

Begin revising by asking yourself these questions: Will an audience understand my purpose? Is there sufficient detail? Are my ideas connected and is my purpose clearly defined?

Copyright © 2007, The McGraw-Hill Companies, Inc. All rights reserved.

Read Critically

EXERCISE 7.14

Examine the following paragraph. Underline the topic sentence and circle transition words or phrases. Look for strengths and weaknesses.

Today's youth encounter many life-threatening obstacles. Beginning with poverty, stress, and temptation. These three things play an important role in many young lives. Poverty starts at home, when parents struggle to make it through daily life and try to make things better for themselves and their children. Some families lack many material and important things like clothes, food, shelter, etc. That leads them to stress, and stress becomes their everyday trial. Stress comes from not having the needed necessities to life. After people stress long enough, they tend to need money immediately. And that may tempt one to do illegal things, such as sell drugs, gamble on the street corners, steal and sell cars, etc. All of the above mentioned things tend to become an everyday lifestyle for many youth of this day and age.

Focus

1. Is the paragraph's subject clear? Will a reader understand why this topic is important?

Detail

2. Does the writer identify clear causes and effects?

3. Are there adequate details and explanation?

Connections

4. Does the writer present details in an order that is effective? Does anything seem out of order or irrelevant?

5. Is the order made clear by connecting words?

Taking a Critical View

6. What are the strengths and weaknesses of the paragraph?

Strengths	Weaknesses

7. What will improve this paper?

Read Peer Papers

EXERCISE 7.15

Form a group of three or four students and take turns reading and discussing your paragraphs. Use the questions from Exercise 7.14 to identify each paragraph's strengths and weaknesses. Offer suggestions for a revision plan.

Rethink Your Work

A cause-and-effect paragraph focuses on a problem. Organize your paragraph to clearly define the problem and state the causes and effects. In addition, your paragraph will be most effective if you explain how the causes are related to the problem.

EXERCISE 7.16

Read the following student paragraph and focus on its organization. Discuss with a classmate whether you think the organization is effective. Is the problem clearly defined? Are the causes connected to the problem? Are the effects clearly stated?

> Growing up, I hated getting in a car with my parents. They both smoked then. The smell in the car and on our clothes was disgusting. I swore I was choking and couldn't breathe. I didn't even like to touch the cigarette pack: it was so gross. However, through my teenage years of rebellion, and peer pressure, I did eventually try smoking. With my friends, it wasn't so gross. It was cool. Everyone did it. Once, my mother saw me driving down the road trying to light a cigarette. When I returned home later that day, she questioned me. I told her it was only once in a while; it wasn't like I was addicted. Nevertheless, I was grounded and told I couldn't smoke in front of them. They hoped this would reduce my smoking and help me kick the habit. I am now twenty-four years old, and I am addicted to smoking. It is not cool, and I choke and can't breathe. The ironic thing is that my favorite time to smoke is as soon as I get in the car.

EXERCISE 7.17

Outline your paragraph to analyze its current order. Then determine if your paragraph's organization is effective.

- Do you clearly state your problem?
- Do you connect your causes to the problem?
- Do you state the effects of the problem?

EDIT

- Eliminate your usual errors
- Focus on one common error— pronoun case and agreement
- Search and correct

Prepare to turn your paragraph in for a grade. Make sure you are not repeating errors you usually make. Then look for new errors that may distract your reader from the purpose and meaning of your writing.

Copyright © 2007, The McGraw-Hill Companies, Inc. All rights reserved.

Eliminate Your Usual Errors

EXERCISE 7.18

Turn to the grids in Chapters 18, 19, and 20 where you have been keeping track of the errors you make. List those errors in the space provided below. Then proofread your paper and correct the errors you find.

_____   _____   _____

_____   _____   _____

Focus on One Common Error—Pronoun Case and Agreement

When writers shift from casual language to "school language," they need to watch their pronouns. Pronoun errors are also common when writers shift their focus from personal subjects to popular and academic subjects.

Pronoun Case

Pronouns come in different forms, or *cases*. Subject pronouns are used as the subjects of sentences; objective pronouns are used with verbs and prepositions.

> **Incorrect pronoun case:** If you were talking to **my sister and I,** you were just wasting your breath!

Try the pronouns separately:

> If you were to talking to my sister . . .
> If you were talking to I . . .

> **Correct pronoun case:** If you were talking to **my sister and me,** you were just wasting your breath!

> **Incorrect pronoun case:** Once again, **me and my sister** are not on speaking terms.

Test the pronouns separately:

> Once again, me is not . . .
> Once again, my sister is not . . .

> **Correct pronoun case:** Once again, **my sister and I** are not on speaking terms.

EXERCISE 7.19

Identify and correct errors with pronoun case in the following sentences. Test the pronouns separately to see if they sound right. Put a C after sentences that are correct.

1. He was a pretty good artist, but Bob and me were better.
2. By this time she was taking drugs. Me and my friends were always smart enough not to do them.
3. My mother was at work. This young lady and I were just fooling around when I heard the door open.
4. We used to go to the babysitter's down the street. She would invite us to go downstairs where she played Barbies with her kids, my friend Marisa, and me.
5. During the summer, my cousin Michelle would come and stay with my grandmother and I.
6. My sisters and me would argue over who was going to be Farrah when we played.

EXERCISE 7.19 continued

7. If you get to know my friends and me, you will see that we are not bad people.

8. About 11:00 p.m. last night, all my buddies and I were hanging out in the downtown area.

9. Lisa took a liking to me from day one. Her and I gradually grew dangerously close.

10. I thought a lot about my friend and what her and her new friends were doing.

Pronoun Agreement

Pronouns take the place of nouns. The nouns they replace are called *antecedents.* The pronoun and antecedent must "agree"; singular pronouns refer to singular antecedents, and plural pronouns refer to plural antecedents.

> **Not in agreement:** I have never known **anyone** who has changed **their** name.
>
> **In agreement:** I have never known **anyone** who has changed **his or her** name. *Or* I have never known **any people** who have changed **their** names.
>
> **Not in agreement:** While the teacher was out of the room, friends and I went to his desk, grabbed his books, and put **it** under the table.
>
> **In agreement:** While the teacher was out of the room, friends and I went to his desk, grabbed his books, and put **them** under the table.

EXERCISE 7.20

Underline the pronouns and circle the antecedents in the following sentences. Correct the errors by changing the pronouns.

1. A responsibility I think everyone should have is taking care of themselves.

2. There is a time in everybody's life when they are going to be responsible for someone or something.

3. It's amazing how many more people are working from his or her house.

4. Nursing is not the only area where a person must remain committed to their jobs.

5. You do not need to hit a child to make them obey you.

6. When a child can control itself she has conquered their inner self.

7. At what point in a teenager's life does it suddenly strike them that it's time to start driving?

8. When a person puts you in charge, they are trying to see if they can trust you.

9. Young people have a vivid imagination, the ability to create things that do not exist, all before the cruel adult world gets hold of him.

10. Not every driver is as good as they should be, but that doesn't mean we are all doomed.

Search and Correct

EXERCISE 7.21

Double-check your grammar. Search for pronouns in your draft and connect them to antecedents. Correct agreement problems you find.

Copyright © 2007, The McGraw-Hill Companies, Inc. All rights reserved.

Destinations: Getting Somewhere (and Knowing How You Did) with Cause and Effect

Targeting Cause, Gauging Effect

1. "The King died, and then the Queen died."

2. "The King died, and then the Queen died of grief."

The difference between these two sentences involves only two words, but a whole world of meaning. Every day, in one way or another, we exercise a basic component of critical thinking: asking ourselves *why* something happened. If you like what happened—let's say, for example, you managed to talk a police officer out of giving you a speeding ticket—you might well ask yourself how you can get it to happen again, by examining the chain of cause-and-effect that led up to the event. Where were you driving? Exactly *how* fast? Why were you speeding? What did you say to the officer when you were stopped? If, on the contrary, you *don't* like what happened—let's say you got the ticket (and a hefty fine)—you'll need to follow the chain of events back far enough so that you can keep it from happening again. (And maybe you'll just slow down.)

Making Your Case in Class

You will often find yourself arguing about cause and effect in papers and in classroom discussion. Remember that every statement you make about "what caused what" is, in fact, a claim, and implies an argument. What were the causes of the Civil War? Why don't more Americans vote? Why didn't the engine start? Why did the mixture of two chemicals form a noxious gas? Being able to argue convincingly for the cause (or combination of causes) you think most relevant will make the difference between persuading your audience or leaving them doubting your conclusions.

Working It Out

Determining the cause(s) of a particular effect is a skill you will need in virtually any job. You may have to assemble data that could explain why sales are down—for example, shifts in consumer buying patterns; new (and perhaps less popular) features in the product you are selling; changes in the way you are marketing it; a downturn in the national economy—and then make an argument for the relevant cause(s) to your boss or to your company's shareholders. The more accurate your determination of the causes of lower sales, the more likely you will be to turn things around and reap the rewards. Why does a certain patient exhibit a persistent rash? You will first need to examine the physical symptoms carefully, consider the patient's history, and perform the necessary tests before making a proper judgment as to the underlying cause. Going the extra mile in analyzing a situation can make the difference between success and failure in your chosen career.

EXERCISE 7.22

Double-check your spelling. Computer spell-checks make mistakes. Therefore, it is essential that you proofread your paper before turning it in for a grade. Focus your close reading on typographical errors.

EXERCISE 7.23

Find a proofreading pal. After you have double-checked your paper, exchange papers with that student and proofread each other's work. Find out what errors your classmate would like you to search for. Using your list from Exercise 7.18, tell your classmate what errors you are inclined to make.

REFLECT

- Identify successes
- Set goals

Each time you write, you build skills and strategies. The last step in the writing process is to reflect and recognize what you did well and what you learned.

Identify Successes

EXERCISE 7.24

Take a few minutes to reflect on your successes. Write one or two sentences that explain two things you have learned from this chapter and how you successfully applied them to your writing. Use a specific example from your work to support your thinking.

Set Goals

EXERCISE 7.25

Now that you have examined your successes, determine what challenges you face. Rate yourself using the following scale—5 indicates a task that you consider a challenge most of the time, and 1 indicates a task for which you have the required skills and strategies.

Stages	Strategies and Skills	5	4	3	2	1
Prewrite	1. I prewrite to explore my ideas and think deeper about a topic.	__	__	__	__	__
Draft	2. I focus my paragraphs with topic sentences.	__	__	__	__	__
	3. I organize my ideas and make connections.	__	__	__	__	__
Revise	4. I read critically to identify and use the successful techniques of other writers.	__	__	__	__	__
	5. I identify the strengths and weaknesses in my papers.	__	__	__	__	__
	6. I apply specific revision strategies to my papers.	__	__	__	__	__
Edit	7. I employ all or some of the following editing strategies:					
	▪ search for pronouns and antecedents, correcting agreement errors as needed	__	__	__	__	__
	▪ use spell-check on my computer	__	__	__	__	__
	▪ read a printed copy of my paragraph aloud to check for spelling errors and typographical errors	__	__	__	__	__

EXERCISE 7.26

Finish the following sentences in order to explore your learning experience and to set goals.

1. My attitude toward writing is

2. I still need to work on

Copyright © 2007, The McGraw-Hill Companies, Inc. All rights reserved.

STUDENT SAMPLE OF THE WRITING PROCESS

STUDENT MODEL

Roberto's Clustering

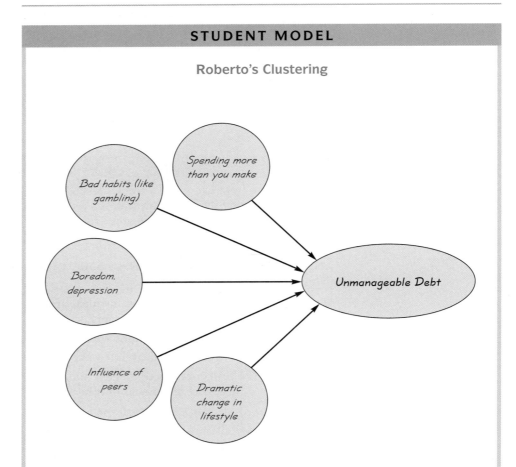

Roberto's Unedited Freewrite

If you have your lifestyle set with a certain job then being terminated, you can have yourself in debt. you would become in debt which would give you abad credit report. When you decide to g et back on your feet, you start to look for a new job. You might be denied the job due to your bad credit report due to being in debt. Most people have a bad habit of spending more money than what they often make. This leaves them in debt with things that are unnecessary to them. When people are bored they tend to want to spend money to pass the time. Once they relize how much they actually spent, they find themselves in trouble. This could lead a person into depression. people have a tendency to want to impress others by spending huge amonts of money. This bad influence could lead to a person becoming in debt. Impressing others to make yourself to like you are livng life to the fullest is not a good idea if you cant live to the fullest comfortably. Another reason why people may find themsefls in debt is them buying things just for pleasure. Not needing an item and still purchasing it just to say you have it leads people into bad jams. These are all causes and effects of what unmanageable debts one might experience.

Roberto's Unedited First Draft

Most people find themselves living with unmanageable debt. There are many causes and effects of unmanageable debt. For instance, you may find yourself in a situation where you have a set lifestyle where you are living comfortably. For some reason, you might be terminated. Which would leave you struggling and could lead you into debt. With you in debt, you receive a bad credit report. When you go and apply for another job, they might deny you due to your bad credit report. Another way you might find youself in debt is that if you spend more money than what you make. People have bad habits of spending money because they are bored or they try and impress others. They lke to present themselves as big spenders and to act as though they are living life to the fullest. This leads a person into debt. Them being in debt may cause them to fall into a state of depressioin. Finally, one other reason why people find themselves living with unmanageable debt is because they gamble. Gambling is a bad habit that leaves many people in extreme debt. Gamblers take money off of credit cards which tend to give credit card holders an extent of money. Not only do you suffer from gambling, but you are also in debt with the credit card companies. Although, you are allowed to pay off credit cards with minimum payments, you still owe money for years to come. These are a few causes and effects of unmanageable debt that you should try avoiding.

Peer Reader's Comments on Roberto's First Draft

topic sentence

There are many reasons for unmanageable debt.
~~Most people find themselves living with unmanageable debt. There are~~

eliminate "you" throughout

~~many causes and effects of unmanageable bedt.~~ For instance, ~~you~~ some people may find

Elaborate on "comfortably"

~~yourself~~ themselves in a situation where ~~you have a set lifestyle where you~~ they are living

comfortably. For some reason, ~~you~~ they might be terminated. Which would leave

consolidate debt?

you struggling and could lead you into debt. With you in debt, you receive a

bad credit report. When you go and apply for another job, they might deny

Examples here?

you due to your bad credit report. Another way you might find youself in

debt is that if you spend more money than what you make. People have _bad_

reason

habits of spending money because they are bored or they try _and impress_

continued

Copyright © 2007, The McGraw-Hill Companies, Inc. All rights reserved.

another reason?

others. They ~~like~~ to present themselves as big spenders and to act as though they are living life to the fullest. This leads a person into debt. Them being in debt may cause them to fall into a state of depressioin. Finally, ~~one other reason why people find themselves living with unmanageable debt is because they gamble.~~ Gambling is a bad habit that leaves many people in extreme debt. Gamblers ~~take~~ charge money ~~off of~~ on their credit cards ~~which tend to give credit card holders an extent of money.~~ Not only do you~~they~~ suffer from gambling, but you~~losses~~ are also in debt with the credit card companies. Although you ~~are allowed to~~ can pay off credit cards with minimum payments, you still owe money for years to come. Gambling is easily avoidable. Stay away from casinos. ~~These are a few causes and effects of unmanageable debt that you should try avoiding.~~ — People bring it on themselves

Roberto's Final Edited Paragraph

There are a variety of reasons for unmanageable debt, many of which are avoidable. For instance, some people find themselves in a situation where they are living comfortably. Rather than being careful with their money, they buy cars, go on vacations, and buy those "extras" they always wanted. Then if they get terminated for some reason, they find themselves in debt. Once they are in debt, they have a bad credit report. If they try to borrow money to consolidate debt, they might be denied because of their bad credit report. If they had been more careful, they might have avoided debt. Another way people get into debt is they spend more money than they make. They buy jewelry or stereos or fancy clothes. Then again, some people spend money when they are bored, or they try and impress others with jewelry or stereos and fancy clothes. This foolish attempt to present themselves as big spenders living life to the fullest can lead to debt. Once again, their debt could have been avoided. Debt causes some people to fall into a state of depression, which they try to get out of by spending even more money. It's a vicious circle. Finally, gambling is a bad habit that leaves many people in extreme debt. Gamblers charge money on their credit cards. Not only do they suffer from gambling losses, but they are also in debt with the credit card companies. Although they can pay off credit cards with minimum payments, some people owe money for years to come. Gambling debt is easily avoidable. Just stay home from the casinos. Sometime debt happens to people, but more often that not, they bring it on themselves.

Roberto's Reflection

Stages	Strategies and Skills	5	4	3	2	1
Prewrite	1. I prewrite to explore my ideas and think deeper about a topic.			X		
Draft	2. I focus my paragraphs with topic sentences.					X
	3. I organize my ideas and make connections.					X
Revise	4. I read critically to identify and use the successful techniques of other writers.				X	
	5. I identify the strengths and weaknesses in my papers.				X	
	6. I apply specific revision strategies to my papers.				X	
Edit	7. I employ all or some of the following editing strategies:					
	▪ search for pronouns and antecedents, correcting agreement errors as needed		X			
	▪ use spell-check on my computer					X
	▪ read a printed copy of my paragraph aloud to check for spelling errors and typographical errors					X

1. My attitude toward writing is *getting better. I actually liked writing this paragraph because the topic was important to me. I know people who gamble. It makes me mad. Writing this gave me a chance to get some of that off my chest.*

2. I still need to work on *pronouns. It took me forever to get my pronouns right in this paragraph. I sort of understand it. No I don't.*

GOING TO THE NEXT LEVEL: MULTIPLE-PARAGRAPH PAPERS

If you have more to say about your subject, or if your instructor would like you to take your writing to the next level, proceed to the following exercises. These exercises invite further exploration and provide suggestions for structuring a longer paper.

Dig Deeper

Use the thinking and writing strategies you have learned so far to explore your topic further. Choose from the following questions to discover more ideas and details relevant to your topic.

Illustration and Example	Narrative	Process
Are there specific examples of your subject?	Can you discuss an incident to make your point?	What people are involved in the process?
Are the examples similar or different?	Who was involved?	Where and when does it occur?
Do those examples lead to more examples? to more specific detail?	When and where did it occur?	Are materials, gear, props, or equipment involved?
	What were the important actions?	
	What was the outcome?	What is the most important detail?

Copyright © 2007, The McGraw-Hill Companies, Inc. All rights reserved.

Talk

> ### EXERCISE 7.27
>
> Sit down with a classmate and explain why you have decided to explore your topic further. Discuss what interests you about the topic and why you think it is important. As you talk, use the preceding questions as a guide to your thinking.

Cluster

> ### EXERCISE 7.28
>
> Choose those questions from the box on page 149 that you like best for clustering and explore your topic further.

Freewrite

> ### EXERCISE 7.29
>
> Write for ten minutes on your topic, using those questions from the box on page 149 that give you the most to say.

Brainstorm

> ### EXERCISE 7.30
>
> List all the new ideas and details you have generated in your prewriting activities. As you list them, think about how they relate to each other and whether time, importance, or place helps you see logical relationships.

Review Essay Structure

Drawing on the new ideas and details you gathered from digging deeper into your subject, write a draft of your essay. Follow the guidelines below for essay structure. Don't forget to include your cause-and-effect paragraph as you take your ideas to the next level.

> ### INTRODUCTION PARAGRAPH
>
> The Introduction arouses the reader's interest in your subject, establishes the importance of your subject, and provides the focus of your essay.
>
> A thesis statement captures the main idea or point of the entire essay.

> ### BODY PARAGRAPHS
>
> The cause-and-effect paragraph you wrote for this chapter might appear in this portion of your essay. Body paragraphs deliver the main content of your paper. The number of body paragraphs depends on how much you have to say and on the length requirements your instructor imposes. Your readers look for substance in body paragraphs. Don't forget topic sentences. Remember your supporting details.

CONCLUSION

Like the introduction, the conclusion paragraph focuses the reader's attention on the main point of the essay.

STUDENT MODEL

Student Sample—Single Paragraph

The main reason my sister and I quarrel is our upbringing. When we were children, our parents taught my sister and me to be independent thinkers. We learned at a young age how to solve our problems, on our own! While I strongly believe this is a skill every child needs, it can be detrimental if taken to the extreme. This is something I tend to do under certain circumstances, especially those circumstances that make me look "weak" in front of my sister. That's another reason we quarrel. I always felt I needed to be the "strong one," always ready to help my sister out of her next catastrophe. But what I didn't learn to do as a child was to let my sister be there for me as well. Unfortunately, the lesson we both learned as children has hindered our ability to support each other now, as adults. Those times when we could benefit from each other's support the most, we often turn away from each other, and the long silent treatment begins again.

Expanded Student Sample—Multiple Paragraphs

The writer begins with a question to draw the reader in.

How long can two people live in the same house without talking? If you were asking that of my sister and me, the answer would be for weeks! Once again, my sister and I are not on speaking terms. That sounds silly, but it really is an unfortunate and sad fact. Despite the love we have for each other, every now and then we find ourselves giving each other the silent treatment. This last round of silence was the result of a dumb argument we had last Thursday. We both were fooled and hurt by a mutual friend. Instead of going to each other for support, we took our anger that we felt for this friend out on each other. We both said things that would never have been said had we not been angry, just like when we were kids.

*The writer uses a short **narrative** to dramatize the topic.*

The main reason we quarrel like this is our upbringing. When we were children, our parents taught my sister and me to be independent thinkers. We learned at a young age how to solve our problems, on our own! While I strongly believe this is a skill every child needs, it can be detrimental if taken to the extreme. This is something I tend to do under certain circumstances, especially those circumstances that make me look "weak" in front of my sister. I always felt I needed to be the "strong one," always

*The writer uses her **cause-and-effect** paragraph.*

continued

Copyright © 2007, The McGraw-Hill Companies, Inc. All rights reserved.

*The writer describes a **process**—how the silent treatment works.*

ready to help my sister out of her next catastrophe. But what I didn't learn to do as a child was to let my sister be there for me as well. Unfortunately, the lesson we both learned as children has hindered our ability to support each other now, as adults. Those times when we could benefit from each other's support the most, we often turn away from each other, and the long silent treatment begins again.

When the silent treatment hits the Connolly sisters, it can be such an ugly and childish sight. First comes the trigger. It can be anything: a thoughtless word or a small, selfish act. Then comes the freeze. We meet each other in the house, we don't look at each other, we don't say anything. The most critical part of the silent treatment is walking out of a room the other person is in. That will fix her. How two grown women living in the same (too small) house cannot talk to each other for weeks at a time is one of the mysteries of my life. Daily I remind myself that we are close relatives, living in very close quarters, aware of personal and intimate secrets we each have. Then I ask myself, "How can two people who really love each other behave so immaturely?" In all these years, I have never come up with a good answer.

The writer uses a problem-solution approach in her conclusion.

My past has taught me many valuable lessons. One lesson I learned from my past is that it is never too late to learn new lessons. After our last argument, another argument that led my sister and me to give each other the silent treatment, I decided it was time for me to "grow up." No longer is it okay to treat my sister the way I did as a child. Instead of taking my anger and frustration for others out on her, I am going to learn how to ask for her support.

Sharpen Your Thesis

A good thesis statement makes all the difference in your essay. It provides the reader with a preview of what is to come in the essay. Following Exercise 7.31 is a final edited version of the preceding essay.

EXERCISE 7.31

Revise the following thesis statements so they include key terms the writer might explore in the body of her paper.

EXAMPLE:

My sister and I argue a lot.

Revised: *Because of <u>the way we were raised</u> and <u>simple habit</u>, we argue until <u>the silent treatment</u> begins.*

1. Good sleep is a necessity.

Copyright © 2007, The McGraw-Hill Companies, Inc. All rights reserved.

EXERCISE 7.31 continued

2. I like to exercise.

3. Family relationships matter a great deal.

4. Acquiring a new skill takes discipline.

5. Online shopping is convenient.

STUDENT MODEL

Expanded Student Sample: Final Edited Essay

How long can two people live in the same house without talking? If you were asking that of my sister and me, the answer would be for weeks! Once again, my sister and I are not on speaking terms. That sounds silly, but it really is an unfortunate and sad fact. Despite the love we have for each other, every now and then we find ourselves giving each other the silent treatment. This last round of silence was the result of a dumb argument we had last Thursday. We both were fooled and hurt by a mutual friend. Instead of going to each other for support, we took our anger that we felt for this friend out on each other. We both said things that would never have been said had we not been angry, just like when we were kids. Because of the way we were raised and simple habit, we argue until the silent treatment begins.

When the silent treatment hits the Connolly sisters, it can be such an ugly and childish sight. First comes the trigger. It can be anything: a thoughtless word or a small, selfish act. Then comes the freeze. We meet each other in the house, we don't look at each other, we don't say anything. The most critical part of the silent treatment is walking out of a room the other person is in. That will fix her. How two grown women living in the same (too small) house cannot talk to each other for weeks at a time is one of the mysteries of my life. Daily I remind myself that we are close relatives, living in very close quarters, aware of personal and intimate secrets we each have. Then I ask myself, "How can two people who really love each other behave so immaturely?" In all these years, I have finally come up with a good answer.

The main reason we quarrel like this is our upbringing. When we were children, our parents taught my sister and me to be independent thinkers. We learned at a young age how to solve our problems, on our own! While I strongly believe this is a skill every child needs, it can be detrimental if taken to the extreme. This is something I tend to do under certain circumstances, especially those circumstances that make me look "weak" in front of my sister. I always felt I needed to be the "strong one," always ready to help my sister out of her next catastrophe. But what I didn't learn to do as a child was to let my sister be there for me as well. Unfortunately, the lesson we both learned as children has hindered our ability to support each other now, as adults. Those times when we could benefit from each other's support the most, we often turn away from each other, and the long silent treatment begins again.

My past has taught me many valuable lessons. One lesson I learned from my past is that it is never too late to learn new lessons. After our last argument, another argument that led my sister and me to give each other the silent treatment, I decided it was time for me to "grow up." No longer is it okay to treat my sister the way I did as a child. Instead of taking my anger and frustration for others out on her, I am going to learn how to ask for her support.

8 *Comparison and Contrast*

*W*hich one is better? Which one is worse? You compare and contrast objects and ideas automatically every day. Exploring similarity and difference leads to thoughtful action. It also leads to thoughtful essays. Comparison involves looking at how two things are alike. Contrast involves looking at how two things are different. To a great extent, your judgments about ideas and concepts are determined by how you perceive similarity and difference:

- Where can I order the best pizza?
- What's the difference between buying products online and in person?
- Why is one therapeutic approach to an illness better than another?
- How is capitalism different from socialism?

You use comparison-and-contrast thinking to answer these questions. You analyze the items to identify the points that are the same and the points that are different.

IN THIS CHAPTER: A PREVIEW

Comparison-and-Contrast Thinking

- Elements of Comparison and Contrast
- Noticing Similarities and Differences
- Point-by-Point Analysis
- Elaborate on a Key Detail

A Process Approach to Writing the Comparision-and-Contrast Paragraph

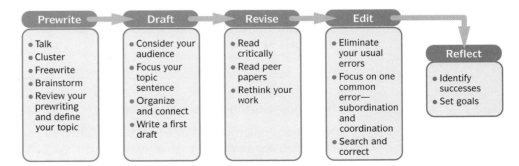

Prewrite	Draft	Revise	Edit		Reflect
• Talk • Cluster • Freewrite • Brainstorm • Review your prewriting and define your topic	• Consider your audience • Focus your topic sentence • Organize and connect • Write a first draft	• Read critically • Read peer papers • Rethink your work	• Eliminate your usual errors • Focus on one common error—subordination and coordination • Search and correct		• Identify successes • Set goals

Copyright © 2007, The McGraw-Hill Companies, Inc. All rights reserved.

Student Sample of the Writing Process

Going to the Next Level: Multiple-Paragraph Papers

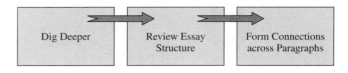

| Dig Deeper | Review Essay Structure | Form Connections across Paragraphs |

WW   Louis Gates Jr.

COMPARISON-AND-CONTRAST THINKING

Comparison-and-contrast analysis begins with a decision about two situations, ideas, or objects from the same category: You want a job, but you can't decide which job will provide the best opportunities. You believe solar energy is preferable to fossil fuels. To think critically about a preference, you examine the common and contrasting characteristics of each alternative. You make lists of points to consider. In addition, you balance the analysis, giving equal consideration to each alternative.

Elements of Comparison and Contrast

Similarity versus Difference	Specific Points	Key Detail
Are the two things mostly alike or mostly different?	In what respect are they alike or different?	Which point or detail is most meaningful? Why?

Similarity versus difference

Specific point 1

Specific point 2

Specific point 3

Key detail

READING: from "The Tapestry of Friendships," by Ellen Goodman

Well, she thought, on the whole, men had buddies, while women had friends. Buddies bonded, but friends loved. Buddies faced adversity together, but friends faced each other. There was something palpably different in the way they spent their time. Buddies seemed to "do" things together; friends simply "were" together. Buddies came linked, like accessories, to one activity or another. People had golf buddies and business buddies, college buddies and club buddies. Men often keep their buddies in these categories, while women keep a special category for friends.

DISCUSSION QUESTIONS

1. Count the number of sentences in this short paragraph. How many sentences discuss friends? How many discuss buddies?

2. What do you notice about sentence structure in this paragraph?

3. Goodman focuses on differences in her short paragraph. List two or three similarities and then formulate sentences, imitating Goodman's sentence structure.

Noticing Similarities and Differences

Noticing similarities and differences is essential to comparison-and-contrast thinking. Often a writer will focus on just similarities or just differences. Notice how Ellen Goodman's thinking is based on contrasting points of related ideas.

SUBJECT: FRIENDSHIP		
Buddies	**Friends**	**Similar or Different**
males have buddies	females have friends	different
bond with each other	love each other	different
face adversity together	face each other	different
"do" things together	"are" together	different
defined by activities they shared	defined as a special category	

Conclusion: Male buddies are "palpably different" from female friends because of the way they spend their time together.

EXERCISE 8.1

List similar and different characteristics and qualities in the following pairs. Then state your conclusion about how the two things are alike or different.

EXAMPLE:

Subject: diets

Healthy Diet	Fad Diet	Similar or Different
cut out junk foods and sweets	*cut out junk foods and sweets*	*similar*
make a permanent change in eating habits	*make a temporary change in eating habits*	*different*
get gradual results	*get fast results*	*different*
weight loss tends to be permanent	*weight loss tends to yo-yo back to prediet weight or higher*	*different*
doctor's permission recommended	*doctor's permission recommended*	*similar*

Conclusion: Healthy diets and fad diets both help a person get the weight off, but the healthy diet has longer-lasting results.

1. Subject: going to college

University	Community College	Similar or Different

Conclusion:

Copyright © 2007, The McGraw-Hill Companies, Inc. All rights reserved.

2. Subject: meeting new people

Blind Dates	Going to Clubs	Similar or Different

Conclusion:

3. Subject: purchasing a car

Compacts	Sport-Utility Vehicles	Similar or Different

Conclusion:

4. Subject: vacation spots

The Beach	Mountains	Similar or Different

Conclusion:

5. Subject: best place to raise children

City	Country	Similar or Different

Copyright © 2007, The McGraw-Hill Companies, Inc. All rights reserved.

EXERCISE 8.1 continued

Conclusion:

Point-by-Point Analysis

Often writers focus their comparison-and-contrast analysis on a few key points and then systematically analyze each item.

EXERCISE 8.2

Go deeper into your analysis of the subjects in Exercise 8.1. Identify key points of similarity or difference. Use these points to analyze the ideas and determine if they are the same or different. Write a sentence in which you state the point of your comparison and contrast.

EXAMPLE:

Subject: diets

Point	Healthy Diets	Fad Diets	Similar or Different
exercise	*essential component*	*recommended but not always essential*	*different*
promoted by	*doctors, hospitals, Weight Watchers and other organizations*	*celebrities, manufacturers, book companies*	*different*
equipment or materials	*calorie counters, fat-gram counters, scales, food-group counters*	*special foods, scales, calorie counters, fat-gram counters, food-group counters*	*similar*
professional aid	*classes, support groups, doctor's care, nutritionist appointments*	*books, tapes, designed programs to follow*	*similar and different*
effects	*improve health and appearance; results can be permanent or temporary*	*improve health and appearance; results can be permanent but are usually temporary*	*similar and different*

The point: *It seems like healthy diets are better, but both seem to be dependent on the willpower of the individual.*

EXERCISE 8.2 continued

1. Subject: going to college

Point	University	Community College	Similar or Different

The point:

2. Subject: meeting new people

Point	Blind Dates	Going to Clubs	Similar or Different

The point:

3. Subject: purchasing a car

Point	Compacts	Sport-Utility Vehicles	Similar or Different

The point:

4. Subject: vacation spots

Point	The Beach	Mountains	Similar or Different

Copyright © 2007, The McGraw-Hill Companies, Inc. All rights reserved.

EXERCISE 8.2 continued

The point:

5. Subject: best places to raise children

Point	City	Country	Similar or Different

The point:

Elaborate on a Key Detail

Not all details are equal. Key details are often a matter of personal preference. Therefore, it is essential to identify and elaborate on a key detail to create emphasis and to convey your personal viewpoint.

EXERCISE 8.3

Select the point of comparison or contrast that is most important to you. Elaborate on it with two sentences.

EXAMPLE:

Subject: friendship (from "The Tapestry of Friendships" by Ellen Goodman)

Key detail: *Buddies seemed to "do" things together; friends simply "were" together.*

Elaboration sentences:

A. *Buddies came linked, like accessories, to one activity or another.*

B. *People had golf buddies and business buddies, college buddies and club buddies.*

1. Subject: going to college

Key detail:

Elaboration sentences:

A.

B.

EXERCISE 8.3 continued

2. Subject: meeting new people

Key detail:

Elaboration sentences:

A.

B.

3. Subject: purchasing a car

Key detail:

Elaboration sentences:

A.

B.

4. Subject: vacation spots

Key detail:

Elaboration sentences:

A.

B.

5. Subject: best place to raise children

Key detail:

Elaboration sentences:

A.

B.

A PROCESS APPROACH TO WRITING THE COMPARISON-AND-CONTRAST PARAGRAPH

The comparison-and-contrast paragraph gives equal consideration to two ideas or objects. Most likely, it will begin with a statement of opinion, which establishes the two ideas or objects as similar or different. Then it systematically lists the points of comparison or contrast that explain the paragraph's conclusion. Following are some suggested topics for your comparison-and-contrast paragraph.

Specific Topics	General Topics
A past job and a current job	Personal Life
A current job and a future job	• relatives
Why it is better or worse to be the boss rather than the worker	• pastimes
	• places of solitude
Which job is better—a desk job or a manual labor job	• conflicts

A healthy habit and an unhealthy habit

An expensive hobby and an inexpensive hobby

Why hobbies fail or succeed

Living at home or getting an apartment

Driving an older car or driving a new car

Why a vacation is successful or miserable

Why are some parties, dates, or vacations more successful than others

School Life
- subject matters you like or dislike
- approaches to learning
- influences on you

Work Life
- coworkers
- shifts
- opportunities to learn

ELEMENTS OF COMPARISON AND CONTRAST

Similarity versus Difference	Specific Points	Key Detail
Are the two things mostly alike or mostly different?	In what respect are they alike or different?	Which point or detail is most meaningful? Why?

STUDENT MODEL

Student Sample

Similarities versus difference

Specific point 1

Specific point 2

Specific point 3

Key detail

At home or in a restaurant, I love eating. While they are both great, they definitely have their differences. First, eating out is much more relaxing. You go to the restaurant, get a seat, and order your food. In just a little while it's ready. At home, you have to thaw it out and spend an hour in front of the stove before you can eat. Restaurant food also tastes better. I'm not a bad cook, but I'm not a professional. Restaurants prepare meals all day. If you don't like the way it is cooked, you can send it back. Try doing that at home. If restaurants are so great, then why does anyone cook? They cook to save money. Restaurants are just too expensive. If I want a steak and baked potato for dinner, I can make it at home for less than ten bucks. It's hard to find a sandwich and fries at a nice restaurant for that price. Drinks are included in a meal at home too. If I were rich, I'd eat out daily. Since I'm not, I'll eat at home.

PREWRITE
- Talk
- Cluster
- Freewrite
- Brainstorm
- Review your prewriting and define your topic

Select one or more of the following prewriting strategies to explore a topic and develop ideas for a comparison-and-contrast paragraph.

Copyright © 2007, The McGraw-Hill Companies, Inc. All rights reserved.

Talk

EXERCISE 8.4

Talk to one or two other students who chose the same topic you did. Discuss the similarities and differences that are important to you. Once each person has shared his or her ideas on the topic, write down what you learned. Use the following questions to guide additional writing:

- On what points did you agree with your peers?
- On what points did you disagree?
- Which of your ideas did your peers find important?
- Which of their ideas did you find important?

Cluster

EXERCISE 8.5

Use the following clustering diagram to explore two ideas or objects (for example, "healthy habits" and "unhealthy habits"). Work back and forth from side to side to develop your thoughts and discover new details.

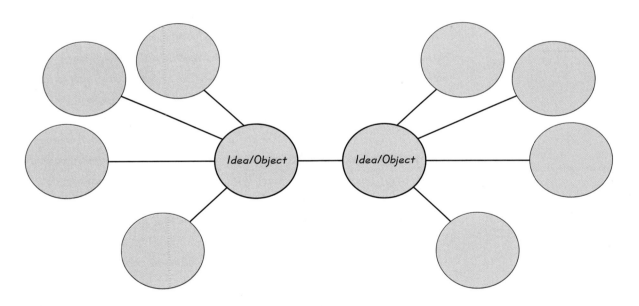

Freewrite

EXERCISE 8.6

Freewrite to explore the similarities and differences in your topic. Then review your freewriting and underline a key word or phrase for each point of comparison or contrast. Compose a sentence or two stating the conclusions you draw from your writing. As you write, consider these questions:

- What similarities or differences stand out? Why are they important to you?
- When did you become aware of these similarities or differences?
- Do you associate these similarities or differences with people or places?

Brainstorm

EXERCISE 8.7

Using Exercise 8.2 as your model, analyze the topic that interests you. List the similarities and differences. Try to find five to seven similarities and differences for each idea or object. Write a sentence that sums up your thinking.

Review Your Prewriting and Define Your Topic

EXERCISE 8.8

Use the following questions to review your prewriting and define your topic for a comparison-and-contrast paragraph.

- Which topic is most interesting and generated the most detail?
- Which topic had a significant impact on you or other people?
- Which one helped you discover something new or interesting about yourself or the subject you selected?

DRAFT

- Consider your audience
- Focus your topic sentence
- Organize and connect
- Write a first draft

Write a draft that organizes your prewriting into a single paragraph. This first draft will establish the subject and state the point of your comparison-and-contrast paragraph.

Consider Your Audience

EXERCISE 8.9

Reread your prewriting to examine all your ideas about your topic. To size up your audience's knowledge of your subject, consider the following dimensions of your topic.

- Why is this topic important to your audience?
- What special meaning does this topic have for you? Why do you want your audience to understand this meaning?
- Will your audience agree or disagree with your thinking? Will you be asking them to think about your subject in a new way?
- Return to the exercises on comparison-and-contrast thinking in this chapter and decide which way of thinking about your topic will help you connect best with your audience.

Copyright © 2007, The McGraw-Hill Companies, Inc. All rights reserved.

Focus Your Topic Sentence

EXERCISE 8.10

Read the following topic sentences and select the one that is focused for a comparison-and-contrast paragraph.

EXAMPLE:

_____ Basketball is a better game than football.

_____ The biggest difference between basketball and football is the ball itself.

__X__ Both basketball and football are very physical games.

1. _____ Community colleges cost less than universities.

_____ Community colleges offer more to the undecided student than universities do.

_____ Last year my cousin went to Indiana University.

2. _____ A noisy public setting can have advantages over a quieter setting for meeting new people.

_____ Meeting new people just isn't that hard.

_____ I had a terrible blind date one time.

3. _____ A car accident can cost thousands of dollars.

_____ The best cars on the road are Fords.

_____ Whether you buy a small car or a large car, there are additional expenses you can't escape.

4. _____ Sunburns can be a problem at both the seashore and the mountains.

_____ I just love to ski!

_____ Whether going to the seashore or the mountains, a person on vacation will find plenty to do.

5. _____ Unlike country kids, city kids are real brats.

_____ Kids in the city are likely to have more recreational opportunities than kids in the country.

_____ I grew up in the city, and I think I turned out just fine.

EXERCISE 8.11

Underline key terms in the following topic sentences. Then indicate whether the writer intends to focus on similarities or differences.

EXAMPLE:

$$1 \qquad\qquad + \qquad\qquad 1$$

<u>Stream fishing and lake fishing</u> involve very different <u>forms of equipment</u>.

    compare: focus on similarities   ~~contrast: focus on difference~~

1. Getting the news from the Internet is not as convenient as getting it from a good newspaper.

    compare: focus on similarities   contrast: focus on difference

2. In order to anticipate effectively, football players on defense have to know many of the same things their opponents on offense know.

    compare: focus on similarities   contrast: focus on difference

Copyright © 2007, The McGraw-Hill Companies, Inc. All rights reserved.

EXERCISE 8.11 continued

3. Similar economic conditions were present prior to the stock market crashes of 1929 and 1999.

   compare: focus on similarities   contrast: focus on difference

4. Digital and conventional cameras have different advantages.

   compare: focus on similarities   contrast: focus on difference

5. Being a parent to a young child and an older child calls for two completely different attitudes.

   compare: focus on similarities   contrast: focus on difference

Organize and Connect

Point of view is a powerful organizing principle in your writing. When you talk about yourself and your own experience, you focus on **I**, which is first person. When you talk about a subject as others experience or understand it, you focus on **he/she/they/it**, which is third person. In informal writing or conversation (for example, when giving directions), you use the second person, **you**. In most academic writing, however, the second-person "you" is avoided. Making conscious decisions to shift from one point of view to the other, or to concentrate exclusively on one, will enhance the structure of your writing.

STUDENT MODEL

Student Sample

Third person
First person

Third person
First person

Third person

First person

Baseball isn't as simple as it seems. A baseball player must be alert and knowledgeable about things like the infield fly rule, which is something I still don't understand. During my baseball years, I would just nod my head and pretend I knew what was going on. Baseball players must also be quick-witted. I wasn't the most attentive kid on the field. All it took was the nearby concession stand to divert my focus. Physically, baseball players must be strong, fast, and coordinated. Unfortunately, my talent for baseball was as good as my attitude for it. In T-ball, I even had difficulty hitting the ball off the tee. When I made the transfer to baseball, it didn't get any easier. Most of the time I would stand there, hoping for a walk or to be hit by the pitch. The coach, who happened to be my father, once made the mistake of having me pitch for one inning. The opposing team scored six runs, all thanks to me.

In the following revision, the writer of the preceding paragraph uses point of view to organize the details. He uses third person at the beginning of the paragraph to provide a general overview of the skills a baseball player needs. Then he shifts to first person to describe his own experience, providing a sharp contrast in the process.

STUDENT MODEL

Student Sample Revised

Third person

Baseball isn't as simple as it seems. A baseball player must be alert and knowledgeable about things like the infield fly rule. In addition, he must be quick-witted. Finally, baseball players must be strong, fast, and coordinated.

continued

First person

> During my baseball years, I was anything but alert. I would just nod my head and pretend I knew what was going on. I wasn't the most attentive kid on the field. All it took was the nearby concession stand to divert my focus. In T-ball, I even had difficulty hitting the ball off the tee. I never made it to strong, fast, and coordinated. When I made the transfer to baseball, it didn't get any easier. Most of the time I would stand there, hoping for a walk or to be hit by the pitch. The coach, who happened to be my father, once made the mistake of having me pitch for one inning. The opposing team scored six runs, all thanks to me. I did not have the essentials of a baseball player.

EXERCISE 8.12

Read the following paragraph and find the shifts in point of view. Indicate those shifts in the margin, marking first person, second person, and third person where the shifts occur. Then rewrite the paragraph. Use third-person and first-person points of view to organize the details.

Singing is a lot harder than it looks. There isn't that much to it, but everything has to be done precisely. You have to be able to breathe well and have strong lungs. This shouldn't really be a problem for me since I've been playing hockey all my life, and my lungs should have pretty good endurance. Secondly you must have finely tuned vocal cords. You would think that you would have this covered. After all you have been using your voice all your life, and you must have mastered it by now. Puberty gave you some trouble, but you're back on your feet and in control of your voice again. Wrong. You have to know how to hit the high notes and make your low notes sound good. The notes a person sings have to be the right pitch, tone, and loudness, and you have to coordinate it perfectly to the music. Then you have to have rhythm. That is really no problem for me. I can dance. I even played percussion in the school band for a while. If you have some of these things, it is really not enough. You have to have all of them.

EXERCISE 8.13

Following are some transition words and phrases commonly used in comparison-and-contrast writing. Read the paragraph below and underline the topic sentence. Then circle transition words and phrases that reflect comparison and contrast.

Compare	Contrast
and	but
also	yet
likewise	while, whereas
in addition	on the other hand
moreover	conversely
similarly	in contrast

EXERCISE 8.13 continued

The experience of kids who are active in sports is similar to the experience of those who participate in the music program. Both programs invite students to join an enjoyable extracurricular activity. In addition, both programs offer primarily positive, supervised activities, helping students avoid immoral or illegal activities. Moreover, both teach children who may or may not be successful academically that they can achieve success in a more personal yet public way through their talents. Then again, both offer rewards in the form of trophies, medals, positions in the band or on the team, and scholarships for demonstrating exceptional talent and accomplishments. The ironic thing is that although they have all of these similarities, they are seen as opposites in the social structure of the school. The jocks do not see that they have anything in common with band or choir geeks. Similarly, the kids in the music program feel exactly the same way.

Write a First Draft

EXERCISE 8.14

Use the following checklist as a guide to draft your comparison-and-contrast paragraph.

_____ Review your prewriting to clarify your purpose and what you want your audience to understand.

_____ Insert details to explain your points of comparison and contrast.

_____ Use the 1+1 approach in your topic sentence.

_____ Insert transitions to connect ideas and details.

REVISE

- Read critically
- Read peer papers
- Rethink your work

Begin revising by asking yourself these questions: Will an audience understand my purpose? Is there sufficient detail? Are my ideas connected and is my purpose clearly defined?

Read Critically

EXERCISE 8.15

Examine the following paragraph. Underline the topic sentence and circle transition words or phrases. Look for strengths and weaknesses.

Given the choice, I would go to a swimming pool rather than a beach any day. For one thing, the accommodations are almost always more comfortable at a pool. There is a cement deck, easy to walk on; comfortable chairs, pleasant to sit on; and nearby, a snack bar, convenient for access to drinks and accessories such as tanning lotion or batteries. Then there is the pool itself. At a well-run facility, the water is usually very clean. There are no leaves floating on the surface and no bacteria waiting to infect the swimmer. And pools almost always have diving boards, which provide the swimmer with a chance for extra fun. A beach, on the other hand, is more likely to have too much nature. Sand is nice. Waves are nice. Walking on the beach can be a thrill. But for just lying on a towel, trying to get a tan, sand is the pits. It gets all over everything. It sticks to lotion, gets in sunglasses and wallets, and somehow finds its way into soft drinks and food. As for the water, there's a little too

Copyright © 2007, The McGraw-Hill Companies, Inc. All rights reserved.

EXERCISE 8.15 continued

much nature in there too. Green leaves are nice in salad; weeds and beach grass make an attractive skirt. These things also tickle the bathers' feet and get lodged between their toes, never a pleasant sensation. And muck? Sandy bottoms are okay; mucky bottoms are simply awful. Finally, there's the water itself. It's full of living things. Fish live in it. Turtles and birds go to the lake for lunch. Some people prefer to appreciate nature from afar. They swim in swimming pools.

Focus

1. Is the paragraph's subject clear? Will a reader understand why this topic is important?

Detail

2. Does the writer clearly identify points of comparison and contrast?

3. Is there a key detail?

Connections

4. Does the writer present details in an order that is effective? Does anything seem out of order or irrelevant?

5. Is the order made clear by connecting words?

Taking a Critical View

6. What are the strengths and weaknesses of the paragraph?

Strengths	Weaknesses

7. What will improve this paper?

Read Peer Papers

EXERCISE 8.16

Form a group of three or four students and take turns reading and discussing your paragraphs. Use the questions from Exercise 8.15 to identify each paragraph's strengths and weaknesses. Offer suggestions for a revision plan.

Rethink Your Work

Clearly stating the main idea is only the first step in a comparison-and-contrast paragraph. Writers need to elaborate on similarities and differences.

Destinations: Choosing Routes with Comparison/Contrast

Making Daily Decisions

Think about the last time you made a major purchase—say you were looking for a car. In order decide which one to buy, you almost certainly compared different models according to the criteria (categories) that were important to you—for example, price; fuel economy; repair history; looks—and you did this more or less "automatically," without thinking explicitly about choosing the criteria. So why do you have to learn about "comparison and contrast" in textbooks? It's important to become fully conscious of what you're doing when you compare and contrast things, in order to apply these same skills to more complicated situations. Let's say, for example, that you are trying to persuade someone to vote for a particular political candidate. In order to do this effectively, you have to be aware of the criteria that matter to that other person and present your candidate accordingly. Comparing and contrasting the candidate according to the criteria that seem obvious to *you* might not do the job.

On the Other Hand . . .

Comparing and contrasting for a particular purpose is an important aspect of critical thinking and, therefore, of writing. You may be drafting a proposal for a solution to a social problem like homelessness and presenting two alternatives (one of which you favor), or you might be presenting two methods of performing an experiment, and explaining why you chose one or the other. In order to make the best case for your position, you'll need to know what the most relevant criteria for your purposes are and what criteria will matter the most to your audience.

Which One Would You Choose?

If you are involved in purchasing anything for your business—from office supplies to next season's clothing—you will be required to choose from among a number of options, and you will have to base your decision on comparing/contrasting available options. Skill in comparison/contrast is not just about buying things, of course. A mechanic would have to compare different repair jobs in order to prioritize them, while a dental assistant would have to compare a patient's X-rays between visits and determine what differences (if any) would require treatment. The more practice you have in comparing and contrasting effectively, the better you will be at your job.

EXERCISE 8.17

Read the following paragraph to identify each point of comparison or contrast. Discuss with a classmate the effectiveness of the points, but also consider whether the points have sufficient elaboration. Could the writer have said more?

My sisters-in-law are very different. Stephanie is very up front and honest with me and gives me her honest opinion on different things. On the other hand, Hope will just tell you what you want to hear just to be nice. Stephanie is very secure about herself, and Hope is always worried about what people think. It can get very annoying because Hope is always overthinking everything she says to people. One thing is for certain, Stephanie is very moody, and you never know if she's in the mood to talk. Hope is always willing to talk to you or set some time aside to listen if you need to talk. Overall though, they are both pretty good friends and family, and I really care about the both of them.

EXERCISE 8.18

Review your paragraph. Divide a sheet of paper into halves by drawing a vertical line down the center. On one half, list your points of comparison; on the other, your points of contrast. Then examine the details you use to elaborate each point. Could you have said more? Revise your paragraph by elaborating on underdeveloped points.

Copyright © 2007, The McGraw-Hill Companies, Inc. All rights reserved.

EDIT

- Eliminate your usual errors
- Focus on one common error—subordination and coordination
- Search and correct

> Prepare to turn your paragraph in for a grade.
> Make sure you are not repeating errors you usually make.
> Then look for new errors that may distract your reader from
> the purpose and meaning of your writing.

Eliminate Your Usual Errors

EXERCISE 8.19

Turn to the grids in Chapters 18, 19, and 20 where you have been keeping track of the errors you make. List those errors in the space provided below. Then proofread your paper and correct the errors you find.

_____ _____ _____

_____ _____ _____

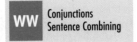
Conjunctions
Sentence Combining

Focus on One Common Error—Subordination and Coordination

College writers often use insufficient connecting words to enhance the structure of their writing. In comparison-and-contrast writing, these connections are essential. They establish a logical relationship between ideas and details. Use coordinate conjunctions, subordinate conjunctions, and conjunctive adverbs with appropriate punctuation.

Coordinate Conjunctions

Use a comma before a coordinate conjunction that begins an independent clause.

> Salesmen travel a lot. They need to wear comfortable clothes.
> Salesmen travel a lot, **so** they need to wear comfortable clothes.

> One of the cars was a piece of junk. The other cost more than it was worth.
> One of the cars was a piece of junk, **and** the other cost more than it was worth.

Subordinate Conjunctions

When a subordinate conjunction begins a sentence, use a comma at the end of the dependent clause:

> **Because** salesmen travel a lot, they need to wear comfortable clothes.

> **Whereas** one of the cars was a piece of junk, the other cost more than it was worth.

When a subordinate conjunction falls in the middle of a sentence, the dependent clause it begins is preceded by a comma:

> One of the cards was a piece of junk, **whereas** the other cost more than it was worth.

Note: Do not use a comma when a subordinate conjunction introduces essential information in the sentence.

> Salesmen need to wear comfortable clothes **because** they travel a lot.

Conjunctive Adverbs

Use a semicolon before a conjunctive adverb and a comma after it.

> Salesmen travel a lot; **consequently,** they need to wear comfortable clothes.
>
> One of the cars was a piece of junk; **furthermore,** the other cost more than it was worth.

EXERCISE 8.20

Following is a list of coordinate and subordinate conjunctions and conjunctive adverbs. Combine the sentences below using these terms. If possible, use more than one approach to connecting the sentences. Use appropriate punctuation.

Coordinate Conjunctions	Subordinate Conjunctions	Conjunctive Adverbs
and, or, nor, for, but, yet, so	after, although, as, because, if, not only, since, when, whenever, whereas, while	consequently, furthermore, indeed, in fact, moreover, nevertheless, for example, however

EXAMPLE:

> My sister is shy. She likes going to parties.
> *Although my sister is shy, she likes going to parties.*

1. You could be a very smart person. You might not know how to run your own business.

2. Violence can be seen as a cry for help. It can also be a call for attention.

3. I learned a lot from my first work experience. I learned how to operate a huge computer.

4. My date was a really good dancer. I was embarrassed and told him I'd rather not dance.

5. It's important to be yourself. You also have to give some consideration to what other people think.

6. I tried listening to classical music. I found it slow and boring.

7. Not many people I knew enjoyed classical music. It wasn't something I had to adjust to.

8. This individual did pretty well in life. When he was younger, nobody thought he would be worth much.

9. He was known as kind of a wise guy. He barely passed high school.

10. Most women aren't looking for a superman. They would just like to find someone who will pitch in a little.

Copyright © 2007, The McGraw-Hill Companies, Inc. All rights reserved.

Search and Correct

EXERCISE 8.21

Double-check your grammar. Search for the connecting words listed in Exercise 8.20 and proofread your paper for errors with subordination and coordination. Correct punctuation as needed.

EXERCISE 8.22

Double-check your spelling. Computer spell-checks make mistakes. Therefore, it is essential that you proofread your paper before turning it in for a grade. Focus your close reading on typographical errors.

EXERCISE 8.23

Find a Proofreading Pal. After you have double-checked your paper, exchange papers with that student and proofread each other's work. Find out what errors your classmate would like you to search for. Using your list from Exercise 8.19, tell your classmate what errors you are inclined to make.

REFLECT
- Identify successes
- Set goals

Each time you write, you build skills and strategies. The last step in the writing process is to reflect and recognize what you did well and what you learned.

Identify Successes

EXERCISE 8.24

Take a few minutes to reflect on your successes. Write one or two sentences that explain two things you have learned from this chapter and how you successfully applied them to your writing. Use a specific example from your work to support your thinking.

Set Goals

EXERCISE 8.25

Now that you have examined your successes, determine what challenges you face. Rate yourself using the following scale—5 indicates a task that you consider a challenge most of the time, and 1 indicates a task for which you have the required skills and strategies.

Stages	Strategies and Skills	5	4	3	2	1
Prewrite	1. I prewrite to explore my ideas and think deeper about a topic.	—	—	—	—	—
Draft	2. I focus my paragraphs with topic sentences.	—	—	—	—	—
	3. I organize my ideas and make connections.	—	—	—	—	—
Revise	4. I read critically to identify and use the successful techniques of other writers.	—	—	—	—	—
	5. I identify the strengths and weaknesses in my papers.	—	—	—	—	—
	6. I apply specific revision strategies to my papers.	—	—	—	—	—

EXERCISE 8.25 continued

Edit   7. I employ all or some of the following editing
strategies:

- search for errors of subordination and
  coordination

  — — — — —

- use spell-check on my computer

  — — — — —

- read a printed copy of my paragraph aloud to
  check for spelling errors and typographical
  errors

  — — — — —

EXERCISE 8.26

Finish the following sentences in order to explore your learning experience and to
set goals.

1. My attitude toward writing is

2. I still need to work on

STUDENT SAMPLE OF THE WRITING PROCESS

STUDENT MODEL

Barbara's Cluster

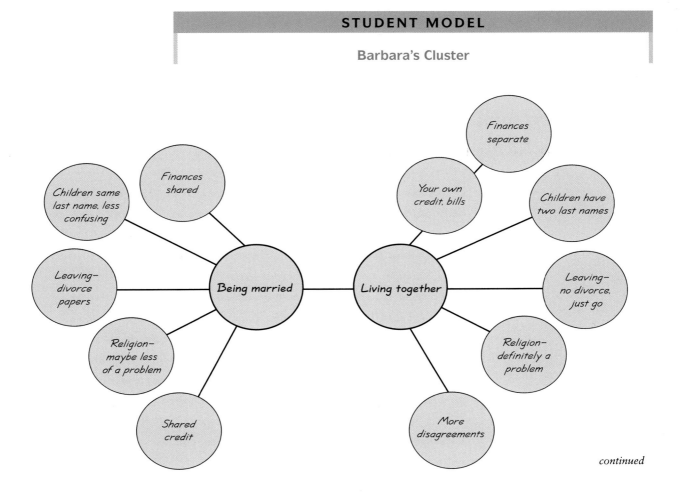

continued

Copyright © 2007, The McGraw-Hill Companies, Inc. All rights reserved.

Barbara's Freewrite

Financial responsibilities is one the biggest differences between a couple living together without being married, and a couple being married and living together. When a couple lives together they have their financial responsibilities and their own money. As where, a married couple has shared responsibilities and a shared account with money. And what if there's children that may be involved. If there are children in marriage they may have the same last name as the parents. If there are children between a couple living together not married, the parents have two different last names, and the children have one or another. It can be confusing to a young child. Religious matters. This subject plays a major role in a couple living together without being married. A married couple living together is accepted in most religions, as where, not being married and living together is not accepted. Married couples usually share a religious belief. A couple living together may have each other's own religious beliefs. Legal matters come into this discussion. A single person has his or her own credit rating, credit cards, loans and etcetera. A married couple usually shares credit cards, loans, and their credit ratings are right around where the other's is. Which plays a role in marriage.

Barbara's Unedited First Draft

There are many differences between being married and living together. Financial responsibilities is one big difference. When a couple lives together they have their own financial responsibilities and their own money. On the other hand, a married couple has shared responsibilities and a shared account with money. Another difference is children. When two people are married, their children have the same last name as the parents. If a couple is just living together, the parents have two different last names, and the children have one or another, if not both. It can be confusing to a young child. Religion is another important matter. A couple living together may have the same religious beliefs. Married couples usually have the same religious belief. Legal matters also come into this discussion. A single person has his or her own credit rating, credit cards, and loans. A married couple usually shares credit cards and loans, and their credit ratings are right around where the other's is. Which plays a role in marriage. Finally, splitting up when married is a complicated process. A divorce has to take place, papers have to be filed and agreements be made. Splitting up while living together is much easier. No divorce, no papers, and very little agreement, if any is required.

Peer Reader's Comments on Barbara's First Draft

It's easier to walk away from a relationship if two people live together instead of getting married

topic sentence — ~~There are many differences between being married and living together.~~ Financial responsibilities is one big difference. ~~When~~ A a couple lives ing together ~~they~~ have ~~their~~ own financial responsibilities and their own money. ~~On the other hand,~~ a married couple has shared responsibilities and a shared

Elaborate. Say more about money matters. — account with money. Another difference ,is children. When two people are between living together & being married married, their children have the same last name as the parents. If a couple is just living together, the parents have two different last names, and the children have one or another, if not both. It can be confusing to a young

This detail doesn't relate to ending a relationship — child. Religion is another important matter. A couple living together may have the same religious beliefs. Married couples usually have the same

Ok—but how does religion relate to ending a relationship? — religious belief. Legal matters also come into this discussion. A single person has his or her own credit rating, credit cards, and loans. A married couple

Organization: I think you covered this already. — usually shares credit cards and loans, and their credit ratings are right around where the other's is. Which plays a role in marriage. Finally, ~~splitting~~ ending a marriage ~~up when married~~ is a complicated process. A divorce has to take place, papers have to be filed ~~and agreements be made.~~ Splitting up while living together is much easier. No divorce, no papers, ~~and very little agreement, if any is required.~~

Barbara's Final Edited Paragraph

It's easier to walk away from a relationship if two people live together instead of getting married. Financial responsibilities are one big difference. A couple living together have their own financial responsibilities and their own money; a married couple have shared responsibilities and a shared account with money. A single person has his or her own credit rating, credit cards, and loans, whereas a married couple usually share credit cards and loans, and their credit ratings go together. Money matters play a significant role in relationships and may keep people together. Another difference between living together and being married is children. People who live together are less likely to have children. For that reason, they will find it easy to leave a relationship. In contrast, married people with children often stay together "for the kids' sake." Religion is another important matter. A couple will probably be condemned by their relatives for living together; married couples, in contrast, are more likely to have religion on their side.

continued

Copyright © 2007, The McGraw-Hill Companies, Inc. All rights reserved.

They usually have the same religious belief. If not, at least no one can say they are "living in sin." The influence of religion can do a lot to keep people together. Finally, legal matters also come into this discussion. Ending a marriage is a complicated process. Papers have to be filed; a divorce has to take place. Splitting up while living together is much easier: no papers, no divorce. Say what you will, there are more things than love keeping married people together. If you think staying together is good, you should get married.

Barbara's Reflection

Stages	Strategies and Skills	5	4	3	2	1
Prewrite	1. I prewrite to explore my ideas and think deeper about a topic.			X		
Draft	2. I focus my paragraphs with topic sentences.					X
	3. I organize my ideas and make connections.					X
Revise	4. I read critically to identify and use the successful techniques of other writers.				X	
	5. I identify the strengths and weaknesses in my papers.				X	
	6. I apply specific revision strategies to my papers.				X	
Edit	7. I employ all or some of the following editing strategies:					
	▪ search for errors of subordination and coordination					X
	▪ use spell-check on my computer					X
	▪ read a printed copy of my paragraph aloud to check for spelling errors and typographical errors					X

1. My attitude toward writing is *right now I'm high. I really liked the compare/contrast thing and especially using the semicolon to say opposite things. This topic was good, too. I just wanted to write about it because some of my girls shack up and have had a really bad time with money stuff especially.*

2. I still need to work on *saying less. I get going on a subject, I say something, then I say it again. I'm always worried about my writing being long enough so I go on and on and on. Bad.*

GOING TO THE NEXT LEVEL: MULTIPLE-PARAGRAPH PAPERS

If you have more to say about your subject, or if your instructor would like you to take your writing to the next level, proceed to the following exercises. These exercises invite further exploration and provide suggestions for structuring a longer paper.

Dig Deeper

Use the thinking and writing strategies you have learned so far to explore your topic further. Choose from the following questions to discover more ideas and details relevant to your topic.

Illustration and Example	Narrative
Are there specific examples of your subject?	Can you discuss an incident to make your point?
Are the examples similar or different?	Who was involved?
Do those examples lead to more examples? to more specific detail?	When and where did it occur?
	What were the important actions?
	What was the outcome?

Process	Cause and Effect
What people are involved in the process?	Does this thing have one or more causes?
Where and when does it occur?	Does it have one or more effects or consequences?
Are materials, gear, props, or equipment involved?	Does it help to think in terms of reasons for this thing?
What is the most important detail?	

Talk

EXERCISE 8.27

Sit down with a classmate and explain why you have decided to explore your topic further. Discuss what interests you about the topic and why you think it is important. As you talk, use the preceding questions as a guide to your thinking.

Cluster

EXERCISE 8.28

Choose those questions from the box on page 179 that you like best for clustering and explore your topic further.

Freewrite

EXERCISE 8.29

Write for ten minutes on your topic, using those questions from the box on page 179 that give you the most to say.

Brainstorm

EXERCISE 8.30

List all the new ideas and details you have generated in your prewriting activities. As you list them, think about how they relate to each other and whether time, importance, or place helps you see logical relationships.

Copyright © 2007, The McGraw-Hill Companies, Inc. All rights reserved.

Review Essay Structure

Drawing on the new ideas and details you gathered from digging deeper into your subject, write a draft of your essay. Follow the guidelines below for essay structure. Don't forget to include your comparison-and-contrast paragraph as you take your ideas to the next level.

INTRODUCTION PARAGRAPH

The introduction arouses the reader's interest in your subject, establishes the importance of your subject, and provides the focus of your essay.

The thesis statement captures the main idea or point of the entire essay.

BODY PARAGRAPHS

The comparison-and-contrast paragraph you wrote for this chapter might appear in this portion of your essay. Body paragraphs deliver the main content of your paper. The number of body paragraphs depends on how much you have to say and on the length requirements your instructor imposes. Your readers look for substance in body paragraphs. Don't forget topic sentences. Remember your supporting details.

CONCLUSION

Like the introduction, the conclusion paragraph focuses the reader's attention on the main point of the essay.

STUDENT MODEL

Student Sample—Single Paragraph

Professional baseball is corrupt. There was a time when professional athletes were honorable people. In the 1960s, Al Kaline was asked if he wanted to be the first baseball player to make $100,000 a year. He turned it down, saying it's ridiculous for a baseball player to make that much money. Now MLB athletes make $2 million per year and want to go on strike. I say let them have their strike. Let them have it forever. I'm not too thrilled that our "national pastime" is nothing but a league of whiny millionaires.

Expanded Student Sample—Multiple Paragraphs

*The writer begins with a **description** of a specific memory, making the point that he's bad at sports*

Everyone else must have been horrible, or I did pretty well for myself. Either way, I was the winner of my high school's 2002 chess tournament. The previous year I made it to the semifinals, but this year I was the best. For the first time in my life, I was a winner. Not third place, not runner up, not "thanks for playing," but grand champion of the school. I have a certificate that says so. Perhaps I have a skill when it comes to meaningless games such as chess, checkers, and video games. But when it comes to real sports, I'm a natural born loser.

Copyright © 2007, The McGraw-Hill Companies, Inc. All rights reserved.

*The writer lists **examples** of sports he can't play*

Narrative—the writer describes his first encounter with baseball

Comparison and contrast— the writer names skills needed for baseball and compares his performance with what it should be

Cause and effect—the writer looks at reasons why he chooses not to worry about baseball

I was usually picked last when we played football in gym. I was in a floor hockey league and scored one goal all season. Several years ago, I was defeated by my grandmother in a game of table tennis. I don't like sports, and evidently they don't like me. If I could name one sport among the many I can't play, I'd name baseball.

It began in the classic summer of 1988. I was four years old. I enjoyed the simple pleasures in life, such as Nintendo, action figures, cartoons, and more Nintendo. That's why it came as an unpleasant shock when my parents signed me up for T-ball. It sounded simple enough as they explained that baseball was as simple as running to first, second, third, and home. I later realized that home was not where you got to sit on the couch and watch TV. It was a white plate, and all it meant was that you had to keep playing this dumb game for two or three more hours.

Baseball isn't as simple as it seems. A baseball player must be alert and knowledgeable about things like the infield fly rule, which is something I still don't understand. During my baseball years, I would just nod my head and pretend I knew what was going on. Baseball players must also be quick-witted. I wasn't the most attentive kid on the field. All it took was the nearby concession stand to divert my focus. Physically, baseball players must be strong, fast, and coordinated. Unfortunately, my talent for baseball was as good as my attitude for it. In T-ball, I even had difficulty hitting the ball off the tee. When I made the transfer to baseball, it didn't get any easier. Most of the time I would stand there, hoping for a walk or to be hit by a pitch. The coach, who happened to be my father, once made the mistake of having me pitch for one inning. The opposing team scored six runs, all thanks to me.

Perhaps I could improve my skill as a baseball player, but I don't want to. For one thing, it's a boring and pointless game. I have far better things to do with my time, such as collecting unusually shaped pieces of cheese. Second, baseball is corrupt. There was a time when professional athletes were honorable people. In the 1960s, Al Kaline was asked if he wanted to be the first baseball player to make $100,000 a year. He turned it down, saying it's ridiculous for a baseball player to make that much money. Now MLB athletes make $2 million per year and want to go on strike. I say let them have their strike. Let them have it forever. I'm not too thrilled that our "national pastime" is nothing but a league of whiny millionaires.

So I'm not a baseball fan, whether it's recreational or professional. Sports are not my thing and never have been. I'll stick to video games instead, where there's no risk of getting hit in the nose, stomach—or worse—by a line drive.

Form Connections across Paragraphs

Your essay is easier to read if you make connections across paragraphs. These connections begin with your introduction, where your thesis should have a key term you repeat or "echo" in body paragraphs. Here are the first and last sentences of each paragraph in the preceding essay. Some words and phrases are boldfaced to enhance connections to the key term in the thesis statement, "natural born loser."

First sentence: Everyone else must have been horrible, or I did pretty well for myself.
Thesis statement: But when it comes to real sports, I'm a natural born loser.

First sentence: **I've been a loser at sports since grade school:** I was usually picked last when we played football in gym.
Last sentence: If I could name one sport among the many I can't play, I'd name baseball.

First sentence: It began in the classic summer of 1988.
Last sentence: It was a white plate, and all it meant was that you had to keep playing this dumb game for two or three more hours. **To me, baseball was for losers.**

First sentence: Baseball isn't as simple as it seems.
Last sentence: The opposing team scored six runs; **we lost,** all thanks to me.

First sentence: Perhaps I could improve my skill as a baseball player, but I don't want to.
Last sentence: I'm not too thrilled that our "national pastime" is nothing but a league of whiny millionaires.

First sentence: So I'm not a baseball fan, whether it's recreational or professional.
Last sentence: I'll stick to video games instead, where **I'm a winner** and there's no risk of getting hit in the nose, stomach—or worse—by a line drive.

EXERCISE 8.31

Write the first and last sentence of each paragraph in your draft. Look for a key term you can repeat to enhance connections across paragraphs. Revise as needed. Following is a final revised version of the essay on page 180.

STUDENT MODEL

Expanded Student Sample: Final Edited Essay

Everyone else must have been horrible, or I did pretty well for myself. Either way, I was the winner of my high school's 2002 chess tournament. The previous year I made it to the semifinals, but this year I was the best. For the first time in my life, I was a winner. Not third place, not runner up, not "thanks for playing," but grand champion of the school. I have a certificate that says so. Perhaps I have a skill when it comes to meaningless games such as chess, checkers, and video games. But when it comes to real sports, I'm a natural born loser.

I've been a loser at sports since grade school: I was usually picked last when we played football in gym. I was in a floor hockey league and scored one goal all season. Several years ago, I was defeated by my grandmother in a game of table tennis. I don't like sports, and evidently they don't like me. If I could name one sport among the many I can't play, I'd name baseball.

It began in the classic summer of 1988. I was four years old. I enjoyed the simple pleasures in life, such as Nintendo, action figures, cartoons, and more Nintendo. That's why it came as an unpleasant shock when my parents signed me up for T-ball. It sounded simple enough as they explained that baseball was as simple as running to first, second, third, and home. I later realized that home was not where you got to sit on the couch and watch TV. It was a white plate, and all it meant was that you had to keep playing this dumb game for two or three more hours. To me, baseball was for losers.

Baseball isn't as simple as it seems. A baseball player must be alert and knowledgeable about things like the infield fly rule, which is something I still don't understand. During my baseball years, I would just nod my head and pretend I knew what was going on. Baseball players must also be quick-witted. I wasn't the most attentive kid on the field. All it took was the nearby concession stand to divert my focus. Physically, baseball players must be strong, fast, and coordinated. Unfortunately, my talent for baseball was as good as my attitude for it. In T-ball, I even had difficulty hitting the ball off the tee. When I made the transfer to baseball, it didn't get any easier. Most of the time I would stand there, hoping for a walk or to be hit by a pitch. The coach, who happened to be my father, once made the mistake of having me pitch for one inning. The opposing team scored six runs; we lost, all thanks to me.

Perhaps I could improve my skill as a baseball player, but I don't want to. For one thing, it's a boring and pointless game. I have far better things to do with my time, such as collecting unusually shaped pieces of cheese. Second, baseball is corrupt. There was a time when professional athletes were honorable people. In the 1960s, Al Kaline was asked if he wanted to be the first baseball player to make $100,000 a year. He turned it down, saying it's ridiculous for a baseball player to make that much money. Now MLB athletes make $2 million per year and want to go on strike. I say let them have their strike. Let them have it forever. I'm not too thrilled that our "national pastime" is nothing but a league of whiny millionaires.

So I'm not a baseball fan, whether it's recreational or professional. Sports are not my thing and never have been. I'll stick to video games instead, where I'm a winner and there's no risk of getting hit in the nose, stomach— or worse—by a line drive.

Copyright © 2007, The McGraw-Hill Companies, Inc. All rights reserved.

9 *Definition*

Wait a minute! We're not talking about the same thing at all. As a college student, you consider definitions more often than you might think. At times you think you know what something is, but when you put it under a microscope, its true nature becomes apparent. Formulating and working with precise definitions involves this kind of careful examination. It is an important step in critical thinking.

- To a scientist, what is the precise meaning of "adaptation"?
- What is "customer service"?
- What is a "tragic flaw," and how does it provide a basis for your understanding of *Hamlet?*
- Does the term "justice" always mean the same thing?

Good definitions are the foundation of clear thinking. You build on them. Shared definitions make effective communication possible.

IN THIS CHAPTER: A PREVIEW

Definition Thinking

- Elements of Definition
- Rename Your Subject
- Define with Negatives
- Definition and Analysis

A Process Approach to Writing the Definition Paragraph

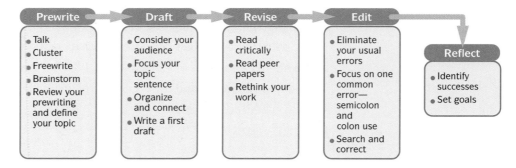

Prewrite	Draft	Revise	Edit	Reflect
• Talk • Cluster • Freewrite • Brainstorm • Review your prewriting and define your topic	• Consider your audience • Focus your topic sentence • Organize and connect • Write a first draft	• Read critically • Read peer papers • Rethink your work	• Eliminate your usual errors • Focus on one common error—semicolon and colon use • Search and correct	• Identify successes • Set goals

Student Sample of the Writing Process

Going to the Next Level: Multiple-Paragraph Papers

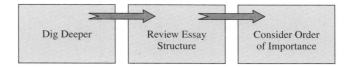

| Dig Deeper | → | Review Essay Structure | → | Consider Order of Importance |

DEFINITION THINKING

WW Paul Theroux

Definitions enable you to establish your territory. When you define your terms, you tell the reader, "I'm writing about *this,* not *that.*" Depending on your purpose and audience, sometimes a one-sentence definition is sufficient. At other times, it helps to develop your definition in a paragraph or throughout an entire essay.

Elements of Definition

Name	Components/Parts	Functions/Purpose	Origins
Does this thing have another name?	Can you take it apart? What does it consist of?	What does it do? What is it good for?	Where does it come from? Does it change over time?

Name

Components/ parts

Name

Components/parts

Origins

Components/parts

Function/purpose

READING: from *Care of the Soul,* by Thomas Moore

Care of the soul is a fundamentally different way of regarding daily life and the quest for happiness. The emphasis may not be on problems at all. One person might care for the soul by buying or renting a good piece of land, another by selecting an appropriate school or program of study, another by painting his house or his bedroom. Care of the soul is a continuous process that concerns itself not so much with "fixing" a central flaw as with attending to the small details of everyday life, as well as to major decisions and changes.

Care of the soul may not focus on the personality or on relationships at all, and therefore it is not psychological in the usual sense. Tending to things around us and becoming sensitive to the importance of home, daily schedule, and maybe even the clothes we wear, are ways of caring for the soul. When Marsilio Ficino wrote his self-help book, *The Book of Life,* five hundred years ago, he placed emphasis on choosing colors, spices, oils, places to walk, countries to visit—all very concrete decisions of everyday life that day by day either support or disturb the soul. We think of the psyche, if we think of it at all, as a cousin to the brain and therefore something essentially internal. But ancient psychologists taught that our own souls are inseparable from the world's soul, and that both are found in all the many things that make up nature and culture.

Copyright © 2007, The McGraw-Hill Companies, Inc. All rights reserved.

DISCUSSION QUESTIONS

1. What is Moore's purpose in writing?

2. Why does he spend so much time talking about therapy?

3. Who is Moore's audience?

Rename Your Subject

A good definition often begins by providing another name for your subject. Think of this approach as the mathematical statement, $x = y$:

> A <u>college education</u> is a <u>passport</u> to new worlds.
> The latest <u>attack</u> was a <u>wake-up call</u> to the country.

In his definition, Thomas Moore tells the reader explicitly what care of soul is. He does so not once, but twice:

> <u>Care of the soul</u> is a fundamentally <u>different way of regarding daily life</u> and the quest for happiness.
> <u>Care of the soul</u> is a <u>continuous process</u> that concerns itself not so much with "fixing" a central flaw as with attending to the small details of everyday life, as well as to major decision and changes.

When you think of another name for your subject, you direct your attention to a new level of meaning.

EXERCISE 9.1

Write a definition sentence in which you provide another name for each of the following terms. After each definition, write an $x = y$ statement in parentheses. Do not use a dictionary.

EXAMPLES:

> Sports are *a distraction for many young people. (sports = distraction)*
> Nature is *an escape for stressed-out people. (nature = escape)*

1. Meat is

2. A horse is

3. Penmanship is

4. Manners are

5. Courage is

6. A computer is

EXERCISE 9.1 continued

7. Temptation is

8. An automobile is

9. Work is

10. Money is

Define with Negatives

When you define with negatives, you focus on misconceptions—what people erroneously think your subject means. You say what your subject is *not*. Thomas Moore uses this approach to definition, telling us what care of soul does not do and what it is not.

> Care of the soul may <u>not</u> focus on the personality or on relationships at all, and therefore it is <u>not</u> psychological in the usual sense.

Often this form of definition is a two-statement maneuver. You state what your subject is *not*; then you state what it *is*.

EXERCISE 9.2

Write a negative definition and then a positive definition of each of the following terms.

EXAMPLES:

> driver's license: *Having a driver's license is not a right. It is a privilege.*
> vegetarianism: *Vegetarianism is not a goofy religion. It is a careful approach to health through nutrition.*

1. a child.

2. strength

3. money

4. studying

5. friendship

Definition and Analysis

To develop your definition paragraph, it may help to consider your subject's **origins,** how it has changed over time, and what **different forms** it takes on. In addition, in many cases, what something *is* can be defined by what it *does*. When you think about **functions,** you explore what your subject does, what it is good for, and what it produces. Also, it may help to dissect your subject, examining its **components** and/or **parts.** Finally, definition thinking is abstract. If possible, connect your definition to

Copyright © 2007, The McGraw-Hill Companies, Inc. All rights reserved.

specific **illustrations.** A chair is an object of furniture upon which a person sits (chair = object of furniture). There is a big difference, however, between a wooden bench and a lazyboy recliner. Both have the same function, but they are very different illustrations of the thing you have defined.

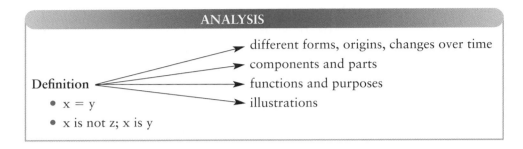

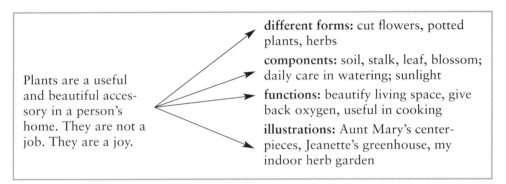

EXERCISE 9.3

Reread your negative and positive definitions in Exercise 9.2. Then analyze the topics using the process illustrated above.

EXAMPLE:

> driver's license
>
> Definition sentence: *Having a driver's license is not a right. It is a privilege.*
>
> Different forms: *permit, operator's license, chauffeur's license, temporary license, laminated "permanent" license*
>
> Components: *photo, name and mailing address, state insignia, license number; knowledge of traffic laws and how to operate a vehicle; sixteen years or older*
>
> Functions: *Driving is the only way to get around in this country. A driver's license is your key to freedom. It's a true indicator that you're not a kid; you're a grown-up. You can get to work, you can get to recreational things, you can go out and buy lightbulbs and a can of soup.*
>
> Illustrations: *The kid next door hasn't had his license for two years. He was arrested for driving under the influence twice. My aunt had her license taken away when she showed signs of having Alzheimer's.*

1. a child

Definition sentence:

Copyright © 2007, The McGraw-Hill Companies, Inc. All rights reserved.

Different forms:

Components:

Functions:

Illustrations:

2. strength
Definition sentence:

Different forms:

Components:

Functions:

Illustrations:

3. money
Definition sentence:

Different forms:

Components:

Functions:

Illustrations:

4. studying
Definition sentence:

Different forms:

Components:

Functions:

Illustrations:

EXERCISE 9.3 continued

5. friendship

Definition sentence:

Different forms:

Components:

Functions:

Illustrations:

A PROCESS APPROACH TO WRITING THE DEFINITION PARAGRAPH

Paragraph-length definitions provide a thumbnail sketch of a topic. When writing a definition, you have a chance to give your special "take" on your subject, your particular viewpoint. In longer papers, the definition may lead to a wider, more exploratory discussion. On its own, however, the definition paragraph should capture the essential features and characteristics of a topic. Following are some suggested topics for your definition paragraph.

Specific Topics	General Topics
A good job	Personal terms
An operation or product that is important in the work you do	• personality traits
	• emotions
A social skill you admire in another person	• items you own or purchase
A family value you know best	An uncommon but important concept or term you use
Discrimination as you see it	• at work
Discipline or self-control	• at home
What work means to you	• at school
Relaxation	Daily experiences and terminology
A type of music you love	• legal
A food you love that might be unusual or unique	• medical
	• cultural
	A definition of your choice

ELEMENTS OF DEFINITION

Name	Components/Parts	Functions/Purpose	Origins
Does this thing have another name?	Can you take it apart? What does it consist of?	What does it do? What is it good for?	Where does it come from? Does it change over time?

STUDENT MODEL

Student Sample

Purpose

Name

Functions/purpose

Functions/purpose

Credit card companies say their cards are a step to financial freedom. Quite the opposite is true. A credit card is a step to financial enslavement. Granted, they do help build your credit. Without credit history, it is almost impossible for a person to get a loan to buy something. Credit cards help put a person on the "financial map." They are also good to have in case of emergency. If an individual runs out of gas or needs to buy something he had not planned on buying, a credit card is really convenient.

Origin

Components/parts

However, the fact is that it is hard for some people to separate necessities from luxuries. The lure to "buy now, pay later" can be very tempting. People buy things they don't really need and can't really pay for. Paying at a later time means they don't have much money left from their paycheck after the credit card and other bills are paid. Worse yet,

Components/parts

sometimes the credit card bills are not fully paid. That is just what credit card companies want. They charge high interest rates and finance charges. Sometimes people end up paying a lot more for purchases than the original price. All credit cards are good for is getting people in debt.

Name

They are not a step to financial freedom; they are a step toward financial disaster.

PREWRITE

- Talk
- Cluster
- Freewrite
- Brainstorm
- Review your prewriting and define your topic

Select one or more of the following prewriting strategies to explore a topic and develop ideas for a definition paragraph.

Talk

EXERCISE 9.4

Choose a topic that interests you and talk to another student about it. Explain your understanding of the topic and the origins of your understanding. Point out how your definition of this topic differs from at least one other person's. Take turns discussing your topics. Then choose another topic and find a new partner. Repeat the process.

Copyright © 2007, The McGraw-Hill Companies, Inc. All rights reserved.

Cluster

EXERCISE 9.5

Select the topic that interests you most and use the following clustering diagram to explore it.

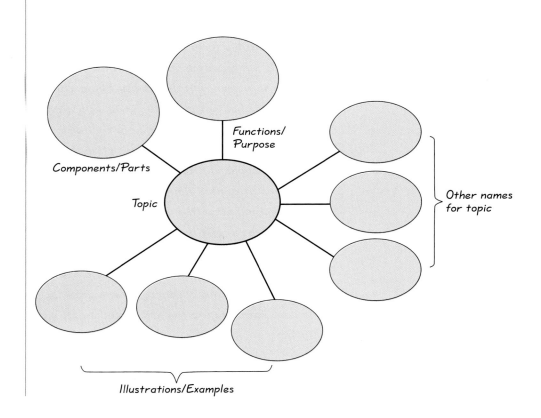

Freewrite

EXERCISE 9.6

Using the following definition questions as a guide, write as much as you can about each topic that interests you. As you write, try to address each of the questions, but concentrate more attention on those questions that give rise to fluent writing.

- What is another name for it? Or to what class of things does it belong to?
- How does it compare to similar things? Can you define your topic negatively, by stating what it *isn't?*
- What is the composition of the thing you are defining? What is it made of? What are its components or parts? What is the key detail?
- What is its function? What is it for? How is it used?
- What is its origin? Where did it come from? How has it changed or evolved over time?
- What examples or illustrations come to mind when you think of this thing you're defining?
- What stories come to mind when you think of this thing?

Brainstorm

EXERCISE 9.7

List all of the important ideas you have become aware of in your prewriting activities. As you list them, pay attention to new ideas and details and add them to your list.

Review Your Prewriting and Define Your Topic

EXERCISE 9.8

Review your prewriting and define your topic with the following questions in mind:

- Which topic struck you as most interesting?
- Which topic were you able to write the most about?
- Which one did your peers respond best to?
- Which one most needs a definition to clarify misunderstanding?

DRAFT

- Consider your audience
- Focus your topic sentence
- Organize and connect
- Write a first draft

Write a draft that organizes your prewriting into a single paragraph. The first draft will establish the subject and state the point of your definition paragraph.

Consider Your Audience

EXERCISE 9.9

Now that you have selected a topic, consider who will read your paragraph. Use the following questions to consider how to convey your point to an audience.

- Why is this topic important to your audience?
- What special meaning does this topic have for you? Why do you want your audience to understand this meaning?
- Will your audience agree or disagree with your thinking? Will you be asking them to think about your subject in a new way?
- Return to the exercises on definition thinking in this chapter and decide which way of thinking about your topic will help you connect best with your audience.

A key detail may distinguish your definition from someone else's. It is the most important quality of the thing you define. For example, to one person, strength might have mainly to do with physical capacity; to another, it might be the mental faculty of concentration. To yet another person, strength might be defined in negative terms: a

Copyright © 2007, The McGraw-Hill Companies, Inc. All rights reserved.

person's ability to *not* react in anger, to *not* give up, to *not* fall back into old habits. Definitions need to be recognizable to others. They need to make sense so the reader can share them and find room for agreement. However, as you write, you may also want to state what is most important or distinctive in your view.

EXAMPLE:

TOPIC: FOOTBALL	
Breakdown	**Detail**
components	Football involves eleven men and their coaches on each side, four quarters in the game, possessions consisting of four downs, running, passing, kicking, and throwing.
origins	Football is related to rugby and soccer. All three sports are played outside and involve getting a ball in a goal. American football is rougher, uses more equipment, and divides offense plays into "downs".
different forms	In any community, there can be middle school football, high school football, and sometimes college football. Kids can play "pickup" games on the sandlot.
illustrations	People unite around their teams when they have tailgate parties before games. In Ann Arbor, 100,000 or so people pack into the stadium to watch the Wolverines. Even bad teams, like the Detroit Lions, have loyal fans.
key detail	To me, the quarterback is what makes football the game it is. He calls the plays, works out strategy, and deploys players on various parts of the field. People are united as they watch the skillful quarterback; they may also be united by their frustration with an ineffective quarterback.

EXERCISE 9.10

Drawing on your prewriting in this chapter, jot down your topic. Then add more specific detail. Indicate your key detail and explain why it is the most important definitive detail.

Focus Your Topic Sentence

EXERCISE 9.11

Underline the key terms in each of the following topic sentences and describe the form of definition the topic sentence promises to use.

EXAMPLE:

$$1 \qquad\qquad + \qquad\qquad 1$$

A parent is not a friend to her child; she is more like a teacher concerned with nurturing, discipline, and growth.

Form of definition: *focus on the purpose of a parent*

EXERCISE 9.11 continued

1. A part-time job is the first step to a young person's financial independence.
   Form of definition:
2. Alternative energy sources are no longer a figment of the public's imagination. They are practical options a smart consumer can choose from.
   Form of definition:
3. Saturday afternoons are an oasis: a time of rest, relaxation, and restoration.
   Form of definition:
4. Chess is the ultimate game of concentration and strategy.
   Form of definition:
5. Many men are beginning to rethink what it means to be a man.
   Form of definition:

EXERCISE 9.12

Using the following example as a model, break down your topic into its components, origins, different forms, and functions. Then, write a two-sentence definition: x is not z; x is y.

EXAMPLE:

Topic Sentence: A good vacation refreshes a person mentally and physically.

A. Components
   1. Rest
   2. Recreation
   3. Quiet

B. Origins
   1. Childhood—summer vacation
   2. Adult—weekend off

C. Forms
   1. Family vacation
   2. Vacation with friends
   3. Being alone—away from everyone and everything

D. Functions
   1. Relief from stress
   2. Connect with people you love
   3. Try new things

Definition: A vacation is not a break from activity altogether; it is a different form of activity that leads to growth.

Organize and Connect
Time, place, and importance are forms of order. Consider presenting ideas of least importance first and most importance last.

Copyright © 2007, The McGraw-Hill Companies, Inc. All rights reserved.

Weak Order of Presentation

Romantic love is a special gift that you can be blessed with.

There's another type of love to talk about, and that is a mother's love toward her child.

Let's talk about another kind of love. It's a brother and sister's love.

Revised Order (based on order of importance)

An important kind of love is a brother and sister's love.

There's another type of love to talk about, and that is a mother's love toward her child.

Finally, there is romantic love between a man and a woman.

EXERCISE 9.13

Review the details in your definition and make an outline for your definition. As you do so, determine which way of ordering the details (time, place, importance) is most appropriate. A definition paragraph draws on a variety of transition terms. Choose those from the following list that relate to the definition approach you take.

Negative	Origins/Change over Time	Functions/ Purpose	Illustration
unlike	initially	first	for example
whereas	to begin with	second	next
although	then	third	in addition
in contrast	now		moreover
on the other hand	ultimately		
	finally		

EXERCISE 9.14

Read the following paragraph and underline the transition terms.

Juveniles are people who don't have the same rights or responsibilities as adults. First, sixteen is the legal driving age for juveniles. However, a guardian must give written permission before a juvenile can receive a driver's license. Second, age determines the amount of hours a young person can work. At fourteen a young person can start working, but only for a few hours per week. As age increases, so does the amount of hours kids can legally work. Third, juveniles are not allowed to vote. They are not considered ready for that responsibility until they reach the age of eighteen. Fourth, juveniles are also prevented from enlisting in the military. The draft age is also eighteen. Before that age, juveniles can enlist, but they need parental consent. Finally, juveniles are not legally responsible for their financial debts; for this reason, they can't enter into a legal contract without permission from their guardian. When they give permission, guardians become responsible for the juvenile's debt. Age is a factor that limits many of the rights that juveniles receive.

Write a First Draft

EXERCISE 9.15

Use the following checklist as a guide to draft your definition paragraph.

_____ Review your prewriting to clarify your purpose and what you want your audience to understand.

_____ Insert details to explain your definition.

_____ Use the 1+1 approach in your topic sentence.

_____ Insert transitions to connect ideas and details.

> **REVISE**
> _____
> • Read critically
> • Read peer papers
> • Rethink your work

Begin revising by asking yourself these questions: Will an audience understand my purpose? Is there sufficient detail? Are my ideas connected and is my purpose clearly defined?

Read Critically

EXERCISE 9.16

Examine the following paragraph. Underline the topic sentence and look for the paragraph's strengths and weakness.

The cell phone is a very good thing to have when you are busy. It's not a convenience; it's a necessity. If you are like me, you want the best phone money can buy. The one I use is about the size of a pager. It doesn't even have an antenna. It has a calculator, a calendar, and about fifty different rings. The most important part of the phone is its ability to store numbers. This phone book enables me to dial people by name instead of keying in a number. It is also convenient because when the phone rings, if the number is in my phone book, the name of the person calling appears on the phone's display. If there is an important date, if I need to go to an appointment, if it's somebody's birthday or I have a test that day, I enter the date in the phone's calendar, and it warns me with an alarm. Finally, on a minor note, the phone can be useful for passing time because it has a few games on it. At one time, you needed a computer genius to tell you how to work all of the buttons on a cell phone. These days, phones are getting to be very user friendly. Without that, I would have a hard time being organized.

Focus

1. Is the paragraph's subject clear? Will a reader understand why this definition is important?

Detail

2. Does the writer provide details on components, origins, form, and function?

Copyright © 2007, The McGraw-Hill Companies, Inc. All rights reserved.

EXERCISE 9.16 continued

3. Is there a key detail?

Connections

4. Does the writer present details in an order that is effective? Does anything seem out of order or irrelevant?

5. Is the order made clear by connecting words?

Taking a Critical View

6. What are the strengths and weaknesses of the paragraph?

Strengths	Weaknesses

7. What will improve this paper?

Read Peer Papers

EXERCISE 9.17

Form a group of three or four students and take turns reading and discussing your paragraphs. Use the questions from Exercise 9.16 to identify each paragraph's strengths and weaknesses. Offer suggestions for a revision plan.

Rethink Your Work

Definition demands specifics. Expanding with specific details that name and clarify the concept being defined is essential. At the same time, clarity can be sacrificed if unnecessary details are inserted. Reexamine your details to determine what clarifies your definition and what confuses it.

EXERCISE 9.18

Read the following paragraph and notice the points that clarify the definition. Discuss with a classmate which points need expansion and which points and details need to be cut.

Point 1

 I have a very strong work ethic. Having a work ethic is not about just working hard. It is a state of mind. When I work, I commit all my time and mind to what I am doing. Even if I am working for someone, I like to think that I am working for myself, as if it was my business. I got it from my father and from his employees.

Point 2

Point 3

Having fun strengthens a work ethic. Joking with other workers and the customers makes the time fly. I learned that when you think that way, work will be much easier. In addition, my ethics have grown stronger because of the nice way my boss treats me. He respects and trusts me. Up until today my strong ethics haven't changed. I still have pride, desire, and respect for what I do. I always have the desire to improve to become better.

Destinations: Giving the Journey Meaning with Definition

What Did You Say Again?

Imagine you are describing a movie you just saw to one of your friends. If you were to say, "It's a screwball comedy, but a little on the dark side," you might well hear this response: "What's a 'screwball comedy'? And what do you mean by the 'dark side'?" Your friend is asking you to define your terms and, in order for the conversation to move forward, you will have to do so. Definition, then, is one way of establishing a basis for an intelligent discussion. You may also find that your notion of a word's meaning will change after talking about it with others.

Definition: A Basis for Argument

In class discussion and projects, you will need to carefully define your terms. Are you discussing assisted suicide? At the outset, you should be sure that you and your listeners or readers understand how you define the term. For example, you might say, "In referring to 'assisted suicide,' I'm limiting this discussion to cases in which terminally ill patients—as opposed to physically healthy persons—are aided by others in ending their lives." Limiting the argument by defining your terms can turn an unmanageably large topic into something you (and your reader) will be able to handle.

Definition on the Job

Definition is obviously key to classroom teaching—"An isosceles triangle is . . ."; "Democracy is most commonly defined as . . ."; "Freud defined the 'ego' as . . ."—but it plays a role in many other jobs as well. A librarian would need to define an "online database" for someone new to the world of electronic research; a physician's assistant might need to explain the phrase "complete work-up" to an anxious patient; an employee training a new hire would have to define the jargon ("requisition," "work order," or "supplier," for example) of his or her particular business. Similarly, the kind of definition that makes a decision, position, or policy clear, is a part of most jobs: for example, a government official might state the technical definition of an "assembly" in discussing the need for a license for a planned public meeting, while a waiter in a restaurant might have to clearly define the "early bird special" in order to avoid an argument with eager customers.

EXERCISE 9.19

Review your definition paragraph to analyze whether your points are supported by sufficient or unnecessary detail.

- Identify the points you use to define your subject.
- Underline the details you use to explain the point.
- Ask if these details are sufficient to clarify the definition.
- Ask if the details are unnecessary. Even if they're interesting, some details may distract the reader from the topic.
- Clarify your definition by adding or cutting details.

EDIT

- Eliminate your usual errors
- Focus on one common error—semicolon and colon use
- Search and correct

Prepare to turn your paragraph in for a grade. Make sure you are not repeating errors you usually make. Then look for new errors that may distract your reader from the purpose and meaning of your writing.

Copyright © 2007, The McGraw-Hill Companies, Inc. All rights reserved.

Eliminate Your Usual Errors

EXERCISE 9.20

Turn to the grids in Chapters 18, 19, and 20 where you have been keeping track of the errors you make. List those errors in the space provided below. Then proofread your paper and correct the errors you find.

_____   _____   _____

_____   _____   _____

Focus on One Common Error—Semicolon and Colon Use

The semicolon and colon are strong marks of punctuation, almost as strong as the period. Used carefully, they can indicate relationships of consecutive ideas.

Semicolon

Use a semicolon between sentences expressing contrasting ideas.

> My mother is an early riser; my father likes to sleep in.
>
> One way to enjoy music is to listen to a CD; another is to perform it.

Colon

Use a colon between two sentences with general and specific content. In the following examples, the second sentence explains the first with specific detail.

> I was very lucky as a kid: I had a lot of things to keep me occupied.
>
> My fourth-grade teacher was great: she was full of life and very creative.

EXERCISE 9.21

Correct the punctuation in the following sentences. Use a semicolon in sentences that express contrasting ideas; use a colon in those sentences with general and specific content. Some sentences may work best with a period.

1. Some people have no knowledge of cars at all, others can take one apart in their sleep. I belong to the former category, my father definitely belongs in the latter category.

2. Working at the bakery offered one special advantage, I could have flexible hours, not everyone took advantage of this option, but I did.

3. I'm not really sure why I'm so shy, I guess it is simply a personality trait I'm stuck with, things could be worse I'm just not sure how.

4. I decided to make the kids clean the whole facility, the girls did the mopping, the boys washed tabletops and windows.

5. The company gave the workers Dixie cups for water, I decided to put lemonade in mine one day they considered that stealing, so they fired me.

EXERCISE 9.21 continued

6. There was one thing I didn't like about the job I had to bring carts into the store when it was cold and there was snow on the ground, it was very difficult work.

7. Professionally I am known as Brandeis, to my friends and family, I'm just Brandi.

8. Soon we were skipping school every day some days we would drive around, hang out at the park, or go the movies other days we went to a shopping mall in the next county.

9. It was our freshman year in high school, we were involved in every after-school activity it was easy to put energy into these things working on homework at night was a different story.

10. The real issue was my father, I didn't know how he was going to react to this, he had hit me once before maybe this time it would be much worse.

Search and Correct

EXERCISE 9.22

Double-check your punctuation. Proofread your paragraph and look for sentences that could be connected by a semicolon or colon. Use a semicolon in sentences that express contrasting ideas; use a colon in those sentences with general and specific content. Then look for other sentences in which you have already used a semicolon or colon and determine whether you have used the punctuation correctly.

EXERCISE 9.23

Double-check your spelling. Computer spell-checks make mistakes. Therefore, it is essential that you proofread your paper before turning it in for a grade. Focus your close reading on typographical errors.

EXERCISE 9.24

Find a proofreading pal. After you have double-checked your paper, exchange papers with that student and proofread each other's work. Find out what errors your classmate would like you to search for. Using your list from Exercise 9.20, tell your classmate what errors you are inclined to make.

Copyright © 2007, The McGraw-Hill Companies, Inc. All rights reserved.

REFLECT
- Identify successes
- Set goals

Each time you write, you build skills and strategies. The last step in the writing process is to reflect and recognize what you did well and what you learned.

Identify Successes

EXERCISE 9.25

Take a few minutes to reflect on your successes. Write one or two sentences that explain two things you have learned from this chapter and how you successfully applied them to your writing. Use a specific example from your work to support your thinking.

Set Goals

EXERCISE 9.26

Now that you have examined your successes, determine what challenges you face. Rate yourself using the following scale—5 indicates a task that you consider a challenge most of the time, and 1 indicates a task for which you have the required skills and strategies.

Stages	Strategies and Skills	5	4	3	2	1
Prewrite	1. I prewrite to explore my ideas and think deeper about a topic.	—	—	—	—	—
Draft	2. I focus my paragraphs with topic sentences.	—	—	—	—	—
	3. I organize my ideas and make connections.	—	—	—	—	—
Revise	4. I read critically to identify and use the successful techniques of other writers.	—	—	—	—	—
	5. I identify the strengths and weaknesses in my papers.	—	—	—	—	—
	6. I apply specific revision strategies to my papers.	—	—	—	—	—
Edit	7. I employ all or some of the following editing strategies:					
	▪ search for appropriate use of semicolons and colons	—	—	—	—	—
	▪ use spell-check on my computer	—	—	—	—	—
	▪ read a printed copy of my paragraph aloud to check for spelling errors and typographical errors	—	—	—	—	—

EXERCISE 9.27:

Finish the following sentences in order to explore your learning experience and to set goals.

1. My attitude toward writing is

2. I still need to work on

STUDENT SAMPLE OF THE WRITING PROCESS

STUDENT MODEL

Bill's Clustering

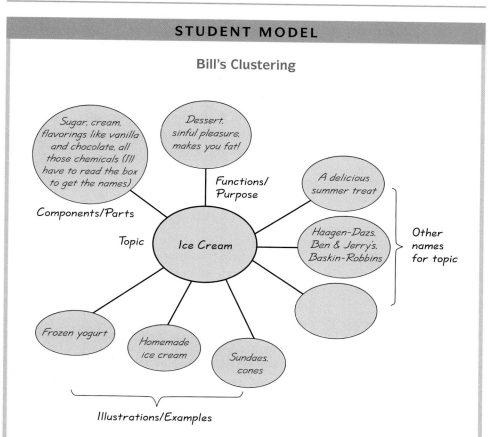

Bill's Unedited Freewrite

Is there anything more wonderful than ice cream? I don't think so. There are cones and sundaes (hot fudge!), and ice cream on a stick. A delicious summer treat, my mother always says. Some people eat it in the winter to. Like me. So ice cream is: cream, ice, flavoring, sugar. It's fattening, that's the worst thing about it. Nowadays it has more chemicals in it than before. But you can get natural ice cream if you want, maybe Ben and Jerrys. Some people make their own, they need a mchine. All knds of new ice creams now; such as frozen yogurt. Low fat. Diet ice cream. Takes the fun out it. Why eat it if its not fattening?

Bill's Unedited First Draft

Ice cream is a treat that is popular on a hot day, it is also enjoyed by many in the dead of winter. It comes in a variety of flavors, too many to mention here. The texture can be from very soft and creamy to quit rigid and icy. Ice cream can be eaten in a bowl, on a stick, or in a cone. Many

continued

Copyright © 2007, The McGraw-Hill Companies, Inc. All rights reserved.

people enjoy toppings on their ice cream; such as fruits, nuts, hot fudge, and cookies. Originally, ice cream was made from frozen cream, sugar, and fruit these days, ice cream has ingredients such as sorbitol, diglycerides, and other hard to pronounce words. If you are willing to pay a higher price, you can always get the more natural type of ice cream. Many people have their own ice cream maker machine; which allows them to use all natural ingredients. As more and more people are struggling with their weight, more and more low-fat ice creams make their way to the stores. For most people, the satisfaction gained from eating this tasty treat makes up for its lack of nutritional value.

Peer Reader's Comments on Bill's First Draft

doesn't have much nutritional value.

Ice cream is a treat that is popular on a hot day, it is also enjoyed by

Why not mention a few flavors?

many in the dead of winter.]It comes in a variety of flavors, ~~too many to~~ ~~mention here~~. The texture can be from very soft and creamy to quit rigid

Reconsider order of details

and icy. Ice cream can be eaten in a bowl, on a stick, or in a cone. Many people enjoy toppings on their ice cream; such as fruits, nuts, hot fudge, and cookies. Originally, ice cream was made from frozen cream, sugar, and fruit;

and

Seems kind of random

these days, ice cream has ingredients such as sorbitol/diglycerides, ~~and~~ ~~other hard to pronounce words~~. If you are willing to pay a higher price, you

; furthermore,

can always get the more natural type of ice cream. Many people have their own ice cream maker machine; which allows them to use all natural ingredients. As more and more people are struggling with their weight, more and more low-fat ice creams make their way to the stores. For most people, the satisfaction gained from eating this tasty treat makes up for its

lack of nutritional value)   *It's so bad. That's why we love it??*

Bill's Final Edited Paragraph

    Ice cream is a tasty treat that doesn't have much nutritional value. The texture can be soft and creamy or rigid and icy. It can be eaten in a bowl, on a stick, or in a cone. Originally, ice cream was made from frozen cream, sugar, and fruit; these days, it has ingredients such as sorbitol and diglycerides. If you are willing to pay a higher price, you can always get the more natural type of ice cream; furthermore, many people have their own ice cream maker machine, which allows them to use all natural ingredients. Ice cream comes in a variety of flavors, such as vanilla, chocolate, strawberry, and blue moon. Many people enjoy toppings on their ice cream too, like fruits, nuts, hot fudge, and cookies. It's popular on a hot day, but it is also enjoyed by many in the dead of winter. Unfortunately, ice cream can be very fattening because of the sugar and fat content. As more and more people are struggling with their weight, more and more low-fat ice creams make their way to the stores. For most people, the satisfaction gained from eating ice cream comes from the feeling that it's a litte bit sinful. It's bad, so it must be really good.

Bill's Reflection

Stages	Strategies and Skills	5	4	3	2	1
Prewrite	1. I prewrite to explore my ideas and think deeper about a topic.	—	—	—	—	X
Draft	2. I focus my paragraphs with topic sentences.	—	—	—	—	X
	3. I organize my ideas and make connections.	—	—	—	—	X
Revise	4. I read critically to identify and use the successful techniques of other writers.	—	—	X	—	—
	5. I identify the strengths and weaknesses in my papers.	—	—	—	X	—
	6. I apply specific revision strategies to my papers.	—	—	—	X	—
Edit	7. I employ all or some of the following editing strategies:					
	▪ search for appropriate use of semicolons and colons	—	—	—	—	X
	▪ use spell-check on my computer	—	—	X	—	—
	▪ read a printed copy of my paragraph aloud to check for spelling errors and typographical errors	—	—	—	—	X

1. My attitude toward writing is *getting a little better. I liked writing this paper because I like the subject and I remembered making ice cream at my grandpa's house when I was a child. My final draft seems organized. That made me happy.*

2. I still need to work on *my spelling. Some of my group members showed me errors I made. I don't write on a computer so how am I supposed to use spell check. This has always been a problem. I think I'm getting a little better at looking for spelling. I like semicolons but I'm still not sure when to use them.*

GOING TO THE NEXT LEVEL: MULTIPLE-PARAGRAPH PAPERS

If you have more to say about your subject, or if your instructor would like you to take your writing to the next level, proceed to the following exercises. These exercises invite further exploration and provide suggestions for structuring a longer paper.

Copyright © 2007, The McGraw-Hill Companies, Inc. All rights reserved.

Dig Deeper

Use the thinking and writing strategies you have learned so far to explore your topic further. Choose from the following questions to discover more ideas and details relevant to your topic.

Illustration and Example	Narrative	Process	Cause and Effect	Comparison and Contrast
Are there specific examples of your subject? Are the examples similar or different? Do those examples lead to more examples? to more specific detail?	Can you discuss an incident to make your point? Who was involved? When and where did it occur? What were the important actions? What was the outcome?	What people are involved in the process? Where and when does it occur? Are materials, gear, props, or equipment involved? What is the most important detail?	Does this thing have one or more causes? Does it have one or more effects or consequences? Does it help to think in terms of reasons for this thing?	In what respects does it resemble another object or idea? In what respects is it different? Is there a key detail of similarity or difference?

Talk

EXERCISE 9.28

Sit down with a classmate and explain why you have decided to explore your topic further. Discuss what interests you about the topic and why you think it is important. As you talk, use the preceding questions as a guide to your thinking.

Cluster

EXERCISE 9.29

Choose those questions from the box on page 206 that you like best for clustering and explore your topic further.

Freewrite

EXERCISE 9.30

Write for ten minutes on your topic, using those questions from the box on page 206 that give you the most to say.

Brainstorm

EXERCISE 9.31

List all the new ideas and details you have generated in your prewriting activities. As you list them, think about how they relate to each other and whether time, importance, or place helps you see logical relationships.

Review Essay Structure

Drawing on the new ideas and details you gathered from digging deeper into this subject, write a draft of your essay. Follow the guidelines below for essay structure.

Don't forget to include your definition paragraph as you take your ideas to the next level.

INTRODUCTION PARAGRAPH

The introduction arouses the reader's interest in your subject, establishes the importance of your subject, and provides the focus of your essay.

The thesis statement captures the main idea or point of the entire essay.

BODY PARAGRAPHS

The definition paragraph you wrote from this chapter might appear in this portion of your essay. Body paragraphs deliver the main content of your paper. The number of body paragraphs depends on how much you have to say and on the length requirements your instructor imposes. Your readers look for substance in body paragraphs. Don't forget topic sentences. Remember your supporting details.

CONCLUSION

Like the introduction, the conclusion paragraph focuses the reader's attention on the main point of the essay.

STUDENT MODEL

Student Sample—Single Paragraph

Love is a special gift that you can be blessed with. As time goes on, it can become stronger and stronger with each day that passes. It takes a strong person to keep love growing. Love consists of several elements, such as communication, trust, compromise, and patience. It can build into something everlasting, but it can also crumble to become nothing. The greatest or worst thing about love is how easily you can fall into it.

Expanded Student Sample—Multiple Paragraphs

I've only really been in love twice in my life. I met my first true love when I was 13 years old. At least that's what I thought. It was a few years ago, at the movie theater. My cousin knew his cousin, and we met up at the movies so we could double-date. We went to get something to eat first, which gave us time to talk face-to-face. We had already talked on the phone. I thought in my mind that he was the one for me to be with. But

*The writer begins with a **narrative** paragraph.*

continued

Copyright © 2007, The McGraw-Hill Companies, Inc. All rights reserved.

*The writer follows with a **definition** paragraph.*

what do we really know at 13 years old? Nothing at all. We talked for a long time and became comfortable with each other right away.

Love is a special gift that you can be blessed with. As time goes on, it can become stronger and stronger with each day that passes. It takes a strong person to keep love going and growing. Love consists of several elements, such as communication, trust, compromise, and patience. It can build into something everlasting, but it can also crumble to become nothing. The greatest or worst thing about love is how easily you can fall into it.

*The writer uses another short **narrative** to explore a different aspect of love.*

There's another type of love to talk about, and that is a mother's love toward her child. I remember one time when I was 7 years old, and I fell out of a tree. I scraped my leg, and I ran in the house crying. My mother wrapped her arms around me and gave me the biggest hug. After she took care of my wound, we went out for ice cream. She always shows me unconditional love. No matter what I do, good or bad, she's always there for me. She shows me a special type of love.

*The writer uses an **extended example** to make another point about love.*

Let's talk about another kind of love. It's a brother and sister's love. I've grown up with one brother for most of my life. When I turned 10 years old, I found out that I had sixteen brothers on my father's side. This was a big shock to me. I got to meet ten of them at age 10. I have twin brothers whose names are Tony and Terry. The three of us are so close. I can talk to them about anything, and they will always understand. They show me how much they love me by always being concerned with my life. They call every weekend to find out what's going on in my life. They come to visit quite often. They can become overprotective of me and who is around me. I feel the same way toward both of them. I never want anything or anyone to hurt them. This love is a hard feeling to explain. It is a bond that cannot be broken no matter what happens.

*The writer returns to the task of **defining** love.*

*The writer **summarizes** some of the content explored earlier in the essay.*

Love consists of many things. Some of the other names for love can be affection, devotion, character, integrity, respect, honesty, giving, and heartfelt unity. Eventually you will build a solid foundation of hope for the future. You will feel relaxed that you've found people who accept you unconditionally and without prejudice. They just love you for who you are inside. They show you all their love they have inside. It can be a mother's love, a child's love, a brother's love, a sister's love, or a romantic love. You'll feel overjoyed for the people showing you this emotion and sharing their life with you. That's what love's all about.

Consider Order of Importance

Consider the order in which you present your ideas. A good strategy is to keep the best for last. Save your most important ideas for the end of the paper, just before the conclusion.

Copyright © 2007, The McGraw-Hill Companies, Inc. All rights reserved.

EXERCISE 9.32

Organize the following topic sentences to reflect order of importance. Save the best for last. Write one or two sentences to explain your reasons for organizing the ideas the way you do.

EXAMPLE:

Thesis statement: Getting good grades is the result of many small decisions a student makes.

Topic sentences:

A good student makes the hard decision to see an instructor about a difficulty in the course. *3*

A good student forms friendships with classmates to form helpful study groups. *2*

A good student decides to go to the library right after class and get started on homework. *1*

Your reasons: *Going to one's instructor with questions and forming effective study groups are helpful to getting good grades, but the most important habit a student can have is doing homework on time, while the material is still fresh.*

1. Thesis statement: Travel is a very important learning experience for a young person.

   Topic sentences:

   Having seen other places and people, the individual may learn to appreciate his own living circumstances even more.

   The individual learns about other customs and ways of life.

   A person can try lots of interesting foods.

   Your reasons:

2. Thesis statement: Senior citizens have acquired wisdom and experience that can benefit younger people, if you only take the time to listen.

   Topic sentences:

   Old people are often ignored because they take a little longer and talk a little slower.

   Seniors have lived through some of the great events in recent world history

   Just hearing the older ladies talk about fashions can be funny and enlightening.

   Your reasons:

3. Thesis statement: A truly valuable hobby is one in which both a person's hands and mind are focused.

   Topic sentences:

   Of course a hobby is good to have because it can help a person keep from wasting his free time.

   Then again, a truly pleasurable hobby often involves actually making something that is beautiful, useful, and important.

EXERCISE 9.32 continued

A valuable hobby may involve learning, expanding a person's skill and ability; it doesn't simply stay the same over time.

Your reasons:

4. Thesis statement: A sense of fashion involves more than knowing how and where to buy clothes; it also means a person knows how to dress to advantage.

Topic sentences:

If you don't know how to wear clothes properly suited to an occasion, the biggest closet and collection of clothes will be worth nothing.

It is certainly true that a person with fashion sense knows how to find bargains and combine clothes in new and interesting ways.

A fashionable person knows how to look; that is, she watches people and sees what they wear, learning about clothes and fashion all the time.

Your reasons:

5. Thesis statement: Being responsible means doing the hard things when everyone else does what is easy.

Topic sentences:

Responsibility is the habit of being dependable and doing the right thing.

A person should be responsible on a daily basis; it is especially important around the home.

At work and in school, there are countless choices a person makes that come down to responsibility.

Your reasons:

EXERCISE 9.33

Write your thesis statement and topic sentences to reflect the order of your ideas in your paper. Then compose a few sentences explaining why this order makes sense. Revise your essay to reflect this new strategy of saving the best for last. Following is the final edited version of the essay on page 207.

STUDENT MODEL

Expanded Student Sample: Final Edited Essay

I've only really been in love twice in my life. I met my first true love when I was 13 years old. At least that's what I thought. It was a few years ago, at the movie theater. My cousin fixed me up on a blind date, and we met at the movies so we could double-date. We went to get something to eat first, which gave my date and I time to talk face-to-face. We had already talked on the phone. I thought in my mind that he was the one for me. But what do we really

Copyright © 2007, The McGraw-Hill Companies, Inc. All rights reserved.

know at 13 years old? Nothing at all. We talked for a long time and became comfortable with each other right away. Love is about comfort, but it is also about commitment to another person.

Love is a special gift that you can be blessed with. As time goes on, it can become stronger and stronger with each day that passes. It takes a strong person to keep love going and growing. Love consists of several elements, such as communication, trust, compromise, and patience. It can build into something everlasting, but it can also crumble to become nothing. The greatest or worst thing about love is how easily you can fall into it.

An important kind of love that lasts is a brother and sister's love. I've grown up with one brother for most of my life. When I turned 10 years old, I found out that I had sixteen brothers on my father's side. This was a big shock to me. I got to meet ten of them at age ten. I have twin brothers whose names are Tony and Terry. The three of us are so close. I can talk to them about anything, and they will always understand. They show me how much they love me by always being concerned with my life. They call every weekend to find out what's going on in my life. They come to visit quite often. They can become overprotective of me and who is around me. I feel the same way toward both of them. I never want anything or anyone to hurt them. This love is a hard feeling to explain. It is a bond that cannot be broken no matter what happens. It will last all my life.

There's another type of love to talk about, and that is a mother's love toward her child. I remember one time when I was 7 years old, and I fell out of a tree. I scraped my leg, and I ran in the house crying. My mother wrapped her arms around me and gave me the biggest hug. After she took care of my wound, we went out for ice cream. She always shows me unconditional love. No matter what I do, good or bad, she's always there for me.

Finally, there is romantic love between a man and a woman. This is the love we often see in the movies. It is violins and love scenes, broken hearts and shining eyes when the two people find each other forever. Most people want this kind of love. In real life, it is harder than that. In real life, love between a man and a woman has more to do with getting up in the middle of the night and taking care of sick kids. A man and woman who love each other take turns. It has to do with coming home tired and washing up a sinkful of dishes. A man and woman who love each other take turns at this too. My mother and father have been married thirty years. Every now and then they go out on a "date." It's usually a movie or just an afternoon with friends. It doesn't seem very romantic, but they are still together after all these years.

continued

Love consists of many things. Some of the other names for love can be affection, devotion, character, integrity, respect, honesty, giving, and heartfelt unity. Eventually you will build a solid foundation of hope for the future. You will feel relaxed that you've found people who accept you unconditionally and without prejudice. They just love you for who you are inside. They show you all their love they have inside. It can be a mother's love, a child's love, a brother's love, a sister's love, or a romantic love. You'll feel overjoyed for the people showing you this emotion and sharing their life with you. That's what love's all about.

PART THREE

Integrating Patterns: Special Assignments

10 *Paraphrase, Summary, and Quotation*

How do I write about what I've read without just repeating what the author says? As a college student, you'll often be asked to write about what you read. In writing about what you have read, you demonstrate **comprehension, recall,** and **critical thinking.** You form connections between what you already know and new information. In writing about what you have read, therefore, you acquire *new knowledge.* As you read, you need to ask yourself the following questions:

- What is the main idea?
- What are the key details?
- What is the writer's viewpoint?

Two basic forms of writing about what you have read are **paraphrase** and **summary.** In paraphrase and summary, you state what you have read in your own words. In doing so, you capture the most important points and provide the reader with an overview. At other times, you will select a **quotation** that captures a writer's idea or point of view in vivid language.

IN THIS CHAPTER: A PREVIEW

Paraphrase
Summary

- Capturing the Main Idea
- Capturing the Details
- Providing an Overview

Quotation

- Introducing Quotations
- Documenting Quotations

Suggestions for Daily Practice

PARAPHRASE

When you paraphrase, you restate an author's ideas in your own words. Paraphrasing is the most basic skill used in summary, and for this reason it deserves continuous practice. Look for **key terms** and the **main idea** in the sentence(s) you paraphrase, and be sure to restate them. In your paraphrase, you will probably have to use some of the author's words. However, if you use more than five consecutive words from the author's sentence, you are no longer paraphrasing. Always remember that in paraphrasing, it is a good idea to keep things simple: a short sentence is almost always better than a long one. The following original sentences come from Richard Sennett's *The Corrosion of Character.*

> **Original:** The bakery was filled with noise; the smell of yeast mingled with human sweat in the hot rooms; the bakers' hands were constantly plunged into flour and water.
> **Paraphrase:** The bakery was noisy, hot, and smelly, and the work was constant.
>
> **Original:** The bakers needed to cooperate intimately in order to coordinate the varied tasks of the bakery.
> **Paraphrase:** Working together was important.
>
> **Original:** The bakery no longer smells of sweat and is startlingly cool, whereas workers used frequently to throw up from the heat. Under the soothing fluorescent lights, all is now strangely silent.
> **Paraphrase:** The bakery is now a cool, quiet place to work.

When you paraphrase effectively, you retain the meaning of the original, use only minimal wording from the original, and avoid expressing your opinion and making judgments.

EXERCISE 10.1

Following are some sentences from Mary Sherry's essay "In Praise of the F Word." For each sentence, select the paraphrase that most effectively states the main idea of the original sentence.

1. Tens of thousands of 18-year-olds will graduate this year and be handed meaningless diplomas.
   A. Lots of high schoolers graduate without full degrees.
   B. Many high school graduates will receive meaningless diplomas this year.
   C. Tens of thousands of high school graduates will be handed meaningless diplomas this year.

2. These diplomas won't look any different from those awarded their luckier classmates.
   A. Their diplomas will look like everyone else's diplomas.
   B. These kids ought to be really angry.
   C. These diplomas aren't worth the paper they are printed on.

3. Their validity will be questioned only when their employers discover that these graduates are semiliterate.
   A. These kids won't know how to do anything on the job.
   B. The meaning of their diplomas won't be questioned until they go to work.
   C. These students won't know their diplomas are worthless until they get a job.

4. Eventually a fortunate few will find their way into educational-repair shops—adult-literacy programs, such as the one where I teach basic grammar and writing.

Copyright © 2007, The McGraw-Hill Companies, Inc. All rights reserved.

EXERCISE 10.1 continued

    A. Educational-repair shops, such as adult-literacy programs, will eventually save a fortunate few.

    B. Some of these graduates will eventually go back to school.

    C. Naturally these poor suckers will lose their jobs and go back for more education.

5. There, high school graduates and high school dropouts pursuing graduate equivalency certificates will learn the skills they should have learned in school.

    A. They will have to hit the books again, in hopes of eventually making some big bucks.

    B. They will pick up basic skills in these programs.

    C. Here, high school graduates and high school dropouts pursuing graduate equivalency certificates will make up for lost time.

6. Passing students who have not mastered the work cheats them and the employers who expect graduates to have basic skills.

    A. Employers who expect graduates to have basic skills should be very angry.

    B. Passing students who haven't learned anything isn't fair to students or employers.

    C. If you asked me, the whole system stinks!

7. We excuse this dishonest behavior by saying kids can't learn if they come from terrible environments.

    A. I came from a bad environment, and I managed to learn a thing or two.

    B. It's the school's fault; they are dishonest.

    C. When kids don't learn, we blame their environment.

8. No one seems to stop and think that—no matter what environments they come from—most kids don't put school first on their list unless they perceive something is at stake.

    A. Environment isn't the issue; it's a matter of kids realizing that school matters.

    B. Most kids have better things to do than go to school and study.

    C. No matter what environments they come from, kids still need to get an education.

9. They'd rather be sailing.

    A. They'd rather be sailing.

    B. They don't want to study.

    C. They have other interests.

10. People of all ages can rise above their problems, but they need to have a reason to do so.

    A. If they don't learn when they're in school, too bad.

    B. Even kids from bad environments can learn, but they have to be motivated.

    C. People of all ages can rise above the problem of having a bad education.

EXERCISE 10.2

Paraphrase the ideas in each of the following original sentences from a sampling of essays. Make sure your paraphrase sentences are short, simple, and to the point. Avoid using more than five consecutive words from the original sentence.

EXERCISE 10.2 continued

EXAMPLE: We may have come a long way baby, but the latest Voices of Women opinion poll suggests we still have a long way to go.

Paraphrase: *Women have made a lot of progress, but more work lies ahead.*

1. The survey found men are beginning to share the same attitudes toward work as women—with like percentages seeking flexible work hours and the ability to work from home.

   Paraphrase:

2. Leaders of the nation's largest drug prevention program, Drug Abuse Resistance Education, announced on Thursday that they were changing DARE's approach, admitting that the vastly expensive program appears to be ineffective.

   Paraphrase:

3. Joan McCord, co-chairwoman of the National Academy of Sciences panel that issued a stinging report on DARE this week, is one of the people who is concerned about the program hurting the children who participate.

   Paraphrase:

4. Ten years ago, David Warm bulldozed cherry fields into fairways. He painted clubhouse walls and built sand traps with his father, helping open one of northern Michigan's scores of picturesque golf courses.

   Paraphrase:

5. Checking players' weight after practice and the following day to monitor excessive weight loss, and taking mandatory rest breaks in the shade and water breaks during practice and at needed intervals are essential to help prevent heatstroke.

   Paraphrase:

6. Rollovers make up a small fraction of all accidents but are responsible for a disproportionate number of deaths, particularly in S.U.V.'s.

   Paraphrase:

7. Few, if any, countries have adapted notions like automation and virtual reality so widely or embraced them so fully as Japan, where animated films, for example, are consistently the biggest hits.

   Paraphrase:

8. While most fancy new gadgets tend to be embraced first by the young, Aibo, the virtual pet, is most popular among lonely elderly people, a category that abounds in Japan.

   Paraphrase:

9. Company officials envision a day when household companions will be sold that can fetch a beer or the newspaper, or even cook a meal.

   Paraphrase:

10. With the arrival of huge dust storms for the third consecutive year, Koreans have begun to grimly resign themselves to the addition of an unwelcome fifth season—already dubbed the season of yellow dust—to the usual four seasons that any temperate country knows.

    Paraphrase:

SUMMARY

A summary is a snapshot of what you have read. You summarize to capture the main idea or the important details of a story. The same rules apply in both paraphrase and summary: use your own words and keep it short.

Copyright © 2007, The McGraw-Hill Companies, Inc. All rights reserved.

Capturing the Main Idea

Capturing the main idea involves selection: you make a choice about what is most important in the work you're summarizing. A rule to guide you in this selection process is to look for general rather than specific details. It's like describing a spectacular touchdown in a football game: you probably wouldn't dwell on a block on the line of scrimmage, but you would instead focus on the runner going into the end zone.

EXERCISE 10.3

Read the following paragraphs from "How Gum Began," from the Wrigley Company, and capture the most important ideas or actions. For each paragraph, write no more than two sentences of summary. For some paragraphs, one sentence will be sufficient.

EXAMPLE: Who was the first person to chew gum? Where was chewing gum invented? No one can be absolutely certain who the first gum chewers were, but historians tell us that civilizations around the world were chewing natural gum thousands of years ago. Before the invention of the electric light bulb, the telephone or even soda pop, people discovered the pleasure and benefits of chewing gum.

Paraphrase: People have chewed gum for thousands of years.

1. In A.D. 50, ancient Greeks were believed to chew mastiche, tree resin from the mastic tree. Researchers also discovered that the Mayans, an Indian civilization that inhabited Central America during the second century, enjoyed chewing chicle. This natural gum comes from the latex of the Sapodilla tree and later became the main ingredient in chewing gum.
   Paraphrase:

2. The American Indians discovered another natural form of gum-like resin by cutting the bark of spruce trees. They introduced the custom of chewing spruce gum to the early North American settlers. These savvy New Englanders created the first commercial chewing gum by selling and trading lumps of spruce. Spruce gum continued to be sold in 19th century America until the 1850s when paraffin wax became the new popular base for chewing gum.
   Paraphrase:

3. Modern chewing gum products appeared in 1869. Mexican General Antonio Lopez de Santa Anna, conqueror of the Alamo, hired New York inventor Thomas Adams to develop a new form of rubber using chicle. Chicle is the same gummy substance people in Mexico had been chewing for centuries. Adams was unsuccessful in developing rubber, but he did succeed in producing the first modern chewing gum. He called it Adams New York No. 1.
   Paraphrase:

4. Gum made with chicle and similar latexes soon became more popular than spruce gum or paraffin gum. Chicle-base chewing gum was smoother, softer and held its flavor better than any previous type of chewing gum. By the 1900s chewing gum was manufactured in many different shapes and sizes (long pencil-shaped sticks, ball form, flat sticks and blocks) and flavors (peppermint, fruit and spearmint).

Copyright © 2007, The McGraw-Hill Companies, Inc. All rights reserved.

EXERCISE 10.3 continued

Paraphrase:

5. Bubble gum was invented in 1928 by Walter Diemer, a cost analyst for the Fleer Company. Many people had tried for years to develop a gum that could be blown into bubbles, but it was Mr. Diemer, a young man who knew nothing about chemistry, who found the right combination of ingredients and created a gum that was strong enough and elastic enough to stretch when filled with air.
Paraphrase:

6. Today, synthetic materials replace natural gum ingredients to create a chewing gum with better quality, texture and taste. There are more than 1,000 varieties of gum manufactured and sold in the United States. You can find gum filled with liquid or speckled with crystals; gum that won't stick or is made without sugar; gum with wild flavor combinations like mango and watermelon or gum in crazy shapes like long rolls of tape.
Paraphrase:

7. Whatever your preference, there is a gum for you!
Paraphrase:

Capturing the Details

To summarize a piece of writing, you need to identify the important details that support the main point. A summary of a story, for example, would include what happened, where and when, who was involved, and the outcome.

EXERCISE 10.4

Read the following news stories and write a summary. Your summary should provide an overview of what happened, when and where, who was involved, and what the outcome was. Underline a few sentences or place check marks in the margin next to the details that help you answer these questions. Then compose your summary. Your summary should be no longer than six sentences.

EXAMPLE:

READING: from "Lives Changed in a Split Second," by Charles Wheelan

Until the early morning hours of January 3, my wife and <u>I had many reasons to drive a sport utility vehicle</u>. As our only car, it offered space for our two children, the dog, and the things we hauled around, like the Christmas tree. We like being in a big vehicle with a high vantage point in a city full of crazy drivers. Since we take public transportation to work and don't drive much, we could rationalize away the bad gas mileage and the high emissions. And to be honest, an S.U.V. projected a different image than a minivan or station wagon.

✓   But our Ford Explorer felt a lot less practical as <u>we lay smashed upside down in it on Interstate 80 at 4:00 a.m. last Wednesday</u>. <u>My wife was trapped in the passenger seat</u>. Our two daughters hung from their car seats, screaming. The dog was silent. <u>After skidding on a patch of ice, the truck flipped</u> and slid across the median to within a foot of traffic going 65 m.p.h. in the other direction.

EXERCISE 10.4 continued

I learned a lot of things very quickly. Each of our girls screams in a slightly different way, and I now know that it is a good thing to hear both screams coming from inside a crushed vehicle—because it means that everyone is alive. I learned that I can unhook a child from a car seat upside down in the dark with hands so cold that they have lost nearly all sensation. I know that when there is no other way to get a six-month-old out of a crushed vehicle sitting dangerously close to traffic, you will drag her through broken glass. I learned that strangers will stop in the middle the night and practice remarkable acts of kindness, including searching through the wreckage for a missing finger.

✓ In the grand scheme of things, we're in a great shape. <u>My three-year-old daughter's hand was smashed, and she has lost her right thumb</u>. I don't want to minimize the challenges she faces, but I often visualize the range of possible outcomes, and this one was very, very good.

Rollovers make up a small fraction of all accidents but are responsible for a disproportionate number of deaths, particularly in S.U.V.'s. And this week the National Highway Traffic Safety Administration gave the Ford Explorer two stars out of a possible five—meaning a 30 to 40 percent chance of flipping in an accident, compared to a less than 10 percent chance for a vehicle with a five-star rating.

✓ Even without the new data, <u>I should have known better</u>. I have followed the Ford Explorer story and have even written about it. True, our truck did not have Firestone tires. Our family was riding on the "good tires"; Ford even sent us a letter to tell us that. But I should have recognized that the tire issue masked the more fundamental problem: S.U.V.'s as a class are more likely to roll over than other vehicles. Indeed, the problem is inherent in vehicles that ride high on a relatively narrow wheel base, which is the most attractive feature of S.U.V.'s.

I do not believe that my family is alive because we were in a big truck. <u>We are alive because of seat belts and car seats</u>. (I will never fully understand how the dog made it, but he did.) I believe that a car with a lower center of gravity would not have been so likely to skid on an icy road, nor would it have flipped so easily when we hit deep snow on the median. Can that be proved in this case? Maybe.

Ford has redesigned the 2002 Explorer to make it less likely to flip and has been eager to settle rollover suits with people involved in far worse accidents than ours in earlier models, including one settled this week involving a Texas woman who was left a quadriplegic. I now know how quickly a rollover can happen.

✓ <u>I never should have put my family in that truck or any other like it</u>.

Summary: Charles Wheelan and his wife drove a Ford Explorer because it was practical. Then came a terrible accident. On a Wednesday morning, around 4:00 a.m., the car skidded on ice and rolled over, trapping Wheelan, his wife, and children in the car. In the end, no one was killed or horribly injured, although his daughter lost a finger. The incident reminded Wheelan that SUVs are not safe, something he already knew but chose to ignore. He believes seat belts and car seats saved his family from harm and regrets ever putting his family at risk by driving an SUV.

Copyright © 2007, The McGraw-Hill Companies, Inc. All rights reserved.

EXERCISE 10.4
continued

READING: from "A Deadly Toll Is Haunting Football," by Ira Berkow

More than 1000 mourners were expected to file into the Cathedral of St. John the Evangelist on St. John Street in Lafayette, La., this morning to pay final tribute to Eraste Thomas Autin, 18, a local high school football hero who died Wednesday.

It was six days after he had collapsed in 102 degree heat following a voluntary freshman workout at the University of Florida—voluntary, that is, under the NCAA rules, for official workouts are not supposed to begin for another two weeks. He had been in a coma since July 19.

Autin, heavily recruited out of St. Thomas More High School, had accepted a football scholarship to Florida. He planned to major in pre-med and follow in the footsteps of his father, Dr. David Autin. Eraste Autin had been a good student in high school, but he was also a talented athlete. At 6-foot-2, 250 pounds, he played fullback and, it was said, had a shot at starting at that position for the Gators.

Autin's was the second college football related death in the state in the last five months. In February, DeVaughn Darling, a Florida State linebacker, also collapsed and died after a so-called voluntary workout during the off-season. He was, like Autin, 18 years old and a freshman.

The coroner's report on Autin stated that he died from complications of heatstroke. An autopsy on Darling, who died after arduous indoor agility drills, found no definitive cause, although the autopsy also reported that a rare sickle-cell trait may have played a role.

Nonetheless, Autin is the 18th high school or college player since 1995 to die from heatstroke, Dr. Fred Mueller of the University of North Carolina sports medicine department tracks these statistics.

"It shouldn't be," he said, regarding the number of football deaths by heatstroke. "There has to be more done to prevent these tragedies, and there can be. I think most are preventable."

Mueller said that such deaths reached a high of eight in one year, in 1970, and then began to decrease.

"For a number of years, there were no deaths at all," he said, "but in the last seven years they've begun to creep back up again."

Checking players' weight after practice and the following day to monitor excessive weight loss, and taking mandatory rest breaks in the shade and water breaks during practice and at needed intervals, he said, are essential to help prevent heatstroke. "Many kids don't want to do this," he said, "so someone has got to be watching."

Mueller also wondered what voluntary really meant.

"I teach a class with football players," he said, "and there's a concern about voluntary practice: if you don't show up, it hardly helps your chances of making the football team, or playing more."

Jeremy Foley, the Florida athletic director, seemed to agree.

"It's a two-edged sword," he said. "You want to get players in shape for the official workouts. On the other hand, you don't want to overwork them, but no matter what you do, many of them are so highly motivated—and concerned for their spot in the team—that they'll work out on their own if they have to."

Foley said, yes, there were rest breaks, that water was plentiful and available, and that six coaches were on the field at all times. "Eraste was a hard-working, dedicated kid who was in excellent physical shape," Foley said. "He didn't stumble around on the field, he showed no signs of distress.

Autin's death may or may not be one of the mysteries of life. His mother, Joanie, said there was no reason to believe there was danger, since Eraste had practiced in the heat of Louisiana summers throughout his junior high school and high school years. "He was never sick," she said.

In Mueller's view, however, the overall reasons for the rise in deaths of high school and college football players due to heatstroke can be guessed.

"Proper precautions," he said, "have apparently been relaxed."

The pressures of football, the macho element in football, surely seem to contribute to relaxing such precautions.

An added suggestion here is that twice a year, the team doctor on every high school and college team read to his players and coaches and school administrators the names of the football dead in recent years, and describe the circumstances. Maybe also run a film of Eraste Autin's funeral.

Morbid? Possibly. But lifesaving, possibly, too.

Summary:

READING: from "Golf Course's Closure Meant to Save Land," by Lori Hall Steele

Ten years ago, David Warm bulldozed cherry fields into fairways. He painted clubhouse walls and built sand traps with his father, helping open one of northern Michigan's scores of picturesque golf courses.

Now, he's defecting from northern Michigan's fairway freeway. This will be the last season for his 18-hole Matheson Greens Golf Course.

Next year, the 290-acre family-owned links, estimated to be worth at least $2.5 million, will start reverting to the wild in a conservation easement.

"This sends a message that people's relationship to the land is much deeper and stronger than we sometimes realize," said Brian Price, director of the Leelanau Conservancy that is working with Warm. "Yes, golf attracts people. But what keeps them coming back is really the beauty of our natural environment."

Warm, 33, made the decision to close the course after he tried for 18 months to sell it. He found interest only from those who wanted to intensely develop the property with condominiums or homes on the hills southwest of Northport.

Copyright © 2007, The McGraw-Hill Companies, Inc. All rights reserved.

EXERCISE 10.4 continued

"I grew up on this land. I wouldn't want to throw a development next to my neighbors' or my own door," said Warm, a partner in the Ada-based Peninsula Oil and Gas Co. "This is a statement about what we value. We value open land."

The conservancy is working with Warm to create a preservation plan, which may include public access. Final details of the easement are pending. Warm's family would retain the deed, but development likely would be prohibited.

Putting the land in a conservation easement has tax benefits, Warm said, but nothing like what he could make by selling the property. His family's other income allows them to make the choice, he said.

Warm and his family, who bought the property in 1971 and moved there in 1979, also are conserving 90 adjacent privately owned acres. The property contains wetlands and is home to coyotes, foxes and deer. Eagles and black bears have been spotted nearby, said Brian Price, the conservancy's director.

Matheson Greens opened in 1991, and Warm took over full management after his father's death in 1995.

Leelanau County officials value the golf course at $1.1 million for taxation purposes. But Suttons Bay real estate agent Cory Beuerle said, "It's worth way more" and estimated the course's value to be about $2.5 million.

"It's a very generous thing they're doing," she said. "We're not used to seeing people give up an investment."

Dick Haughton, president of McKay Golf Properties, a Lansing-based national golf course real estate brokerage and appraisal firm, said developing a quality 18-hole golf course today could cost from $2.5 million to $5 million or more.

And *Golf Digest* magazine has given Matheson Greens a best-value four-star rating.

"This is a noble decision," said Mike Grant, of the Traverse City–based Northern Michigan Environmental Action Council.

For the past five years, Michigan has led the nation in new golf course openings. Last year, 30 courses opened, and the state now has more public links—nearly 800—than any other state, said Susy Avery, director of Travel Michigan.

More than 160 courses operate in the northern Lower Peninsula.

Summary:

Providing an Overview

EXERCISE 10.5

Read the following short essays and place check marks in the margin next to the important points. Then compose a short summary in which you state the main points in your own words. Do not make more than four check marks in the margin. Your summary should be no longer than six sentences.

EXERCISE 10.5 continued

EXAMPLE:

READING: from "Housework Still Women's Work" (from applesforhealth.com)

✓   We may have come a long way baby, but the latest Voices of Women opinion poll suggests we still have a long way to go. Sixty-one percent of the women questioned for the survey—to be released Friday in Chicago—were employed. But 41 percent said they think their spouses assume housework is women's work, and 36 percent feel guilty for not getting all the housework done.

✓   More than 80 percent of the 2,177 women and 826 men surveyed say it's acceptable for men and women to share the household chores and child-rearing responsibilities when both spouses work. However, women still do 76 percent of the laundry, 76 percent of ironing, 71 percent of routine cleaning, 67 percent of the cooking, 58 percent of the carpooling of children, 58 percent of the grocery shopping and 56 percent of taking children to friends' homes. The only jobs that were evenly split were planning the family vacation and making investment decisions. The survey found men have responsibility for doing the household repairs (59 percent) and having the car serviced (57 percent).

✓   Although a majority of women say a satisfying life must include marriage, career and children, the stress of trying to pursue all three at the same time leads to a lower degree of satisfaction. Things may be changing, however. The survey found men are beginning to share the same attitudes toward work as women—with like percentages seeking flexible work hours and the ability to work from home.

> Summary: *Women with jobs are still expected to do most of the housework. Men and women both say the idea of sharing housework and child-care responsibilities is acceptable. In practice, however, a Voices of Women poll shows that wives and mothers who work do most of the housework and experience a lot of stress as a result.*

READING: from "Just Say No to DARE," by Dawn MacKeen

For nearly two decades, the majority of schoolchildren in the United States have been required to memorize three little words: "Just say no." They have been taught that dabbling with drugs even once can harm you, that peer pressure to use drugs is a lurking menace to be dodged and rejected at all costs. They have written thousands of essays decrying drug use, and worn T-shirts, hats, ribbons and badges to ward off the encroaching threat of narcotics.

But the days of "Just say no" may just be over. Leaders of the nation's largest drug prevention program, Drug Abuse Resistance Education, announced on Thursday that they were changing DARE's approach, admitting that the vastly expensive program appears to be ineffective. Indeed, research has indicated that DARE may actually have contributed to greater drug use by high school students.

DARE administrators announced that the program will adopt a new strategy for school-based drug prevention, and begin testing it in 80 high schools and 176 middle schools in the fall. Around 50,000 students will be involved.

Destinations: Staying on Course with Quotation, Summary, and Paraphrase

Summary: A Key to Understanding

Summarizing is a valuable skill, in and out of the classroom. The plot summary of a movie, say, or the summary of an interesting magazine article you read, could come in handy in a casual conversation. If you encounter something you know you'll want to explain or otherwise use later, in writing or in person, consciously identifying and reviewing main ideas, key details, and impressions can enhance your memory and understanding of anything from a news item to a long, involved novel.

Avoid Plagiarism: Quote, Quote, Quote!

The process of finding and correctly documenting quotes and other information is necessary to avoid *plagiarism*. Plagiarism, which has serious ethical and legal repercussions, means taking credit for someone else's work. Using someone else's exact language without giving that person credit is considered plagiarism, but so is paraphrase (putting their thoughts in your own words), if it is not properly attributed. When you document your sources with internal cita-

tions and put together a "Works Cited" page, you give credit where credit is due and inform your reader that specific material in your paper belongs to specific sources.

In Other Words: The Art of Paraphrasing

At some jobs, you will be given instructions that, at first, you may not be entirely sure you understand. In these situations, it is sometimes helpful to ask a question by paraphrasing or summarizing what your supervisor has just said. For example, instead of asking for a re-explanation, you might say, "So I need to make two photocopies of the file: One to keep in the office, and one to send out to the client. Is that right?" By paraphrasing an instruction, you will be able to quickly pinpoint whether you have correctly understood your assignment.

EXERCISE 10.5 continued

"The new curriculum gives students the skills to make positive, quality-of-life decisions," reads DARE's press release. "It also discusses the conditions leading up to violent behavior, how to identify potentially violent situations, and some basic ways to avoid or defuse such situations."

Critics of DARE say the time is long overdue to dismantle the program and make sure, before exposing children to it, that it is not only effective but, most important, not harmful. They also worry that these changes, like much-heralded changes in the past, will not be significant enough to completely revamp the failing program.

Joan McCord, co-chairwoman of the National Academy of Sciences panel that issued a stinging report on DARE this week, is one of the people who is concerned about the program hurting the children who participate.

"It's a mistake to assume that you can simply design a program and know in advance whether it will be harmful," says McCord. "I think of those who created thalidomide. They had good intentions, and look what happened. The harm comes from the failure of programs and programs must be evaluated for safety."

She and others assert that politics is what has kept the much-criticized program around for so many years, despite a mountain of evidence contesting its efficacy.

Don Lynam, who issued a report two years ago questioning the effectiveness of DARE, feels vindicated after Thursday's announcement. But he fears that the new DARE program won't depart enough from its old curriculum.

Copyright © 2007, The McGraw-Hill Companies, Inc. All rights reserved.

EXERCISE 10.5 continued

Summary:

READING: from "Toy Story: Looking for Lessons," by Lisa Guernsey

On the Tuesday before Christmas, parents with good intentions were swarming through the second floor of the Toys "R" Us store in Times Square.

There, amid columns of bright green plastic and the flashing headlights of a singing school bus, were shelves of products by LeapFrog Enterprises, a company based in Emeryville, Calif., that in six years has become one of the fastest-growing toy makers in the nation. Its best-selling product is the LeapPad, an electronic talking book that some analysts say is even outselling Harry Potter merchandise.

"We like to buy things that are learning-based, more than just toys," said Dianne Chodaczek of Riverside, Conn., as she made her way out of the crowd with a $49.99 LeapPad tucked under her arm. She said she had come on an errand for her grown daughter, who had already bought a LeapPad for her 4-year-old son and had decided to get one for her 6-year-old son, too.

"They were out of them in her town in New Jersey," said Ms. Chodaczek before dashing for the checkout line.

Some parents may cringe at the notion of pricey electronics' becoming more popular than Play-Doh. But LeapFrog is bounding ahead, propelled by the financial muscle of its majority owner, the global education conglomerate Knowledge Universe. Founded in part by Michael R. Milken, the former junk-bond trader who has recently focused on educational projects, Knowledge Universe has enabled LeapFrog to run multiple television commercials for its products and to spread its gospel by paying calls on influential education experts.

LeapFrog has joined other companies like Educational Insights and VTech in the winning combination of coupling technology with that word that parents love to hear: educational.

By taking advantage of ever smaller chip sizes and improved speech synthesis, electronic toys like the LeapPad, the Piccolo Touch and Talk Interactive Discovery Center and Alphabert & Sprocket unite two factors that most educators see as integral to the learning process. They are multisensory, combining elements that children can see, hear and touch, and they are interactive, enabling children to take charge of their play instead of passively receiving whatever stimuli are beamed their way.

With the LeapPad, for example, a child has to merely touch the word "cat" with a stylus and the machine will say the word. Other words and buttons trigger the start of stories or word games or specific sounds. The idea is that by hearing a word while seeing and touching it, children will get a leg up in learning to read. Children a few years older—ages 7 and 8—are encouraged to use the LeapPad Pro, a $64.99 product that does not recite stories but does pronounce new vocabulary words.

Copyright © 2007, The McGraw-Hill Companies, Inc. All rights reserved.

EXERCISE 10.5 continued

"They can pick up a LeapPad, pick out a book and read on their own," said Mike Wood, LeapFrog's founder and president. But while the word "educational" may be splashed across their packaging, no broad studies have been done to assess whether these toys actually teach anything, something even the manufacturers acknowledge.

"I can't imagine that these toys make much of a difference," said Alison Gopnik, a psychologist and child-development expert at the University of California at Berkeley who wrote "The Scientist in the Crib: Minds, Brains and How Children Learn" (William Morrow, 1999). "Especially not as much as sitting children down on a sofa with some hot chocolate and reading a good story."

So far, research on such toys has consisted only of small experiments. LeapFrog says its tests showed reading improvement among children who use its literacy products in school settings. And teachers reported that two class groups using two Educational Insights products, the MathShark and the LaunchPad, showed significant gains in math and reading. But again, the sample sizes were too small to yield general conclusions.

Summary:

READING: from **"A Green Light for Sinful Drivers: It's Election Time,"** by Suzanne Daley

What do traffic violations have to do with a presidential election?

In France, a great deal.

Political tradition dictates that whoever is elected makes his first decree an amnesty on traffic fines.

Parisians have been turning creative parking into an art form lately, gambling that the winner this year will once again annul fines worth millions of dollars.

"It is just a way of saying thank you for voting for me," said Laetitia Contri, the owner of a Honda Civic, who has accumulated 10 parking tickets so far this year. "I wouldn't vote for someone just because he promised to do it, but I would like him better."

Charles de Gaulle was the first to wipe the slate clean, in 1965. Pretty much everybody thought it was a grand idea. But since then, road safety advocates have grown more and move vocal, saying a surprise amnesty is different from one that everyone expected. These critics say that a pattern has developed, with people driving any way they please during an election year.

This year, even the country's mayors joined the chorus against the amnesty. They contend that it is already hard enough to regulate circulation on French roads without having to deal with the effects of such presidential magnanimity.

"This thing is from another era, and it just makes our job more difficult," said Pierre Herisson, a vice president of the Association of French Mayors. "People have absolutely no respect for the rules during an election year. We think it's time it was abolished."

Some road safety advocates say there is a clear correlation between road deaths and elections. Claude Got, the vice president of the European Center for Safety Studies and Risk Analysis in Paris and an adviser to the National Road Safety Council, says that road deaths rose sharply before François Mitterrand's re-election in 1988 and in the seven months leading up to President Jacques Chirac's election in 1995.

"Some 600 people died because of the elections," said Mr. Got recently. "Who can reasonably endorse these amnesties?"

Three of France's largest road safety groups have banded together to circulate a petition to stop the practice. "This tradition really belongs in oblivion," said Pierre Gustin, a spokesman for one of the groups, the 200,000-member Road Safety Association. "It seems like something from the Middle Ages when you bought indulgences. It drives people to do whatever they want on the road for a year. It's time for the politicians to say enough."

Not everyone agrees that a connection is so clear. Jean Orselli, an engineer at the Ministry of Public works, calls Mr. Got's conclusions naïve. He says there are vacillations in the number of road deaths about every 18 months, though the general trend is sharply down. He sees nothing wrong with the amnesty.

"The president of the United States gives amnesties too," he said. "Such gestures have a role. You see them in every society. It helps form a social cohesion. It teaches us to pardon one another. The question goes far beyond road safety.

"You cannot tell me that some drunk is going to drink and drive more because of an amnesty. Or that someone who doesn't drink is going to start drinking."

France's leading candidates for the presidency, Mr. Chirac, a conservative, and Prime Minister Lionel Jospin, a Socialist, appear ready to try to please both sides.

Summary:

READING: from "Tree Rings Show a Period of Widespread Warming in
                 Medieval Age," by Kenneth Chang

A new study of old tree rings shows that 1,000 years ago, long before power plants and sport utility vehicles, temperatures across North America, Europe and Asia rose in a period of unusual warmth.

In warm weather, trees thrive and grow a thick ring of wood in their trunks for that year. In cold years, growth slows and the tree ring is thin.

Temperatures were known to be warm in Europe between 900 and 1100, what is known as the Medieval Warm Period. Collecting wood samples in 14 locations

EXERCISE 10.5 continued

that cover a swath of the globe from New Orleans north to the top of Alaska, researchers from Columbia University's Lamont-Doherty Earth Observatory and the Swiss Federal Research Institute found evidence that the warm temperatures extended to much of the Northern Hemisphere.

Writing in the current issue of the journal *Science*, the scientists say the data demonstrate that temperatures naturally rise and fall over the centuries. The scientists, however, add that their data do not argue against the view that artificial emissions—so-called greenhouse gases—have set off the global warming of recent decades.

"I never intended or meant to imply that that's the case," said Dr. Edward R. Cook, an author of the *Science* paper and an expert at Lamont-Doherty on reconstructing climate from tree rings.

Greenhouse gases like carbon dioxide from factories and cars trap heat in the atmosphere. Globally, temperatures have risen about 1 degree Fahrenheit over the last century.

Although the climate has repeatedly swung between warm and cold over the Earth's 4.5-billion-year history, the usual interpretation is that the climate has been quite stable since the end of the last ice age 10,000 years ago.

"This record suggests that the amplitude of natural variability is larger than the other records have suggested in the past," Dr. Cook said.

The data may help scientists refine their climate models to provide better predictions of future warming.

An earlier reconstruction of temperatures over the past millennium by Dr. Michael E. Mann, a professor of environmental sciences at the University of Virginia, found a much smaller temperature rise in the Medieval Warm Period, but the different numbers do not necessarily contradict each other.

Dr. Mann's data covered the entire Northern Hemisphere—in addition to tree rings, he included other indicators of past temperature like coral reefs and ice cores from Greenland. Temperatures in the tropics vary much less than those in the higher latitudes, he said.

Because the authors of the *Science* paper averaged their data over 40 years to smooth out year-to-year fluctuations, their temperature curve does not reflect the most recent warming.

"They've kind of smoothed out the record," Dr. Mann said. "It doesn't support the conclusion that the medieval warmth was comparable to the latter 20th century warmth."

Rather, the peak temperatures in the Medieval Warm Period are similar to those seen in the first half of the 20th century, and that warming, most scientists agree, was induced naturally, by a brightening of the sun.

Summary:

Copyright © 2007, The McGraw-Hill Companies, Inc. All rights reserved.

EXERCISE 10.5
continued

READING: from "Two Portraits of Children of Divorce: Rosy and Dark," by Mary Duenwald

Divorce often hurts children, everyone agrees. It can cause great pain, anger, anxiety, confusion and behavior problems in the first couple of years after the breakup. And for some it leads to lasting anxiety, insecurity and fear of having close relationships with other people.

Most children recover, though it may take years, and go on to find happiness and success in marriage, work and life. Experts agree about that, too.

But from this general accord arises a heated dispute between those who emphasize the pain and those who think more attention should be paid to the children's recovery.

Dr. E. Mavis Hetherington, emeritus professor of psychology at the University of Virginia, has recently accentuated the more positive prognosis for children of divorce with the publication of her new book, "For Better or for Worse: Divorce Reconsidered," written with John Kelly and published in January by Norton.

And in doing so, she has brought this long-running argument among social scientists back into the public spotlight.

"Divorcing is a high-risk situation," Dr. Hetherington said. "But most kids are able to adapt. They're resilient in the long run."

Her studies over the past 30 years have found that 20 percent to 25 percent of children whose parents divorce are at risk for lifelong emotional or behavioral problems, compared with only 10 percent of children whose parents stay married.

"Now, that twofold increase is not to be taken lightly," Dr. Hetherington said. "It's larger than the association between smoking and cancer. But it also means that 75 to 80 percent are functioning in the normal range, and some are functioning remarkably well."

The other side of the debate is represented by Dr. Judith S. Wallerstein, a co-author of "The Unexpected Legacy of Divorce: A 25-Year Landmark Study" (Hyperion, 2000), written with Dr. Julia M. Lewis and Sandra Blakeslee, a contributing science writer for the *New York Times*. The book concentrates on how children of divorce struggle with loneliness and anxiety, especially over love and commitment.

Dr. Wallerstein found that children of divorce, after suffering the breakups and then growing up in fragmented families, end up ill prepared to form their own intimate relationships.

"I am not saying these young people don't recover," Dr. Wallerstein said. "I'm saying they come to adulthood burdened, frightened and worried about failure. They want love. They want commitment. They want what everybody else wants. But they're very afraid they'll never get it."

The differences between the two researchers are partly of the half-full or half-empty kind. "We're not against each other," Dr. Hetherington said. "When I read Judy's books, I always learn something. But you know Judy has a gloom and doom approach to divorce."

Copyright © 2007, The McGraw-Hill Companies, Inc. All rights reserved.

Exercise 10.5 continued

"I don't have a gloom and doom approach," Dr. Wallerstein responded, "but I do think we've underestimated the cost on the child."

Their differences also have to do with how the researchers went about their work. Each spent the past three decades studying white middle-class families, mainly those that broke apart in the early 1970's, when the divorce rate was taking its last giant step to 50 percent of all marriages.

Summary:

**Plagiarism
Commas
Quotation Marks**

QUOTATION

A well-chosen quotation can add both authority and color to your writing, but it must be both skillfully introduced and properly identified in order to be a real asset.

Introducing Quotations

For the sake of variety, learn to use both **partial quotes** and **complete quotes**. A partial quote is a phrase you build a sentence around; a complete quote is a grammatical sentence that begins with a capital letter and ends with a period.

> **Original** (from the *Washington Post* 24 Aug. 1986, C1+): As many as two-thirds of America's high-school juniors and seniors now hold down part-time paying jobs, according to studies. Many of these are in fast-food chains, of which McDonalds is the pioneer, trend-setter and symbol.
>
> **Partial quote:** The *Washington Post* reports that a large number of high school students work at fast-food restaurants and that McDonald's serves as "the pioneer, trend-setter and symbol."
>
> **Complete quote:** Many high school students work part-time jobs. According to the *Washington Post*, "Many of these are in fast-food chains, of which McDonalds is the pioneer, trend-setter and symbol."

	Punctuation	Capitalization
Partial Quote	No comma before the quote	No capital necessary unless first word in quote is a proper noun
Complete Quote	Comma or colon before the quote	Capitalize first word of quote

All quotes must be identified in some manner. In the following section, "Documenting Quotations," we will briefly look at the Modern Language Association's system, a formal method of identifying quotations. For now, though, we will look at a less formal means of identifying the author or source of a quote:

1. In the case of a magazine or newspaper article, identify the name of the publication and the author, if there is one.

2. Identify authors and speakers by name and include a phrase describing their credentials:

Bernard P. Horn, political director for the National Coalition Against Legalized Gambling, observes, "The American Psychiatric Association and the American Medical Association recognize pathological gambling as a diagnosable mental disorder."

Atlanta psychologist Michael White says, "What we love is the illusion of danger. Because of safety regulations, we know roller coasters are not really dangerous."

If you include a second quote by the same author or speaker, use that person's last name only:

Horn adds that gambling problems in the United States are reaching "epidemic proportions."

Most people at amusement parks, White points out, "flock to roller coasters like moths to flame."

3. Identify an author by name and refer to the article, essay, or book you are quoting:

Frances Mayes says of her home in *Under the Tuscan Sun,* "Much of the restoration we did ourselves, an accomplishment, as my grandfather would say, out of the fullness of our ignorance."

In *Dakota: A Spiritual Biography,* Kathleen Norris appreciates "the harsh beauty of a land that rolls like the ocean floor it once was, where dry winds scour out buttes, and the temperature can reach 110 degrees or plunge to 30 degrees below zero for a week or more."

EXERCISE 10.6

Read the following short excerpts. Select a partial quote and a complete quote, and write them in the space provided.

1. (From *Days of Atonement,* by Richard Rodriguez) Something hopeful was created in California through the century of its Protestant development. People believed that in California they could begin new lives. New generations of immigrants continue to arrive in California, not a few of them from Mexico, hoping to cash in on comedy. It is still possible in California to change your name, change your sex, get a divorce, become a movie star. My Mexican parents live in a house with four telephones, three televisions, and several empty bedrooms.

Partial quote:

Complete quote:

2. (From the *New York Times*) There is still no sexual equality in comedy. For women, historically too easily despised and made the butt of the jokes, the victory is in pulling off a comic character that is both laughable and laudable: Lucy Ricardo in the 50's, Mary Richards in the 70's, and Carrie Bradshaw in the 90's. For men, humor lies in blurring the line between lovable and loathsome: Ralph Kramden, Archie Bunker, and now Larry David.

Copyright © 2007, The McGraw-Hill Companies, Inc. All rights reserved.

EXERCISE 10.6 continued

Partial quote:

Complete quote:

3. (From *Galileo's Daugher,* by Dava Sobel) December 1615 thus brought Galileo to Rome brandishing new support for Copernicus—derived from observations of the Earth, not the heavens. The tidal motions of the great oceans, Galileo believed, bore constant witness that the planet really did spin through space. If the Earth stood still, then what could make its water rush to and fro, rising and falling at regular intervals along the coasts?

Partial quote:

Complete quote:

EXERCISE 10.7

Scan several articles from a newspaper or a news magazine. Find at least five examples each of partial quotes and complete quotes. Copy them exactly as they appear in the article you select, and cite the source.

EXAMPLE:

Partial quote: *Mr. Kaplan is "a superb craftsman, someone working on an important subject and doing justice to it," said Robert Darnton, a Princeton historian who specializes in seventeenth- and eighteenth-century France.*

Complete quote: *Roger Chartier, a French cultural historian and visiting professor at the University of Pennsylvania, said, "He has a very profound, deep knowledge of the archives."*

Source: *Deborah Baldwin. "Helping an Old French Art Rise." New York Times 27 Nov. 2003: A15+.*

Documenting Quotations

Identifying the source of quotations is a legitimate and useful form of name-dropping. Documenting a quote—that is, providing the location where a quote can be found—allows your readers to look it up and (if they like) read further on the topic.

The rules for documenting sources vary, but many college courses use the system developed by the Modern Language Association (MLA). Essentially, this is a two-part process: in the body of the paper itself, you briefly identify the source and the page number on which you found the quote; and in a "works cited" section appended to your paper, you provide more detailed information about where and when the source of the quotation was published.

Here, we will concern ourselves only with the information provided in the body of the paper itself. (For information on "works cited" and more on MLA documentation, see Chapter 11, "Finding and Using Sources.")

Original: (from *Discover* magazine, June 2000, p. 21): Clinical trials for a memory-enhancing drug are just two to five yars away, say Jerry Yin and Tim Tully of Cold Spring Harbor Laboratory on Long Island, New York. At the center of their work is a protein that helps nerve cells in the brain store memories. A sudden increase in the activity levels of the protein sends the memory-making process into overdrive and allows neurons to make long-lasting storage structures immediately, without the slow work of repetition.

Partial quote: *Discover* magazine reports that memory improvement will involve "a protein that helps nerve cells in the brain store memories" (21).

Complete quote: According to *Discover* magazine, "Clinical trials for a memory-enhancing drug are just two to five years away" (21).

EXERCISE 10.8

Write a paragraph in which you list two or three examples of television's negative effects on children. Be sure to explain and elaborate on each example. Then read the following article. Select a quotation from the article to support a point you make in your paragraph. Revise your paragraph to include the quote (either partial or complete).

READING: from "Effects of TV on Kids Becoming Less Remote," by
Janet Kornblum (*USA Today*, 10 Nov. 2003, p. 9)

Every day, 2-year-old Marion Hall-Zazueta wakes up thinking about one thing: a video featuring Maisy, a lovable animated mouse. "It's the first thing she asks for in the morning," says her mom, Ilen Zazueta-Hall of Sebastopol, Calif. "We have to convince her to do other things." Usually, Marion watches about a half-hour of Maisy a day, but some days a half-hour turns into $1\frac{1}{2}$ hours.

Does that make Marion a mini couch potato, prone to the same types of problems, such as laziness and obesity, as adult couch potatoes? Probably not—as long as the viewing is moderate, experts say. But the truth is, says Ellen Wartella, dean of the College of Communication at the University of Texas–Austin, "We don't know the long-term consequences of such early media use, particularly electronic media use, on children's development." Wartella co-wrote a study in late October by the Kaiser Family Foundation that surprised even those who have hypothesized that babies and children are exposed to more media than ever before, including TV, computers, DVDs, videos and video games. The study found that 68% of Americans 2 and younger spend an average of two hours a day in front of a screen. And children under 6 spend as much time in front of electronic media as they do playing outside.

Other studies of children have linked TV with obesity and lower reading levels. Studies vary on effects of PC use. One recent study showed that children ages 4 to 13 who used computers up to eight hours a week had slightly improved reading levels. But when use topped eight hours a week, reading levels were the same as for kids who had no computer use, says Paul Attewell, sociology professor at City University of New York. In addition, the kids spending more time on PCs were heavier than kids who spent little or no time on the computer. It may be that larger, non-athletic kids are choosing to stay on the computer rather than playing outside, Attewell says. The cause and effect are not clear, but the study shows PC use can be beneficial in moderation and detrimental in excess, he says.

Copyright © 2007, The McGraw-Hill Companies, Inc. All rights reserved.

EXERCISE 10.8 continued

Moderation—and common sense—are key when figuring out how much TV and computer use to allow kids, says Daniel Anderson, professor of psychology at the University of Massachusetts–Amherst. Parents still should monitor what their kids watch and do their best to keep it to a minimum. But some, including the American Academy of Pediatrics, recommend that kids 2 and younger avoid TV and other screen media altogether. That is partly why the recent Kaiser study alarmed so many in the field. Though many studies have focused on habits of children, the Kaiser study is considered landmark because it looks into viewing habits of infants and toddlers, which has not been comprehensively studied before.

Preliminary numbers from the Kaiser study indicate there may be a correlation in very young kids between heavy TV watching and lower reading levels. Kids in homes where the TV is on nearly all the time—not necessarily being watched— tend to read less than others: 34% of 4- to 6-year-olds in heavy-TV homes can read, compared with 56% of those in homes that watch less TV. The numbers should be a "wake-up call that we better do some studies to find out the impact of such early screen viewing," Wartella says. "It's not just a few kids who are doing this. It's a lot."

Marion's father, Craig Hall, says he and his wife always have been careful about what their kids can view. They generally allow them to watch only videos and DVDs. His opinion on background TV changed when he and his wife were watching *The Godfather* five years ago. Their older daughter, Fiona, was only about 5 months old at the time and wasn't even watching. But she was in the room when an extremely violent scene was shown, and she became "inconsolable." "We said, 'This is clearly having a negative effect,'" Hall says.

Though experts can't say what the long-term consequences are of early media saturation, they can say that kids are affected, positively and negatively, by what they see on television, on the computer or anywhere else. They tend to imitate characters they see on TV or video games, so parents need to be mindful about exposure to negative characters. "Given that kids are watching TV a lot, it's critical that we continue as a society to develop more programming that is really aiming to support their development," says Stacey Matthias of Insight Research Group, a market research firm that has studied children and the media. "When kids are watching television that is appropriate to their age, it is used to enforce skills and knowledge that they're working on in the rest of their lives." But kids model themselves on TV, regardless of the content. "They are like sponges."

Like most parents, Melissa Alvarez, the mother of a 14-month-old, is doing her best to walk that tightrope. But it's not always easy. Alvarez, of Castro Valley, Calif., observed the effect of TV on kids as an au pair putting herself through college. She noticed that kids who watched a lot of TV tended to "have a lot more undirected, crazy energy." So she restricts her child's access, which includes encouraging her husband to keep the TV off.

"Sometimes it's a necessary evil. We all know what it feels like to come home and flip on our favorite TV show and just veg for an hour. It feels really good, and so it's really easy to do that for children," she says. "Unfortunately, easy isn't always the best way to go."

SUGGESTIONS FOR DAILY PRACTICE

1. At the end of class, write a short summary of the main points or activities covered.

2. Select a sentence from your textbook. Count the number of words. Write a paraphrase that restates the idea in half the number of words.

3. Select an article from the newspaper that interests you and write a short summary.

4. Keep a journal. Make journal entries that summarize your daily activities.

5. Write summaries of movies or television programs you find entertaining.

6. Find a newspaper or magazine article on a subject that interests you. Copy the article's quotations. Count the number of partial and complete quotes.

11 *Finding and Using Sources*

*H*ow do I find information on a subject that interests me—and then what do I do *with it?* If you're attending college today, you have an abundance of information at your fingertips. In fact, the Internet provides information in *such* abundance that it is easy to be overwhelmed by it.

Of course, all Internet sources are not alike; neither are they all equally credible. Traditional sources such as newspapers, magazines, periodicals, and books tend to be more reliable because the information in them has generally been checked by editors or other authorities. But this is not invariably the case—nor is it the case that everything on the Internet is worthless. For this reason, critical literacy means being *selective.* Careful college writers learn to evaluate all of their sources carefully and critically.

Once you've found trustworthy and relevant sources, however, your work has just begun. You still need to make good *use* of these sources in the following ways:

- Take notes to process information.
- Cite statistics and use quotes in your papers.
- Mention the names of authorities and institutions to show you have found reliable sources of information.
- Provide references so that a reader can consult your sources.

USING SOURCES

When you make good use of outside sources, you're able to think more deeply, by thinking *with* or *against* other writers about issues and ideas that matter to you. Effective use of source material—whether an interview or printed or electronic

Copyright © 2007, The McGraw-Hill Companies, Inc. All rights reserved.

material—places you in a community of learners. It is an essential skill in college writing.

As an example, here is a student essay on the negative effects of television. Dan has drawn on his personal experience and observation to explore the topic.

STUDENT MODEL

Dan's Edited Draft

Trouble with the Tube

They watch in the morning. Then they come home and watch after school. Don't forget every single night. Some kids even watch TV in bed. All this television can't be good for our young people of today. They could be reading or playing outside, exercising their imaginations, doing anything besides sitting there like zombies or couch potatoes watching the same darn show they have already seen twenty-five times. Nevertheless, that's the way it is nowadays. TV is a negative fact of life.

One problem with TV is it cuts in on school time. My sister is in the eleventh grade, and she is having a hard time in some of her classes. She brought home a terrible report card a few weeks ago. She does all of her homework sitting in front of the TV. Some nights I look at her and she isn't doing any homework at all. She is watching Friends reruns. When he saw her grade, my dad grounded her from TV. We'll see if it works.

Another problem with TV is the violence. It's either sex or violence every night. That's what sells. That's what people want to see. The trouble is, every time you turn on the news, you hear about an actual kid that got into trouble with violent crime. Look at Columbine. Those two guys walked into a school and opened fire just like it was a movie set. Only it was real kids, real blood on the floor, and all those parents grieving the loss of their kids. Look at the young people dealing drugs and shooting each other up in the streets. That probably wouldn't be happening if it weren't for TV. TV glamorizes violence.

Finally, the U.S. is fatter now than it has ever been before. It should come as no surprise. We sit on the couch and change channels with a remote, munching on the latest snack food advertised on the tube. I saw a bumper sticker the other day. "Kill your TV," it said. I agree. We would be better off without it, or at least with less of it.

This essay makes its point. However, Dan might want to read up on television's effects on kids and incorporate into his paper what some authorities have to say about the topic. Well-chosen statistics and quotations can transform a paper into a more authoritative statement on your subject. (At the end of this chapter is Dan's final edited essay, which illustrates how the use of source materials can help a writer support his or her viewpoint on a topic.)

WW Resources for Research

FINDING SOURCES

Searching the Internet

Internet searches are done with search engines. These powerful applications search literally hundreds of thousands of sites for key words that you supply.

INTERNET SEARCH ENGINES	
www.google.com	www.lycos.com
www.metacrawler.com	www.altavista.com

Because it is not uncommon to find thousands of Web sites that relate to your topic, you need to be as specific as possible in your searches. Follow this four-step process when you do an Internet search:

1. After accessing the search engine of your choice, enter key words that relate to your topic. To avoid an unreasonably large number of "hits," be as specific as possible and use as many terms in a single search as you think apply to your topic. *Tip:* If you precede each of your terms with "+" signs, a search engine like Google will return only sites that contain all of the specified terms (as opposed to one of the terms or a combination). Adding quotation marks to a phrase (say, "effects of television") will return only sites with that exact phrase:

   +"effects of television" +children +research

Results of a Google search on television's effects on kids. © 2004 Google, Inc. Used with permission.

2. Scan the list of sites your search engine returns. Look at the Internet addresses (URLs, or universal resource locators) of the Web sites to determine whether

Copyright © 2007, The McGraw-Hill Companies, Inc. All rights reserved.

Address ☐ http://www.screendigest.com/yp_99-05(1).htm

	issue
ABOUT US	
MONTHLY NEWSLETTER	
RESEARCH	**CHILDREN'S TELEVISION: A**
FILM / CINEMA	**globalised market**
TELEVISION	

· Europe's cable power players:
Consolidation prelude to growth
June 2001
· Over 100 new European channels
each year
March 2001
· European cable
markettransformation
October 2000
· European TV programme market
buoyant
April 2000
· Digital terrestrial television
March 2000

The spread of multichannel TV reception around the w
an exponential growth in the number of channels targeti
Over 50 of the 87 channels listed here have launched in
years - a reflection of the extra capacity and lower tran
offered by digital.

The USA, which saw the launch of the first children's cl
Nickelodeon, in 1979, has been the hotbed of channel
and has provided the main funding model. Although ser
Nickelodeon (owned by MTV Networks, part of Viac
most of their revenue from advertising, subscription rev
very significant element of their funding.

URL

About
the
source

A quick look at screendigest.com shows this information has more to do with marketing and the entertainment industry than with television's effects on kids. © Screen Digest Ltd. Used with permission.

they are sponsored by a commercial group (.com), an educational institution (.edu), a government organization (.gov), or a nonprofit organization (.org). (Since .com sites are selling something, you should be wary. In a search like the one Dan is performing, .org, .edu, and .gov sites are likely to have the most useful—and reliable—information.)

3. Go to sites that are likely to have useful information and continue your evaluation. Quickly scroll top to bottom in the site. Check for dates to see if the information is current. Look for "About Us" or "Who We Are" links to learn more about the source of the information.

4. If the site passes these initial tests, bookmark it using the "Favorites" or "Bookmarks" function of your Internet browser. (It helps to create a folder for specific projects or searches in your "Favorites" folder.) Then, either on a notecard or in a computer file, record the source and title information, a description of the information you found, and the date you accessed it.

Author/source: Parents Television Council
Title: "'It's Just Harmless Entertainment.' Oh Really?"

Description: How much TV kids watch, its effects

Notes:

- PTC is a group that would like to make television a socially responsible form of entertainment. There are over 800,000 members.
- More than a thousand studies have focused on the link between violence on TV and kids' behavior.
- The average American kid watches 25 hours of television a week and plays video games for 7 hours.
- By 18 years of age, the American kid has seen over 10,000 murders and 200,000 acts of violence on TV.

Date accessed: 12/6/03   *URL:* http://www.parentstv.org/ptc/facts/mediafacts.asp

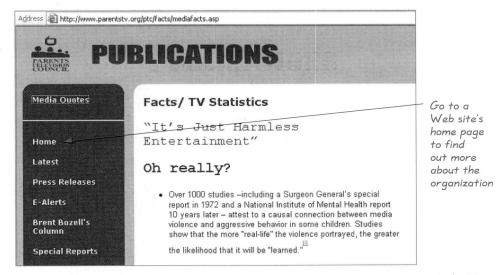

A quick look at this Web site suggests it provides relevant information. © Parents Television council. All rights reserved.

EXERCISE 11.1

Use an Internet search engine to find a few statistics on out-of-wedlock birth trends in the United States. Look at three sources and select the one that seems most reliable and significant to you. Use the following notecard to record information on the source. Be sure to paraphrase. In the space provided beneath the card, explain in a sentence what you know about the source of your information.

Author/source:	*Description:*
Title:	
Notes:	
Date accessed: *URL:*	

About this source:

Searching Periodicals Databases

College and public libraries offer a variety of online periodicals databases to help writers search print sources of information more efficiently. Using key words, you

Copyright © 2007, The McGraw-Hill Companies, Inc. All rights reserved.

Gen'l Reference Ctr Gold
_____

Subjects containing the words: violence in television
_____

Violence in Television
[View]   492 Newspaper references
[View]   1136 Periodical references or   [Narrow]   by sub-division
[See also] Related Subjects
_____

A search in General Reference Center Gold produces these sources on the subject of violence in television. © 2004 Gale Group, a division of Thomson Learning, Inc.

can search for articles much as you do on the Internet. Among the databases you might find are:

> **Infotrac:** citations from thousands of magazines, journals, and newspapers, many in full text; includes the current year of the *New York Times;* excellent coverage of current events, health, business, and much more.
>
> **FirstSearch:** specialized databases, many with full-text periodical articles, in fields from accounting to zoology; includes WorldCat (access to the book catalogs of the world's libraries), and WilsonSelect (full-text articles from magazines and journals).
>
> **General Reference Center Gold:** available twenty-four hours a day via the Internet, General Reference Center Gold provides one-stop access to general interest magazines, business periodicals, reference books, maps, historical images, and newspaper articles. Records are available with a combination of indexing, abstracts, image, or full-text formats.
>
> **Electric Library:** content from more than 100 full-text magazine, newspaper, book, and transcript sources, plus thousands of maps and pictures.

Key-word searches may lead to subtopics, enabling your to narrow your search and be more specific. Follow this four-step process when you do a database search:

1. Enter terms into the search window of the database. *Tip:* As in Internet searches, it is critical to narrow your search as much as possible at this stage. (See the tip on Internet searches on page 239.) Unlike most Internet search engines, however, most periodicals databases allow for "Subject," "Author," "Title," and "Key Word" searches, among other options. Check the "Help" section of the database you're using to see how to narrow your searches most efficiently—for example, whether it accepts + signs, quotation marks, and/or Boolean operators like *AND, OR, NOT,* etc.

2. Make a quick evaluation of the results of your search. In addition to looking at content descriptions (if any), titles, length, and authorship, consider the types of periodicals in which the articles appear. Are they from popular sources, such as *USA Today, Time,* and *Newsweek,* or from more academic or professional publications, such as *Teaching College English*? Which is more appropriate to your topic?

3. If an article that looks good is available online, skim it. Quickly scan the article top to bottom, reading headings and the first sentence of each

Copyright © 2007, The McGraw-Hill Companies, Inc. All rights reserved.

Gen'l Reference Ctr Gold

Subdivisions of: Violence in Television

addresses, essays, lectures
View   5 articles

advertising
View   1 article

analysis
View   68 articles

anecdotes, cartoons, satire, etc.
View   1 article

associations and societies
View   2 articles

attitudes
View   3 articles

australia
View   1 article

A narrowed search sorts articles into subtopics. © 2004 Gale Group, a division of Thomson Learning, Inc.

Author/source: Jib Fowles   *Description:* Reasons why TV
Title: "The Whipping Boy"   violence is a popular subject

Notes:

We assume television makes kids violent. Fowles writes, "Although television violence has never been shown to cause hostile behavior, its sinister reputation lives on."

No one sticks up for TV violence. Everyone condemns it, even the people who make a lot of money off it.

Date of publication: 12/7/03   *Page:* 27

---

paragraph. Check for dates to see if the information is current. If your hunch about it was right—that is, if it still seems useful—print it out (if possible), or record detailed information about it—the author's name, the name of the publication, the title of the article, a description of the information you found, the date, and page number—on a notecard or computer file.

4. If your search yields only a *citation* (the name and publication information, rather than a full text), print out or copy down the publication information for articles that look useful and consult the library for a print (or microfilm) copy.

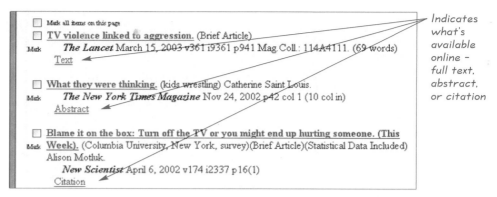

General Reference Center Gold indicates how much of the article is available in the database: "Text" (the article as it appears in the publication), "Abstract" (a brief overview of the article), and "Citation" (publication information). © 2004 Gale Group, a division of Thomson Learning, Inc.

Gen'l Reference Ctr Gold

◀ —— **Article 20 of 81** —— ▶

☐
Mark   ***Reason***, March 2001 v32 i10 p27

The Whipping Boy. *Jib Fowles.*

Full Text: COPYRIGHT 2001 Reason Foundation

The hidden conflicts underlying the campaign against violent TV

Although television violence has never been shown to cause hostile behavior, its sinister reputation lives on. This is because the issue masks a variety of other struggles. Many of these conflicts are suppressed because they may pose a threat to social order or are considered unseemly topics for public discussion. Hence, we hear only the polite versions of the conflicts between races, genders, and generations, although these struggles roil national life. Because they are denied full expression, such conflicts are transferred into other debates, including and perhaps especially the issue of television violence.

The text of some articles can be seen onscreen.

EXERCISE 11.2

Using a periodicals database in your college or public library, find an article about out-of-wedlock births. Narrow the search based on the subtopic that interests you. Scan three sources and select the one that seems most reliable and significant to you. Use the following notecard to write down a few facts or ideas relevant to your interest. Be sure to paraphrase. Select a short quotation and write it on the notecard, using quotation marks to separate it from the rest of your notes. In the space provided beneath the card, explain in a sentence what you know about the source of your information.

Destinations: Finding and Using Sources, Online and Off

Hungry for More?

Ever see a movie and find yourself hungry for more information on who was in it, who made it, or what it was based on? In order to find out, it helps to know how to do research quickly and efficiently. Whether you want to know who played Frodo in Peter Jackson's *The Lord of the Rings* movies or what critics and writers—including W. H. Auden—were saying about *The Fellowship of the Ring* when it was first published in the fall of 1954, online and print sources offer much more than facts; they are a great resource for reviews and other kinds of conversation about the books, films, or music you love.

The Internet vs. the Printed Page

The Internet offers a wealth of information that is literally at your fingertips; type a few key words into a search engine, and your computer will return hundreds of sites related to your chosen topic. Be warned, however: many of these sites will contain irrelevant, highly personal, or downright erroneous information. Anyone with access to a computer and some basic tools can post a site, so be sure to check a site's credibility before citing it. Who wrote it, and who sponsors the site? Why, and for what kinds of readers? Is it well written and carefully edited? Are sources cited? Do the facts presented on the site check out when you compare them to other sources? Evaluating all sources for credibility will ensure that you choose the right ones to cite.

Doing Research on the Job

The research skills you hone during college won't simply gather dust after graduation; finding and managing outside information is an important aspect of many jobs. You could be asked, for example, to locate reliable sales figures (internally) or news stories (externally) that relate to a project you're doing; you might be asked to design a field survey that will help your company determine whether or not to embark on a new venture. Whether you find yourself plowing through years of sales receipts or surfing the Internet for new techniques for building a mousetrap, research skills will aid you in almost any job.

EXERCISE 11.2 continued

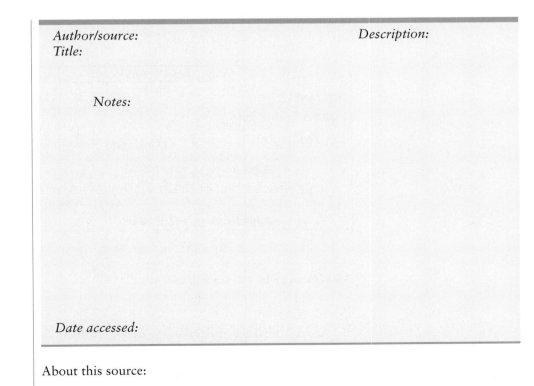

Author/source:
Title:

Description:

Notes:

Date accessed:

About this source:

Copyright © 2007, The McGraw-Hill Companies, Inc. All rights reserved.

Searching the Library Catalog

At one time students searched card catalogs and the Reader's Guide for sources of information. Today, searches are likely to be electronic. Library catalogs can be searched in a variety of ways—usually at least by "Subject," "Author," "Title," and "Key Word." Again, in order to search most efficiently, be as specific as possible and include as many search terms as are relevant. (Consult the "Help" section of your library's online system in order to determine the most efficient means of limiting your searches.)

SUBJECT ⌄	television	View Entire Collec

Result page:Prev 1 2

Save Marked Records	Save All On Page

Num	Mark	SUBJECTS (13-19 of 19)
Television		
13		-- See also Nurses in television
14		-- See also Sex in television
15		-- See also Sex role in television
16		-- See also Television display systems
17		-- See also Video art
18		-- See also Violence in television

A catalog search with "television" as the subject.

Save Marked Records	Save All On Page

Num	Mark	SUBJECTS (1-3 of 3)
Violence In Television		
1	☐	Children In Front Of The Small Screen / Grant Noble.
		Adult Services; 791.45 NOB
2	☐	Stop Teaching Our Kids To Kill : A Call To Action Against TV, Movie & Video Game Violence / Dave Grossman And Gloria DeGaetano.
		Adult Services; 302.2308 GRO
3	☐	Violence In Film And Television / James D. Torr, Book Editor.

Books listed under "Violence in television."

As with Internet or database searches, evaluate catalog sources (i.e., the actual books or periodicals) for relevance and trustworthiness: check authorship, publication information, dates, and any other clues you find in the catalog to determine which sources are likely to be useful. Once you've found a book or periodical that passes these initial tests, consult the table of contents and index to find sections and pages that address your topic.

Copyright © 2007, The McGraw-Hill Companies, Inc. All rights reserved.

EXERCISE 11.3

Using the online or card catalog in your college or public library, find a book that provides information on out-of-wedlock births. Select two or three books. Scan the table of contents and index to find relevant passages. Use the following notecard to write down a few facts or ideas relevant to your interest. Be sure to paraphrase. Select a quotation and write it on the notecard, using quotation marks to separate it from the rest of your notes. In the space provided beneath the card, explain in a sentence what you know about the source of your information.

Author/source: *Description:*
Title:

        Notes:

Date of publication: *Page:*

About this source:

Plagiarism, Quotation Marks, Research, APA, MLA

INTEGRATING SOURCES INTO YOUR PAPER

Finding useful statistics and quotations is only the first step in making effective use of source material in your paper. A second and equally important step in this process is working this material into your paper. To integrate your reading into your work, you should cite your sources by name in your paper, include parenthetical references, and provide a list of works cited.

Citing Your Sources within Your Paper

Avoid simply dropping a statistic or quote into your paper. Citing sources is a four-step process. Your goal is to integrate the information you have found into your paper as smoothly as possible. Effective integration involves:

1. Naming your sources
2. Citing statistics or quotations

3. Providing parenthetical references to specific page numbers

4. Providing full publication information in a "works-cited" list

Include *minimal information* in your parenthetical reference. For traditional sources such as magazines and books, include a page number in parentheses.

> In his article in *Reason* magazine, Jib Fowles states that "television violence has never been shown to cause hostile behavior" (8).

For Internet sources, page numbers are usually not provided; in this case, simply give your reader enough information to direct her or him to full-source information in your list of works cited.

> According to the Web site of the Parents Television Council, a group of more than 800,000 parents concerned about the impact of television on kids, American kids watch 25 hours of television a week. By 18 years of age, they have seen over 10,000 murders and 200,000 acts of violence on TV.

Practice using verbs to introduce your sources: *says, reports, states, explains, argues, observes.* The more variation you use when you set up your quotes, the smoother the integration process.

> The Parents Television Council, a group of more than 800,000 parents concerned about the impact of television on kids, **reports** on its Web site that American kids watch 25 hours of television a week. By 18 years of age, they have seen over 10,000 murders and 200,000 acts of violence on TV.
>
> The Parents Television Council, a group of more than 800,000 parents concerned about the impact of television on kids, **observes** that . . .
>
> The Parents Television Council, a group of more than 800,000 parents concerned about the impact of television on kids, **states** that . . .

Be sure to distinguish between partial and complete quotes, observing rules for capitalization and punctuation. (See Chapter 10 for additional information on quotations.)

> **Complete quote:** In *Reason* magazine, Jib Fowles states, "Although television has never been shown to cause hostile behavior, its sinister reputation lives on" (27).
>
> **Partial quote:** Jib Fowles, writing for *Reason* magazine, points out that television's "sinister reputation lives on," even though there is no evidence that it actually causes kids to be aggressive (27).

College writers often include too much information in the body of their papers. The idea is to provide only enough detail to help your reader clearly identify your source. Do not include publishing companies or Internet addresses. Save this information for your list of works cited.

EXERCISE 11.4

Following are two notecards with information on out-of-wedlock births. Compose a short paragraph for each notecard in which you refer to the information given. In one paragraph, cite a statistic; in the other paragraph, cite either a partial or complete quote. Be sure to set up your quotes properly and provide a parenthetical reference in each paragraph.

Copyright © 2007, The McGraw-Hill Companies, Inc. All rights reserved.

EXERCISE 11.4 continued

Author/source: National Center for Health Statistics   *Description:* 2002 stats
Title: "Nonmarital Childbearing in the United States, 1940–99"

Notes: Since 1994, roughly 34 percent of births in the United States were out of wedlock. That equals around 1,300,000 births each year.

Less than 3 in 10 of out-of-wedlock births are to teenagers, but most teen mothers have their babies out of wedlock.

The number of teen births fell by 2 percent from 1998 to 1999.

Date accessed: 12/8/03
URL: http://www.cdc.gov/nchs/releases/00facts/nonmarit.htm

Page:

About this source: A division of the Centers for Disease Control, funded by the U.S. Government

Short paragraph:

Author/source: Newsweek   *Description:* Impact of single-parent families
Title: "Unmarried, with Children"

Notes: "Half the kids born in the 1990s will spend at least part of their lives in a single-parent home."

"Demographers and politicians will likely spend years arguing about what this all means and whether the shifts are real or just numerical flukes."

"But one thing everyone does agree on is that single mothers are now a permanent and significant page in America's diverse family album."

Date of publication: May 28, 2001   *Page:* 46

Short paragraph:

Listing Works Cited at the End of Your Paper

Once known as the bibliography, the works-cited section of your paper provides the reader with publication information. Think of this as a favor you do for an interested reader who might want to learn more about your subject. The information you provide here would enable him to go to the Internet or traditional print sources and learn from the same sources you used to write your paper. How you cite your sources here depends on the kind of source it is.

Web site

Author(s). Name of Page/"Title of Article." Date of Posting/Revision [if any]. Name of Institution/Organization Affiliated with the Site. Date of Access. <Electronic address>.

Notice the "hanging indent." The first line is tight to the margin; all additional lines are indented.

Magazine

Author(s). "Title of Article." Title of Source Date: Pages.

Use periods, commas, and colons as shown. Punctuation matters.

Book

Author(s). Title of Book. Place of Publication: Publisher, Year of Publication.

Dan's research on television violence led him to Web sites, a magazine article, and a book. Using the preceding forms as a model, his Works Cited would be written as follows. Note that sources are listed in alphabetical order and that turnover lines are indented.

> Fowles, Jib. "The Whipping Boy." Reason March 2001: 27.
>
> Grossman, Dave and Gloria DeGaetano. Stop Teaching Our Kids to Kill: A Call to Action Against TV, Movie, and Video Game Violence. New York: Crown, 1999.
>
> Parents Television Council. "'It's Just Harmless Entertainment.' Oh Really?" 6 December 2003. <http://www.parentstv.org/ptc/facts/mediafacts.asp>.

EXERCISE 11.5

Using the preceding forms as a model, write the Internet and magazine sources in Exercise 11.4 as they would appear in the works-cited list of a paper on out-of-wedlock births.

Copyright © 2007, The McGraw-Hill Companies, Inc. All rights reserved.

EXERCISE 11.6

Return to the notecards you produced for Exercises 11.1, 11.2, and 11.3. Write them as they would appear in a works-cited list of a paper on out-of-wedlock births.

Following is Dan's final edited paper. He has gone through the process of finding, evaluating, and processing sources. This work enabled him to integrate facts, paraphrases, and quotes into his earlier draft on page 238.

STUDENT MODEL

Dan's Final Edited Paper

Trouble with the Tube

They watch in the morning. Then they come home and watch after school. Don't forget every single night. Some kids even watch TV in bed. All this television can't be good for our young people of today. They could be reading or playing outside, exercising their imaginations, doing anything besides sitting there like zombies or couch potatoes watching the same darn show they have already seen twenty-five times. Nevertheless, that's the way it is nowadays. TV is a negative fact of life.

Revised topic sentence.

One problem with TV is how much time it takes. According to the Parents Television Council, a group of over 800,000 parents who would like to improve the quality of television, the average American kid watches 25 hours of television a week and plays video games for 7 hours. It is hard to see how kids find time to do any school work. My sister is a case in point. She is in the eleventh grade, and she is having a hard time in some of her classes. She brought home a terrible report card a few weeks ago. She does all of her homework sitting in front of the TV. Some nights I look at her and she isn't doing any homework at all. She is watching *Friends* reruns. When he saw her grade, my dad grounded her from TV. We'll see if it works.

Statistic supports the claim that kids watch too much

Another problem with TV is the violence. It's either sex or violence every night. That's what sells. That's what people want to see. The Parents Television Council reports that by 18 years of age, the American kid has seen over 10,000 murders and 200,000 acts of violence on TV. The trouble is, every time you turn on the news, you hear about an actual kid who got into trouble with violent crime. Look at Columbine. Those two guys walked into a school and opened fire just like it was a movie set. Only it was real kids, real blood on the floor, and real parents grieving the loss of their kids. Look at the young people dealing drugs and shooting each other up in the streets. That probably wouldn't be happening if it weren't for TV. TV glamorizes violence.

Statistic shows how much violence there is on TV

continued

Quotation shows the supporting view

Jib Fowles, writing for *Reason* magazine, points out that television's "sinister reputation lives on," even though there is no evidence that it actually causes kids to be aggressive (27). He may be right, but there is no evidence that television *doesn't* cause kids to be aggressive. At least we can say this: the U.S. is fatter now than it has ever been before. It should come as no surprise. We sit on the couch and change channels with a remote, munching on the latest snack food advertised on the tube. I saw a bumper sticker the other day. "Kill your TV," it said. It's a violent solution, but I agree. We would be better off without it, or at least with less of it.

Works Cited

Use hanging indents in Works Cited

Fowles, Jib. "The Whipping Boy." <u>Reason</u> March 2001: 27.

Grossman, Dave, and Gloria DeGaetano. <u>Stop Teaching Our Kids to Kill: A Call to Action Against TV, Movie, and Video Game Violence</u>. New York: Crown, 1999.

Parents Television Council. "'It's Just Harmless Entertainment.' Oh Really?" 6 December 2003. <http://www.parentstv.org/ptc/facts/mediafacts.asp>.

12 *The Essay Test*

What will I do when I have to write in class? Instructors regularly require students to complete assignments in class, often in the form of essay tests. These tests require many of the same types of writing you studied in Part 2: illustration and example, narrative, process, cause and effect, comparison and contrast, and definition. Although essay tests may seem more stressful than objective, multiple-choice exams, both students and teachers report that they lead to deeper, longer-lasting learning.

IN THIS CHAPTER: A PREVIEW

Types of Essay Responses

- Sentence-Length Short Answer
- Paragraph-Length Short Answer
- The Essay Test

Investigating Essay Responses in College Classes

TYPES OF ESSAY RESPONSES

Essay tests are widely used to evaluate learning in college classes. While the content may vary from class to class, most instructors have similar expectations. They look for answers written in complete sentences. They also look for detailed answers that show you have paid attention in class and retained important course content. You will encounter essay tests that fall into three categories:

- Sentence-length short answer
- Paragraph-length short answer
- Essay-length long answer

Sentence-Length Short Answer

You will use sentence-length short answers for definitions. Your teachers are looking for complete thoughts, which means your answers should always be formulated in complete sentences. An effective sentence-length definition begins with the term to be defined, contains a present-tense linking verb (e.g., *is* and *are*), and ends with an elaborated idea.

Copyright © 2007, The McGraw-Hill Companies, Inc. All rights reserved.

Inadequate definition: Precipitation—rain.

Satisfactory definition: Precipitation is any form of water or moisture that condenses in the upper atmosphere and falls to earth, including snow, sleet, rain, mist, and dew.

Precipitation	is	any form of water	that . . .
(term to be defined)	(linking verb)	(idea)	(elaboration begins)

Inadequate definition: Alliteration—words with same letter at the beginning

Satisfactory definition: Alliteration is a literary device in which two or more consecutive words begin with the same consonant.

Alliteration	is	a literary device	in which . . .
(term to be defined)	(linking verb)	(idea)	(elaboration begins)

EXERCISE 12.1

Write definitions for the following terms. Consult a dictionary if necessary, but do not copy the definitions. Be sure to write in complete sentences.

1. parking meter:

2. bread:

3. floppy disk:

4. television:

5. latitude:

6. election:

7. florist:

8. camera:

9. flu:

10. janitor:

EXERCISE 12.2

Select important terms from another course (or courses) and define them on a piece of paper. If necessary, use study guides as well as textbooks from your courses to find relevant ideas and details to help you formulate your definitions. Use the same sentence structure you practiced in Exercise 12.1.

Paragraph-Length Short Answer

Paragraph-length short answers will be evaluated for three qualities: **focus, detail,** and **grammatical and mechanical correctness.** The focus of your paragraph-length

Destinations: Getting the Most Mileage from Timed Writing

The Heat Is On

Pressure. We've all felt it. There is an intensity in the air, a sense of urgency, and a lump in your throat. In an academic setting, the most intense pressure arrives at exam time, though regular quizzes and in-class writing may constantly keep you on your toes. And, fortunately or unfortunately, pressure doesn't end with graduation. Throughout life, you will face high-stakes, time-sensitive situations, and the sooner you learn to cope with such scenarios, the better. If you can execute a well-crafted essay in the pressure cooker of a classroom, you will find it that much easier to deal with "pressurized" situations in your non-academic life. It's 11:00 p.m. on April 15th and you suddenly realize you forgot to file your taxes—no problem, right?

Showing What You Know

Professors can't grade you on what you know; it's what you can *show* you know that counts. No matter how well-prepared you are, if you write an incoherent, threadbare essay exam, your teacher will likely assume that your knowledge and ideas are just as incoherent and threadbare. Bridging the gap between what you have learned and what you can write is an essential academic skill. Learning to write an effective exam essay is an important move toward closing this gap. The techniques you use to master the essay exam will help you surmount other academic tasks as well.

Working against the Deadline

The working world is filled with deadlines. Clients need answers, projects must be submitted, bosses demand reports . . . and all this work has to be completed by a specific time on a particular day. Even the best prepared professionals sometimes find themselves in the deadline crunch, with work that needs to be done yesterday. Unfortunately, time pressure is never an excuse for lack of quality. Mastering the ability to work well in a limited amount of time will benefit you greatly in any work setting. If you can approach a "time sensitive" situation calmly and work rationally toward its conclusion, you will be a valuable contributor to whatever field you work in.

answer depends on your reading the question carefully and identifying key terms. Those terms should become part of the topic sentence of your paragraph and should be repeated at least once in the paragraph-length answer.

Short-essay question: Give one <u>drawback</u> or <u>problem</u> with using <u>utilitarianism</u>.

Key terms

Topic sentence: One <u>drawback</u> to using the <u>philosophy of utilitariansim</u> is that actions or ways of life that have no observable use or effect cannot be evaluated as good.

Short-essay question: What did <u>Epicurus</u> conclude about how to <u>maximize pleasure</u>?

Key terms

Topic sentence: To <u>maximize pleasure</u>, <u>Epicurus</u> concluded that a person must make conscious choices in life to create situations where pleasure will be the outcome.

Be alert to what thinking and writing strategy the essay question is based on. Whether it asks for examples, causes, or a comparison, use what you know about thinking and writing strategies to develop your answer.

Copyright © 2007, The McGraw-Hill Companies, Inc. All rights reserved.

Short-essay question: Explain <u>three ways</u> in which <u>mass media</u> acts as an <u>agent of gender socialization</u> during childhood.

——— Key terms

Topic sentence: The <u>mass media</u> acts as an <u>agent of gender socialization</u> during childhood in <u>three important ways</u>. (thinking and writing strategy: illustration and example)

Short-essay question: Explain the <u>feminist perspective</u> on crime. In your answer, be sure to include what the perspective identifies as the <u>central cause.</u>

Key terms ———

Topic sentence: In the <u>feminist perspective</u> on crime, the <u>central cause</u> of crime is the unsatisfied desire to dominate. (thinking and writing strategy: cause and effect)

Finally, it is important that you use proper grammar and mechanics in any writing you do in college. You may think, *Well, this isn't an English class, so* how *I write isn't as important as* what *I write.* Nothing could be further from the truth. All your college teachers care about the way you write. You will never be criticized for writing clear sentences and using correct grammar.

EXERCISE 12.3

Underline the key terms in the following short-essay questions and write a topic sentence. Indicate which thinking and writing strategy you would use in your answer.

1. What were some of John Quincy Adams's concerns in his deliberations on the Amistad?

2. In what way are the genes "selfish" in Dawkins's view? What is the primary consequence of the gene being selfish?

3. Explain how Steinbeck did both primary and secondary research as he prepared to write *The Grapes of Wrath*.

4. Describe two general differences between Puritan and Native American societies.

5. Explain three challenges in studying past Native American culture and family life.

The Essay Test

On an essay test, your job is to display your grasp of course content. You will be evaluated for your essay's focus, detail, and mechanical and grammatical correctness. You may use more than one thinking and writing strategy as you formulate your answer. If you do not know the essay question before the date of the test, prepare for the test by anticipating questions.

Preparing for the Essay Test

1. Review notes you took during lectures and class discussion.

2. Review the course syllabus and circle unit titles and themes.

3. Review reading material.

4. Outline answers to possible questions.

5. Compose sentence- and paragraph-length answers to establish the language you will use on the day of the test.

At the Beginning of the Essay Test

1. Underline key terms in the essay question.

2. Drawing on your memory of the pretest outline you made, quickly list key terms, concepts, and details from the course content that you must mention in your essay.

3. Identify thinking and writing strategies that will help you organize and focus your answers.

While Writing Your Essay Answer

1. Include key terms from the test question in your first sentence.

2. Get to the point. Avoid introduction paragraphs and wordy preludes.

3. If ideas occur to you as you write, make quick changes and additions to your outline.

4. Do not pause too long to consider spelling and grammatical problems; place light check marks in the margin of your paper to signal those areas that require attention during the editing phase of your writing.

5. Use what you know about thinking and writing strategies. If you are asked to cite examples, be sure to explain each example. If you are asked to discuss causes and effects, be sure to use those key terms and provide sufficient elaboration.

6. Keep an eye on your outline. Check off key details you have integrated into the essay; plan ahead to structure answers to the remaining key details.

7. Leave enough time at the end of the exam period for proofreading. Erase or lightly cross out misspelled words or grammatical errors, and make corrections. Unless you are told otherwise, do not copy your paper over.

EXERCISE 12.4

Read the following essay questions and underline key terms. Indicate what thinking and writing strategies you would use in answering the questions and how many paragraphs you would need for a detailed answer. (*Suggestion:* plan on one or two paragraphs for each key term in the test question.)

1. What were your perceptions of geography before signing up for this class? Has your initial view of geography changed? If so, how and why? What do you see as the value of utilizing geography's approach to address contemporary problems and issues?

Thinking and writing strategies:

Number of paragraphs:

Copyright © 2007, The McGraw-Hill Companies, Inc. All rights reserved.

2. Define the "shadow" side of the personality. Use Goffman's ideas on the "presentation of self" to explain how the shadow side develops. Discuss one of your shadow traits and use Goffman's ideas to explain how it developed.

Thinking and writing strategies:

Number of paragraphs:

3. Relate the three characteristics of tragedy we discussed in class to Arthur Miller's *Death of a Salesman*. What, in your opinion, makes this a peculiarly American tragedy? In your answer, refer to at least three characters in detail.

Thinking and writing strategies:

Number of paragraphs:

INVESTIGATING ESSAY RESPONSES IN COLLEGE CLASSES

I want to be prepared. Know what to expect from your college classes. Investigate the types of in-class and examination writing you will be doing.

EXERCISE 12.5

Survey members of your class for writing on tests they have done. If possible, collect specific questions for four or five tests. Analyze the language of each test question and circle the type of answer required (sentence, paragraph, or essay), list the key terms, recommend the best thinking and writing strategies for answering the question, and estimate the number of paragraphs (if an essay) required to answer it.

EXAMPLE:

American History

Test Question: *Explain the concept of "impressment" and its consequences in U.S. and British relations.*

Type of answer: sentence, paragraph, essay

Key terms: *impressment, consequences, U.S.–British relations*

Thinking and writing strategies: *definition, cause and effect*

Number of paragraphs (for essay questions): *1*

13 *The Expository Essay*

Discuss. Explain. Consider. Explore. Write a paper about . . . The instructions for your writing assignments in college will often contain terms like these. When your college teachers, instructors, and professors use these terms, their expectation is that you will write an expository essay.

The expository essay is a multiple-paragraph paper. At the very least, your readers will expect to see three or four, possibly five or six paragraphs in the essays you write. They will read for both structure and content. An expository essay has an introduction, a body, and a conclusion. Using the forms of thinking and writing you have learned in Part 2, an essay conveys information in an organized fashion. The content may be personal observation that supports your view of a subject or information you get from assigned reading in class or from library and Internet sources. In an expository essay, you might explore topics such as these:

- the latest evidence of global warming
- the significance of natural selection in the theory of evolution
- economic factors contributing to the formation of an underclass
- "spin-off" benefits of the space program

WW Essay Writing

IN THIS CHAPTER: A PREVIEW

Thinking in the Expository Mode
- Elements of Exposition
- Assignments as Road Maps
- Outline and Organization

A Process Approach to Writing the Expository Essay

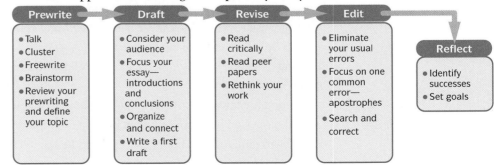

Prewrite	Draft	Revise	Edit	Reflect
• Talk • Cluster • Freewrite • Brainstorm • Review your prewriting and define your topic	• Consider your audience • Focus your essay—introductions and conclusions • Organize and connect • Write a first draft	• Read critically • Read peer papers • Rethink your work	• Eliminate your usual errors • Focus on one common error—apostrophes • Search and correct	• Identify successes • Set goals

Student Sample of the Writing Process

Copyright © 2007, The McGraw-Hill Companies, Inc. All rights reserved.

WW Maya Angelou

THINKING IN THE EXPOSITORY MODE

Writers compose essays to hold up their end of the conversation in a public exchange of ideas, whether in the classroom or on the editorial page. Sometimes their desire to write begins with an incident that gets them thinking. At other times, they decide to write because of something they have read.

Elements of Exposition

Writers structure their essays with a thesis statement and topic sentences, supporting their ideas with specific details. They often combine thinking and writing strategies in their expository essays to present their ideas in a variety of ways: illustration and example, narrative and description, process, cause and effect, comparison and contrast, and definition.

READING: from "A Simple Glass of Water," by Ted Fishman

Narrative

    Recently, on a day so blistering in Chicago that authorities issued a heat warning, telling people to stay inside when possible, I was out early with my wife and 10-year-old son, hoping to run errands before the temperature topped 90. Alas, at 9:45 a.m., we were too late, and the heat hit. We wanted water. We went into a coffee shop and ordered a latte for my wife, an iced coffee for my son, and please, a glass of water for me. "I can only give you a small cup," the clerk told me. That would be fine, I told him. He came back with a thimble-sized cup with roughly one ounce of liquid in it. Was it possible to get more? I asked. "No," said the clerk. "That's all we can give out. We do sell water, though."

Thesis statement

Definition

    These days it seems that providing a simple drink of water is not so much an exercise in quenching the thirsty as in soaking them. Worldwide, bottled water is a $35 billion business. Over the next four years, the bottled water market is expected to grow 15 percent annually. That dwarfs the growth rates for fruit beverages, beer and soft drinks, all under 2 percent. Of course, sometimes bottled water does taste better or is more convenient or safer than tap water—and is worth paying for. That's nothing new. More novel is the pervasive push by businesses to sell bottled water by depriving customers of tap water.

Examples

    For the past few years, the movie theaters I frequent have been declining requests for water, pushing—at $2.50 each—the bottled product instead. Seen a water fountain at a gasoline station lately? Not likely. Bottled water is one of the highest selling items—after cigarettes—in the stations' convenience stores. In restaurants, waiters now frequently ask for your drink order before they bring you tap water, in the hope that you can be talked into buying bottled water. A waitress I asked called this the "beverage greeting" that her manager required her to say before bringing a glass of water.

Comparison and contrast

    During my travels nearly 20 years ago through Indonesia's coffee-growing regions, I would often stop by a bamboo-thatched lean-to for a drink. Water in the land of the coffee bean rarely comes from a tap; it has to be hauled from wells, strained and boiled. Often I was served by rail-thin old men or women in fraying sarongs who subsisted on a few dollars a week. Yet, ask for water and they brought it. At first I asked to pay, not for the water, but for the work behind it. They'd refuse even the smallest coin. The custom of sharing water was too elemental to gum up with finagling.

In India, the Sarai Act mandates that an innkeeper give a free glass of drinking water to any passerby. Indeed, in most places around the world, giving strangers water is the bare minimum of humane behavior. Why is that not so here?

DISCUSSION QUESTIONS

1. Fishman begins his expository essay with a short narrative. Why does he tell this story?

2. What detail does Fishman provide to describe the water business?

3. "In most places around the world," Fishman asserts, "giving strangers water is the bare minimum of humane behavior." What does this assertion suggest about selling water in the United States?

Assignments as Road Maps

Expository essays often begin with a class assignment. Assignments are usually carefully worded to provide students with suggestions for focusing and organizing their work. Learn to read assignments as road maps for the essays you will write.

EXERCISE 13.1

Read the writing assignments below and identify the key terms you would focus on if you were writing an essay. Look also for specific directions on how to organize and structure the paper. Using the following box as a guide, indicate which thinking and writing strategies the assignments suggest you use. Explain how you would use those strategies.

Thinking and Writing Strategies	
Illustration and Example: Can you look at specific instances to be more specific?	**Cause and Effect:** Are reasons and causes an issue in your topic? Are consequences an important consideration?
Narrative: What stories can you tell to explore the topic?	**Comparison and Contrast:** Can you talk about similarities or differences?
Process: Does it help to explain how something works?	**Definition:** Does it help to define a key term? Is there a difference of opinion about the meaning of words or events?

EXAMPLE: Everywhere we turn these days, the world is going digital. Everything, it seems, is computerized or will soon become digital. Discuss the advantages and disadvantages to the widespread use of computers in daily life. Draw on examples and firsthand experience where possible.

Copyright © 2007, The McGraw-Hill Companies, Inc. All rights reserved.

EXERCISE 13.1 continued

Key terms: *going digital, advantages and disadvantages to the widespread use of computers in daily life, examples, firsthand experience*

Thinking and writing strategies: (1) *illustration and example—cite examples of different places where computers are used in daily life;* (2) *narrative—tell a story about a time when a computer definitely worked to my disadvantage (couldn't order any food because the computers were down);* (3) *narrative, comparison and contrast—tell a story about a time when a computer worked to my advantage*

1. Role models can make a decisive difference in a person's life. Discuss a role model's influence on you. Focus on before and after, explaining how you have changed in an important way and what this person did to help bring about that change.

   Key terms:

   Thinking and writing strategies:

2. Everyone does something well, whether it's taking care of a child or a car. Choose something you are especially good at and explain your approach or method and why it is so successful.

   Key terms:

   Thinking and writing strategies:

3. Write an essay defending or opposing sexual freedom. Explain what you mean by sexual freedom and then tell why this kind of behavior is right or wrong.

   Key terms:

   Thinking and writing strategies:

4. How have you and/or others that you know adjusted your lifestyles to avoid becoming crime victims?

   Key terms:

   Thinking and writing strategies:

EXERCISE 13.1 continued

5. It's said that travel is educational. What have you learned from trips you've taken?

Key terms:

Thinking and writing strategies:

EXERCISE 13.2

For assignments that do not contain key terms or a road map for writing, the writer's job is essentially the same. You bring your personal knowledge and experience to a topic. Your critical-thinking activity is to explore what you have to say about your topic. Practice this thinking with the following topics. Determine which strategies you would use to explore what you know about the topic and write a sentence giving your dominant impression of the topic.

EXAMPLE:

chewing gum

Thinking and writing strategies:

A. *Narrative: I can tell the story about waking up in the morning with gum in my hair.*

B. *Illustration and example: other examples of gum as a nuisance (stuck underneath desks, spit out on the sidewalk and getting stuck to your shoe).*

C. *Process: how to chew gum responsibly.*

Dominant impression: *Gum is a pain in the neck!*

1. pets

Thinking and writing strategies:

A.

B.

C.

Dominant impression:

2. amusement parks

Thinking and writing strategies:

A.

B.

C.

Copyright © 2007, The McGraw-Hill Companies, Inc. All rights reserved.

Dominant impression:

3. study habits

Thinking and writing strategies:

A.

B.

C.

Dominant impression:

4. traffic safety

Thinking and writing strategies:

A.

B.

C.

Dominant impression:

5. music

Thinking and writing strategies:

A.

B.

C.

Dominant impression:

Outline and Organization

Having identified thinking and writing strategies that will help you explore your topics, your next task is to explore in more detail the experience and knowledge you bring to the assignment. An outline helps you identify specific detail; it also helps you see the structure and organization of your ideas.

EXERCISE 13.3

Choose two topics from Exercise 13.1 and from Exercise 13.2 and expand your initial exploration into a more detailed outline. Once you have completed your outline, formulate a thesis statement that captures the main idea of the essay you would write. Use the following example as a guide.

EXAMPLE:

chewing gum

Thinking and writing strategies:

Copyright © 2007, The McGraw-Hill Companies, Inc. All rights reserved.

EXERCISE 13.3 continued

1. *Narrative: waking up in the morning with gum in my hair*
   A. *I'm eight years old.*
   B. *I have really short hair, so it's not that big of a problem.*
   C. *I've seen other kids with gum in their hair (Forest Whitman actually came to school with a gob on the back of his head).*
   D. *How my mother gets it out.*
2. *Illustration and example: Gum is almost always a pain in the neck.*
   A. *Under tables and chairs at school, in drinking fountains. (Why do people do this?)*
   B. *On sidewalks. (Tell about stepping on gum at the beach. It felt like a hot coal stuck to my foot.)*
   C. *A person chewing gum looks ugly (at stoplights, in shopping centers). Their jaws are working when they don't think anyone is watching. Open-mouth chewing versus closed-mouth chewing.*
3. *Process: It is possible to be discrete.*
   A. *Minimize the wad size (half a stick, please).*
   B. *Keep the wrapper in your pocket.*
   C. *No bubble blowing. (Another example of being a pain in then neck. Talk about this in the example paragraph.)*
   D. *Keep your mouth closed and chew slowly.*
   E. *Dispose of it by wrapping the chewed gum in a wrapper and dropping it in a wastebasket.*

Thesis statement: *Chewing gum is almost always a nuisance.*

A PROCESS APPROACH TO WRITING THE EXPOSITORY ESSAY

The expository essay is a snapshot of a subject. It provides a focused, detailed, and purposeful picture that enables you to explore, explain, and clarify your point of view. An essay enables you to make sense of your subject for your reader. Following are some suggested topics for your expository essay.

EXPOSITORY ESSAY TOPICS

1. Many college students have full- or part-time jobs. Discuss the ups and downs of being a working student. What is a good job? What is a bad job? Discuss your work, if applicable, or the work of other students you know. Be specific by giving examples of pros and cons.
2. Fast food is widely criticized by young and old alike. Nevertheless, fast food has become an increasingly important industry in our economy. Rather than criticize fast food, discuss two or three important benefits it provides. Support your assertions with specific detail.
3. Describe how you are different from your parents. How are their beliefs, values, and lifestyles different from yours? What things do you sometimes argue about? What things are important to you but unimportant to your parents, and vice versa?
4. We have all known people who seemed to fit a type: the neighborhood bully, the sissy, the grouch, the gentleman, the joker, the macho man. Give an account of one such person you have known. Tell what effect this person had on you. Describe at least one incident involving you and that person.

STUDENT SAMPLE

Not a Child of Nature

Thesis statement

Reasons the writer doesn't enjoy camping

I just do not get the concept of camping. Bring the indoors outside? What's the point? There is too much manual labor that goes into camping. There is preparation for the trip and making sure you have everything you are going to need. Then there is getting to the campground after a long drive, where you still need to start setting up your site. Sleeping outside under a tent with all the bugs, wild animals, wearing bug spray, and making a fire to keep warm? No, camping is not for this gal.

Illustration-and-example paragraph

Camping appeals to a certain group of people. First, there is the "nature nut." These people find peace of mind in the outdoors. They have a great passion for the way nature works. Another type of person that enjoys camping is the adventurer. It is a satisfying feeling to be challenged to survive in the great outdoors. This is the type of person who takes advantage of all the outdoors has to offer. They find nothing more satisfying than canoeing down a river until they find the right spot to pitch a tent for the evening and catch their dinner.

Narrative paragraph

I had the worst camping experience when I was a senior in high school. My friend decided to plan a camping trip. Of course, I did not want to be left out, so I said "Why not?" I had no idea what I was in for when I agreed to this whole camping idea. It was about a six-hour drive out to the campsite. When we got there, we were five miles from any type of civilization. It took us 30 minutes to pitch the tent and another 30 minutes to unload the car. We broke up into groups. Some people collected wood, while others dug the fire pit. After about two hours of work, we were settled. That is when all the bugs started biting, so we combated this with tons of bug spray. Then as night hit, it got cold even with the fire. There was no toilet and nowhere to get fresh water. It was so bad that we had to drive into town to get bottled water to brush our teeth. Everyone was covered with bug bites and smelled like sweat and bug spray mixed. Our backs hurt from sleeping on the hard ground. It took us two and a half hours to pack up camp, and worst off, we still had a six-hour ride home.

Michael J. Smith of Kampgrounds of America says, "We all need an oasis once in a while." A weekend in the woods can restore your soul. KOA has over 500 campgrounds and many provide amenities such as laundry facilities, camp stores, and restaurants. Paul E. Marsh of Camping Magazine says, "Camping helps create a positive sense of self."

Maybe camping is an affordable getaway. You just pack up your car and drive away. The camper finds peace of mind in the great outdoors. But not me. I say leave the great outdoors outside where it belongs. I'll watch it from my hotel window.

> **PREWRITE**
>
> - Talk
> - Cluster
> - Freewrite
> - Brainstorm
> - Review your prewriting and define your topic

Select one or more of the following prewriting strategies to explore a topic and develop ideas for an expository essay.

EXERCISE 13.4

Read your assignment as a road map. Using Exercise 13.1 as a guide, identify the key terms in the topic on page 265 that interests you the most. Look for specific directions on how to organize and structure the paper. What thinking and writing strategies does the assignment suggest you use? How would you use those strategies?

Thinking and Writing Strategies	
Illustration and Example: Can you look at specific instances to be more specific?	**Cause and Effect:** Are reasons and causes an issue in your topic? Are consequences an important consideration?
Narrative: What stories can you tell to explore the topic?	**Comparison and Contrast:** Can you talk about similarities or differences?
Process: Does it help to explain how something works?	**Definition:** Does it help to define a key term? Is there a difference of opinion about the meaning of words or events?

Talk

EXERCISE 13.5

Pair off with another student and talk about the topic that interests you the most. Use the thinking and writing strategies you identified to help organize your discussion.

Cluster

EXERCISE 13.6

Explore the topic that interests you the most. Use the following clustering diagram to discover subtopics and supporting details relevant to the topic.

Copyright © 2007, The McGraw-Hill Companies, Inc. All rights reserved.

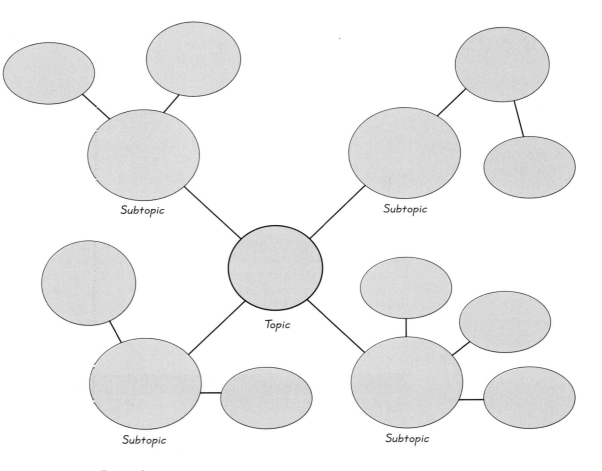

Freewrite

EXERCISE 13.7

Using your clustering as a guide, write as much as you can in ten to fifteen minutes about your topic. As you write, keep in mind your reading of the assignment as a road map. Draw on the thinking and writing strategies for specific details to elaborate on your ideas.

Brainstorm

EXERCISE 13.8

List everything that you discovered about your topic in the previous prewriting exercises. Add to your list anything you thought of since you talked to your classmate about the topic.

Review Your Prewriting and Define Your Topic

EXERCISE 13.9

Use the following questions to review your prewriting and define your topic for your expository essay.

- What is your topic and why is the topic important to you?
- What important ideas and details did you discover in your prewriting? Why are they important?

Copyright © 2007, The McGraw-Hill Companies, Inc. All rights reserved.

EXERCISE 13.9 continued

- Which ideas and details in your prewriting will you probably not explore further? Why?
- What do you need to know more about in order to get started on your essay?

DRAFT

- Consider your audience
- Focus your essay—introductions and conclusions
- Organize and connect
- Write a first draft

Write a draft that organizes your prewriting into an expository essay. Your first draft will establish the subject and explore the point you wish to make in multiple paragraphs.

Consider Your Audience

EXERCISE 13.10

Now that you have selected a topic, consider who will read your paragraph. Use the following questions to consider how to convey your point to an audience.

- Why is this topic important to your audience?
- What special meaning does this topic have for you? Why do you want your audience to understand this meaning?
- Will your audience agree or disagree with your thinking? Will you be asking them to think about your subject in a new way?
- Return to the exercises on expository thinking in this chapter and decide which way of thinking about your topic will help you connect best with your audience.

Focus Your Essay: Introductions and Conclusions

Many student writers say introductions and conclusions are the hardest paragraphs to write. They save their focused ideas for the body of the paper. Consequently, their introductions are vague and bland. They feel the need to repeat themselves in their conclusions, but doing so seems awkward.

Unfocused introduction: In our world today, everyone has to do things they don't want to do. These things are called jobs. Or maybe even chores. There are jobs you do at home, jobs you do at work, and jobs you do at school. One of the chores a person has to do around the house is vacuum the rug.

Focused introduction: Every morning I wake up and find dog hair all over the house. It's on the area rug in the living room, the carpet in my room, and the stairs that lead to the basement and upstairs. My dog Cheyenne is a Norwegian elkhound. Her very thick hair sheds a lot in the summer. I hate seeing dog hair in the house, but I don't like leaving her outside on hot summer days. That is why I depend on my vacuum cleaner. If I didn't have a vacuum cleaner, there is no way I could have a dog like Cheyenne in the house. The carpet and the rugs in the house would be covered with dog hair if I didn't vacuum every day. The vacuum is just one convenience device I use on a regular basis.

Unfocused introduction: There are many benefits to watching a movie, whether it's at the theater or renting a video. Some people enjoy both ways, and some only like one. Movies are a source of entertainment for many American people today, although there are other forms of entertainment. But really, ask yourself who can turn down a really good movie? It all depends on what type of person you are inside. That's the key to knowing which form you like. Personally, I enjoy a great video instead of a crowded theater.

Focused introduction: The floor was sticky. The place was packed. I sat straight up in my seat, afraid of what might get in my hair if I leaned back. That is how I felt the last time I went to the movies. It was a couple months ago. I went with three of my friends. The movie was "Dude, Where's My Car?" We went to a dollar theater. It never used to be as run down as it is now. The seats were broken, and the curtains were ripped. It wasn't stadium seating like most new theaters, so you couldn't see over the person's head in front of you. I now wish I had waited another month and rented the movie. It's almost always better to see a movie on video.

Some Guidelines for a Focused Introduction

1. Start with snappy first sentence.

> My hard drive crashed.
>
> Every morning I wake up and find dog hair all over the house.
>
> She washed my mouth out with soap, then smacked my face.
>
> I remember when only doctors and drug dealers had pagers.
>
> When I was old enough to know better, I could have divorced my parents.
>
> In my fifth-grade class, there were five Jennifers.

2. Use one of the thinking and writing strategies to get your paper started.

Narrative introduction: She washed my mouth out with soap, then smacked my face. She had me run out to the apple tree in our yard to pick a switch. Grandma explained to me that she was going to whip my bottom with the switch that I brought back. She also told me that if the switch wasn't just right, I would be punished even more. To hear her say this to me was unbelievable. My sweet, loveable grandma wanted to hurt me. I remember crying as I chose my weapon. I slowly took the switch to her and received my punishment. I felt ashamed of the vulgar language I had used, and now I had to endure physical pain. Punishment taught me a lesson that time (and many other times).

Illustrations-and-examples introduction: Growing up, I loved math. I had an advanced level of math education, far from a traditional one. In middle school, for example, we learned special shortcuts people in regular math classes didn't learn. Then in eighth grade came algebra. After that I took algebra II, geometry, trig/pre-calculus, and physics. (Although physics is a science class, it's mostly math.) My physics teacher made up a problem involving cockroaches. The problem was about a cannon on the roof of a house firing at a specific angle toward an oncoming line of cockroaches. Given some of the figures, distances, and angles, we were supposed to calculate which roach was going to get it. Throughout my schooling, math was always fun, challenging, and practical.

Summary introduction: The essay "On Compassion" talks about feeding the homeless. The writer asks why people feel compelled to give gifts to the homeless. She came to the conclusion that people do it out of compassion. What does she mean by compassion? Compassion, she says, "is a feeling of pity or empathy." These people are not homeless, nor do they know how it feels to be homeless, but somehow they can relate. They probably have been in a situation that required someone else's help. Helping a homeless person makes them feel better about themselves. For this reason and other reasons, helping others is important.

3. Formulate a thesis statement. The thesis states the point you want to make in your essay. It sums up the paper. It can appear at the beginning, middle, or end of your introduction paragraph.

4. Retrieve a specific detail from your introduction or the body of your paper and begin your conclusion. Use that specific detail to emphasize the main point of your paper.

> **Unfocused conclusion:**   In this paper I have talked about the three main points that are important to me about keeping my house clean.

> **Focused conclusion:**   Cheyenne sheds. There's just no way around it. Nevertheless, I have found ways of keeping up with dog hair and most of the other problems with keeping my house clean.

> **Unfocused conclusion:**   In conclusion, there are many people who like seeing movies on video and many who like seeing them in the theater. In the end, each individual must decide for himself which he prefers.

> **Focused conclusion:**   So the floor might be sticky and the crowds might be noisy, but the theater definitely offers some big advantages over seeing a movie at home.

EXERCISE 13.11

Write an introduction to your essay in which you use narrative or illustration and example to structure your ideas. Begin with a snappy first sentence. End your introduction with a focused thesis sentence.

EXERCISE 13.12

Revise each of the following thesis statements so that it provides a focused preview of the expository essay. Then list three subtopics related to the thesis.

EXAMPLE:

Relatives can certainly make a person's life interesting.

Revised: *Relatives, especially older ones, can teach a young person valuable lessons.*

A. *Lessons about overcoming adversity (Uncle Stan and the war).*

B. *Lessons about the past (Great Grandma's stories about the Depression).*

C. *Lessons about family history (Dad).*

1. Spending money foolishly is easy to do.

A.

B.

C.

2. Exercise is the key to a quality of life.

A.

B.

C.

Copyright © 2007, The McGraw-Hill Companies, Inc. All rights reserved.

EXERCISE 13.12 continued

3. Kids use many electronic gadgets in school nowadays.

A.

B.

C.

4. Religion is as important today as ever.

A.

B.

C.

5. Everyone needs a hobby.

A.

B.

C.

Organize and Connect

EXERCISE 13.13

Use key words and repetition to establish connections between your introduction and the body of your paper. Use the following example as a model.

EXAMPLE:

Thesis Statement: _Relatives, especially older ones, can teach a young person valuable lessons._

Topic sentence: _I learned a lot about overcoming adversity from my Uncle Stan, who told me about being a Marine during the war in Vietnam._

Topic sentence: _My great grandmother tells stories about the Depression to make sure we know how good we have it in this day and age._

Topic sentence. _My dad has two or three stories he tells over and over again so we all "know where we came from."_

Write a First Draft

EXERCISE 13.14

Use the following checklist as a guide to draft your expository essay.

_____ Review your prewriting to clarify your purpose and what you want your audience to understand.

_____ Insert details to develop your ideas.

_____ Focus your thesis and topic sentences.

_____ Insert transitions to connect ideas and details.

_____ Include a focused introduction and conclusion.

Destinations: Expository Writing on the Go

Exchanging Ideas: Thinking in "Expository Mode"

If you find yourself in disagreement with a friend or family member about a political or personal issue, think about how and why you disagree. Supporting your beliefs with details and examples, and conveying them in a civil, respectful tone will contribute to the strength and coherence of your message. Through a full exchange of ideas, you will come to a better understanding of your companion's opinions *and* your own.

Studying Techniques

An important part of studying is knowing *what* to study. When studying for an exam, be sure to consider its format—essay, multiple-choice, short answer, or a combination of all three. If the exam includes an essay component, ask yourself about the key points in the material the exam covers, list these points, and make a note of examples and details that support them. If the exam is multiple-choice, you may want to concentrate more heavily on memorizing facts, such

as dates or formulas. Every class is different, but it's usually wise to focus on material that your professor devoted the most class time to, so check your notes.

Multitasking: Staying Organized

At work, it isn't unusual to be faced with several tasks simultaneously. This is where your skills at organizing and outlining come into play. Many people find it helpful to write out a to-do list that outlines what needs to be done and in what order. By setting aside a little time to plan out and structure your day, you will find that the tasks at hand may suddenly seem less daunting than you initially expected. Up-to-date organizing will help you get the job done more quickly and effectively.

REVISE

- Read critically
- Read peer papers
- Rethink your work

Begin revising by asking yourself these questions: Will an audience understand my purpose? Is there sufficient detail? Are my ideas connected and is my purpose clearly defined?

Read Critically

EXERCISE 13.15

Examine the following essay. Underline the thesis statement and topic sentences and look for the essay's strengths and weakness.

I was 17 years old when I first moved out of my parent's house and into my own. I was pregnant at the time. At night it was difficult for me to sleep. I used television as a sleeping aid. It was a 13-inch color television with a remote. It was my most important possession. After watching it for hours, it finally coaxed me into falling asleep. Later during the years when my child was able to walk and touch things, he tripped over the cord. That made the television fall off the crate and the picture tube had blown. It had to be replaced. I was without of a television for months, and I learned just how important television is to me.

Television is one machine that revolves around my life. It is square shaped and has a glass face. It illustrates information like the news and other important things. It also gives you a source of entertainment of shows from comedy to thrillers. Most televisions are cable ready and can get premium channels installed. Television comes with a remote so you can turn to the movie you prefer.

Copyright © 2007, The McGraw-Hill Companies, Inc. All rights reserved.

Television has changed a lot over time. When I was a little girl, television was shown in black and white. I enjoyed watching Felix the Cat the cartoon. Now television is shown in color. Watching movies in black and white looks drab, and it gives me no exiting feeling now. Color television shows a lot of personality, and it gives you a vivid outlook on the background. Most people prefer color. Other than color, you can choose the size of television that suits your viewing pleasure. It comes in sizes from 5 inches to 52 inches. I own a 36 inch, which I have in my living room so everyone can get a good panorama. In my bedroom I have a 27 inch. The larger you go in television, the better view you will have. Smaller televisions are not as enjoyable because you can't really see all the details such as the background and maybe the props that are being used.

You can select from many types of televisions other than just size. They come in digital and flat screen. My friend has a digital one. When I first saw the television, I was really impressed because the clarity was great. You couldn't see the little dots that put the whole picture together. On my television you could. On the digital one it was clear. That type of television is much more expensive than a regular one. Flat screen television is good for people with a limit of space. Some can be mounted on the wall. I once saw one in a magazine advertisement. It took up less space, therefore, you don't necessarily need an entertainment center. Others you do because of the bulkiness in the back of the screen. Those are usually placed on a television cart.

My dependence for the television is a little bad. I consider it to be normal. If I could not see the news daily, then it would become a problem. I watch the news on channel 2 as early as 7 a.m. all the way until 9 a.m. It's the best one to watch in the morning time. When noon comes, I watch channel 4 news to get information that channel 2 might not have gotten. If I'm home during the evening time, I watch channel 7 from 5 p.m. until 6:30. I make my last round at 11 p.m. on channel 4. On the other hand, my friend Quincy does not watch television at all. He would rather listen to the radio. I've never seen a television in his home. He seems to think it takes up too much personal time. He doesn't depend on television like I do. It's imperative that I can see the news rather than hear it on the radio. I like seeing personal reaction like when someone's family member has been killed in a fire or car accident. I have compassion for those who are hurting. My heart goes out to them. Unlike hearing them on the radio, you can't really get the feeling that they endure.

When I was seventeen, television was just a sleep aide for me. Now I see it can be an educational tool, such as finding out what the weather may be, stock information, what's going on in other countries, and different other things that may interest you. Some may rather read the newspaper or listen to the radio. Television is my favorite.

Focus

1. Is the essay's subject clear? Will a reader understand why this topic is important?

EXERCISE 13.15 continued

Detail

2. What thinking and writing strategies does the writer employ?

3. Does the writer provide adequate details to develop ideas in the essay?

Connections

4. Does the writer present the ideas in an order that is effective? Does anything seem out of order or irrelevant?

5. Is the order made clear by connecting words?

Taking a Critical View

6. What are the strengths and weaknesses of the paper?

Strengths	Weaknesses

7. What will improve this paper?

Read Peer Papers

EXERCISE 13.16

Form a group of three or four students and take turns reading and discussing your papers. Use the questions from Exercise 13.14 to identify each paper's strengths and weaknesses. Offer suggestions for a revision plan.

Copyright © 2007, The McGraw-Hill Companies, Inc. All rights reserved.

Rethink Your Work

EXERCISE 13.17

Review your essay and make the following revisions as necessary.

- Revise your introduction so it makes a strong first impression.
- Identify the point of your essay, sharpening your thesis statement and topic sentences as needed.
- Emphasize key details in each paragraph by elaborating and providing additional detail.
- Cut nonessential details.
- Reorganize your paper so the most important ideas come near the end.
- Focus your conclusion with an important detail from the introduction or body of your paper.

EDIT

- Eliminate your usual errors
- Focus on one common error— apostrophes
- Search and correct

Prepare to turn your essay in for a grade. Make sure you are not repeating errors you usually make. Then look for new errors that may distract your reader from the purpose and meaning of your writing.

Eliminate Your Usual Errors

EXERCISE 13.18

Turn to the grids in Chapters 18, 19, and 20 where you have been keeping track of the errors you make. List those errors in the space provided below. Then proofread your paper and correct the errors you find.

_____   _____   _____

_____   _____   _____

Focus on One Common Error—Apostrophes

The apostrophe is an easy mark of punctuation to overlook or misuse. It is properly used to form contractions and possessives; however, it is often misused in simple plurals.

No Apostrophe with Simple Plurals

Most nouns in English are made plural by adding the letter *s*. Avoid adding an apostrophe to the *s* to make a noun plural.

We ate ice cream cones (not *cone's*).

Traffic was stopped by two stalled trucks (not *truck's*).

Apostrophe with Possessives

The apostrophe with the letter *s* shows possession: my best friend's car, the football team's record, the visitors' decision. If the possessor does not end in the letter *s*, add apostrophe *s* (*'s.*) If the possessor ends in the letter *s*, add an apostrophe following the *s*.

the car of my <u>best friend</u>	my best friend's car
record of the <u>football team</u>	the football team's record
the decision of the <u>visitors</u>	the visitors' decision

Apostrophe with Contractions

The apostrophe replaces missing letters when two words are joined in a contraction. (*Note:* Use contractions sparingly in academic writing.)

cannot	can't
will not	won't
have not	haven't

EXERCISE 13.19

Proofread the following sentences for words with missing or misused apostrophes. Eliminate apostrophes in simple plurals and add apostrophes as needed to form possessives and contractions.

EXAMPLES:

We rode bike's across my moms lawn, front and back, up and down the driveway.
   (simple plural)   (possessive)
We rode bikes across my mom's lawn, front and back, up and down the driveway.

He grabbed me and my friend's and took us down to the principals office.
         (simple plural)   (possessive)
He grabbed me and my friends and took us down to the principal's office.

1. All of this happened in a few second's. I fell asleep, and that was that.

2. My sisters Mustang was upside down in the ditch.

3. The first time at anything can leave a vivid image in ones' mind.

4. My rehearsal's were at 10:00 a.m. on Saturdays and Sundays.

5. I dont remember the rest of the cast's part's, but they had roles on the stage.

6. My whole family, including my mother's aunt's, came to see the events.

7. A lot of student's at school loved that teacher.

8. When they answered rudely to the substitute teacher, I was surprised at my classmates behavior.

Copyright © 2007, The McGraw-Hill Companies, Inc. All rights reserved.

EXERCISE 13.19 continued

9. During my first year's at college, I was on the deans list, until distraction's started to have an impact.

10. I wasnt able to break down math problem's and solve them correctly.

Search and Correct

EXERCISE 13.20

Double-check your punctuation. Proofread your essay and look for apostrophe errors. Eliminate unnecessary apostrophes from simple plurals; add apostrophes for possessives.

EXERCISE 13.21

Double-check your spelling. Computer spell-checks make mistakes. Therefore, it is essential that you proofread your paper before turning it in for a grade. Focus your close reading on typographical errors.

EXERCISE 13.22

Find a proofreading pal. After you have double-checked your paper, exchange papers with that student and proofread each other's work. Find out what errors your classmate would like you to search for. Using your list from Exercise 13.18, tell your classmate what errors you are inclined to make.

> ### REFLECT
> - Identify successes
> - Set goals

Each time you write, you build skills and strategies. The last step in the writing process is to reflect and recognize what you did well and what you learned.

Identify Successes

EXERCISE 13.23

Take a few minutes to reflect on your successes. Write one or two sentences that explain two things you have learned from this chapter and how you successfully applied them to your writing. Use a specific example from your work to support your thinking.

Set Goals

EXERCISE 13.24

Now that you have examined your successes, determine what challenges you face. Rate yourself using the following scale—5 indicates a task that you consider a challenge most of the time, and 1 indicates a task for which you have the required skills and strategies.

Copyright © 2007, The McGraw-Hill Companies, Inc. All rights reserved.

EXERCISE 13.24 continued

Stages	Strategies and Skills	5	4	3	2	1
Prewrite	1. I prewrite to explore my ideas and think deeper about a topic.	—	—	—	—	—
Draft	2. I focus my essays with thesis statements and topic sentences.	—	—	—	—	—
	3. I organize my ideas and make connections.	—	—	—	—	—
Revise	4. I read critically to identify and use the successful techniques of other writers.	—	—	—	—	—
	5. I identify the strengths and weaknesses in my papers.	—	—	—	—	—
	6. I apply specific revision strategies to my papers.	—	—	—	—	—
Edit	7. I employ all or some of the following editing strategies:					
	■ search for apostrophe errors in simple plurals and possessives	—	—	—	—	—
	■ use spell-check on my computer	—	—	—	—	—
	■ read a printed copy of my essay aloud to check for spelling errors and typographical errors	—	—	—	—	—

EXERCISE 13.25

Finish the following sentences in order to explore your learning experience and to set goals.

1. My attitude toward writing is

2. I still need to work on

STUDENT SAMPLE OF THE WRITING PROCESS

STUDENT MODEL

Vickie's Freewriting

Drinking is how many people relieve stress. Family and friends always ask me to go out to the bar with them. They say I need to go out and relax, but getting drunk has never relieved my stress, in contrast it has always increased my stress. When I drink, especially at a bar, I always over drink, argue with people at the bar, and wake up with a hangover that lasts for three days. I

continued

don't think drinking really can be described as relaxing. Gardening is a great hobby. Planting flowers and vegetables is very relaxing. Its wonderful to watch them grow, knowing that it's because of the care that you have given them. I know it's a lot of work. "It's much easier to buy my vegetables from the store." People always tell me, but if they could eat a garden fresh tomato sandwich, they would realize the benefits from gardening are not just the relaxation, but the realize how great fresh vegetables taste. I prefer watching TV to reading. Movies that are made from novels are my favorite types of movies. Many people have told me that if I were to read the book, I would never enjoy the movie, but I just don't enjoy reading novels.

Bar patrons enter the bar slowly adjusting their eyes to the lighting. They examine the other patrons seeing if they recognize any of them. They proceed to an available seat and order their first drink. Some sip their first drink, while others rapidly swallow it and order another one. After their first drink, they become sociable and begin to talk with other patrons. Four or five drinks later, depending upon the patron, they begin to become drunk. This is when the type of drinker they are emerges, like the angry drunk, he becomes very load, so that the other patrons will notice him, the social drinker, he leaves at this point, and the quite drinker, he just sits in a corner looking at all of the other patrons.

There are a variety of different types of people that go to bars. There are the alcoholics who go to the bar to drink. They usually go to the bar directly after work and stay until the bar closes. They are usually irresponsible drinkers who think they are able to drive after drink for hours. This is why most alcoholics don't have a driver's license. Another type of people who patronize bars is the social drinker. They will go to the bar after work, however they usually only have a few drinks then they go home. They are the responsible drinkers who always leave before they are to intoxicate to drive home. People who drink to forget their problems are the worst type of bar patrons. They usually get angry or sad after they become drunk. The angry drunk always wants to fight, and usually with patrons who are having the most fun. However, they also flirt with other patron's dates trying to causes a fight. The sad drunk lays their head on the bar and cries.

Vickie's Unedited First Draft

Drinking is how many people relieve stress. Family and friends have always asked me to go out to the bar with them. They say I need to go out and relax, but getting drunk has never relieved my stress, in contrast it has always increased my stress. When I drink, especially at a bar, I always over drink and wake up with a hangover that lasts for three days. I don't think drinking really can be described as relaxing. Gardening is a great hobby. Planting flowers and vegetables is very relaxing. Its wonderful to watch them grow, knowing that it's because of the care that you had given them. I know it's a lot of work. "It's much easier to buy my vegetables from the store." People always tell me, but once they eat a garden fresh tomato sandwich, they realize the benefits from gardening are not just the relaxation, but how great fresh vegetables taste. I prefer watching TV to reading. Movies that are made from novels are my favorite types. Many people have told me that if I were to read the book, I would never enjoy the movie, but I just don't enjoy reading.

There're a variety of different types of people that go to bars. There're the alcoholics who go to the bar to drink. They usually go to the bar directly after work and stay until the bar closes. They're usually irresponsible drinkers who think they're able to drive after drinking for hours. This is why most alcoholics don't have a driver's license. Another type of people who patronize bars is the social drinker. They will go to the bar after work, however they usually only have a few drinks then they go home. They're the responsible drinkers who always leave before they're to intoxicate to drive home. People who drink to forget their problems are the worst type of bar patrons. They usually get angry or sad after they become drunk. The angry drunk always wants to fight, and usually with patrons who are having the most fun. The sad drunk lays their head on the bar and cries.

I don't patronize bars, because I always drink until I am drunk. I resemble the alcoholic, who stays until the bar closes, but I can only handle a few drinks like the social drinker. I always embarrass myself. I'm loud and laugh at everything. This angers the angry drinker. They don't like people who are laughing and having fun, so they usually want to start a fight with me, which results in me getting kicked out of the bar. My sister and I went to a karaoke bar my starting college. This was a mistake, they know I can't handle alcohol, but they took me to the bar. They regularly go to the bar, so they started a tradition of singing a song by Hank Williams Jr., called "A Family Tradition". We began singing, we sounded awful. I started laughing. "You sound like dogs howling at the moon." A woman yelled from the audience, she was probable the angry drunk. This made me laugh harder. "At least we don't look like one." I yelled back. She and Her friend's jumped up from their table and started towards the stage. A few men grabbed them and held them back. My sister grabbed my arm and we ran from the bar. The next day my head was pounding from a headache. I suffered for three days with a hangover.

continued

Copyright © 2007, The McGraw-Hill Companies, Inc. All rights reserved.

People who patronize bars should be responsible drinkers. The article "The Hazards of Alcohol" By Nick reports, "Almost one fifth of all road accidents are caused by drivers who have been drinking." Also, according to the British Medical Association "alcohol is a factor in:

- *60-70% of homicides*
- *75% of stabbings*
- *70% of beatings*
- *50% of fights and domestics assaults"*

The British Journal of Addiction reported about the drinking behavior of criminals' "fours hours prior to their arrest.

Offence	% reporting alcohol intake
Drunkenness	*100*
Drink Driving	*100*
Criminal Damage	*88*
Breach of the peace	*83*
Assault	*78*
Theft	*41*
Miscellaneous	*37*
Burglary	*26*
Total % reporting alcohol intake	*64"*

With these statistics, I believe most people shouldn't patronize bars. However if people choice to drink they need to respect this thing called alcohol.

Vickie's Final Edited Essay

On the Rocks

When I drink, especially at a bar, I always overdrink and wake up with a hangover. One night of fun cannot persuade me to suffer for three days with a hangover. Nevertheless, drinking at the bar is a favorite pastime for many people. For them, the weekend signifies a night out at the bar. Laughing and having fun sound great. However, what about the hangover? Anyway you look at it, going to a bar and drinking involves a huge waste of time and a number of risks.

The bar patron waves his hand in the air towards the waitress. As his eyes meet hers, he points towards the bar, indicating he wants another drink. He waits until the drink is set on the bar and slides his money toward her. "This is for you," he announces, then slides a tip towards her. In between ordering

Copyright © 2007, The McGraw-Hill Companies, Inc. All rights reserved.

drinks, he talks and laughs with other patrons. This ritual continues until he becomes drunk or runs out of money. Then he staggers out the door, gets into his car, and drives home.

Bar patrons are a diverse population. The social drinker only goes to the bar for a few drinks and a short chat with friends. He is very much like the occasional drinker. He's not a regular drinker, so if he overdrinks, he will be more of a danger to himself than to others and most likely wake up with a hangover. The alcoholic goes to the bar to get drunk. He's what many call a regular. There's no telling how these people get home: maybe in a taxi but probably a car they drive. Then there are the ones who go to the bar to forget their problems. Their type represents the worst type of all. After becoming drunk, they become angry or sad. The sad drunk lays her head on the bar and cries. The angry drunk always wants to fight, more often than not, with patrons who are having the most fun. They are a threat to people on the road and to people sitting right next to them.

I had an encounter with an angry drunk a while ago. After I started college, my sisters and I went to a karaoke bar. I'd only been to one maybe once or twice and never sang, but after a few drinks my sisters easily persuaded me to get on stage and sing. They selected the song. It was "A Family Tradition" by Hank Williams Jr. Both my sisters knew the words; I didn't. I just stood there laughing. From the audience, a woman yelled, "You sound like a pack of dogs." This made me laugh even harder. "At least we don't look like one," I yelled back. She must have been the angry drunk because she and her friends jumped up from their table and started toward the stage. A few men grabbed them and held them back while my sisters and I ran from the bar. The next day my head was pounding. I suffered for three days from a hangover. I had a lot of fun. However, the hangover I experienced prevented me from returning to the bar for a long time. Plus, I remembered the angry drunk. Who needs that?

One night of fun can turn deadly real fast. According to The National Association of Probation, "30% of offenders on probation and 58% of prisoners have severe alcohol problems and alcohol is a factor in their offense or pattern of offending." Also the British Crime Survey (BCS) reports that of all violent crimes, 40% of assailants were under the influence of alcohol. Although most people consume alcohol responsibly, they need to remember that alcohol is a drug, and that its effects are not always positive.

continued

Stages	Strategies and Skills	5	4	3	2	1
Prewrite	1. I prewrite to explore my ideas and think deeper about a topic.		X			
Draft	2. I focus my essays with thesis statements and topic sentences.	X				
	3. I organize my ideas and make connections.					
Revise	4. I read critically to identify and use the successful techniques of other writers.					
	5. I identify the strengths and weaknesses in my papers.			X		
	6. I apply specific revision strategies to my papers.			X		
Edit	7. I employ all or some of the following editing strategies:		X			
	▪ search for apostrophe errors in simple plurals and possessives		X			
	▪ use spell-check on my computer	X				
	▪ read a printed copy of my essay aloud to check for spelling errors and typographical errors				X	

1. My attitude toward writing is *a little embarrassed on this paper. I talked about myself, and about getting loaded, which was kind of embarrassing. I really like the way my intro and conclusion came out. It was good repeating the term "one night of fun" in my conclusion after I said it in my intro. It made my conclusion seem like it was working. I'm a little confused too. I read a lot of stuff on this, but you said I should take out all those statistics I put at the end.*

2. I still need to work on *commas. I read out loud. It kinda helps.*

14 *The Argumentative Essay*

*M*ake a case. *Convince your reader. Argue your point.* You will often be asked to present arguments in your college courses. When you construct an argument, you consider different viewpoints and the reasons for those viewpoints. Then you take a position, present evidence, and persuade your reader that one viewpoint is more acceptable than another. In your college classes, you may argue about:

- interpretations of literary works
- values and social practices
- the significance and meaning of historical events
- conclusions from a lab procedure

Argumentation is a special form of problem solving. When you argue, your goal is to understand a problem and articulate a coherent perspective on it. Doing so involves settling matters in your own mind first, then changing your reader's mind and possibly motivating him to act.

IN THIS CHAPTER: A PREVIEW

Thinking and Argumentation

- Elements of Argument
- Exploring Multiple Viewpoints
- Using Forms of Proof

A Process Approach to Writing the Argumentative Essay

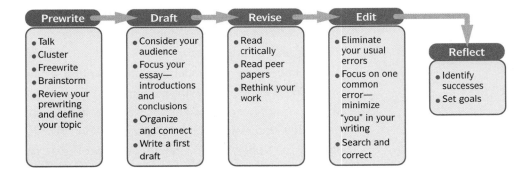

Prewrite	Draft	Revise	Edit		Reflect
• Talk • Cluster • Freewrite • Brainstorm • Review your prewriting and define your topic	• Consider your audience • Focus your essay—introductions and conclusions • Organize and connect • Write a first draft	• Read critically • Read peer papers • Rethink your work	• Eliminate your usual errors • Focus on one common error—minimize "you" in your writing • Search and correct		• Identify successes • Set goals

Student Sample of the Writing Process

Copyright © 2007, The McGraw-Hill Companies, Inc. All rights reserved.

WW | Argument Persuasion

THINKING AND ARGUMENTATION

Argumentation occurs when there is a difference of opinion. In the reading below, Kathy Seal argues that kids these days have too much homework. She uses various forms of evidence to convince her reader that she is right. Her discussion of the problem, however, is not one-sided. She also looks at the issue from the point of view of both parents and teachers, which makes her discussion of the issue balanced. To argue effectively, it is important to take all views into consideration.

Elements of Argument

Writers structure their essays with thesis statements and topic sentences, supporting their ideas with specific details. They often combine thinking and writing strategies in their argumentative essays to present their ideas in a variety of ways: illustration and example, narrative and description, process, cause and effect, comparison and contrast, and definition.

READING: from "Too Much Homework, Too Little Play," by Kathy Seal

Narrative

When I was in junior high school, my parents gave me a typewriter. My friends Amy Neff and Carol Stein often walked with me to my house after school, and we closed my bedroom door and spent the afternoon giggling—or rolling on the carpet, howling with lunatic laughter—as we tapped out silly limericks and satirical stories on my sage-green Hermes. Once we even wrote a play.

Definition

Our after-school typing was not homework. We rambled wherever our teenage imaginations took us; we explored words wildly for the pure fun of it, with no exams, report cards or SAT's in mind. We practiced literary risk-taking and problem solving, honed our language skills and learned perseverance, all with no fear of failure—

Contrast

because we were playing. Few children today have time for this kind of after-school play. There's too much homework. Parents' concerns about overload have become a familiar story as schools all over the country pile on homework in a mis-aimed response to criticism that they were teaching too little. Some elementary teachers routinely assign time-consuming work in each of three or four academic subjects every night.

Cause and effect

Contrast

Amy Neff, one of the friends who helped me enjoy my typewriter in junior high, learned at a school meeting in May that in fifth grade her 10-year-old daughter would have an hour and a half to two hours of homework seven days a week, plus special projects. "The idea is that, under an avalanche of work, children should learn to organize their time efficiently," she wrote to me in an e-mail message. "Nobody has mentioned creativity: ideas, content of what is learned. Just doing LOTS, FAST!" The

Examples

parents and grandparents of today's children had time for "playing around" with stamp collections or model airplanes, writing a fairy tale, selling lemonade or indulging a fascination with space travel. What many people do not realize is that these kinds of interests and hobbies are just as important as academic learning.

Examples

Many successful adults have a childhood history of freewheeling play. Louis Ignarro, a Nobel Prize winning pharmacologist, had six successively complex chemistry sets and played with model rockets. When Letty Cottin Pogrebin, president of the Authors Guild, an association of published writers, was 9, she spent afternoons writing and drawing for a monthly magazine she printed on a primitive press called a hectograph. She charged friends and family 3 cents a copy and then mailed each copy with a 3-cent stamp. She recalls now, "I never understood why the magazine didn't make a profit." But that's just the point: when kids play, they are free to experiment and learn from their experiences, without worrying about how well they're performing.

Thesis statement

Though homework has a clear benefit in high school, there is no research showing that any amount of it advances the education of elementary school kids. They may be stuffing a great deal of information into their heads, but after an hour or two, children lose any eagerness or joy they had in learning. That's important, because research has shown decisively that when children enjoy it, their learning is deeper, richer, and longer-lasting.

Cause and effect

Parents do have some recourse. They can meet with principals and teachers, organize other parents, and protest. Parents in several communities, including Piscataway, N.J., have prevailed upon school districts to enact homework limits. For their children, at least, there may still be time to indulge in the ancient and powerful medium for learning known as play.

EXERCISE 14.1

There are various reasons for and against assigning lots of homework. Use the following chart to record your thoughts.

Reasons for assigning lots of homework	Reasons against assigning lots of homework

Exploring Multiple Viewpoints

EXERCISE 14.2

For each of the following issues, explore opposing points of view. List several reasons supporting each point of view. In a sentence, state your viewpoint on the issue.

EXAMPLE:

Issue: body piercing

Reasons for piercing	Reasons against piercing
Attractive to look at	*Painful*
A fun thing to do	*Makes parents mad*
Makes me feel like part of my generation	*Infection*

Copyright © 2007, The McGraw-Hill Companies, Inc. All rights reserved.

Your viewpoint: *Body piercing is not something I would choose to do.*

1. Issue: requiring young people to do community service

Reasons for	Reasons against

Your viewpoint:

2. Issue: using calculators in math class

Reasons for	Reasons against

Your viewpoint:

3. Issue: going on a crash diet

Reasons for	Reasons against

Your viewpoint:

4. Issue: attending a community college

Reasons for	Reasons against

Your viewpoint:

Copyright © 2007, The McGraw-Hill Companies, Inc. All rights reserved.

EXERCISE 14.2 continued

5. Issue: living together before marriage

Reasons for	Reasons against

Your viewpoint:

Using Forms of Proof

Seal uses three forms of proof in her short essay on page 286. The essay begins with her own personal testimony. She had playtime when she was a kid, so she knows the value of it. This discussion is a form of **ethical proof.** It demonstrates that she knows through firsthand experience what she is talking about. Seal also uses **emotional proof** by appealing to the reader's feelings: Depriving children of their playtime is an emotional issue. Shouldn't we let kids be kids? Finally, she uses **logical proof** by presenting additional evidence, in the form of her friend's testimony and in the form of examples.

Forms of Proof		Conveyed Through:
Ethical	Persuades the reader that you, the speaker, are informed and reliable	Personal narrative, your tone of confidence and control of the subject
Emotional and Logical	Persuades the reader that your topic and arguments are important and timely; makes an appeal to the reader's sense of what is right and reasonable	Illustration and example, narrative, process analysis, cause-and-effect analysis, comparison-and-contrast analysis, and definition
Evidence and Testimony	Persuades the reader, with facts, data, opinion, and expert testimony	Factual and statistical information, quotations from experts and authoritis

Ethical Proof

EXERCISE 14.3

In a short narrative paragraph, explain your personal connection and knowledge of the following topics. If you do not have firsthand experience, tell a story about someone you know, using his or her experience to convey your knowledge of the issue.

EXAMPLE:

Body Piercing

Once, when I was fifteen, I talked my mom into taking me to get my belly button pierced. I wanted to get it done really bad. Almost all of the girls in my classes had it done. Everyone thought it was the coolest thing. My best friend wanted to have it done too, so she came along. There were tattoos all over the walls when we got there. It looked like a place where bikers would hang out. It was kind of scary. I paid my sixty dollars and went first. It didn't hurt too bad. Anna was next. We were relieved when it was over. When I woke up the next day, my belly button was swollen. It was horrible. It hurt just to sit up. Here I had spent all of this money to be in pain. I ended up taking it out. It just wasn't worth it.

1. Issue: requiring young people to do community service

2. Issue: using calculators in math class

3. Issue: going on a crash diet

4. Issue: attending a community college

5. Issue: living together before marriage

Emotional and Logical Proof

EXERCISE 14.4

For each of the following topics, write a sentence that states your position on the issue. Then cite three or four reasons that support your viewpoint. Indicate whether your reason is ethical, emotional, and/or logical.

EXAMPLE:

Issue: body piercing

Position statement: *Body piercing may seem like a cool thing to do, but it has too many unpleasant side effects.*

Copyright © 2007, The McGraw-Hill Companies, Inc. All rights reserved.

EXERCISE 14.4 continued

A. *Piercing has been around for centuries and is widely practiced in many cultures as a way of adorning the body. (logical)*

B. *Some piercings get infected and pose additional health risks. (logical)*

C. *It makes some people feel prejudiced against you when they see your piercings. (emotional/logical)*

D. *It's painful having it done in the first place. (emotional/logical)*

1. Issue: requiring young people to do community service
   Position statement:

   A.

   B.

   C.

2. Issue: using calculators in math class
   Position statement:

   A.

   B.

   C.

3. Issue: going on a crash diet
   Position statement:

   A.

   B.

   C.

4. Issue: attending a community college
   Position statement:

   A.

   B.

   C.

5. Issue: living together before marriage
   Position statement:

EXERCISE 14.4 continued

A.

B.

C.

Evidence and Testimony

With some topics, personal narrative and anecdotal evidence go only so far. For example, to talk about the health risks associated with body piercing, you would have to do some research. Facts and statistics would add to the power of your argument.

- **Facts** are verifiable pieces of information that cannot be disputed. That Thomas Edison went deaf is a fact. It cannot be disputed. That he was America's greatest inventor is a matter of opinion. That the polar ice caps are shrinking is a fact. It cannot be disputed. The causes of this shrinkage, however, may be open to question.

- **Statistical evidence and data** come from studies. Studies are conducted under careful circumstances. When their results are reported, the data become part of the news, part of the conversation about the subject. Most students cannot present numerical data off the top of their head. They have to read and become informed on their subjects.

- **Expert opinion and testimony** help you make a case. Just as in a court proceeding, where expert testimony helps persuade a judge and jury, the arguments you make in college will be more powerful and persuasive if you make use of expert testimony. Sentences beginning "According to the *New York Times* . . ." or "The *Wall Street Journal* reports . . ." have power because of the prestige of those publications. As a writer, you say to the reader, "I'm not the only one who thinks this way; the *Christian Science Monitor* does too."

Reading, learning, and generally "doing your homework" will help you identify additional information to use as evidence.

EXERCISE 14.5

Read the following excerpts and select a quotation and two facts from each that you could use in an argumentative essay. Use appropriate punctuation when copying quotations and write facts in paraphrased form. For more information on these skills, see Chapter 10.

EXAMPLE:

Issue: body piercing

READING: from "Piercing Opens Body to Potential Health Risks," by Sherice L. Shields (*USA Today*)

Periodontist Jeffrey Linfante hadn't seen anything like it. A 32-year-old-man came to his office with sore gums, and it wasn't the result of poor gum care. The man had a small barbell-shaped piece of jewelry in his pierced tongue. He had developed a habit of rubbing the ball of his jewelry along the front of his gums, making the area sore and raw. After 18 months, gingivitis developed.

Copyright © 2007, The McGraw-Hill Companies, Inc. All rights reserved.

EXERCISE 14.5 continued

Linfante, of the University of Medicine and Dentistry of New Jersey Dental School, called in two other dentists to examine the man. It was the first case they had seen linking tongue jewelry to gum complications. The doctors replaced the damaged tissue with tissue from the back of the patient's mouth. The case study, to be reported later this month in *General Dentistry,* comes at a time when experts are worrying that the rising popularity of body piercing also will bring a rise in serious health complications. Beyond gum disease, there are other, more serious possibilities, including hepatitis and HIV infection, health specialists say. "Everybody's worried about broken teeth—forget about that," says Manuel Cordero, spokesman for the Academy of General Dentistry in Chicago. "[Piercing is] a portal entry to potentially killing viruses—and that's nasty."

Research into the effects of body piercing is too new to see a direct relationship between it and disease, but doctors are concerned about delayed effects. Adding to concerns is that body piercing is largely an unregulated industry, and practitioners don't have to answer to any licensing authority. State health departments don't check piercing establishments regularly—only after a customer complaint. And piercers learn through one- to two-year apprenticeships; there is no school for the trade.

Whether body piercing is a time bomb won't be known for years.

Quotation: *According to* USA Today, *"Experts are worrying that the rising popularity of body piercing also will bring a rise in serious health complications."*

Fact/data/opinion: *The body piercing industry is not carefully regulated by state health departments. Consequently, unsafe practices can be overlooked until there is an incident.*

Fact /data/opinion: *Body piercing is an opening in the body where dangerous viruses such as HIV can enter.*

1. Issue: requiring young people to do community service

READING: from "Service-Learning Satisfies Young People's Desire for Public Service" (from Education Development Center)

When young people so readily joined the nation's massive outpouring of generosity following September 11, their public spiritedness came as no surprise to one group of people—the K–12 teachers who use service-learning in their classrooms. Service-learning is a teaching strategy that combines classroom curriculum with community service, to enrich learning, teach civic responsibility, and strengthen communities. According to a report released recently by the National Commission on Service-Learning, chaired by former Senator John Glenn, service-learning offers the chance to actively engage young people by channeling the inclination to help others into activities that promote academic achievement.

Service-learning stands at the intersection of civic and academic engagement. For example, Miami High School in Oklahoma is close to one of the nation's worst toxic clean-up sites and when a group of students and community members learned that children in their community had high levels of lead in their blood, they formed the Cherokee Volunteer Society to increase community awareness of the hazards of exposure to lead and other heavy metals found in local water.

The teachers at Miami High School collaborated with Cherokee tribal leaders and the Environmental Protection Agency and biology students conducted sophisticated water monitoring procedures, language arts classes engaged in creative writing essays and research projects related to toxic waste, and journalism classes tackled public relations, public-health communications and community awareness issues. The students at Miami High School reaped numerous academic benefits while helping the community. Similarly, in West Philadelphia, a neighborhood that had been consistently undercounted by the U.S. Census, eighth graders at Turner Middle School came up with strategies to make sure that people there were fully counted. After a year-long project that applied math, social studies and language arts skills, their neighborhood had the most complete census count of any in the city.

Studies show that large numbers of young Americans are not fully engaged— intellectually or otherwise—in the teaching and learning enterprise. As many as half of all high school students find their classes boring, and substantial majorities see no particular reason to get good grades in school or to refrain from cheating on tests. Disengagement also extends to activities fundamental to democratic society, such as voting and keeping up with current events. Service-learning has proved to be a powerful antidote to student disengagement.

Quotation:

Fact/data/opinion:

Fact/data/opinion:

2. Issue: using calculators in math class

READING: from "Calculators in Class: Freedom from Scratch Paper or 'Crutch'?" by Mark Clayton

It's just after 8 a.m., and Jacqueline Stewart is closely monitoring calculator use in her first-hour math class at Okemos High School. Students are graphing: $y = (x - 3)n$. "All right, you can use calculators on this problem," she says with a light Scottish lilt, "but I want you to conjecture about the expected shape [first]."

This isn't just any math class. It is Core-Plus Mathematics, one of only five math programs designated as "exemplary" by the US Department of Education. The course emphasizes real-life problems, group learning, and weaving together subjects from algebra to trigonometry. It also uses calculators. A lot.

Ms. Stewart and others say calculators are needed to engage students with problems like figuring out how fast college costs are growing, or working out statistical problems in manufacturing processes. Critics, however, say calculators are overused in US middle and high schools. They warn that a wave of "new new

Copyright © 2007, The McGraw-Hill Companies, Inc. All rights reserved.

EXERCISE 14.5 continued

math" programs that employ calculators much more than traditional approaches are entering grade schools, threatening basic math skills. David Klein, a math professor at California State University in Northridge, says calculators should "not be used at all in grades K–5, and only sparingly in higher grades." That's not where America's schools are headed, however. Calculators are an important part of Mathland, Everyday Math, Connected Math, and other new math-reform programs touted by the Education Department last fall as "exemplary" or "promising." One reason such programs use calculators more than traditional math is that they are aligned with the 1989 National Council of Teachers of Mathematics standards. Those standards strongly advocated using more "technology."

"Do we really need to do long division with decimals, with pencil and paper? Calculators give kids the tools for thinking about math ideas they didn't have before," says James Fey, a math professor at University of Maryland.

Quotation:

Fact/data/opinion:

Fact/data/opinion:

3. Issue: crash diets

READING: from "Fad Diets" (from the American Heart Association)

The American Heart Association has declared war on fad diets. Many fad diets—like the infamous Cabbage Soup Diet—can undermine your health, cause physical discomfort and lead to disappointment when you regain weight soon after you lose it.

Fad diets usually overemphasize one particular food or type of food. They violate the first principle of good nutrition: Eat a balanced diet that includes a variety of foods. If you are able to stay on a fad diet for more than a few weeks, you may develop nutritional deficiencies, because no one type of food has all the nutrients necessary for good health. The Cabbage Soup Diet is an example. This so-called fat-burning soup is eaten mostly with fruits and vegetables. The diet supposedly helps heart patients lose 10–17 pounds in seven days before surgery.

Fad diets also violate a second important principle of good nutrition: Eating should be enjoyable. Fad diets are so monotonous and boring that it's almost impossible to stay on them for long periods. A liquid protein diet, using digested collagen with little or no essential substances added, became popular several years ago. But in 1977 this diet was blamed for at least 60 deaths.

In what other ways are fad diets flawed? Many don't encourage physical activity—for example, walking 30 minutes most days of the week. This helps you maintain weight loss over a long period. Physical inactivity is a major risk factor for heart disease and increases the risk of stroke. Because fad diets require drastic changes in eating patterns, you can't stay on them for long. Fad dieters don't learn anything about permanently changing their eating patterns.

Quotation:

Fact/data/opinion:

Fact/data/opinion:

4. Issue: attending a community college:

READING: from "Making Your Own Map—Success at a Two-Year College"
(from www.colleges.com)

It is sometimes assumed that attending a community or technical colleges is "easier" than attending a 4-year college or university. Not only is this false, the reverse is often true. Community and technical colleges can be more challenging than their 4-year counterparts. The classroom experience at both 2- and 4-year colleges is of equal difficulty for equal courses. English 101 at a large university should not differ in any significant way from English 101 at a community college. Of course, every college has different levels of teaching expertise and the quality of the faculty can vary. One of the biggest differences between 2- and 4-year colleges is what happens outside the classroom.

The average age at many 2-year colleges is over 30. Community and technical colleges are convenient to adults returning to higher education. Unlike many 18–24 year old students, adults have little interest is the many activities and support services provided by colleges outside of the classroom. At many 2-year schools, these activities or services are entirely optional. For young adults these services may provide essential counseling, advising or tutoring support but it is up to the individual to seek out these support areas. The challenge is in deciding which services or activities are appropriate.

At 4-year colleges, students are counseled more closely on their extra-curricular choices. Often, a student's academic progress is also monitored to be sure that the college is aware of potential problems. This seldom happens at 2-year colleges. Here, it is necessary for each student to consider their own progress and decide if additional campus resources are needed. Don't expect to be coached through admission, financial aid or registration. The student at a community or technical college who waits for someone to guide them through campus life will not be rewarded.

Quotation:

Fact/data/opinion:

Fact/data/opinion:

Copyright © 2007, The McGraw-Hill Companies, Inc. All rights reserved.

EXERCISE 14.5 continued

5. Issue: living together before marriage

READING: from "Study Finds '20-Something' Dating Culture Focused More on Seeking 'Low-Commitment' Relationships Than Finding Marriage Partners" (from Rutgers University)

Today's "20-something" young adults aren't looking for marriage partners when they date. Instead, they are focusing on fun, casual sex and low-commitment relationships, according to "Sex Without Strings, Relationships Without Rings," a new study by the National Marriage Project at Rutgers.

"Today's singles scene is not oriented toward marriage, nor is it dedicated to romantic love as it has been in the past," said David Popenoe, co-director of the National Marriage Project and professor of sociology at Rutgers.

"Although the study participants expect their future marriages to last a lifetime and to fulfill their deepest emotional and spiritual needs, they are involved in a mating culture that may make it more difficult to achieve this lofty goal," said Barbara Dafoe Whitehead, co-director of the National Marriage Project.

The study found that young men and women enter their 20s with nearly identical goals and attitudes: to achieve individual financial and residential independence before marriage and to delay marriage to an indefinite future.

However, timetables for marriage begin to diverge during the second half of their 20s. Men report a reluctance to give up single life and independence, but remain optimistic about finding the right woman when they are ready to settle down. Women become more serious about the search for a marriage partner, but the older they get the more disenchanted they become with the pool of prospective mates and the likelihood of finding a husband.

The study also reports that young men and women are likely to favor living together before marriage or as an alternative to marriage; identify the fear of divorce as a key reason for living together and for postponing marriage; idealize marriage but also see the experience of being married as hard and often difficult work; see marriage as a potential economic liability, due to the high rate of divorce, rather than as a way to get ahead economically; support marriage preparation and relationship education as an effective way to prevent divorce and unhappy marriages.

Study respondents also see marriage as a couples relationship designed for intimacy and love rather than as an institution designed for parenthood and childrearing.

Quotation:

Fact/data/opinion:

Fact/data/opinion:

A PROCESS APPROACH TO WRITING THE ARGUMENTATIVE ESSAY

The argumentative essay looks at a topic about which there is a difference of opinion. It considers both sides of the topic and uses proof—ethical, emotional and logical, and evidence and testimony—to persuade a reader that one view is preferable to the other. Following are some suggested topics for your argumentative essay.

ARGUMENTATIVE ESSAY TOPICS

Banning loud music in public places
Prohibiting profanity in public
Public displays of affection
Babies in restaurants or movies
Physical education requirements in schools

STUDENT MODEL

Student Sample

Thesis statement

Ethical proof

There is a need for dress codes in school. I can understand that students need to express themselves, but there have to be boundaries. When I attended high school, every young girl wanted to emulate Madonna. Today it's Britney Spears or Lil' Kim, and all the young men want to look like "thugs" or "players" in their baggy jeans showing their underwear. It is true that teens, even preteens, love fashion trends, but schools have to maintain some kind of order so they can educate students. It is important for students to learn that they cannot always do as they please.

Logical proof

Kids have their reasons for wanting to be fashionable. School is their primary meeting place. Up-to-date fashions are fun to wear. Also, certain fashions can identify kids with a particular group. Kids like that. Simply put, they want to fit in. Then there's shock value, plain and simple. School can be a dull place. Wearing something wild simply cuts down on the boredom of school. Kids feel they are expressing their individuality. All this may be true, but it's possible to go too far.

Ethical proof

How far is too far? When I entered into school one winter morning, another student was being escorted to the principal's office by security guards for wearing a full-length fur coat and fedora-style fur hat. I did not think of him as cool, but more like a show-off. Designer clothing? I believe certain designer items should not be allowed in school at all, like expensive handbags, jackets, and even some designer belts. How about fluorescent hair color? How can a student focus on a teacher's lecture with a fluorescent, hot-pink lightbulb sitting in front of them? At one time, schools worried about short skirts and made rules about hemlines. Now they have to deal

Expert testimony

with "skin-is-in fashions." According to *Education Week*, "The new look is everywhere: back-to-school issues of the magazines YM and Teen Magazine are replete with advertisements for girls' jeans that ride low and tight on the hips and shirts that expose bellies, backs, cleavage, and shoulders." Students need to remember that schools are trying to prepare them for the "real world." Employers are not going to hire someone with cotton-candy-colored hair.

Emotional proof

Girls are the worst offenders when it comes to a dress code. Young ladies are always trying to push the envelope, wearing everything from tube tops to booty shorts. Girls love attention and know how to get it, but see-through tops and miniskirts short enough to show their buttocks are not the right clothing for school. It is in every school's best interest for young girls to come to school dressed appropriately. Everyone needs to remember it's an education show, not a style show.

Restating the thesis

Clothes are just the beginning. Students also want to bring pagers, cell phones, and video games to school just to show off. They want to wear gold jewelry, leather, and fur just to show what they can afford. All that junk has no place in a learning atmosphere. Limitations have to be put in place in order for students to learn.

PREWRITE

- Talk
- Cluster
- Freewrite
- Brainstorm
- Review your prewriting and define your topic

Select one or more of the following prewriting strategies to explore a topic and develop ideas for an argumentative essay.

Copyright © 2007, The McGraw-Hill Companies, Inc. All rights reserved.

Talk

EXERCISE 14.6

Pair off with another student and talk about the topic that interests you the most. Use at least two thinking and writing strategies to help organize your discussion.

Cluster

EXERCISE 14.7

Explore the topic that interests you the most. Use the following clustering diagram to discover subtopics and supporting details relevant to the topic.

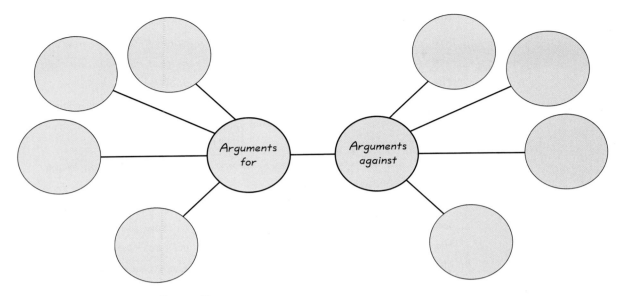

Freewrite

EXERCISE 14.8

Using your clustering as a guide, write as much as you can in ten to fifteen minutes about your topic. As you write, keep in mind the need to look at this issue from more than one point of view.

Brainstorm

EXERCISE 14.9

Keep in mind the thinking and writing strategies you have learned. List everything that you discovered about your topic in the previous prewriting exercises. Add to the list anything you thought of since you talked to your classmate about the topic. As you work, connect the details and ideas to a thinking and writing strategy you can use to structure your writing.

Thinking and Writing Strategies		
Illustration and Example	**Narrative**	**Process**
Are there specific examples of your subject?	Can you discuss an incident to make your point?	What people are involved in the process?
Are the examples similar or different?	Who was involved?	Where and when does it occur?
Do those examples lead to more examples? to more specific detail?	When and where did it occur?	Are materials, gear, props, or equipment involved?
	What were the important actions?	What is the most important detail?
	What was the outcome?	
Cause and Effect	**Comparison and Contrast**	**Definition**
Does this thing have one or more causes?	In what respects does it resemble another object or idea?	Does this thing have components or parts?
Does it have one or more effects or consequences?	In what respects is it different?	What is its function or purpose?
Does it help to think in terms of reasons for this thing?	Is there a key detail of similarity or difference?	What are its origins?
		How does it change over time?
		How does it differ from things similar to it?

Review Your Prewriting and Define Your Topic

EXERCISE 14.10

Use the following questions to review your prewriting and define your topic for your argumentative essay.

- What is your topic and why is the topic important to you?
- What important ideas and details did you discover in your prewriting? Why are they important?
- Which ideas and details in your prewriting will you probably not explore further? Why?
- What do you need to know more about in order to get started in your essay?

DRAFT

- Consider your audience
- Focus your essay— introductions and conclusions
- Organize and connect
- Write a first draft

Write a draft that organizes your prewriting into an argumentative essay. Your first draft will establish the subject and explore the point you wish to make in multiple paragraphs.

Consider Your Audience

EXERCISE 14.11

Now that you have selected a topic, consider who will read your paragraph. Use the following questions to consider how to convey your point to an audience.

- Why is this topic important to your audience?
- What special meaning does this topic have for you? Why do you want your audience to understand this meaning?
- Will your audience agree or disagree with your thinking? Will you be asking them to think about your subject in a new way?
- Return to the exercises on argumentative thinking in this chapter and decide which way of thinking about your topic will help you connect best with your audience.

Focus Your Essay—Introductions and Conclusions

Argumentative essays address a problem or a difference of opinion. Your introduction should quickly state the problem and pull the reader into the essay. Your thesis statement should help the reader see a range of viewpoints.

Some Guidelines for a Focused Introduction

1. Start with a snappy first sentence.

   Citizenship matters.

   Two plus two? Just a second, let me get my calculator.

Copyright © 2007, The McGraw-Hill Companies, Inc. All rights reserved.

Lose a few pounds, make yourself sick: Welcome to the modern age of dieting.

They know their professors, and their professors know them.

Bill and Pam had been living together for six weeks when it stopped being fun.

2. Use one of the thinking and writing strategies to get your paper started.

Illustration-and-example introduction: Bill and Pam had been living together for six weeks when it stopped being fun. First the bills came. Rent, gas, electricity, phone—altogether, they were over $650. They argued about whose calls were whose. Then Pam lost her job. After that it didn't matter how many calls she'd made. Bill had to pay the phone bill and all the other bills, too. Pam's parents were unhappy about the "living arrangement." Pam missed her mom but didn't feel she could just go home, not after the way she had moved out. Living with Bill wasn't such a great idea.

Comparison-and-contrast introduction: Kids need to work. If they don't know how, they can't survive. But work isn't by definition a good thing. Many years back you would see children as young as 8 or 9 years old working in coal mines and many other very dangerous positions. Today's generation of kids are working in what we call McJobs. These jobs include such positions as cashiers and cooks at fast-food places like McDonald's, Burger King, or Arby's. While these jobs can help our youth become accustomed to the workforce, they also come with risks.

Summary introduction: In her essay "Breaking the Chain" M. F. K. Fisher recalls being punished by her father. She tells about a time she dropped her baby brother and her father hit her out of anger for it. She then went upstairs and waited. Her father finally came up and gave her a spanking for what she had done. As he was leaving, he told her it was "the last time." Fisher learns that her father had been beaten as a kid and that he had promised to never do that to his children. But he did. That's the problem with corporal punishment. It may seem useful, but too often it is used in anger and ends up hurting rather than helping.

3. Formulate a thesis statement. The thesis captures the range of viewpoints you will explore. It sums up the paper. It can appear at the beginning, middle, or end of your introduction.

4. In an argumentative essay, a conclusion emphasizes the reasons for a logical viewpoint and/or states the writer's opinion.

Logical viewpoint: Clothes are just the beginning. Students also want to bring pagers, cell phones, and video games to school just to show off. They want to wear gold jewelry, leather, and fur just to show what they can afford. All that junk has no place in a learning atmosphere. Limitations have to be put in place in order for students to learn.

The writer's opinion: I don't believe that we should send every juvenile offender to prison for life. Discipline is important, but rehabilitation is key. If we can make productive citizens of young offenders, we have not only punished but we have taught as well. There are certain horrific crimes that deserve a life sentence, but most juveniles deserve a chance to reform. There must be a middle ground.

EXERCISE 14.12

Read the following thesis statements and indicate whether they are too broad, satisfactory, or too specific. Revise those statements that are too broad or too specific.

Copyright © 2007, The McGraw-Hill Companies, Inc. All rights reserved.

EXERCISE 14.12 continued

EXAMPLE:

Body piercing is a cool thing to do.

(Too Broad)   Satisfactory   Too Specific

Revised: *Body piercing may have some disadvantages, but it's a fashion statement that some young people want to make.*

1. Last spring, young people from Stevenson High School were involved in a two-week community service project.

   Too Broad   Satisfactory   Too Specific

   Revised:

2. If they are used after kids have learned some basic math, calculators can be useful in some math classes.

   Too Broad   Satisfactory   Too Specific

   Revised:

3. Crash diets can be very harmful.

   Too Broad   Satisfactory   Too Specific

   Revised:

4. Community colleges cost less than four-year institutions.

   Too Broad   Satisfactory   Too Specific

   Revised:

5. Living together before marriage may seem like a good idea, but there are definitely problems that come with it.

   Too Broad   Satisfactory   Too Specific

   Revised:

Organize and Connect

EXERCISE 14.13

Use key words and repetition to establish connections between your introduction and the body of your paper. Use the following example as a model.

EXAMPLE:

Thesis statement: *People should not be <u>free</u> to smoke when and where they want to, especially if their smoking is an <u>irritant</u> or <u>health risk</u> to nonsmokers.*

Topic sentence: *For a long time, smoking was <u>freely</u> accepted in public; it was even considered attractive.*

EXERCISE 14.13 continued

Topic sentence: *In recent years, however, as fewer people smoke, the <u>irritation</u> factor in smoking increases.*

Topic sentence: *Studies show that even more than being an <u>irritant</u>, second-hand smoke may be a definite <u>health threat</u> to nonsmokers.*

Manage Opposing Points of View

In your haste to prove that your point of view is preferable, you may dismiss the opposing argument before adequately explaining it. To make sure you don't, devote a separate paragraph to discuss the opposing viewpoint. The following student samples serve as illustration.

STUDENT MODEL

Unedited Student Sample—Single Paragraph

I love video games. There are not a waste of time; they are a great form of entertainment. They don't really makes kids fat. Eating a lot of junk food does that. And video games don't turn your brain to mush. They involve thinking and sometimes instant decision making. They may cost a lot of money, but you can use the games over and over again, which really means that you are saving money. They don't make kids into anti-social morons. Often kids get together for entire afternoons of socializing together as they play their games.

Revised Student Sample—Multiple Paragraphs

I love video games. I can't understand why anyone would have any reason to dislike them. They are not a waste of time. They are a great form of entertainment. Video games can be more action packed, scarier, or even more dramatic than most movies. They also last longer than a movie. On top of that, you control everything in a video game. Then there is the challenge. Video games challenge your coordination, reflexes, problem-solving abilities, and more. They help you become better at all of these things. Before I started kindergarten, I learned to read a little and do some simple math from video games. So I guess you could say they have educational value, too.

Then why would anybody hate them? Well, for many reasons. Some people would rather play sports, hang out with friends, or go to a party. Others would rather listen to music, read a book, or watch TV. It's just an entertainment preference. Video games are repetitive, which some find frustrating. And there are games filled with mindless violence. Perhaps the biggest problem is that video-game haters have yet to try the right game. Sometimes a person will play a bad game and think, "That game was stupid. Video games are stupid." That's like losing all hope in television because you've seen a few substandard TV shows.

Destinations: Mapping Arguments

The Need to Convince

Chinese or Mexican food? Comedy or romance? Democrat or Republican? Ours is a society of choices, and we often make choices as members of a group: The family chooses a restaurant, the couple chooses a movie, the nation chooses a president. Hence, the ability to argue convincingly and effectively for our own point of view is an essential skill to master. If we want our desires and opinions to be taken seriously, we need to be able to support them with well-considered evidence, and to present them in a coherent, compelling form. Whether you are in the midst of discussing a crucial family decision, or just deciding where to eat dinner, the skills you acquire in learning to write an effective argumentative essay will benefit you in many aspects of your daily life.

Making Your Case, Supporting Your Points

The argumentative essay is one of the most critical kinds of college writing. Far from being limited to English courses, the argumentative essay spans nearly every academic discipline. A student in a nutrition class defending her interpretation of a case study; a political science major analyzing the results of an election; a student of social work writing in favor of a particular public health initiative: all of these individuals are making arguments. Each has arrived at a thesis and each uses evidence from his or her research or field work to support and give shape to a central argument.

Hear Me Out on This One, Boss

The importance of making effective arguments in the workplace cannot be stressed enough. In the business world, decisions can affect not just your daily job, but also your long-term future and potential prosperity. Consequently, it is essential that you are able to make your views and desires understood by your coworkers and your employer. Remember, just because your boss occupies a higher rung on the corporate ladder does not mean that he or she is always right. Learning to convince your boss of a certain course of action without seeming disrespectful and learning to convince coworkers without alienating them is a crucial business skill.

EXERCISE 14.14

Make an outline of your paper. Group your discussion of opposing viewpoints in separate paragraphs. In each paragraph, concentrate on one reason or argument at a time. For each argument, provide explanation and elaboration.

Read for Testimony and Evidence

The ideas of authorities and experts make your argument more persuasive. Your goal is to convince your reader that you are well informed. Practice summarizing what you read and integrating this material into your paper. For more extensive practice on summarizing, see Chapter 10.

EXERCISE 14.15

Read the passage below that relates to your topic. Write a two- or three-sentence summary of content that would be useful in your paper. Be sure to paraphrase.

1. Issue: banning loud music in public places

READING: from "A High-Volume World Takes a Toll on Ever Younger Ears," by Linda Kulman

Everyday life is growing noisier and as it does, more Americans are losing their hearing sooner. Long accustomed to treating senior citizens, a growing number of hearing specialists now report that patients in their 40s and 50s—and sometimes even in their teens—are turning up in their waiting rooms complaining that things

Copyright © 2007, The McGraw-Hill Companies, Inc. All rights reserved.

don't sound as clear as they should. "I see middle-aged patients," says Dr. Thomas Balkany, a professor of otolaryngology at the University of Miami, "who have the kind of hearing we'd expect to see in their parents."

Statistics are starting to bolster the experts' observations. The National Health Interview Survey shows that from 1971 to 1990, hearing problems among people ages 45 to 64 shot up 26 percent, and among those ages 18 to 44, they grew by 17 percent. A study conducted in Alameda County, Calif., over three decades shows that hearing loss for men between the ages of 50 and 59 leapt by more than 150 percent. Perhaps more troubling, a study published last year in the *Journal of the American Medical Association* showed that nearly 15 percent of young people 6 to 19 years old showed signs of hearing loss. "You expect your kids to be better off than you are," says John Wheeler, president of the Deafness Research Foundation. "But I had to turn the radio up louder when I reached 50, and my son will probably have to do it at 40."

For nearly one third of the 28 million Americans with hearing loss, "toxic noise" is the main culprit. Loud workplaces remain the most common source. Over the years, legions of Americans lost their hearing working unprotected in steel mills and mines. Other people lost it in the military. But today, a growing source of hearing impairment is the tools and toys of recreation. Americans are pounding their ears with gas-powered leaf blowers and high-amplified stereos, with Nascar races and 1,875-watt hair dryers, even, remarkably, with children's playthings.

Yet the public remains largely unaware of the damage that modern living may be doing to the delicate organs attached to the sides of their heads. Warning labels on noisy appliances are virtually nonexistent. And while Americans are bombarded with admonitions to wear helmets while bike riding and condoms while having nonmonogamous sex, they rarely think to wear earplugs while mowing the lawn. "You don't bleed when you suffer hearing loss," says Les Blomberg, executive director of the Noise Pollution Clearinghouse in Montpelier, Vt., "so people do not recognize the damage they're doing."

Summary:

2. Issue: prohibiting profanity in public

READING: from **"Oh #$@%*!: The Rise in Public Profanity,"** by **Samantha Bennett**

It's shocking to hear a string of obscenities trumpeting from a mouth that still also contains baby teeth. Sometimes I just want to take the urchin aside and explain that, like sex and nudity, strong language should be a relatively private, discreet form of communication in order to maintain its unique power. But the analogy would probably be lost on the little Visigoths anyway. Especially if it were expressed in words of more than four letters.

Copyright © 2007, The McGraw-Hill Companies, Inc. All rights reserved.

EXERCISE 14.15 continued

And let's not overlook the issue of volume. It's a fine and therapeutic thing to hiss your venom to an understanding pal or two, but some expressions are simply not meant to be shouted heartily across a crowded city street at lunchtime in the presence of children, old ladies and, for all you know, actual members of the clergy.

I suppose partly to blame are the parents I see, in the stores and on the sidewalks, scolding their wee cherubs with blue barrages that would be startling from a sailor in a brothel.

I think back to the quaint interjections of my own dear mother, who censored herself at least until my adolescence with exclamations like "holy cow," "oh, sugar," "what the Sam Hill" and an inscrutable bit of blasphemy in Welsh. I only hope I can similarly clean up my own colorful banter in the event of motherhood.

It's silly, to me, to assert that we don't need profanity, and that in situations of extreme vehemence and duress we should be satisfied by a heartfelt "Phooey!" True, Col. Potter of "M*A*S*H" could exclaim "Horse hockey!" with admirable conviction, but most of us lack Harry Morgan's delivery.

A now-retired colleague of mine used to press ordinary words into duty as curses with bizarre effects. It's hard not to laugh when a grown man loses his patience, stands up in a newsroom and thunders, "Oh, MILK!" We have these words in our language for a reason, you see. We need them. They serve a purpose. Sometimes, "You're full of beans" and "I'm terribly nonplussed by this turn of events!" just isn't going to cut it.

But like anything else that is overused, strong words can lose their power and become meaningless. And then we'll have to find other words to shock people. I nominate "propriety."

Summary:

3. Issue: public displays of affection

READING: from **"Keep Your Hormones outside the Classroom!"**
by P. M. Fabian

The couple sits quietly, pretending to listen to what's going on around them, but they secretly exchange longing looks, gazing deep into each other's eyes. The boy rubs his beloved's back, and leans over to whisper sweet nothings in her ear. The girl responds by blushing profusely, and tries to suppress a giggle as the boy nuzzles her neck, and plants tiny kisses up and down her arm and neck.

Sounds like some cheesy romance novel, doesn't it? Believe it or not, the preceding scene was similar to something I witnessed during one of my lectures. Public displays of affection in the classroom make the rest of us look bad by projecting a negative image of the typical student; professors and graduate students may take the immature behavior of others and chalk it up to the flippancy of the

EXERCISE 14.15 continued

insolent undergraduate. In their minds, if some students act that way, then they all must act that way, too.

Of course, there are those who may question my motivations behind criticizing this peculiar courtship practice. I anticipate that some people would think I'm some kind of embittered, jaded coed who is destined to a future of spinsterhood, and that I'm just lashing out because I'm insanely jealous of what I don't have.

First of all, my personal life is nobody's business but my own. Second of all, my opinion on this matter has no bearing whatsoever on my personal status; the point is, PDA in the classroom is just plain rude.

Ask anyone, single or attached, their opinion on the subject. I guarantee they'll agree that mushiness during a lecture is pretty darn juvenile and embarrassing.

So to those couples who just can't keep their hands off each other in class, I say to you: grow up. This isn't high school any more. If you and your sugarplum kumquat of love are just going to sit there and make googly eyes at each other throughout the lecture, then there's no real point of coming to class, now, is there?

You can spout off all you want about the idealistic nobility of romance. You can defend the sincerity of your feelings toward your cuddlecakes. You can engage in a little PDA out in public. But please, do us all a favor and fawn all over your schmoopie after lecture lets out. You're making the rest of us sick.

Summary:

4. Issue: babies in restaurants or movies

READING: from "Screaming Me Me's," by Christina Waters

Small children allowed to run loose in the aisles, to scream, fuss and throw food, all without a word from adults, are unlovable monsters of the future. They and their adult companions should be asked to leave.

A few things are clearly at work here, social forces conspiring to create auditory mayhem in a variety of public places—restaurants, movie theaters, libraries, airplanes, churches—places we share with other like-minded citizens in search of sanctuary, food, entertainment and mobility. These fellow citizens have paid for these privileges and are entitled to a certain amount of fair exchange for keeping their end of the social contract.

Check out John Stuart Mill's "On Liberty" for the clearest statement of the arrangement. We're free to exercise our liberty up to the point where our actions infringe on someone else's freedom. In other words, we're all in this together. By going into a public place to dine, or to purchase coffee and read the newspaper, we each agree to abide by tacit rules of politeness and mutual respect. I don't sit at a table that is obviously already occupied by someone else's coffee and books. That's a violation of someone's prior right to this territory.

Let's apply this pragmatic theory to noise conduct. When you enter a public zone, a space you share with others who similarly expect to be entering a public

EXERCISE 14.15 continued

zone geared to a common purpose, e.g., dining, movie going, football-watching, you have to realize that you're one of many people engaged in the activity. The 747 does not exist just to transport you and your brood from San Jose to Newark and back. There are 235 other people who also paid money to take the trip. It's not your private party. And not everyone is equally charmed by Jonah's ability to recite the alphabet at the top of his lungs while running up and down the aisle.

Here's the deal. Many of the people sitting at tables around you, struggling not to throw down their forks and give you a piece of their minds, are dining out as a break from dinner with the little rugrats. Unlike you, they actually shelled out cash money and hired a babysitter so as not to inflict their rambunctious toddlers on total strangers. If your children aren't ready for prime time, keep them at home until they are.

Summary:

5. Issue: physical education requirements

READING: from "New Phys Ed Favors Fitness over Sports," by Kathy Slobogin

For many baby boomers, physical education class was daily torture. Slow children were sitting ducks for dodge ball, while klutzes were subject to humiliation, hoping against hope they wouldn't be picked last for a team. Not only were there scars, but it now appears those P. E. classes weren't especially good at developing long-term fitness.

"Our old focus was on athletic skill and focusing on about 30 percent of the population—the athletes," said Phil Lawler, a physical education instructor in Naperville, Illinois. "But most of those athletes' careers ended three or four years after they left us and many times they were not athletic after their athletic careers. So what value did we bring to their lives?"

The National Association for Sport and Physical Education recommends that elementary school students should have a minimum of 60 minutes of moderate and vigorous activity every day while middle and high school students should have 30 minutes. The focus on competitive sports also sidelined some of the children who needed physical education the most, according to Lawler. "I think we turned off thousands of children to exercise over the years when they were embarrassed that they weren't one of the best in the class and they kind of hid away."

Lawler is a guru of "the new P. E.," a model he has pushed in his school district for the last 10 years. The new P. E. focuses on the 70 percent of kids who will never be varsity athletes. It's about fitness skills, not athletic competition.

Madison Junior High School in Naperville is a model of the new P. E. The gym is designed as a health club, with weight lifting, exercise bikes and running machines. Rollerblading and a rock-climbing wall get as much attention as competitive sports. Although team sports are still played, Lawler picks the teams.

Copyright © 2007, The McGraw-Hill Companies, Inc. All rights reserved.

EXERCISE 14.15 continued

Students are graded on how well they stay within their heart-rate zones, not how many baskets they shoot. "I now can have a child literally running a six-minute mile at this age, and a 14-minute mile, and each child will get the same grade based on the number of minutes they put in their zone," explained Lawler. "If the best they can do is walk and they're in their zone, that's great."

Each child at Madison gets a computer printout that records things such as his or her cholesterol, heart rate and body fat. The physical transcript follows the student through 12th grade. Lawler said the school's monitoring detected some form of heart disease in at least six students over the last few years.

The movement is spreading. About 30 percent of Illinois schools have changed to the new model, said Lawler, and officials from over 100 schools around the country have visited Madison in the last two years. But the national picture is bleak. At the same time that childhood obesity has reached epidemic levels—doubling in the last 30 years—physical education classes are vanishing.

According to the Centers for Disease Control, 10 years ago, 42 percent of high school students attended daily P. E. class—today it's only 25 percent. A 1997 survey found that a quarter of all U.S. students get no P. E. at all. As schools are pressured to improve students' academic performance, P. E. often gets squeezed out of the curriculum.

One bright spot is the recently passed Physical Education for Progress Act, which provides $5 million in grants for selected school districts to improve their P. E. programs. The grants average $300,000 per district. Lawler's setup at Madison Junior High cost about $75,000, but he said it can be done for less with creative scavenging and donations. In any case, he said the investment pays off far beyond a student's school years.

"I can't grade you on whether you're healthy or not," said Lawler. "Life is going to have a way of grading you. When you go to the doctor, when you're 30 and 40, we're going to find out if you passed or failed."

Summary:

Write a First Draft

EXERCISE 14.16

Use the following checklist as a guide to draft your argumentative essay.

_____ Review your prewriting to clarify your purpose and what you want your audience to understand.

_____ Insert details to develop your ideas and explain points of view.

_____ Focus your thesis and topic sentences.

_____ Insert transitions to connect ideas and details.

_____ Include a focused introduction and conclusion.

Copyright © 2007, The McGraw-Hill Companies, Inc. All rights reserved.

REVISE

- Read critically
- Read peer papers
- Rethink your work

Begin revising by asking yourself these questions: Will an audience understand my purpose? Is there sufficient detail? Are my ideas connected and is my purpose clearly defined?

Read Critically

EXERCISE 14.17

Examine the following essay. Underline the thesis statement and topic sentences and look for the essay's strengths and weakness.

According to an article in the *Washington Post,* jobs for teenagers are not beneficial. The article claims that fast-food jobs do not give teenagers the experience they need. Most teenagers who hold such jobs do poorly in school. Some of them drop out of school. Everything is done for them so they do not learn much. It is a waste of time for kids to work eight hours a day at a job they gain nothing from.

Teenage jobs have some advantages. They teach kids how to make their own money. Therefore, they don't need to run to mom and dad every time they need something. If something happened to their parents, they would know how to work for themselves. It also gives them something to do instead of getting into trouble with their friends. However, there are many disadvantages as well. It is difficult for kids to concentrate in school when their mind is on work. They are not able to devote all their time to studying because their job takes up a lot of their time. They don't gain skills from flipping burgers or mopping floors. It is a waste for kids to work at such jobs when they benefit very little.

I worked in a gas station with my father when I was fifteen years old. It was very difficult for me to focus on school and work at the same time. I couldn't do my homework because I had to wait on customers. Sometimes I couldn't get up for school the next day because I had to stay up late to do my homework. I didn't gain many skills. I only got stressed out. I knew that I would be better off if I got to work in a better environment.

Working wouldn't be so bad if teenagers were able to work at better jobs. Kids should work in fields that prepare them for the work they would like to go into. They need experience in a variety of areas. They should be able to work with doctors and lawyers. Such experience would educate them and expand their minds. They would do better in school if they worked with educated people. Kids who grow up in educated fields tend to succeed in life. Kids who work with riffraff usually do not get very far.

As stated in the article in the *Washington Post,* "There is no room for initiative, creativity, or even elementary rearrangements in fast food jobs." Allowing kids to work at such jobs leads them to believe that is it okay for them to do this type of work for the rest of their life. It is unfair to cheat kids out of the training and education they need because employers need low-income workers. Using young kids to do other people's dirty work has got to stop. If kids are not given proper training when they are young, they will grow up to be stepped on like the floors they are ordered to mop.

EXERCISE 14.17 continued

Focus

1. Is the essay's subject clear? Will a reader understand why this topic is important?

Detail

2. What thinking and writing strategies does the writer employ?

3. Does the writer provide adequate details to develop ideas in the essay?

Connections

4. Does the writer present the ideas in an order that is effective? Does anything seem out of order or irrelevant?

5. Is that order made clear by connecting words?

Taking a Critical View

6. What are the strengths and weaknesses of the paper?

Strengths	Weaknesses

7. What will improve this paper?

Read Peer Papers

EXERCISE 14.18

Form a group of three or four students and take turns reading and discussing your papers. Use the questions from Exercise 11.16 to identify each paper's strengths and weaknesses. Offer suggestions for a revision plan.

Rethink Your Work

EXERCISE 14.19

Review your essay and make the following revisions as necessary.

- Revise your introduction so it makes a strong first impression
- Identify the point of your essay, sharpening your thesis statement and topic sentences as needed.

Copyright © 2007, The McGraw-Hill Companies, Inc. All rights reserved.

EXERCISE 14.19 continued

- Emphasize key details in each paragraph by elaborating and providing additional detail.
- Cut nonessential details.
- Reorganize your paper so the most important ideas come near the end.
- Focus your conclusion with an important detail from the introduction or body of your paper.

> ### EDIT
>
> - Eliminate your usual errors
> - Focus on one common error—minimize "you" in your writing
> - Search and correct

Prepare to turn your essay in for a grade. Make sure you are not repeating errors you usually make. Then look for new errors that may distract your reader from the purpose and meaning of your writing.

Eliminate Your Usual Errors

EXERCISE 14.20

Turn to the grids in Chapters 18, 19, and 20 where you have been keeping track of the errors you make. List those errors in the space provided below. Then proofread your paper and correct the errors you find.

_____ _____ _____

_____ _____ _____

Focus on One Common Error—Minimize "You" in Your Writing

Because the argumentative essay is a very formal assignment, you should try to avoid excessive use of the pronoun "you." Sentences like "You might choose to get a tattoo to express your individuality" should be rewritten as "A young person might choose to get a tattoo to express her individuality."

EXERCISE 14.21

Revise each of the following sentences to eliminate the pronoun "you."

EXAMPLE:

Teenage jobs have some advantages. You learn how to make your own money. Therefore, you don't need to run to mom and dad every time you need something.

Revised: *A job can have some advantages. It teaches kids how to make their own money. Therefore, they don't need to run to mom and dad every time they need something.*

1. I was about five years old. We lived on Cornell Street in a house with an upstairs. The street was gravel. It was hard riding your bike. You would hit a pile of rocks, and it messed up your steering and balance.

EXERCISE 14.21 continued

2. A responsibility I think all young people should have is taking care of themselves. Make sure you are doing what you have to do in your life to be a good person.

3. I have two beautiful young girls. Luckily they are healthy and active. They keep you going all day. As a single parent I could never imagine having constant responsibility of both children.

4. My father plays golf a lot, and he enjoys it. He says that sometimes he gets frustrated but that you just have to relax and slow yourself down.

5. What people do for a job might become a career. Choose something that you will enjoy and can take great pride in. If you don't enjoy what you do, then your life is just wasted, and what pride is there in that?

6. There are many ways a person can protect herself from fools on the road. The person next to you might not realize he is crossing into your lane.

7. This could be a problem with some people. If a person disagrees with them, they'll argue with you until you feel that they're right.

8. In my parents' generation, if a guy had a piercing, you were weird.

9. In sales, especially if you work for a commission, you should make it your duty to satisfy the customer.

10. This was not the kind of job you could slack off at. I had to be prepared at any second because with kids you never know what is going to happen.

Search and Correct

EXERCISE 14.22

Double-check your work. Proofread your essay and make revisions to minimize the frequency of "you" in your paper.

EXERCISE 14.23

Double-check your spelling. Computer spell-checks make mistakes. Therefore, it is essential that you proofread your paper before turning it in for a grade. Focus your close reading on spelling errors caused by spell check.

EXERCISE 14.24

Find a proofreading pal. After you have double-checked your paper, exchange papers with that student and proofread each other's work. Find out what errors your classmate would like you to search for. Using your list from Exercise 14.19, tell your classmate what errors you are inclined to make.

> **REFLECT**
> - Identify successes
> - Set goals

Each time you write, you build skills and strategies. The last step in the writing process is to reflect and recognize what you did well and what you learned.

Identify Successes

EXERCISE 14.25

Take a few minutes to reflect on your successes. Write one or two sentences that explain two things you have learned from this chapter and how you successfully applied them to your writing. Use a specific example from your work to support your thinking.

Set Goals

EXERCISE 14.26

Now that you have examined your successes, determine what challenges you face. Rate yourself using the following scale—5 indicates a task that you consider a challenge most of the time, and 1 indicates a task for which you have the required skills and strategies.

Stages	Strategies and Skills	5	4	3	2	1
Prewrite	1. I prewrite to explore my ideas and think deeper about a topic.	__	__	__	__	__
Draft	2. I focus my essays with thesis statements and topic sentences.	__	__	__	__	__
	3. I organize my ideas and make connections.	__	__	__	__	__
Revise	4. I read critically to identify and use the successful techniques of other writers.	__	__	__	__	__
	5. I identify the strengths and weaknesses in my papers.	__	__	__	__	__
	6. I apply specific revision strategies to my papers.	__	__	__	__	__
Edit	7. I employ all or some of the following editing strategies:					
	▪ search for "you" and minimize or eliminate it	__	__	__	__	__
	▪ use spell-check on my computer	__	__	__	__	__
	▪ read a printed copy of my paragraph aloud to check for spelling errors and typographical errors	__	__	__	__	__

Copyright © 2007, The McGraw-Hill Companies, Inc. All rights reserved.

EXERCISE 14.27

Finish the following sentences in order to explore your learning experience and to set goals.

1. My attitude toward writing is

2. I still need to work on

STUDENT SAMPLE OF THE WRITING PROCESS

STUDENT MODEL

Marilyn's Clustering

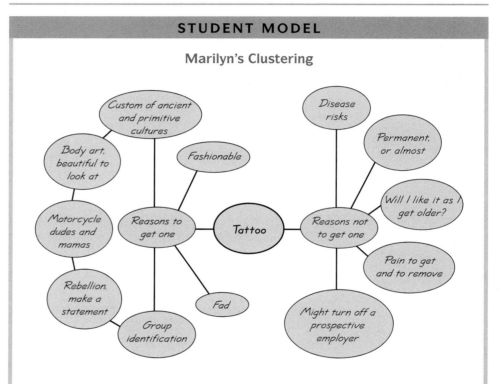

Marilyn's Freewriting

Tattoos, who could do that to their body? If you get a tattoo where people can see it, what can you possibly get that won't look ridiculous when you're sixty? But, if you get one where no one will see it what's the point? Forget about if it can be seen or not, it hurts, and you're going to be paying someone for the pain.

The fan of body art has sentimental feelings about tattoos. He puts a lot of thought into the art he gets. His tattoos are a collection of significant and meaningful things in his life. He is able to display his devotion on his skin for all to see. By understanding his tattoos, you begin to understand him. His tattoos tell a story about him and his life without any words. He didn't just walk into a tattoo shop and pick something off the wall without any

Copyright © 2007, The McGraw-Hill Companies, Inc. All rights reserved.

thought. His tattoos are based around the things he loves. An enthusiast has poured over dozens, perhaps hundreds, of images in order to find just the right one, he may even design one of his own. Once he has made his decision, he can't wait to get under the needles. This isn't his first, it's been several body parts ago since he was considered a newbie. He doesn't show any signs of apprehension, he does not flinch when the needle punctures his skin, he just grits his teeth against the vibrating pain. He appreciates the cliché, "no pain, no gain." The time spent in pain will be worth it when it's over. When he takes off the bandage and sees the symbol he chose to represent some part of his life, he will feel nothing but pride.

Who gets tattoos? Young people, trying to express themselves, will endure ritualistic pain, in order to get an image put into their skin. They are showing the world what an individual they are. They thumb their noses at society's view of tattoos. Someone who is going though a midlife crisis would put himself through the pain of a tattoo, anything to look and feel young again. A tattoo would be a symbol for their youthful daring and rebellion. Gang members get tattoos to show their unity, that they belong to a group. They wear tattoos like a badge of courage, or a barcode, depending on who's viewing it.

The first time I looked in the mirror and saw a thirty-something mom looking back at me, I thought of getting a tattoo. What better expression of youth is there? Vandalizing one's own body seems to be a trend. I'm very sensible, so I decided to think long and hard about the image I would have forever stamped on my body. The next consideration was where would I have it put? I didn't want it anywhere too obvious, but if it were hidden completely from sight, what would be the point?

I decided on a somewhat small, oriental design, to be put on the back of my neck. My husband suggested I go to the same place he had his last tattoo done. It sounded good to me, so off I went. I mustered up my courage and accompanied by my husband, walked into the tattoo shop. While I waited for my turn, I studied the other people there, all of whom already had several tattoos. I tried to picture what they would look like in twenty years. Then I pictured what I would look, with a tattoo, in twenty years. Ridiculous is the only word that came to mind. I did pay for a tattoo that day, and my husband still loves the tribal that HE received. I guess in the end my sensibility won out.

There are many reasons people will get a tattoo; their parents will hate it, to use their body as a symbol of self- expression, to belong to a group, they think they are sexy, or because they simply had a moment of insanity.

continued

Marilyn's Unedited First Draft

There are many reasons people will get a tattoo; their parents will hate it, to use their body as a symbol of self-expression, to belong to a group, they think they are sexy, or because they simply had a moment of insanity. The web page, CRAZYFORTATTOO, is one mans list of these reasons.

There are a myriad of reasons why people get tattoos. The reasons why are as varied as the people that get them. Young people, trying to express themselves, will endure ritualistic pain, in order to get an image put into their skin. They are showing the world what an individual they are. They thumb their noses at society's view of tattoos. Someone who is going though a midlife crisis would put himself through the pain of a tattoo, anything to look and feel young again. A tattoo would be a symbol for their youthful daring and rebellion. On the other end of the spectrum are gang members. Gang members wear tattoos like barcodes, identifying them, not as individuals, but as part of a whole. Once branded, members are forever part of that whole. Whether a person is, or was, a Blood or Marine they will always be associated with that group, through their tattoo.

These reasons for getting tattoos are also good reasons not to get them. They may show what you stand for when you are young, but you may not stand for the same things when you are older. If you get one to feel or look young again, you might wish you just dyed your hair. The people that get them because of the gang or group they are involved with need to consider if they will always be part of that group.

If you get a tattoo where people can see it, what can you possibly get that will still be attractive when you are sixty? However, if you get one where no one will see it what is the point? Forget about if it can be seen or not, it hurts, and you are going to be paying someone for the pain. The demand for advancements in tattoo removal should wake people up; obviously many people decide their tattoos were a mistake.

Skeptics that do not understand another's love for living art have to look at the fan. The fan of body art has sentimental feelings about tattoos. He puts a lot of thought into the art he gets. His tattoos are a collection of significant and meaningful things in his life. He is able to display his devotion on his skin for all to see. By understanding his tattoos, you begin to understand him. His tattoos tell a story about him and his life without any words. He did not just walk into a tattoo shop and pick something off the wall without any thought. His tattoo center around the things he loves. An enthusiast has poured over dozens, perhaps hundreds, of images in order to find just the right one, he may even design one of his own. Once he has made his decision, he cannot wait to get under the needles. This is not his

Copyright © 2007, The McGraw-Hill Companies, Inc. All rights reserved.

first; it has been several body parts ago since he was a newbie. He does not show any signs of apprehension, he does not flinch when the needle punctures his skin, he just grits his teeth against the vibrating pain. He appreciates the cliché, "no pain, no gain." The time spent in pain will be worth it when it is over. When he takes off the bandage and sees the symbol he chose to represent some part of his life, he will feel nothing but pride.

The first time I looked in the mirror and saw a thirty-something mom looking back at me, I thought of getting a tattoo. What better expression of youth is there? Vandalizing one's own body seems to be a trend. I am very sensible, so I decided to think long and hard about the image I would have forever stamped on my body. The next consideration was where would I have it put. I did not want it anywhere too obvious, but if I hide completely from sight, what would be the point? I decided on a somewhat small, oriental design, to go on the back of my neck. My husband suggested I go to the same place he had his last tattoo done. It sounded good to me, so off I went. I mustered up my courage and accompanied by my husband, walked into the tattoo shop. While I waited for my turn, I studied the other people there, all of whom already had several tattoos. I tried to picture what they would look like in twenty years. Then I pictured what I would look, with a tattoo, in twenty years. Ridiculous is the only word that came to mind. I did pay for a tattoo that day, and my husband still loves the tribal that HE received. I guess in the end my sensibility won out.

Marilyn's Final Edited Essay

Too Sensible for Tattoos

There are many reasons people get a tattoo: to make their parents mad, to use their body as a symbol of self-expression, to belong to a group, to look sexy, or just to act kind of crazy. The reasons are as varied as the people who get them. Young people, trying to express themselves, will endure ritualistic pain in order to get an image put into their skin. They are showing the world what an individual they are. They thumb their noses at society's view of tattoos. Someone who is going through a midlife crisis will suffer the pain of a tattoo to look and feel young again. A tattoo is a symbol of the remains of their youthful daring and rebellion. At the other end of the spectrum are gang members. Gang members wear tattoos like barcodes that identify them not as individuals but as part of a group. Once branded, members are forever part of that group. Whether a person is a "Blood" or a Marine, they will always be associated with that group because of their tattoo.

continued

These reasons for getting tattoos are also good reasons not to get them. They may show what a person stands for when she is young, but she may not stand for the same things when she is older. If a person gets one to feel or look young again, she might wish she had just dyed her hair. The people who get them because of the gang or group they are involved with need to consider if they will always be part of that group. The demand for advancements in tattoo removal should wake people up; obviously many people decide their tattoos were a mistake.

Skeptics who do not understand another's love for living art have to look at the fan. The fan of body art has sentimental feelings about tattoos. He puts a lot of thought into the art he gets. His tattoos are a collection of significant and meaningful things in his life. He is able to display his devotion on his skin for all to see. To understand his tattoos is to understand him. His tattoos tell a story about him and his life without any words. He did not just walk into a tattoo shop and pick something off the wall without any thought. His tattoos center around things he loves. An enthusiast has pored over dozens, perhaps hundreds, of images in order to find just the right one. He may even design one of his own. The pain will be worth it. When the bandage comes off, all he will feel is pride.

The first time I looked in the mirror and saw a thirty-something mom looking back at me, I thought of getting a tattoo. What better expression of youth is there? Vandalizing one's own body seems to be a trend. I am very sensible, so I decided to think long and hard about the image I would have forever stamped on my body. The next consideration was where to put it. I did not want it anywhere too obvious, but if I hid it completely from sight, what would be the point? I decided on a small oriental design to go on the back of my neck. My husband suggested I go to the same place he had his last tattoo done. I mustered up my courage and, accompanied by my husband, walked into the tattoo shop. While I waited for my turn, I studied the other people there, all of whom already had several tattoos. I tried to picture what they would look like in twenty years. Then I pictured how I would look, with a tattoo, in twenty years. Ridiculous is the only word that came to mind. I did pay for a tattoo that day. My husband loves the tribal that HE received.

I guess in the end my sensibility won out. Covering my gray turned out to be less dramatic. So much for youthful daring and rebellion. I can't go that far. If I'm in midlife crisis, I guess I'll take care of it with hair dye rather than a tattoo on the back of my neck. Hair dye is temporary; the tattoo is not. I'll just be what I am: a permanent member of that group that says no to tattoos.

Marilyn's Reflection

Stages	Strategies and Skills	5	4	3	2	1
Prewrite	1. I prewrite to explore my ideas and think deeper about a topic.	—	—	—	—	X
Draft	2. I focus my essays with thesis statements and topic sentences.	—	—	—	X	—
	3. I organize my ideas and make connections.	—	—	—	X	—
Revise	4. I read critically to identify and use the successful techniques of other writers.	—	—	—	X	—
	5. I identify the strengths and weaknesses in my papers.	—	X	—	—	—
	6. I apply specific revision strategies to my papers.	—	—	—	X	—
Edit	7. I employ all or some of the following editing strategies:					
	▪ search for "you" and minimize or eliminate it	—	—	X	—	—
	▪ use spell-check on my computer	—	—	—	—	X
	▪ read a printed copy of my paragraph aloud to check for spelling errors and typographical errors	—	—	—	X	—

1. My attitude toward writing is *getting better. I really enjoyed writing this paper. I had been thinking about my tattoo experience for a while. It was fun to write about it. I feel like I understand the subject a little better now. I still don't want one. I'm glad I chose not to have one done on me.*

2. I still need to work on *how much I write. I get going and can't stop. I used to worry about not having enough to say. Now I just keep going and say too much. I need to work on saying just the right things and leaving out all the extras.*

Copyright © 2007, The McGraw-Hill Companies, Inc. All rights reserved.

PART FOUR

A Tool Kit

15 *Building Vocabulary*

How do I build my vocabulary? This is a good question, because a rich vocabulary is essential for the increasingly difficult speaking, reading, and writing demands of college courses.

IN THIS CHAPTER: A PREVIEW

Strategies to Build Your Vocabulary

- Develop a Daily Approach
- Read and Write with a Dictionary and Thesaurus on Hand
- Improve Your Writing with Careful Word Choice
- Learn Commonly Misused Words

WW Word Choice
Word Memory Power

STRATEGIES TO BUILD YOUR VOCABULARY

You build vocabulary with every new experience. Some words you acquire in conversation with friends; others you learn at school, at home, or on the job. To speed the process of building your vocabulary, be strategic. Consciously apply the following strategies as you study or while speaking, reading, writing, or editing your college papers.

- Develop a daily approach.
- Read and write with a dictionary and thesaurus on hand.
- Improve your writing with careful word choice.
- Learn commonly misused words.

Develop a Daily Approach

Each day add a few words to your vocabulary. All of your subjects in college have basic vocabularies. Simply select a few essential words used in your class discussions, lectures, or textbooks. Five new words a day add up to twenty-five new words a week. If five words are too many, add two words a day. Even two new words a day add up to ten new words a week, forty new words a month, one hundred fifty new words in a semester. Use the following three-step approach to systematically select, study, and use new words:

Step 1: Develop a system.

- Devote ten pages in the back of your notebook to vocabulary.

- Flag new words as you read and compile a list of them later.
- Carry a small notebook devoted to word study.

Step 2: Select words.

- Gather technical vocabulary from lectures or textbooks.
- Look for unfamiliar vocabulary that appears repeatedly in your textbooks.
- Focus on concept words that relate to specific subjects or appear in assignments.
- Note unusual or interesting words you want to incorporate in your speech and writing.

Step 3: Study and use each new word in speaking and writing.

- Incorporate the word as you talk.
- Write the word and its meaning.
- Write a sentence using the word. Later in the week, write a new sentence.
- Reread your lists of new words.

Read and Write with a Dictionary and Thesaurus on Hand

Dictionaries
Thesauruses

Expanding your reading and writing vocabulary is a lifelong goal. You will always be building your vocabulary as you are exposed to new courses, work experiences, or personal interests. Speed up your vocabulary growth by getting acquainted with a dictionary and a thesaurus.

Getting Acquainted with a Dictionary

Dictionaries provide much more than definitions. They also provide detailed information on words. By working with a dictionary, you will learn the history of a word, its pronunciation, the word's multiple meanings, and its function or part of speech. *The American Heritage Dictionary* provides the following information on the word *soul:*

Part of Speech
n.—indicates that *soul* is a noun.

Illustrations of the Word in Use

Pronunciation Guide
This is a one-syllable word that is pronounced with a long *o* sound.

Definitions
Soul has a range of definitions, from the spiritual sense to the meaning associated with African American culture.

Origin, or Etymology, of the Word

soul (sōl) *n.* **1.** The animating and vital principle in humans, credited with the faculties of thought, action, and emotion and often conceived as an immaterial entity. **2.** The spiritual nature of humans, regarded as immortal, separable from the body at death, and susceptible to happiness or misery in a future state. **3.** The disembodied spirit of a dead human. **4.** A human: "*the homes of some nine hundred souls*" (Garrison Keillor). **5.** The central or integral part; the vital core: "*It saddens me that this network . . . may lose its soul, which is after all the quest for news*" (Marvin Kalb). **6.** A person considered as the perfect embodiment of an intangible quality; a personification: *I am the very soul of discretion.* **7.** A person's emotional or moral nature: "*An actor is . . . often a soul which wishes to reveal itself to the world but dare not*" (Alec Guinness). **8.** A sense of emotional strength or spiritual vitality held to derive from Black and especially African-American cultural experience, expressed in areas such as language, social customs, religion, and music. **9.** A strong, deeply felt emotion conveyed by a speaker, performer, or artist. **10.** Soul music. [Middle English, from Old English *sāwol*.]

Copyright © 2007, The McGraw-Hill Companies, Inc. All rights reserved.

EXERCISE 15.1

Use your dictionary to clarify the definition of each word in bold type in the following passage.

- List all the definitions given in your dictionary for each word.
- Carefully reread the passage to understand Moore's intended meaning for each boldfaced word.
- Circle the definition from your list that matches Moore's intended meaning.

READING: from *Care of the Soul,* by Thomas Moore

Care of the soul is a fundamentally different way of regarding daily life and the **quest** for happiness. The emphasis may not be on problems at all. One person might care for the soul by buying or renting a good piece of land, another by selecting an appropriate school or program of study, another by painting his house or his bedroom. Care of the soul is a continuous process that concerns itself not so much with "fixing" a central **flaw** as with attending to the many details of everyday life, as well as to major decisions and changes.

Care of the soul may not focus on the personality or on relationships at all, and therefore it is not psychological in the usual sense. Tending to things around us and becoming **sensitive** to the importance of home, daily schedule, and maybe even the clothes we wear, are ways of caring for the soul. When Marsilio Ficino wrote his self-help book, *The Book of Life,* five hundred years ago, he placed emphasis on choosing colors, spices, oils, places to walk, countries to visit—all very concrete decisions of everyday life that day by day either support or disturb the soul. We think of the **psyche,** if we think of it at all, as a cousin to the brain and therefore something essentially internal. But ancient psychologists taught that our own souls are inseparable from the world's soul, and that both are found in all the many things that make up nature and **culture.**

1. quest
   Definitions:

2. flaw
   Definitions:

EXERCISE 15.1 continued

3. sensitive

Definitions:

4. psyche

Definitions:

5. culture

Definitions:

Getting Acquainted with a Thesaurus

A thesaurus helps you select the most precise word. It provides synonyms and antonyms in an easy-to-read list. Like a dictionary, a thesaurus presents words in alphabetical order. Unlike a dictionary, a thesaurus does not provide definitions. To effectively use a thesaurus:

- **Do** read all the synonyms before choosing one to replace your word.
- **Do** use the context of your sentence to make your choice. Choose strong words to make your point.
- **Do** look up words you do not know. A synonym is a word that has *essentially* the same meaning, but it may not have *exactly* the same meaning.
- **Don't** use a word because it sounds sophisticated. Well-chosen simple words are more effective than sophisticated words that are confusing.

Webster's New World Thesaurus provides the following information on the word *explain.*

Copyright © 2007, The McGraw-Hill Companies, Inc. All rights reserved.

Part of Speech
v.—indicates that *explain* is a verb.

Synonym
Syn.—indicates that the words listed have similar meanings.

Alphabetical Entries

explain, *v.*—*Syn.* interpret, explicate, account for, elucidate, illustrate, clarify, illuminate, make clear, describe, expound, teach, manifest, reveal, point up *or* out, demonstrate, tell, refine, read, translate, paraphrase, render, put in other words, decipher, assign a meaning to, construe, define, disentangle, justify, untangle, unravel, make plain, unfold, come to the point, put across, throw light upon, show by example, restate, rephrase, get to, annotate, comment *or* remark upon *or* on, make *or* prepare *or* offer an explanation *or* an exposition (of), resolve, clear up, get right, set right, put (someone) on the right track, unscramble, spell out, go into detail, get over, get to the bottom of, figure out, speak out, emphasize, cast light upon, get across *or* through, bring out, work out, solve, make oneself understood; both (D): hammer into one's head, put in plain English.—*Ant.* puzzle, confuse, confound.

explorer, *n.*—*Syn.* adventurer, traveler, pioneer, wayfarer, pilgrim, voyager, space traveler, investigator, inventor, seafarer, mountaineer, mountain climber, scientist, globe-trotter, navigator, circumnavigator, spelunker, creator, founder, colonist, Conquistador.

Part of Speech
n.—indicates that *explorer* is a noun.

Antonym
Ant.—indicates that the words listed have opposite meanings.

Usage
(D)—indicates that these synonyms may be considered informal for some audiences.

EXERCISE 15.2

A writer uses a thesaurus to find the most effective word. Not all synonyms will work. In the following exercise, use the preceding thesaurus information for the words *explain* and *explorer* to make the word choice more precise.

- Underline the words in each sentence that clarify the meaning of *explain* or *explorer*.
- Use the thesaurus entry above to select a more precise word.
- Select two good choices and one weak choice.

EXAMPLE:

	Good Choices	Weak Choice
Please **explain** your comment on the new tax laws because I did not understand it.	*restate* *rephrase*	*render*

1. It was difficult to **explain** the confusion between my sister and my mother.

2. The meaning of metaphors in poetry is difficult to **explain.**

3. **Explain** the meaning of this word.

4. I knew I was really an **explorer** the day I crawled around caves with a tiny light attached to my hat.

5. I am always thrilled to be the first to do anything; I love the thought that I am an **explorer.**

EXERCISE 15.3

Writers often choose words for their emotional impact on a reader. Read the following excerpt to determine the emotional tone.

- Look up each word in bold type in a thesaurus.
- List the synonyms.
- Circle the words in your list that could serve as good replacements.
- Then determine the emotional effect of these words. What tone does John Simpson create with his word choice?

READING: from "Tiananmen Square," by John Simpson

It was humid and airless, and the streets around our hotel were empty. We had set out for Tiananmen Square: a big, **conspicuous** European television team—reporter, producer, cameraman, sound-recordist, translator, lighting man, complete with gear. A cyclist rode past, shouting and pointing. What it meant we couldn't tell. Then we came upon a line of soldiers. Some of them had bleeding faces; one **cradled** a broken arm. They were walking slowly, **limping.** There had been a battle somewhere, but we couldn't tell where?

When we reached Changan Avenue, the main east–west thoroughfare, it was full of people as in the days of the great demonstrations—a human **river.** We followed the **flow** of it to the Gate of Heavenly Peace, under the **bland,** moonlike portrait of Chairman Mao. There were hundreds of small groups, each concentrated around someone who was **haranguing** or **lecturing** the others, using the familiar, heavy public gestures of the Chinese. Other groups had formed around radios tuned to foreign stations. People were moving from group to group, pushing in, **crushing** round a speaker, arguing, moving on, passing along any new information.

1. conspicuous

2. cradle

3. limping

4. river

Copyright © 2007, The McGraw-Hill Companies, Inc. All rights reserved.

EXERCISE 15.3 continued

5. flow

6. bland

7. haranguing

8. lecturing

9. crushing

10. What emotional tone is created by these words?

WW Word Choice

Improve Your Writing with Careful Word Choice

Powerful writing begins with precise nouns and verbs. A single word can evoke a mental pictures and create an emotional response in the reader. For example, the word *matron* instead of *woman* creates the picture of an older, plain-looking woman. Likewise, the word *scrutinize* instead of *watch* creates the picture of a person looking closely and examining something with great care. Creating these vivid, emotional pictures requires the selection of precise nouns and verbs.

A **noun** is a person, place, or thing.

General diction: woman

Precise diction: lady, maid, girl, matron, broad, doll, dame, spinster

A **verb** describes an action or a state or condition. Most writers prefer **action verbs.**

General diction: walk

Precise diction: hike, traipse, march, saunter, wander, trudge, stroll, cruise

EXERCISE 15.4

Precise nouns and verbs create a concrete image for the reader. The following excerpt from "On Compassion" by Barbara Lazear Ascher provides a powerful image of the homeless. Her description creates a strong contrast between a homeless man and the others on a street corner. This brief encounter poses an important question to prompt a reader to think more deeply about homelessness.

- Pay close attention to the boldfaced nouns and boldfaced and italicized verbs.
- Then answer the questions that follow the essay.

Copyright © 2007, The McGraw-Hill Companies, Inc. All rights reserved.

EXERCISE 15.4
continued

READING: from "On Compassion," by Barbara Lazear Ascher

The man's grin is less the result of circumstance than dreams or madness. His buttonless **shirt,** with one **sleeve** missing, *hangs* outside the waist of his baggy **trousers.** Carefully plaited **dreadlocks** bespeak a better time, long ago. As he crosses Manhattan's Seventy-ninth Street, his gait is the shuffle of the forgotten ones held in place by gravity rather than plans. On the corner of Madison Avenue, he *stops* before a blond **baby** in an Aprica **stroller.** The baby's **mother** *waits* for the light to change and her **hands** *close* tighter on the stroller's **handle** as she sees the man approach.

The others on the corner, five **men** and **women** waiting for the crosstown bus, *look* away. They daydream a bit and gaze into the weak rays of November light. A **man** with a **briefcase** *lifts* and *lowers* the shiny **toe** of his right **shoe,** watching the light reflect, trying to catch and balance it, as if he could hold and make it his, to ease the heavy gray of coming January, February, and March. The winter months that will send snow around the **feet, calves,** and **knees** of the grinning **man** as he heads for the shelter of Grand Central or Pennsylvania Station.

But for now, in his last gasp of autumn warmth, he is still. His **eyes** *fix* on the **baby.** The **mother** *removes* her purse from her shoulder and *rummages* through its contents: **lipstick,** a lace **handkerchief,** and **address book.** She *finds* what she's looking for and *passes* a folded dollar over her child's head to the **man** who *stands* and *stares* even though the light has changed and traffic navigates about his **hips.**

His **hands** *continue* to dangle at his sides. He *does not know* his part. He *does not know* that acceptance of the gift and gratitude are what make this transaction complete. The **baby,** weary of the unwavering stare, *pulls* its blanket over its head. The man *does not look* away. Like a bridegroom waiting at the altar, his **eyes** *pierce* the white veil.

The **mother** *grows* impatient and *pushes* the **stroller** before her, bearing the **dollar** like a **cross.** Finally, a black **hand** *rises* and *closes* around green.

Was it fear or compassion that motivated the gift?

1. Carefully analyze Ascher's word choice. Word choice is the basis for constructing an emotional response in the reader. Insert the highlighted nouns and verbs used to describe the actions of the homeless man, the mother and baby, and the other men and women on the street corner into the table below. Then answer the questions that follow.

The Homeless Man		The Mother and Baby		The Other Men and Women	
Nouns	Verbs	Nouns	Verbs	Nouns	Verbs

EXERCISE 15.4 continued

2. What is your emotional response to the characters in the narrative?

The homeless man:

The mother and baby:

The other men and women:

EXERCISE 15.5

Review the words you analyzed in Exercise 15.4. Then answer the question Ascher poses at the end of the excerpt: "Was it fear or compassion that motivated the gift?" Use specific words that she chooses to support your opinion.

EXERCISE 15.6

Word choice adds an emotional charge to writing. Writers carefully choose words to express emotions and emphasize a point.

Copyright © 2007, The McGraw-Hill Companies, Inc. All rights reserved.

EXERCISE 15.6 continued

1. The photograph shown on p. 332 was taken at a train station parking lot. Consider two different responses to the car using the scenarios described below. List nouns and verbs to describe the car and your emotional reaction.

Scenario	Nouns	Verbs
Scenario 1: You are returning from a three-day trip. This is your car.		
Scenario 2: You are a regular train traveler. This car is part of an art exhibition featuring graffiti artists, which is currently showing at the train station.		

2. Select one of the scenarios above. Write 100 words that describe your encounter with the car. Use careful word choice to suggest a positive or negative emotional response.

Learn Commonly Misused Words

Careful word choice is often complicated by a variety of commonly misused words. There are two varieties of frequently misused words:

- those that sound alike but have different spellings and different meanings
- those that sound similar but have different spellings and different meanings

Develop an awareness of these words and then consciously monitor your usage. Do the following exercises to assess your knowledge and skill at managing these words. Then develop a system to aid you. Some words have unique spellings that make them easy to remember. Take *principle* and *principal*. Remembering that a school *principal* is your *pal* creates a system to distinguish the two words. However, not all words with different meanings have unique spellings, so having a reference book handy or using the reference tools on your computer will help.

Commonly Misused Words—Set 1

Sound alike:	Sound similar:
all ready/already	accept/except
all right/alright	advice/advise
all together/altogether	conscious/conscience
hear/here	choose/chose
its/it's	lie/lay
knew/new	leave/let
their/there/they're	loose/lose/loss
to/too/two	raise/rise
whose/who's	set/sit
your/you're	than/then

EXERCISE 15.7

Commonly misused words sound alike or sound similar but have different meanings. In most cases, they are also different parts of speech. Use your dictionary to look up the common meaning and part of speech of the following words and write them in the space provided. If you already know the definition, check to be sure you are right when you search for the word's part of speech.

EXAMPLE:

part of speech   definition

accept/except

accept: verb—to receive, to understand, to take hold, to allow in

except: preposition—otherwise, than, to the exclusion of
conjunction—unless
verb—to take out

1. advice/advise

2. all ready/already

3. all right/alright

4. all together/altogether

5. conscious/conscience

6. choose/chose

Copyright © 2007, The McGraw-Hill Companies, Inc. All rights reserved.

EXERCISE 15.7 continued

7. hear/here

8. its/it's

9. knew/new

10. lie/lay

11. leave/let

12. loose/lose/loss

13. raise/rise

14. set/sit

15. than/then

16. their/there/they're

17. to/too/two

18. whose/who's

19. your/you're

EXERCISE 15.8

Read the following sentences and select the word whose meaning and part of speech is correct. Circle the correct answer.

1. I have (all ready/already) placed the children's books in the boxes, so these boxes are (all ready/already) to go.

2. I (hear/here) there is a (knew/new) restaurant downtown, but anyplace you choose is (all right/alright) with me.

3. (Their/There/They're) will be more to eat at the party (than/then) you can imagine.

4. If you have to (leave/let) early, please (leave/let) me know at the beginning of the class.

5. I never give (advice/advise) to friends, but (your/you're) an exception (to/too/two) my rule.

6. (Whose/Who's) going to the game with us?

7. Will they bring (their/there/they're) own picnic?

8. Everyone (accept/except) you will be at the party, so plan (to/too/two) come (to/too/two).

9. I have trouble with mathematics so I have given up on it (all together/altogether).

10. I will (choose/chose) a new course for my schedule, so I can (raise/rise) my grades.

11. The boys will stand (all together/altogether) for the picture.

12. I am (conscious/conscience) of the confusion between the (to/too/two) of you.

13. (Its/It's) very late for me to (accept/except) a phone call. Tell the caller that I am not (hear/here).

14. If you let the rope (loose/lose/loss), I can (lie/lay) it flat on the ground.

EXERCISE 15.8 continued

15. Before I (lie/lay) down for a nap, will you (sit/set) down and talk with me about your decision?

16. I never (sit/set) the mail on the counter because I'm afraid I will (loose/lose/loss) something important.

17. I'd rather go to the ball game (than/then) the movies.

18. If we (choose/chose) blue dishes (than/then) we can't buy orange placemats.

19. (Raise/Rise) before dawn and enjoy the beauty of the morning.

20. I (advice/advise) you not to lie because (your/you're) (conscious/conscience) will bother you if you do anything wrong.

21. I knew I might not like the outfit, but I (choose/chose) it to be adventurous.

22. Samantha (knew/new) her cat loved (its/it's) squeaky-toy, but she (choose/chose) to throw it away.

23. (Whose/Who's) dog is sitting on the curb?

24. If you give me (your/you're) phone number, I'll call you when the parts are (all together/altogether).

25. After the game was over, the team waved to (their/there/they're) cheering fans.

26. Amoral people think in terms of someone else's (loose/lose/loss) and their gain.

27. My friends are not coming to the party because (their/there/they're) working tonight.

Commonly Misused Words—Set 2

Sound alike:	Sound similar:
allowed/aloud	behalf/behave
capitol/capital	breath/breathe
hole/whole	clothes/cloth
know/no	complement/compliment
led/lead	propose/purpose
passed/past	safe/save
seen/scene	scared/scarred
threw/through	where/were

EXERCISE 15.9

Commonly misused words sound alike or similar but have different meanings and different spellings. In most cases, they are also different parts of speech. Use your dictionary to look up the common meaning and part of speech of the following words and write them in the space provided. If you already know the definition, check to be sure you are right when you search for the word's part of speech.

EXAMPLE:

part of speech   definition

allowed/aloud

allowed: verb—permissible, permitted

aloud: adjective—audible, capable of being heard

1. behalf/behave

Copyright © 2007, The McGraw-Hill Companies, Inc. All rights reserved.

EXERCISE 15.9 continued

2. breath/breathe

3. capitol/capital

4. clothes/cloth

5. complement/compliment

6. hole/whole

7. know/no

8. led/lead

9. passed/past

10. propose/purpose

11. safe/save

12. scared/scarred

Copyright © 2007, The McGraw-Hill Companies, Inc. All rights reserved.

EXERCISE 15.9 continued

13. seen/scene

14. threw/through

15. where/were

EXERCISE 15.10

Read the following sentences and select the word whose meaning and part of speech is correct. Circle the correct answer.

1. The kids from the next street over (threw/through) rocks at passing cars and people walking in the park. My brother was (scared/scarred) by a huge rock that hit him above the eye. After that, we were (allowed/aloud) to play only with kids on our own block.
2. My cousin would always (behalf/behave) better at school than at home.
3. There are two sides to every story. However, it usually begins with two men who (breath/breathe) sports.
4. The domestic economy siphons off (capitol/capital) needed for foreign investment.
5. Since I gained weight, I am always hunting through my (clothes/cloth) trying to find an outfit that is loose.
6. While camping in New England, my friend and I were awakened by a herd of sheep grazing around our tent. We tried to find (where/were) they might be escaping from. Then we noticed a (hole/whole) in the fence across the road.
7. My (hole/whole) family loves bargain shopping. My sister will drive fifteen miles to (safe/save) even a single dollar.
8. (Know/No) matter how unpleasant a summer job might be, you have to remember that the primary (propose/purpose) is to make money.
9. You can be a very smart person, but you might not (know/no) how to run your own business.
10. I panicked during the exam when the (led/lead) in my only pencil broke.
11. I never lie to my parents about anything major. I'd rather have them (know/no) what I'm up to. They (where/were) kids once too.
12. Sometimes I lied. This (led/lead) my mother to mistrust me.
13. The (capitol/capital) building is beautiful at night.
14. A couple of days (passed/past), and my father began to worry about his paycheck.
15. At the end of the journey, my patience worked out in my (behalf/behave).
16. I heard (threw/through) the grapevine that Kinesha's boyfriend is going to (propose/purpose) to her.
17. I ran home and put my money in a (safe/save) place.

EXERCISE 15.10 continued

18. At that moment, I was very proud of Willie but also very (scared/scarred) at the same time. I had never (seen/scene) such a huge audience.

19. There would often be a violent (seen/scene) in the movie.

20. The United States releases more greenhouse gases than any other country. In the (passed/past), the government did not regulate industry to control gas emissions.

21. I have a bad habit of reading (allowed/aloud) on the bus and irritating people.

22. The best (clothes/cloth) for hiking gear is wool. It wicks away moisture and dries quickly.

23. I love garlic bread, but it gives me the most horrible (breath/breathe).

24. His eyes were (complemented/complimented) by his sandy brown hair.

25. She (complemented/complimented) her employee for a job well done.

Commonly Misused Words—Set 3

Sound alike:	Sound similar:
altar/alter	affect/effect
brake/break	council/counsel/consul/console
born/borne	desert/dessert
cite/site/sight	later/latter/last
coarse/course	moral/morale
discreet/discrete	quiet/quite
do/due	real/really
fourth/forth	
principal/principle	
stationary/stationery	

EXERCISE 15.11

Commonly misused words sound alike but have different meanings. In most cases, they are also different parts of speech. Use your dictionary to look up the common meaning and part of speech of the following words and write them in the space provided. If you already know the definition, check to be sure you are right when you search for the word's part of speech.

EXAMPLE:

part of speech   definition

brake/break

brake: noun—something used to slow down or stop a vehicle

  verb—to stop

break: noun—an interruption; a change in subject; opening shot in a game of pool; separating after a clinch in boxing

  verb—to separate into parts; to ruin or rupture; to end or close; to end a relationship; to divide into groups

1. affect/effect

Copyright © 2007, The McGraw-Hill Companies, Inc. All rights reserved.

EXERCISE 15.11 continued

2. altar/alter

3. born/borne

4. cite/site/sight

5. coarse/course

6. council/counsel/consul/console

7. desert/dessert

8. discreet/discrete

9. do/due

10. fourth/forth

11. later/latter/last

12. moral/morale

13. principal/principle

14. quiet/quite

15. real/really

16. stationary/stationery

EXERCISE 15.12

Read the following sentences and select the word whose meaning and part of speech is correct. Circle the correct answer.

1. I was (real/really) hungry, so I took the (later/latter/last) two pieces of chicken.
2. She wanted only (real/really) flowers at the (altar/alter).
3. The (council/counsel/consul/console) voted to reduce taxes in our town.
4. The (desert/dessert) is (quiet/quite) beautiful in the spring.
5. The (coarse/course) requires you to (cite/site/sight) specific examples of (moral/morale) (principles/principals).
6. I purchased new (stationary/stationery) for the office.
7. The doctor told Bill that any further (affects/effects) from the accident would take months to appear.
8. The (principal/principle) brought (fourth/forth) a new set of rules to be accepted by the Board of Education.
9. It is illegal to (altar/alter) your driver's license.
10. He was (born/borne) on the fourth of July.
11. William has difficulty keeping secrets: he has never been very (discreet/discrete).
12. The farther she walked down the road, the surer she was that she was lost and in need of (council/counsel/consul/console).
13. A (stationary/stationery) bike is great for winter workouts.
14. Students knew work was (do/due) at the beginning of the hour.
15. I'd rather you (do/due) the dishes right after (desert/dessert).
16. Research projects require students to assemble the (discreet/discrete) parts of a paper.
17. The group has (born/borne) the responsibility of the assignment without thinking how it might (affect/effect) their grades.
18. The building (cite/site/sight) has been fenced to stop further vandalism.
19. He did not (brake/break) the stereo.
20. The team's (moral/morale) dropped after their third loss.
21. (Later/Latter/Last), when everyone was (quiet/quite), we could hear the woodpecker in the distance.
22. I didn't know where to go after the (fourth/forth) quarter ended.
23. The Italian (council/counsel/consul/console) asked to stay on the top floor of the Hotel Ritz.
24. I sold my compact car and bought a 4-wheel drive, and after driving in the snow, I prefer the (later/latter/last).
25. I was so angry that I didn't want to (council/counsel/consul/console) my sister after she lost my mother's favorite ring.
26. The fabric softener did not (altar/alter) the (coarse/course) fabric.
27. (Brake/Break) gradually when a stop sign is in (cite/site/sight).

Copyright © 2007, The McGraw-Hill Companies, Inc. All rights reserved.

16 *Sentence Basics*

I *don't think about sentences. I'm too busy trying to get ideas.* Learning the basics of sentence structure will put you on the road to effective writing. Even great ideas can be lost in choppy or tangled sentences. Writing good sentences is another way of getting good ideas. Learn your basic sentence structures:

- the simple sentence
- the compound sentence
- the complex sentence

Basics of Sentence Construction

Glossary, Sentence, Parts of Speech, Sentence Sense

THE SIMPLE SENTENCE

The sentence is a writer's most basic tool. The simple sentence is a building block for more sophisticated writing and thinking. Your task as a writing student is to learn the grammar and mechanics of the complete simple sentence. Your skill with more sophisticated sentences will grow from your skill with the simple sentence.

A **simple sentence** contains two parts: a **subject** and a **predicate.** These two parts form the kernel of the sentence.

subject	+	predicate
family		drove
hair		blew

Two words, however, cannot express much. With modifiers, the simple sentence begins to take on more meaning:

subject	+	predicate
The entire Wilson **family**		**drove** to the seashore on Sunday.
Alice's long dark **hair**		**blew** in the strong ocean breezes.

Some simple sentences are short, others long. However, they all have something in common: one subject and one predicate.

The Subject

All sentences have a subject. The subject is usually stated at the beginning of a sentence. The **simple subject** is the person, place, or thing that does something or is being discussed. The **complete subject** contains the simple subject and the words and/or phrases that describe it.

simple subject

The oldest *sister* always worked harder than the rest of the family.

complete subject

In the preceding sentence, *sister* is the simple subject, the person being discussed. The oldest *sister* is the complete subject; it describes which sister is being discussed.

simple subject

Checkout *lines* in any grocery store are a great place to catch up on Hollywood gossip.

complete subject

In this sentence, *lines* is the simple subject; it is the place where people catch up on Hollywood gossip. Checkout *lines* in any grocery store is the complete subject; it tells us which lines provide the best gossip.

simple subject

My new *puppy* chewed the toes off my new tennis shoes.

complete subject

Puppy is the simple subject in this sentence; it is the thing that acted. My new *puppy* is the complete subject, describing which puppy did the chewing.

In the three preceding examples, the subjects are nouns. Often, however, pronouns serve as subjects. The following box lists common pronouns that serve as subjects.

Personal Pronouns

I	you	she	he	it	we	they

Indefinite Pronouns

all	each	few	no one	somebody
any	either	neither	nothing	someone
anybody	everyone	nobody	one	something
both	everything	none	several	

Copyright © 2007, The McGraw-Hill Companies, Inc. All rights reserved.

simple subject

We ate cold spaghetti quickly.

complete subject

We is a pronoun that names the people doing the action. It is both the simple subject and the complete subject, because *we* has no words to describe it.

simple subject

All *of the* girls went on a trip.

complete subject

All is the pronoun that names the people doing the action; *of the girls* describes who *all* is and which people did the action of going on the trip.

These tips will help you identify the simple and complete subjects in sentences.

- Identify the simple subject first. It is usually a noun or pronoun. It is the doer of the action or the thing being described. The simple subject is the most important part of the complete subject. Ask: Who or what did the action or is being described?

  The underground parking *structure* was crammed with construction equipment.

  simple subject

  In this sentence, the *structure* is being described as "crammed."

- Identify the complete subject next. The complete subject contains the simple subject and the words that describe or explain it. The complete subject is usually the first part of a sentence. Ask: What words describe or explain the simple subject?

  Dozens of black birds crowded on the leafless trees each morning.

  complete subject

  In this sentence, *dozens* is the simple subject; of black birds completes the subject by both explaining and describing it.

- The simple subject is never *part* of a prepositional phrase, although a prepositional phrase may be part of a complete subject:

  simple subject

  Winter in the mountains is absolutely breathtaking.

  complete subject

Winter is the thing being discussed; in the mountains is a prepositional phrase that describes the simple subject *winter*. *Note:* Although the simple subject is never *part* of a prepositional phrase, a prepositional phrase itself is occasionally both the simple subject and the complete subject:

  simple subject

  After daybreak is the best time to catch fish.

  complete subject

After daybreak is a prepositional phrase and is the thing being discussed. It serves as both the simple subject and the complete subject.

Sometimes, however, a prepositional phrase serves as neither the simple subject nor the complete subject:

  simple subject

  After the football game, the entire *team* will watch the game films.

  complete subject

In this sentence, "After the football game" is not part of the complete subject. Although it appears at the beginning of the sentence, it does not explain or describe *team,* the simple subject. Instead, it defines when the watching will take place. The complete subject is <u>the entire</u> *team;* it explains who will watch.

The following box lists words that often begin a prepositional phrase.

COMMON PREPOSITIONS			
about	before	during	over
above	behind	for	through
across	beside	from	to
after	between	in	under
against	beyond	into	until
around	by	of	with
at	down	on	without

- In questions, the simple subject is harder to find. Turn the question into a statement.

Question:	Why can't Bill stop smoking?
Statement:	Bill can't stop smoking.
Simple subject:	*Bill*

- In commands, the simple subject is always "you." It is understood that "you" is the subject.

Command:	Serve the soup cold.
Simple subject:	(*You*) Serve the soup cold.

EXERCISE 16.1

Underline the complete subject and circle the simple subject in the following sentences.

EXAMPLE:

(One) of my coworkers was sick.

1. He called the manager an hour late.
2. Everyone grumbled about his absence.
3. Lay the papers on the table in the kitchen.
4. The quarterback is a sitting duck without a strong offensive line.
5. Sit next to the heater to get warm.
6. By the end of the concert, the band had played all their top hits.
7. What time does the history class begin on Monday?
8. Before sunset will be a perfect time to get the photographs.
9. The beginning of the concert was the most enjoyable.

The Predicate

All sentences have a predicate. The **simple predicate** is the **verb,** which expresses an action, a state of being, or a sense in the past, present, or future. The **complete predicate** contains the verb as well as words and/or phrases that modify the verb. An

Copyright © 2007, The McGraw-Hill Companies, Inc. All rights reserved.

action verb names the action of the subject. Use the subject to help identify the verb. Ask these questions: What did the subject do? What action did the subject take?

action verb

The oldest sister always *worked* harder than the rest of the family.

complete predicate

The action verb is *worked*. It describes what action the subject ("sister") did. The complete predicate, always *worked* harder than the rest of the family, describes how the sister worked.

action verb

My new puppy *chewed* the toes off my new tennis shoes.

complete predicate

The action verb is *chewed*. It describes what action the subject ("puppy") did. The complete predicate, *chewed* the toes off my new tennis shoes, describes what the puppy chewed.

action verb

All of the girls *went* on the trip.

complete predicate

Went is the action verb. It is the action of the subject ("all"). The complete predicate, *went* on the trip, describes where all of the girls went.

A linking verb connects a subject to the words that explain or describe it. These words follow the verb and are called the **subject complement.**

Common Linking Verbs			
am	are	can be	shall be
is	be	could have been	will be
was	being	has been	may be
were	been	have been	must have been
Other Linking Verbs				
appear	feel	look	smell	taste
become	grow	seem	sound	touch

linking verb

All the girls *look* beautiful.

subject complement

The linking verb *look* connects the subject ("girls") to the word that describes them. The subject complement beautiful describes the girls.

linking verb

The oldest sister *was* the hardest worker of the family.

subject complement

The linking verb *was* connects the subject ("sister") to the word that describes her. The subject complement worker describes the sister.

A helping verb is part of a complete verb phrase. A verb phrase contains a helping verb and a main verb. It helps clarify the action or statement of the verb. Helping verbs can be used with action verbs.

COMMON HELPING VERBS				
am	are	is	was	were
do	did	can	may	must
has	have	had	be	been
shall	will	could	would	should

helping verb

All of the girls *are* <u>coming</u> to the dance this Friday.

complete verb phrase

The helping verb *are* clarifies the action verb "coming," suggesting the action of the girls is definite. The complete verb phrase, *are* <u>coming</u>, is the action of the subject ("girls").

The following tips will help you identify the verbs and complete predicates in sentences.

- Identify the verb first. The verb states an action or position.

verb

Vernon and Alice *bought* <u>a new car for their vacation to Alaska</u>.

complete predicate

The verb *bought* states the action of Vernon and Alice. The complete predicate, *bought* <u>a new car for their vacation to Alaska</u>, explains the action.

- Helping verbs, words that describe the action, or subject complements are part of the complete predicate.

verb + helping verb

The teachers *are sending* <u>their students to the library for research</u>.

complete predicate

The verb and helping verb, *are sending,* state the action of the subject ("teachers"). The complete predicate, *are sending* <u>their students to the library for research</u>, explains the action.

- *Note:* The word *not* is never part of a verb phrase:

verb + helping verb

Instructions *have* <u>not</u> *been helpful* <u>to me in the past</u>.

complete predicate

The verb and helping verb, *have been helpful,* explain the use of the subject ("instructions"). The word <u>not</u> is part of the complete predicate. It describes the helpfulness of the instructions, the same as <u>to me in the past</u> describes the helpfulness of the instructions.

EXERCISE 16.2

In the following sentences, underline the complete predicate and circle the verb and any helping verbs.

EXAMPLE:

One of my coworkers (was sick) for two weeks with the flu.

1. He called the manager an hour late.
2. Everyone grumbled about his absence.

Copyright © 2007, The McGraw-Hill Companies, Inc. All rights reserved.

EXERCISE 16.2 continued

3. Lay the papers on the table in the kitchen.

4. Who is the quarterback?

5. The quarterback is a sitting duck without a strong offensive line.

6. Sit next to the heater to get warm.

7. By the end of the concert, the band had played all their top hits.

8. What time do classes begin on Monday?

9. Employee selections for the job will be made after the final interview.

10. The beginning of the concert was the most enjoyable.

EXERCISE 16.3

Identify the complete subject and complete predicate in the following sentences.

- Underline the complete subject once and the complete predicate twice.
- Circle the simple subject.
- Indicate the verb and any helping verbs with an arrow.

EXAMPLE:

A few weeks ago, my girlfriend took me to a fast-food restaurant for dinner.

1. It was terrible.

2. The lines extended to the door.

3. I did not want to stay.

4. We stood in line for forty-five minutes.

5. She laughed at me the whole time.

6. Even at a bad restaurant, we always have fun.

7. Some of the other customers gave us dirty looks.

8. The manager offered everyone coupons as an apology for the wait.

9. I will never go to a fast-food place during the lunch rush again.

10. A rough-and-tumble fistfight will quickly draw a crowd of cheering onlookers.

EXERCISE 16.4

Build on what you practiced in Exercise 16.3. Identify the complete subject and complete predicate in the following sentences.

- Underline the complete subject once and the complete predicate twice.
- Circle the simple subject.
- Indicate the verb and any helping verbs with an arrow.

1. It will be the end of the semester in two weeks.

2. After the election, the Democrats gained five senate seats.

3. How will I ever learn to dance without lessons?

4. All of us wanted to see the new cars at the auto show.

5. The significant difference between the male and female brain is the subject of brain research.

6. Henry and I confirmed that no one enjoys cleaning house.

7. Get back to the starting line.

8. The number of blondes in the United States has increased since the advent of peroxide.

9. The sudden increase in tuition makes college costs difficult for many students.

10. After the first frost, the flowers were shriveled and brown.

Expanding the Simple Sentence

Writing good sentences will naturally lead to writing detailed paragraphs if you think of your sentences as building blocks. One sentence leads to another. Elaboration begins when you learn how to expand your simple sentences.

EXERCISE 16.5

Expand the following simple sentences by adding three to eight words that give additional detail. Indicate the subject and verb in each new sentence.

EXAMPLE:

Simple sentence—3 words:

subject	verb	
The	bus	stalled.

Copyright © 2007, The McGraw-Hill Companies, Inc. All rights reserved.

Expanded simple sentence—6–8 words:

                      subject   verb

The	city	bus	stalled	on	the	boulevard.

Expanded simple sentence—7–11 words:

                                                subject verb

Filled	with	passengers,	the	crowded	city	bus	stalled	on	the	boulevard.

1.

Simple sentence—3 words:

               subject   verb

The	phone	rang.

Expanded simple sentence—6–8 words:

Expanded simple sentence—7–11 words:

2.

Simple sentence—3 words:

               subject   verb

The	sun	set.

Expanded simple sentence—6–8 words:

Expanded simple sentence—7–11 words:

3.

Simple sentence—3 words:

               subject   verb

A	dog	barked.

Expanded simple sentence—6–8 words:

Copyright © 2007, The McGraw-Hill Companies, Inc. All rights reserved.

EXERCISE 16.5 continued

Expanded simple sentence—7–11 words:

4.

Simple sentence—3 words:

subject	verb	
A	whistle	blew.

Expanded simple sentence—6–8 words:

Expanded simple sentence—7–11 words:

5.

Simple sentence—3 words:

subject	verb	
The	woman	stared.

Expanded simple sentence—6–8 words:

Expanded simple sentence—7–11 words:

EXERCISE 16.6

Write a simple sentence about a person or activity you enjoy.

- Circle a word in that sentence that you can expand on in two additional sentences.
- Try both expansion techniques demonstrated below.

EXAMPLE:

Original: *My grandfather's cellar is full of canned* (vegetables)

List: *He has green beans, squash, and tomatoes from his garden.*

          1   2   3

Stacking prepositional phrases:
He shelved the jars <u>with a label</u> <u>in the center</u> <u>of each jar.</u>
1   2   3

1. Original:

List:

Stacking prepositional phrases:

2. Original:

List:

Stacking prepositional phrases:

3. Original:

List:

Stacking prepositional phrases:

4. Original:

List:

Stacking prepositional phrases:

5. Original:

List:

Stacking prepositional phrases:

EXERCISE 16.7

Using action verbs is another technique to expand your sentences. Write two sentences about five family members or friends.

- The first sentence will make a statement.
- The second sentence will use an action verb and elaborate on the first sentence.
- Underline the verb in each sentence.

EXAMPLES:

My father <u>was</u> a truck driver.
He <u>delivered</u> farm gas and fuel oil for thirty-five years.

My mother <u>is</u> a secretary.
She <u>keeps</u> track of purchasing, payroll, and inventory.

EXERCISE 16.7 continued

1.

2.

3.

4.

5.

6.

7.

8.

9.

10.

The Simple Sentence and Coordination

Coordination involves connecting two things. The most common forms of coordination are compound subjects and compound verbs. A **compound subject** is two or more subjects that share the same verb. Two or more subjects are connected by a **coordinating conjunction**—usually *and* or *or*.

single subject

Single subject + verb: *Bob* drove to the seashore alone.

compound subject

Compound subject + verb: *Bob* <u>and</u> *Alice* drove to the seashore on Saturday.

coordinating conjunction

compound subject

Wilma <u>or</u> *Elisha* will probably offer to work the night shift.

coordinating conjunction

Copyright © 2007, The McGraw-Hill Companies, Inc. All rights reserved.

EXERCISE 16.8

Underline the compound subjects in the following sentences. Circle the coordinating conjunctions.

EXAMPLE:

Male <u>birds</u> (and) female <u>birds</u> do not always share the duties of hatching young.

1. A bouquet of flowers and a box of candy are popular gifts on Valentine's Day.
2. Mustard and onions on a hot dog cannot be beat.
3. Angelica or I will be at the concert early enough to get a front-row seat.
4. The windows in the house and the windows in the barn were made of handblown glass.
5. Bicycle racing and women's volleyball are two exciting but forgotten sports.

A **compound verb** is two verbs (action verbs or linking verbs) that share the same subject and are connected by a **coordinating conjunction**—usually *and, or,* or *but.*

single verb

Subject and single verb: Anderson *raced* to the door, escaping the rain.

compound verb

Subject and compound verb: The girls *argued* <u>and</u> *complained* about the homework assignment.

coordinating conjunction

EXERCISE 16.9

Underline compound verbs in the following sentences. Circle the coordinating conjunctions.

EXAMPLE:

During the game, the crowd <u>cheered</u> (and) <u>jeered</u> the team.

1. My accountant invested my money but made very poor choices.
2. We sat on the dock and watched the blue water glisten in the sun.
3. The doctor sent a bill and charged me for two visits instead of one.
4. Conway wants a raise and has complained about his job assignment.
5. My friend complains about her boyfriend constantly but still dates him.

EXERCISE 16.10

Write a simple sentence with a single subject and a single verb.

- Then revise it by adding a second subject and a second verb.
- Underline the compound subject once and the compound verb twice in the second sentence.
- Circle the coordinating conjunctions in the second sentence.

Copyright © 2007, The McGraw-Hill Companies, Inc. All rights reserved.

EXERCISE 16.10 continued

EXAMPLE:

Sylvia planned a vegetable garden for the small plot behind her house.

Sylvia and her mother planned a vegetable garden and planted it in a small plot behind her house.

1.

2.

3.

4.

5.

THE COMPOUND SENTENCE AND COORDINATION

Compound sentences connect ideas or actions that are related. Unlike compound subjects and verbs, **compound sentences** contain two complete thoughts that are connected by a comma and a coordinating conjunction.

COORDINATING CONJUNCTIONS	
and	or
but	nor
yet	for
so	

Complete sentences: Escorts are one of the most common cars for teenagers. You see them all over the place.

Compound sentence: Escorts are one of the most common cars for teenagers, <u>and</u> you see them all over the place.
coordinating conjunction

Complete sentences: I travel a lot.
I need a very comfortable car.

Compound sentence: I travel a lot, <u>so</u> I need a very comfortable car.
coordinating conjunction

Complete sentences: A guy approached me and asked me to dance.
I turned him down.

Compound sentence: A guy approached me and asked me to dance, <u>but</u> I turned him down.
coordinating conjunction

EXERCISE 16.11

Write a compound sentence by combining the following sentence pairs. Circle the coordinating conjunctions.

1. I will bring the desserts.
   You can bring the drinks.

2. Britta and Clem wanted to know how to salsa at their wedding.
   They took ballroom dancing lessons.

3. I scheduled my next annual physical a year in advance.
   I hope that I remember the appointment.

4. Fedora is willing to go to the football game.
   Fedora is willing to go the movie.

5. My worst subject in school was geometry.
   I also did not like and was terrible in choir.

EXERCISE 16.12

Read the following sentences and circle the coordinating conjunctions. Some are simple sentences with compound subjects or verbs. Some are compound sentences. Put an asterisk next to compound sentences.

1. I saw a car standing by the side of the road this morning, and the tire was flat.
2. I hate doing the dishes and taking out the garbage.
3. My sister's boyfriend went to France last summer, and this year, she wants to go.
4. My mom works afternoons and doesn't really have time to cook dinner.
5. My boyfriend and I go to the grocery store and buy the ingredients for the meal we decide to make.
6. We like to make salads a lot, so we always buy some kind of vegetables to go with the meal.
7. We usually make something that is simple and doesn't require a whole lot of cooking time.
8. We often make spaghetti or taco salad.
9. My mom likes refried beans and guacamole.
10. I mostly cut up the vegetables and cook the meat, and James, my boyfriend, sets the table and does the dishes afterward.

EXERCISE 16.13

Write two sentences about your job, a hobby, or a vacation.

- Write the first one as a simple sentence.
- Then write a compound sentence to expand or explain the first one.
- Circle the coordinating conjunctions that connect the two sentences to create a compound sentence. Underline the subjects once and the verbs twice in the revised sentence.

EXAMPLE:

I have decided to give up stamp collecting.

You have to buy stamps and keep them in books, (and) I just do not have the time.

1.

2.

3.

4.

5.

THE COMPLEX SENTENCE AND SUBORDINATION

Using subordination and complex sentences is another way writers can express relationships between two ideas. Unlike coordination, subordination joins elements that are dependent on each other for meaning. Sentences making use of subordination are called **complex sentences** because if separated, the subordinate elements do not express a complete thought. **Subordination** occurs when an independent clause (containing a subject and verb) is made into a dependent clause by joining it to another independent clause using a **subordinating conjunction**.

SUBORDINATING CONJUNCTIONS			
after	because	since	when
although	before	so that	whenever
as	even though	than	where
as if	if	though	wherever
as long as	in order that	unless	whether
as though	provided that	until	while

Copyright © 2007, The McGraw-Hill Companies, Inc. All rights reserved.

Complete sentences: A great-looking guy approached me and asked me to dance. I turned him down.

subordinating
conjunction

Complex sentences: <u>Although</u> a great-looking guy approached me and asked me to dance, I turned him down.

Complete sentences: Escorts are one of the most common cars for teenagers. They are economical on gas.

subordinating
conjunction

Complex sentence: Escorts are one of the most common cars for teenagers <u>because</u> they are economical on gas.

Complete sentences: I travel across the country. I need a very comfortable car.

subordinating
conjunction

Complex sentence: <u>Whenever</u> I travel across the country, I need a very comfortable car.

EXERCISE 16.14

Read the following sentences and identify the complex sentences.

- Circle the subordinating conjunctions.
- Underline the subject and verb in each clause.
- Put an asterisk next to sentences that are *not* complex sentences.

1. As long as I am winning, I like playing any game.
2. After the game, I went to the dance at the youth center.
3. I study every night from seven until midnight so that I can get a scholarship.
4. Whether you go or not, I plan to see the Degas art exhibit on dance.
5. My boss requires all his employees to submit vacation requests six months in advance because he wants to accommodate as many as possible.
6. Why did you remove the tile in the bathroom next to the guest bedroom?
7. I do not want to go to the movies unless you can convince me otherwise.
8. Although I always wanted a dog, my brother's allergies kept us from having one.
9. Before the performance, Mark broke his hand while he was moving scenery around the stage.
10. When you decide to quit your job, let me know so that I can apply for it.

EXERCISE 16.15

Write two sentences about your job, a hobby, or a vacation.

- Then combine the sentences by creating a complex sentence.
- Add the dependent clause to the beginning or end of the independent clause.
- Circle the subordinating conjunction.

EXAMPLE:

I want to take ballroom dancing lessons.
I love the tango and fox trot.

(Because) *I love the tango and fox trot, I want to take ballroom dancing lessons.*

1.

2.

3.

4.

5.

EXPERIMENTING WITH SENTENCE VARIETY

Sophisticated writing begins with sentence variety. Using a combination of simple, expanded simple, compound, and complex sentences will help make your writing style interesting.

EXERCISE 16.16

Using the following example as a model, write a paragraph fifteen to twenty-five sentences long about one of the first jobs you ever had.

- Using simple, compound, and complex sentences, write six sentences that answer the questions who? what? when? where? why? and how? Label each sentence type.
- Write two to four additional sentences for each of the six original sentences.
- Circle subordinating conjunctions and underline coordinating conjunctions.

Copyright © 2007, The McGraw-Hill Companies, Inc. All rights reserved.

EXAMPLE:

WHY: *When I was pregnant with my daughter, I worked as a telemarketer.* *(Complex)*

WHERE: *I worked for a heating and cooling company, Air Control Systems.* *(Simple)*

WHEN: *We had to work on Saturday mornings, and there were a lot of rude people. (Compound)*

WHO: *I worked with a room full of women who drove me crazy. (Simple)*

HOW: *That job taught me about how to keep a job, and it taught me how to like a job. (Compound)*

WHAT: *Working commission can be both a good thing and a terrible thing.* *(Simple)*

> WHY: *When I was pregnant with my daughter, I worked as a telemarketer.*
> 1. *I could sit down and relax because there would be no pressure on my feet.*
> 2. *I talked all day to people while the rest of the world did much more strenuous jobs.*
>
> WHERE: *I worked for a heating and cooling company, Air Control Systems.*
> 1. *This company fixed and replaced furnace and central air units.*
> 2. *I did free estimates on furnace, central air system, and duct cleanings.*
>
> WHEN: *We had to work on Saturday mornings, and there were a lot of rude people.*
> 1. *Most people would just say no, and they would slam the phone.*
> 2. *Some people would hang up in our faces, and we wouldn't even say a word.*
> 3. *Some would curse us out for calling, and they would slam the phone.*
>
> WHO: *I worked with a room full of women who drove me crazy.*
> 1. *I used to think they hired only good-looking women because every woman there was good looking.*
> 2. *Then I realized that we were good talkers, and nobody saw us anyway.*
> 3. *We didn't get along even though we worked well together.*
> 4. *There was a lot of fussing and fighting sometimes about women's issues, but when push came to shove, we got our work done with no problem.*
>
> HOW: *That job taught me about how to keep a job, and it taught me how to like a job.*
> 1. *I got to work on time, or I lost pay.*
> 2. *I learned to work with people, or I learned to live with people I didn't like.*
>
> WHAT: *Working commission can be both a good thing and a terrible thing.*
> 1. *You get $50 for every lead or furnace.*
> 2. *You get $100 for every air conditioner unit.*
> 3. *However, selling anything over the phone isn't easy.*
> 4. *You have to have the gift of gab or be just plain lucky.*

17 *Sentence Variety and Style*

How can I connect with my audience? Careful sentence construction makes an essay clear and purposeful, but sentence variety and style engage a reader

WW Advanced Sentence Writing Techniques

IN THIS CHAPTER: A PREVIEW

Strategies for Sentence Variety and Style

- Vary Sentence Length
- Vary the Placement of the Subject and Verb
- Use Repetition and Parallelism

WW Sentence Sense

Vary Sentence Length

Sentence length is a key element of writing style. Short sentences pack a punch. They have a dramatic effect. Longer sentences pace the delivery of the information; they build emphasis. Learn to vary your sentence length by studying other writers' styles.

EXERCISE 17.1

In the following readings—the first two from magazine articles and the third a student sample—the writers use sentence length to create an emotional impact. Count the words in each sentence and fill in the blank bar graphs accordingly. Then answer the questions to explore the effects of sentence length on meaning.

READING: from "Why Has Our Weather Gone Wild?" by Joseph D'Agnese

As you read this, flip your eyes over to the window. The sky is clear, the wind light, and the sun brilliant. Or maybe not—Mother Nature is full of surprises these days. The calendar says it's spring, but there could just as easily be a winter blizzard, a summer swelter, or an autumn cold snap on the other side of that glass pane. Almost in an instant, it seems, the weather shifts from one season to another. And wherever it swings, it seems increasingly likely to be extreme.

Copyright © 2007, The McGraw-Hill Companies, Inc. All rights reserved.

Consider what Mother Nature slung our way last year in May, typically the second worst month for tornadoes. In less than 24 hours, more than 70 hellholes of wind rampaged through Oklahoma and Kansas, killing 49 and causing more than $1 billion in damages. In June, it was heat, as the Northeast began roasting through weeks of the worst drought since the 1960s; 256 people died. Last September, Hurricane Floyd forced the largest peacetime evacuation in U.S. history, as 2.6 million people scurried for safety, and huge sections of the East Coast went underwater, drowning hundreds of thousands of farm animals. This year in January, blizzards pounded the nation from Kansas to the Atlantic Ocean. In April, 25 inches of snow fell on parts of New England.

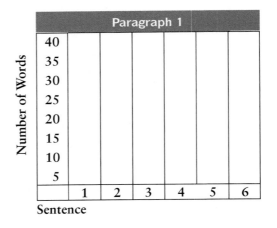

1. The majority of the sentences are approximately the same length. However, one sentence is extremely long. What does the longest sentence emphasize?

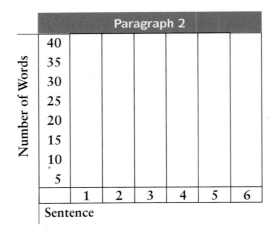

2. What does the longest sentence emphasize?

EXERCISE 17.1 continued

3. What is the effect of the final shorter sentences at the end of the second paragraph?

READING: from "Brave, Braver, Bravest," by Stewart Massad

"I've been dreaming about having a baby," said Ashley. That's not a strange thing for a childless 36-year-old woman to tell her gynecologist, but it surprised me because this patient is HIV-infected. Having a baby implies having a future, something that those of us who have watched women die of AIDS once never dared hope for.

But Ashley has always been tenacious. Six years ago, the boyfriend who introduced her to heroin and HIV died of pneumonia, leaving her resolved to convince others not to duplicate her mistakes. She began speaking in schools, women's shelters, and half-way houses, wherever she could find an audience for warnings about unsafe sex and dirty needles. Before long she met Ron, another former drug user whose HIV diagnosis had shocked him into getting clean. Their collaboration in the fight against AIDS inspired a love bold enough to include the prospect of having a child.

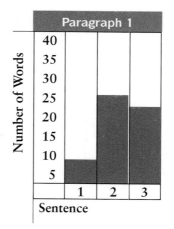

1. What does the shortest sentence emphasize?

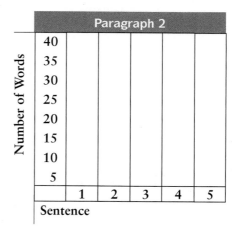

Copyright © 2007, The McGraw-Hill Companies, Inc. All rights reserved.

2. What does the shortest sentence emphasize?

3. What do the long sentences emphasize?

STUDENT SAMPLE

Back during the summer of 2001, I believe in June, I got a bright idea that I was going to dye my hair green. So I went out and bought the stuff. My brother did all the bleaching and then dyed my hair. It turned out to be yellow and green swirls. It looked totally crazy. I freaked everyone out. There were some people who laughed at me, but others knew me to be sort of an exhibitionist, so they expected me to do something foolish. My new "do" got me a lot of attention; however, some of the attention I didn't need, but you have to take the bad with the good when doing something like that, so I decided to keep the color until one day when my two-year-old daughter said, "Dad you look funny. Cut hair now." It was time. My daughter had the fun of cutting the green and yellow clumps off.

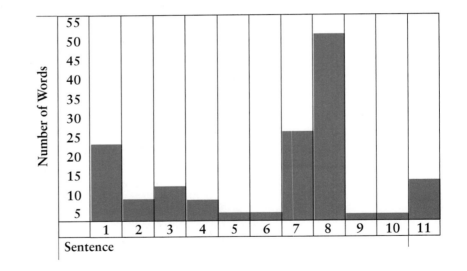

1. What do the short sentences emphasize?

2. Which sentence creates the biggest impact on the reader? Explain your thinking.

EXERCISE 17.2

Write a paragraph describing the photograph "Hand Play (Juego de manos)." Assume your reader cannot see the photograph.

EXERCISE 17.2 continued

Hand Play (Juego de manos)

- Briefly describe the photograph.
- Explain your emotional reaction to the photograph. Use a personal experience to explain your reaction. What do you think of when you look at the photo? What do you remember?
- Vary the length of your sentences.

EXERCISE 17.3

Count the number of words in each sentence of your paragraph from Exercise 17.2 and chart them below. Then answer the questions that follow.

Number of Words	1	2	3	4	5	6	7	8	9	10	11	12
55												
50												
45												
40												
35												
30												
25												
20												
15												
10												
5												
Sentence												

Copyright © 2007, The McGraw-Hill Companies, Inc. All rights reserved.

1. Write your longest and shortest sentences below.

Longest:

Shortest:

2. Which sentence has the most emotional impact?

3. Do you prefer long or short sentences? Why?

4. Select one long sentence from your description and divide it into two or three short sentences.

Original sentence:

Shortened sentences:

A.

B.

C.

5. Select a short sentence and expand it by adding details.

Original sentence:

Expanded sentence:

Vary the Placement of the Subject and Verb

Many writers vary their sentence structure by altering the placement of the subject and verb. Notice in the following chart how the emphasis shifts from the subject and verb to the details simply by shifting the placement of the subject and verb.

Location of Subject and Verb	Sentences	Emphasizes
Beginning	The **man limped** across the street.	person and action
Interrupted	The <u>man</u>, **tipping slightly to one side with each step,** <u>limped</u> across the street.	details
End	**Tipping slightly to one side,** the <u>man limped</u> across the street.	details

EXERCISE 17.4

Following are a number of sentences from Barbara Lazear Ascher's essay "On Compassion." Underline the subject and verb, and circle which part of the sentence seems to be emphasized.

1. His buttonless shirt, with one sleeve missing, hangs outside the waist of his baggy trousers.
2. As he crosses Manhattan's Seventy-ninth Street, his gait is the shuffle of the forgotten ones held in place by gravity rather than plans.
3. On the corner of Madison Avenue, he stops before a blond baby in an Aprica stroller.
4. The others on the corner, five men and women waiting for the crosstown bus, look away.
5. His hands continue to dangle at his sides.
6. The baby, weary of the unwavering stare, pulls its blanket over its head.
7. The man does not look away.
8. The New York Civil Liberties Union is watchful.
9. We cannot deny the existence of the helpless as their presence grows.
10. As he stands, the scent of stale cigarettes and urine fills the small, overheated room.

EXERCISE 17.5

Write a description of the photograph "Chicken Dinner." Assume your reader cannot see the photograph. Consider what you write to be a "verbal sketch" that enables your reader to "see" the photo. Also, feel free to write about your reaction to

"Chicken Dinner"

Copyright © 2007, The McGraw-Hill Companies, Inc. All rights reserved.

EXERCISE 17.5 continued

the photograph: what it makes you remember and your emotional reaction to the people and situation.

- Be as thorough as possible in this description. Structure your sentences to emphasize your detailed descriptions.
- Use all three types of subject-verb placement: beginning, interrupted, and end.
- Vary the length of your sentences.

EXERCISE 17.6

Count the number of words in each sentence of your paragraph from Exercise 17.5 and chart them below.

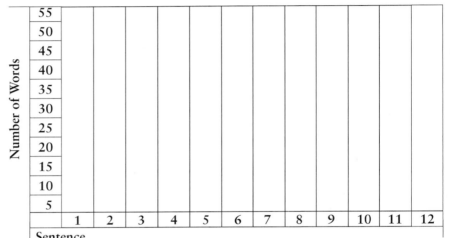

EXERCISE 17.7

Referring to your paragraph from Exercise 17.5, analyze the emphasis you created with subject-verb placement. Chart your findings below. Then answer the questions that follow.

Location of Subject and Verb	Sentence											
	1	2	3	4	5	6	7	8	9	10	11	12
Beginning												
Interrupted												
End												

1. What is the location of the subject and verb in your shortest sentence?

2. What is the location of the subject and verb in your longest sentence?

3. Which sentence has the most emotional impact? Explain your answer.

Use Repetition and Parallelism

Repetition and Parallel Lists

Speakers and writers understand the power of repetition and parallel lists. The combination can create an emotional impact, make connections, or emphasize a point. Parallel lists can appear in a single sentence or in a series of sentences. In the following paragraph,

- Notice the repeated use of "I" and "never," which have been circled. The writer uses repetition to emphasize the consistency of her routine and the impact it has made on her life.
- Notice the parallelism in the sentence structure, which has been underlined. The writer uses parallelism to illustrate the ritual approach to her morning routine.

> My morning routine is an essential ritual to prepare me for the day. (I) hit the snooze once to give myself seven calm minutes to start the day. (I) do a sunrise yoga routine to energize my body. (I) take a long shower to relax my muscles. (I) make oatmeal with butter and brown sugar to provide a great start. (I) grab my purse, books, and backpack waiting for me next to the door. (I) leave the house early to avoid the hectic pace of rush hour. I (never) rush, (never) forget things, and (never) arrive frazzled.

EXERCISE 17.8

Martin Luther King's "I Have a Dream" speech presents a list of demands. He combines repetition and parallel lists to emphasize the importance of taking action. Underline the parallel lists.

READING: from "I Have a Dream," by Martin Luther King Jr.

We have also come to this hallowed spot to remind America of the fierce urgency of now. This is not the time to engage in the luxury of cooling off or to take the tranquilizing drug of gradualism. Now is the time to make real the promises of democracy. Now is the time to rise from the dark and desolate valley of segregation, to the sunlit path of racial justice. Now is the time to lift our nation from the quicksands of racial injustice to the solid rock of brotherhood. Now is the time to make justice a reality for all of God's children.

EXERCISE 17.9

The following paragraph makes a powerful statement about the dignity of work and the peril of theft. Identify and underline the parallel lists. Then answer the questions that follow.

READING: from *With These Hands,* by Daniel Rothenberg

I am a real migrant worker. I earned that name. I been knocked down with the bruise. I been kicked down with the bumps. I fell a lot. I rolled. Yes, I stumbled. I got my little nose scarred. I got knocked in the head. But I didn't steal. For a

Copyright © 2007, The McGraw-Hill Companies, Inc. All rights reserved.

EXERCISE 17.9 continued

working man, the money you earn is good money. Just going out and pulling a gun sounds good. You sure can get a Cadillac in one walk. "Let's hit this store." Boom, bam! But it ain't no good. Once you learn that pulling a gun ain't good, there's nothing for you to do but to get your hands in order. Fast hands—quick on pulling leaves, quick on picking oranges, quick on cutting cabbages, quick on picking bell peppers, fast on peaches, superfast when it comes to the potatoes. Just make those hands real slow when it comes to stealing.

1. What is the emotional impact of each list?

2. The narrator creates parallel lists to make his point about dignity. Which list has the most emotional impact?

EXERCISE 17.10

Parallelism is based on repetition. Using repetition, compose three sentences about each of the following topics. A word or phrase is suggested for repetition.

EXAMPLE:

Topic: vitamins

Repeat: "to some people"

To some people, vitamins are the solution to all their problems. To some people, they are a substitute for actual food. To some people, they are just another pill they forget to take.

1. Topic: snow

Repeat: "a little snow"

2. Topic: birthdays

Repeat: "no big deal"

EXERCISE 17.10 continued

3. Topic: smoking
Repeat: "secondhand smoke"

4. Topic: cell phones
Repeat: "while driving"

5. Topic: dress codes
Repeat: "when a dress code"

EXERCISE 17.11

Rewrite the following sentences. Break longer sentences into short parallel sentences and use repetition to create emphasis. Underline the parallel constructions in the revised sentences. Feel free to add details in your revised sentences.

EXAMPLE:

People do goofy things when they use drugs. These things include saying inappropriate things, getting crazy, and committing crimes.

Revised: *People do goofy things when they use drugs. They say inappropriate things. They get crazy. They commit crimes.*

1. Every day computers become outdated, more complex, and confusing. System conflicts and programming errors hinder access to the Internet.
Revised:

2. For many families, television is a way to have fun together and simply enjoy time with each other. They make a bowl of popcorn and get some pop. Everyone grabs a chair, a spot on the couch, or a pillow. Someone reads the TV guide to determine what to watch. Someone clicks on the set, and the laughter or tears begin.
Revised:

Copyright © 2007, The McGraw-Hill Companies, Inc. All rights reserved.

3. Many young adults these days have credit cards. Without thinking, they buy anything they want and end up with bad credit.

Revised:

4. When we were very small, my dad taught us that guns were not toys and that the guns he kept in our home were strictly off-limits.

Revised:

5. All of a sudden a huge guy comes running out of the dressing room. He jumps in the ring and starts demolishing his opponent. The crowd goes crazy. The audience is ecstatic. He picks his opponent up over his head and drops him head-first to the canvas. Many people jump to their feet and applaud.

Revised:

6. I learned many things working in a pizza carryout restaurant, such as how to make pizza, prepare the dough and have things ready for the rush times, manage crabby customers, and operate the cash register.

Revised:

7. Charity is never done as a chore or out of a sense of obligation.

Revised:

8. Intelligence can be many things. For example, some people know lots about automobiles, and others are good with computers.

Revised:

9. Watching a movie at home gives you lots of opportunities that a theater can't offer, like rewinding when you miss a part or talking to your friends and

Copyright © 2007, The McGraw-Hill Companies, Inc. All rights reserved.

EXERCISE 17.11 continued

laughing as loud as you want. Plus you can stop it and go to the bathroom or make popcorn. And if the movie is bad, you can just turn it off.
Revised:

10. Teenagers should have a better understanding about right and wrong. In particular, they need to realize that their actions have consequences and that they can make a mistake that can follow them for the rest of their life. The impact of a single moment, even a small wrong moment, can be devastating.
Revised:

Parallelism in Compounds

Compounds are created when writers put two or more things together in a sentence. Compound subjects and compound verbs are the most common forms of compounds. Making these things parallel can enhance one's writing style, make a clearer connection, create emphasis, and highlight contrast.

Not parallel: After the long ride home, Henry <u>wanted</u> lunch and <u>to take</u> a nap.
(verb—past tense) (verb—infinitive)

Parallel: After the long ride home, Henry <u>ate</u> lunch and <u>took</u> a nap.
(verb) (verb)

Not parallel: My high school science teacher was <u>impatient</u>, <u>eccentric</u>, and <u>was grumpy</u>.
(adjective) (adjective) (verb phrase)

Parallel: My high school science teacher was <u>impatient</u>, <u>eccentric</u>, and <u>grumpy</u>.
(adjective) (adjective) (adjective)

EXERCISE 17.12

Read the following sentences from Gail Sheehy's essay "Predictable Crises of Adulthood." Sheehy uses compounds throughout her essay. Underline the parallel compound parts in each sentence.

1. The tasks of this passage are to locate ourselves in a peer group role, a sex role, an anticipated occupation, an ideology or world view.
2. As a result, we gather the impetus to leave home physically and the identity to begin leaving home emotionally.
3. Taken to the extreme, these are people who skip from one trial job and one limited personal encounter to another, spending their twenties in the transient state.
4. Some of us follow the lock-in pattern, others the transient pattern, the wunderkind pattern, the caregiver pattern, and there are a number of others.
5. The trouble with his advice to his wife is that it comes out of concern with his convenience, rather than with her development.

EXERCISE 17.13

Revise the following sentences, making the compound parts parallel. The conjunctions are identified for you in bold type.

- Underline the parts of the sentence that need to be parallel.
- Rewrite the sentence. Some cutting or adding may be necessary. Try to preserve the exact meaning of the sentence.
- Underline the parallel compound parts in your revised sentences.

EXAMPLE:

In my childhood years, I'd tend to forget <u>homework</u> **or** <u>doing a chore</u>.
Revised: In my childhood years, I tended to forget <u>homework</u> or <u>chores</u>.

1. So if I were to own a small business **and** looking to give you a job, you would have to be knowledgeable about the products in my business.
   Revised:

2. I want someone I can trust, rely on, **and** be very good with customers.
   Revised:

3. They should feel comfortable working with others **and** not someone who tries to do work without asking questions when they are confused.
   Revised:

4. As an elementary school paraprofessional, I learned to make cutout letters, preparing bulletin boards, **and** manage student discipline.
   Revised:

5. First the problem had to be defined, a meeting of the minds was called, **and** lastly, organizing committees around the world under the watchful eyes of the UN.
   Revised:

6. One leader was dubbed by his own people to be incompetent **and** a disaster as Secretary of the Environment.
   Revised:

7. I was stuck swimming in the hotel pool **and** ocean by myself. That was about all there was to do besides miniature golf **or** going for a boat ride.
   Revised:

Copyright © 2007, The McGraw-Hill Companies, Inc. All rights reserved.

EXERCISE 17.13 continued

8. I tried to outsmart him by speeding up **or** turn quickly so I could confuse him.
Revised:

9. We'd play cops and robbers until one of us got called in for dinner, for the night, **or** if we got tired.
Revised:

10. My sisters **and** all the rest of my friends on the block played soccer in the streets.
Revised:

EXERCISE 17.14

Build on what you practiced in Exercise 17.13. Revise the following sentences, making the compound parts parallel. The conjunctions are identified for you in bold type.

- Underline the parts of the sentence that need to be parallel.
- Rewrite the sentence. Some cutting or adding may be necessary. Try to preserve the exact meaning of the sentence.
- Underline the parallel compound parts in your revised sentences.

1. I will always remember the scene in the *Bone Collector* where a gun ripped off a man's fingers, toes, **and** shot through his heart.
Revised:

2. Without guns there would be less war, senseless death, **and** more peace.
Revised:

3. I wanted to make the right choice in size, price, **and** good running car for me.
Revised:

4. Charity is never done as a chore **or** doing something because you have to.
Revised:

5. A few friends and I were practicing for a race. The track was real sandy **and** loose mud.
Revised:

6. He started becoming very irresponsible. He would miss curfew, slack off in college, **and** he began to drink.
Revised:

7. Television can be used for many things, including entertainment, **and** finding facts.
Revised:

EXERCISE 17.14 continued

8. She was fun to be around, very friendly **and** a very nice person.
Revised:

9. Because my name is fairly common, it's easy to remember, easy to pronounce **and** to spell.
Revised:

10. Mathematics consists of numbers, signs, angles, degrees, **and** calculating.
Revised:

EXERCISE 17.15

Write a paragraph in which you describe and react to the photograph "Noire et blanche (Black and White)." Assume your reader cannot see the photograph. Use parallelism in your paragraph. Vary the length of your sentences.

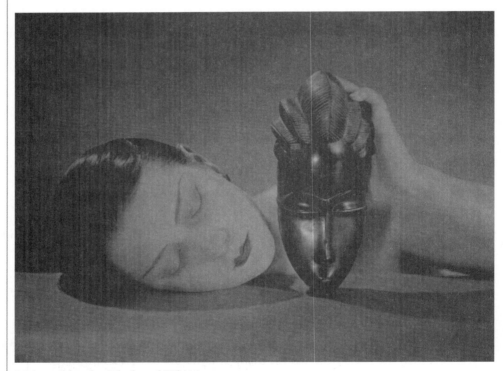

Noire et blanche (Black and White)

EXERCISE 17.16

Count the number of words in each sentence of your paragraph from Exercise 17.15 and chart them below. Highlight or bracket two sentences containing parallelism. Then answer the questions that follow.

EXERCISE 17.16 continued

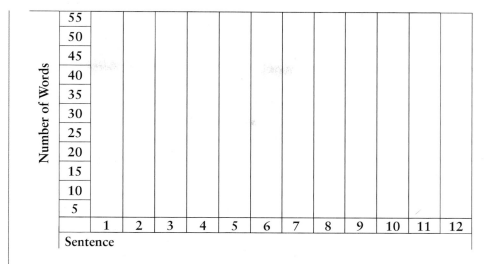

1. In how many sentences do you use parallel structure?

2. Which type of parallelism did you use (compounds, parallel lists, or repetition)?

Copyright © 2007, The McGraw-Hill Companies, Inc. All rights reserved.

18 *Repairing Sentences*

Use the following grid to help you keep track of common sentence errors in your writing. When your instructor makes marginal note of these errors in your papers, keep a tally on this grid. For example, in your second writing assignment, your instructor might point out three commas splices and two run-ons. You would then enter those numbers in the appropriate spaces below. As you proceed from one writing assignment to the next, use the grid to monitor your progress. Complete the exercises in this chapter to help you identify and understand common sentence errors. Then become a focused proofreader: search out and correct these errors when you edit final drafts of your work.

	Writing Assignment									
Error	1	2	3	4	5	6	7	8	9	10
Fragment										
Comma Splice										
Run-on										

WW Sentence Sense

IN THIS CHAPTER: A PREVIEW

Fragments

- Fragments and Punctuation
- Fragments and Dependence
- Fragments and Connecting Words
- Fragments and Phrases
- The Intentional Fragments

Comma Splices

- Comma Splices and End Punctuation
- Comma Splices and Connecting Words

Run-ons

- Run-ons and End Punctuation
- Run-ons and Connecting Words

Parallel Structure

- Words and Phrases
- Parallelism in Clauses and Consecutive Sentences

Dangling Modifiers

FRAGMENTS

The sentence fragment looks like a complete sentence. It begins with a capital letter and ends with a period. A fragment, however, does not express a meaningful and complete idea on its own.

> A flock of geese descended on the parking lot.
>
> Roger George, a funny guy who sits behind me in political science class.

The first sentence conveys a complete, meaningful idea. The second, a fragment, does not. What about Roger George? The fragment does not "make a statement." It does not express a meaningful idea.

EXERCISE 18.1

Write *S* next to each of the following items that is a complete sentence. Write *F* next to each fragment.

1. Sparkling blue eyes with a dash of gold in the middle.
2. A look of pure distrust enveloped their cola-stained, worry-free faces.
3. Girls and boys holding hands, most of them dancing, swaying back and forth to the music as if they were hypnotized.
4. We met back in November of 2000.
5. I was living life day by day, wondering what tomorrow would bring.
6. A normal day with many phases and challenges that await.
7. Every Friday on the eve of C-day as we called it.
8. We would go to Autozone to get materials for our job.
9. As I sit thinking back a couple years to my childhood days.
10. It seems like yesterday that we met.

EXERCISE 18.2

Build on what you practiced in Exercise 18.1. Write *S* next to each complete sentence. Write *F* next to each fragment.

1. Large enough to seat four people.
2. Michelle is my sister.
3. The kind of jewelry that turns your fingers green, but I didn't care.
4. If Michelle does not understand something, she asks a question or looks for an answer.
5. Something you don't hear every day.
6. When we sat down and talked about it, Margaret didn't look mad anymore.

Copyright © 2007, The McGraw-Hill Companies, Inc. All rights reserved.

7. Security Square Mall, which is in Baltimore, Maryland.

8. Not just my stepchildren or nieces and nephews, but everybody's children.

9. I had to memorize the name of the rocks.

10. It is not good for your health to eat when you're surrounded by cigarette smoke.

Fragments and Punctuation

Fragments commonly occur because a writer uses end punctuation where it doesn't belong. The error is corrected by linking the fragment to the sentence it properly belongs to. In some cases, a comma is needed to join the fragment to the main sentence; in other instances, no punctuation at all is required.

> **Incorrect:** Some soccer players get hurt. In fact, I read an article by Rebecca Harrison. <u>About a player who ran for his life from a gang who slammed him</u>
>
> fragment
>
> <u>against a wall, knocking him unconscious.</u>

No punctuation is needed to correct this fragment:

> **Correct:** Some soccer players get hurt. In fact, I read an article by Rebecca Harrison about a player who ran for his life from a gang who slammed him against a wall, knocking him unconscious.

> **Incorrect:** My boyfriend is also very good at math. <u>Which surprises me because</u>
>
> fragment
>
> <u>he seems to take no interest in anything.</u>

Substitute a comma for the period to correct this fragment:

> **Correct:** My boyfriend is also very good at math, which surprises me because he seems to take no interest in anything.

EXERCISE 18.3

In the following exercise, underline each fragment. Correct the error by making the fragment part of the sentence it belongs to. Modify the punctuation as needed. Some of the sentences may be correct.

1. There are many things that can make a person happy. Such as family, friends, a good job, and even a love interest.

2. Once we got to the little hole-in-the-wall restaurant. We gave the waiter our order.

3. I do not have the concentration to be an organized person. Especially when it comes to organizing parts of my life that do not excite me.

4. Because I am organized, I am always prepared for anything. If my friend comes over to my house without telling me he is coming. It doesn't bother me in the least.

5. My husband and I are experts on already-prepared foods. We have a tendency to pick up something quick on our way home for dinner. Instead of going home and actually taking time to cook dinner.

EXERCISE 18.3 continued

6. Employees must be willing to take on the responsibilities of opening and closing the store if needed. And also be able to make it to work on time. Finally, they must be friendly and informative.

7. In many homes, American children watch an average of three hours of TV in the morning. And an average of seven hours in the afternoon and evening.

8. I didn't think I got into that much mischief as a child. Until I remembered how I loved to do things out of the ordinary. I guess I did get out of line once in a while.

9. Larry got into a lot of trouble when he was a kid. When he was thirteen years old. He was at that daredevil age when he would try a whole lot of different daring things. Like sneaking out of the house, staying out late, sneaking company over, or even taking his stepfather's truck.

10. When the police came looking for us, we had to stay hidden under a bridge until school was out. Then we went home. We knew we had all been caught. The school had called our parents. We were really in trouble.

EXERCISE 18.4

Build on what you practiced in Exercise 18.3. Underline each fragment. Correct the error by making the fragment part of the sentence it belongs to. Modify the punctuation as needed. Some of the sentences may be correct.

1. We used things to our advantage to have a good time. One thing we did I am not very proud of. We often made fun of kids in the neighborhood. Like this one little girl in particular named Sarah, who was so clueless. She often became the butt of our jokes.

2. My idea was a good one. If I pretended I was a good religious kid, I could avoid work. It was the perfect plan. Until one day when my plan was discovered. My mom thought I was praying. For some reason she walked in and saw that I was reading a magazine and not praying.

3. These occupational courses give students a little taste of everything. Nail tech, for example. Then after high school, if a student is interested in them, she can take more of those classes.

4. Jake and I loved to play, watch, or just talk about football. Unfortunately, not all the other kids we played football with shared our enthusiasm. If it had been up to us, we would have made everyone play every day.

5. I don't think Joe even noticed his ball was missing. Then he rode his bike by my house and saw me and Jake playing with his ball.

6. I recently learned a lesson about friendship. No matter what, one should never compromise himself for a friend. Because any good friend accepts a person for what he is. This new acquaintance, I soon learned, was no friend.

Copyright © 2007, The McGraw-Hill Companies, Inc. All rights reserved.

EXERCISE 18.4 continued

7. On senior pride day at my high school. The students were very happy. They had to dress up and look nice.

8. When I was thirteen, I started working at a local country club. As a caddy. It was my summer job for three years.

9. It was around 8:00 p.m. on a Friday in the cold month of October. Just before Halloween. I was in the eighth grade, which made me fourteen years old.

10. The purpose of punishment is to correct an action that was wrong. To let the child know he or she cannot do wrong, unlawful, or harmful things without being disciplined It's as simple as that.

Fragments and Dependence

Fragments do not express a complete idea. They may precede or follow the sentence that they "depend" on. Changing punctuation joins the fragment to its related sentence. In the following examples, the fragments are underlined. The arrow indicates which sentence the fragment belongs to.

The first path led to the "mud hole." It was shaped like a saucer. <u>Shallow on the edges and a bit deeper in the center</u>. Someone always fell in.

The first path led to the "mud hole." It was shaped like a saucer, shallow on the edges and a bit deeper in the center. Someone always fell in.

I have so many memories of this time and place. <u>When my sister and I would sneak out at night</u>. We always went down to the beach to see the stars. My dad used to scare us and tell us a bear was going to come along.

I have so many memories of this time and place. When my sister and I would sneak out at night, we always went down to the beach to see the stars. My dad used to scare us and tell us a bear was going to come along.

The summer I turned five, my father started taking my family and me up north to Lupton. <u>Where my grandpa's cabin was</u>. There was nowhere in the world like that.

The summer I turned five, my father started taking my family and me up north to Lupton, where my grandpa's cabin was. There was nowhere in the world like that.

EXERCISE 18.5

In the following exercise, underline each fragment. Draw an arrow above the fragment to indicate which sentence it belongs to. Correct the error by joining the fragment to the appropriate sentence. Some of the sentences may be correct.

1. Every day I used to kick the fence and throw rocks and sticks at the neighbors' dogs, hoping they would get dirty or hurt. I was only four years of age. I didn't care about those dogs. Until this one particular day I was in front of my house.

2. One day on our way to the store. My dad and I had an incident with this angry dog. It was a warm Friday afternoon.

EXERCISE 18.5 continued

3. The thought of safety didn't enter my mind. As I stared in awe at this beast charging in my direction, ready to devour me. Just as it closed in, my guardian angel scooped me up from behind and placed me on top of the car.

4. As I look back on it now, I really don't think the dog was going to hurt me. Because it didn't bite my dad or even really bark. But ever since then, I have been scared of my neighbors' dogs.

5. I really learned my lesson. Which was to keep an eye on little infants and what they have in their mouths. I also learned to help an infant when its life is in danger.

6. Once my friends found the perfect spot for the prank, they unloaded their gear. The most important of which were the Polaroid camera, a recorder, and a flashlight. My duty was lookout. I had to let the other boys know if the security guard was around.

7. I never saw a real gun until I was ten years old. When a guy drove up to me and pulled out a gun on me. I was never so scared in my life.

8. We played "jailbreak" when we were kids. The bad guy would be thrown into our makeshift jail, and moments later, he or she would break out. Repeating the same cycle of running, hopping fences, and eventually getting caught. We had fun like this the entire summer.

9. I wasn't afraid of crossing the bridge itself. I was just afraid of falling into the water below. The bridge seemed like it was a million miles long, and time seemed to slow down. I thought we would never get to the other side.

10. The sun had gone down. It was a cool night. Sitting by the riverbank, smoking our first cigarettes. We felt like the coolest guys alive.

EXERCISE 18.6

Build on what you practiced in Exercise 18.5. Underline each fragment. Draw an arrow above the fragment to indicate which sentence it belongs to. Correct the error by joining the fragment to the appropriate sentence. Some of the sentences may be correct.

1. I called my friend and told him I had changed my mind about joining the police force. I never thought being a police officer would be so hard. Especially if you have to quit something you like, which in my case was college. I just couldn't do it.

2. My cousin and my uncle are both very smart. My cousin sets up auto shows so people can come and look at cars. She also travels around the world and talks to many different people. She's a very intelligent person, perhaps because of the experiences she has had and the people she meets. She has practical intelligence. Whereas my uncle has booksmarts. He reads all the time and is just as intelligent as my cousin, but in a different way.

Copyright © 2007, The McGraw-Hill Companies, Inc. All rights reserved.

EXERCISE 18.6 continued

3. Being responsible is important to me. When I wake up and am on time for class. I am showing my teachers that I want to learn and that I'm a responsible person.

4. An immoral person considers his gain and only his gain. Never really thinking of the person who is losing. On the other hand, the honest person puts himself in another person's place.

5. The opposite of honesty is dishonesty. It's also connected with the idea of care. If a person doesn't care about himself. He sure as hell won't care about you.

6. In our culture, parents tend to give boys more leeway to do what they please. Boys are often allowed to stay out till midnight. While girls usually have a curfew of 8 p.m. or, if they're lucky, 9 p.m. Because of their greater freedom, boys are more likely to make mistakes.

7. A smart bike rider carries everything he needs in his backpack. A spare tire, pump, first aid kit, water, and anything else useful for riding. That way, he can handle almost any emergency.

8. As a teen I was in some minor trouble, nothing too bad as I remember. But I did have to be disciplined from time to time.

9. Gangs used to be pretty big around my neighborhood. Everyone thought it was cool. Especially the younger kids. Some of the neighborhood girls started hanging around with the gang members. They ended up getting in trouble.

10. Some adults dislike kids for foolish reasons. Like my mom, for example. She did not like my friend Mike because of the way his hair was styled.

Fragments and Connecting Words

Look for connecting words at the beginning of a word group. Connecting words, such as those listed in the box below, indicate places where fragments may begin. A fragment that begins with a connecting word belongs either to the sentence that comes before it or after it:

My favorite hobby is reading. <u>Although I also enjoy sports.</u>
My favorite hobby is reading, although I also enjoy sports.

<u>Until I was in high school</u>. I wasn't really much of a basketball player.
Until I was in high school, I wasn't really much of a basketball player.

I still remember many rocks we studied in geology class. <u>**For example,** crystal rock, extrusive and intrusive rocks, granite, obsidian, basalt, gneiss, slate, shale, and more.</u>

I still remember many rocks we studied in geology class, for example, crystal rock, extrusive and intrusive rocks, granite, obsidian, basalt, gneiss, slate, shale, and more.

Common Connecting Words

as	until	whether
after	unless	which
although	whereas	who
because	when	whoever
before	while	like
even though	that	such as
if	whatever	for example
since	once	for instance
so		

EXERCISE 18.7

Circle the connecting words in the following sentences. Some of the sentences with connecting words state a complete idea; others do not. Alter the punctuation to correct the fragments.

1. When will I ever have to know how many degrees are in an octagon? The answer is never, unless I become an engineer. Which I choose not to be. So all those engineers can just enjoy their math. I'm doing fine without it.

2. When we first moved to this country, I would help my dad balance his checkbook. Usually after he had mailed out all of his bills. Some math knowledge came in handy then.

3. I currently work as a waiter. More than likely, technology will not take my job. Unless they build robots to serve people, I'm going to be all right. Although not too many people are in my shoes. At least I can say for the time being that I'm not worried about new technology.

4. Smoking should be banned in restaurants. Because some people have asthma, and secondhand smoke in public places makes them sick. That's just the simple fact of the matter.

5. Once, without permission, I gave a lot of my mother's things to charity, which made her pretty mad. When we sat down and talked about it, my mother didn't look mad any more. For the next few years, until I grew out of it. My mom designated a charity box for everyone in the family to contribute to.

6. When people ask questions about my name, it gives me a story to tell. About my father, how I was named after him, and how he got his name. No one believes it, but it's true.

7. There are some famous people who have the same name I do. For instance, Gary Shandling. Another is Gary Peters. He was a senator.

Copyright © 2007, The McGraw-Hill Companies, Inc. All rights reserved.

8. When I was nine years old, my brother, my friend, and his brother. We used to collect chestnuts. We used to have buckets full of chestnuts.

9. I played a lot of sports when I was a kid. On some teams I became a leader, which I valued a lot because it made me the better person that I am today.

10. I worked in customer service. That meant all the upset people came to me. I handled all the Better Business Bureau complaints. Which meant talking to some irate people and getting them results. Sometimes I really wanted to quit.

EXERCISE 18.8

Build on what you practiced in Exercise 18.7. Circle the connecting words. Some of the sentences with connecting words state a complete idea; others do not. Alter the punctuation to correct the fragments.

1. When I was little, my friends used to call me Missy. I hated that. Probably because people think of Missy as someone with an attitude.

2. Throughout my life I have had many jobs. Many of which I am proud of. Most recently I worked with a tile man installing ceramic tile in new homes. That was hard work, but I really learned a lot.

3. The teacher picked me to play an angel. Since that's the part I'd raised my hand for. I was very excited.

4. During an afternoon recess, my friends and I decided to play touch football. Everyone was enjoying the game. Until a girl named Stephanie ran right into me. I lost both the ball and my self-control. I grabbed her and threw her to the ground.

5. My mom worked from 8 a.m. to 5:30 p.m. and came home around 7:00 p.m. Meaning that she wouldn't be home when we wanted to skip school. So my friends asked me if they could have their party at my house. I was hesitant, but I agreed.

6. Chores are something that everyone has to do. I personally hate chores. There were many things that I had to do around our house. Like dusting, vacuuming, cleaning the bathrooms, etc. As I got older, I started working, and the number of my chores decreased.

7. There wasn't really a certain physical punishment; in my case, it was a matter of privileges being taken away from me for a long period of time. For example, talking on the phone and going out with friends. That was all it took for me to behave.

8. I was hanging out with the wrong crowd. Parties were the highlight of my life. When all it was doing was ruining me. My grades were dropping, and my family was falling apart.

Copyright © 2007, The McGraw-Hill Companies, Inc. All rights reserved.

EXERCISE 18.8 continued

9. Cars are convenient to have all year. Whereas you can use motorcycles only when it is warm. If a person lives in a cold climate, a car is a necessity.

10. If the cold persists after a week or so, you should consult a doctor. After seeing the doctor and ruling out other infections. You should go home and start taking prescription medication.

Fragments and Phrases

A sentence is a word group that contains a subject and a verb and expresses a complete idea. A word group lacking either a subject or a verb is a phrase. A fragment is frequently a phrase that needs to be linked to a complete sentence that comes before or after it.

Phrase	Fragment	Corrected
Noun Phrase	A dog is a friend. *The best friend a kid could ever have.*	A dog is a friend, the best friend a kid could ever have.
Verb Phrase	My mother thought the cake was done, so she took it out of the oven. *Frosted it and set it aside.*	My mother thought the cake was done, so she took it out of the oven, put frosting on it, and set it aside.
Verbal Phrase (*-ing* Forms)	When I was thirteen, I started working at a local country club. *Carrying 30- to 40-pound bags on my shoulder anywhere from four to eight hours.*	When I was thirteen, I started working at a local country club, carrying 30- to 40-pound bags on my shoulder anywhere from four to eight hours.
Verbal Phrase (*to* Forms)	The purpose of punishment is to correct wrongful action. *To let the child know he cannot do harmful things without being disciplined.*	The purpose of punishment is to correct wrongful action, to let the child know he cannot do harmful things without being disciplined.
from . . . to Forms	Every day was a new adventure. *From playing every kind of pick-up sport, to playing tag with toy guns, to collecting baseball cards.*	Every day was a new adventure, from playing every kind of pick-up sport, to playing tag with toy guns, to collecting baseball cards.

EXERCISE 18.9

Underline the phrases in the following items. Determine which sentences they depend on and alter the punctuation as needed.

1. How do I use math in my life now? I'll cite just one important example. Cutting coupons for shopping and knowing how much I'm actually saving.

2. There's no better feeling than driving a shiny red car, with the top down and the hum of the large motor under the hood. The feeling of power and control, the sheer excitement. You can't help thinking, "Don't I look cool?"

3. As a kid, there were many things I did to pass the time. Everything from playing video games, to riding bikes, to playing sports. What made it even better was the fact that I was surrounded by really good friends.

4. With a stern voice, my mother said I should get in the car. And told me we were going home. I knew I was in trouble.

5. From helping my little brothers with homework to taking the garbage out every Monday I really had a lot of responsibilities. A kid's work was never done.

6. Working under extremely hot conditions. Chasing golf balls, cleaning golf balls, and cleaning golf clubs after every use. This was not an ideal job for a girl.

7. I taught the campers how to blow bubbles with their fingers when we washed our hands. It gave me a feeling I will never forget. Just to see their smiling faces every time I taught them something new or just played with them.

8. The job I now have has some good and bad qualities. I'm a waitress, which gives me excellent experience with people. All types of people. Which also helps me develop patience.

9. I started working when I was 15 years old. I worked at Meijers. I was too young to be a cashier. I was a bagger, which was more than just bagging groceries. I had to clean the entranceways. Get change for the cashiers. Get items that customers forgot and put items back that customers did not want.

10. Then came high school. It started out just like elementary school. The teachers calling me Debra and my friends calling me Debbie.

EXERCISE 18.10

Build on what you practiced in Exercise 18.9. Underline the phrases. Determine which sentences they depend on and alter the punctuation as needed.

1. I know of many people with my name. My childhood neighbor, Suzy, for example. Then there are also three or four people I have met in college.

2. It took a while to vacuum the whole house. We had a dining room, a living room, bedrooms, hallways, and even carpeted stairs. I also had to vacuum all the corners of every room. Working on my knees and pushing furniture around so I could reach into the corners. It was a tremendous amount of work.

3. I lay in the middle of the floor screaming as loudly as possible. I rolled around on the floor. Demanding that my mother purchase something for me.

Copyright © 2007, The McGraw-Hill Companies, Inc. All rights reserved.

EXERCISE 18.10 continued

4. My little sister will raise her voice, use hand gestures, throw things such as shoes, slippers, and toys. Depending on the situation. In essence, she will do anything to get attention.

5. I promised my mother and father I would do better. All along lying to them and myself. They caught me from time to time.

6. Some things are meant to be forgotten. Like that smart remark your sibling made that caused you to become so angry. You don't want to be angry your whole life.

7. The face of dawn is creeping over the horizon as the runner finishes his stretching routines and tightens his shoelaces. He takes his position. Then pushes loose asphalt and concrete from under his feet as he springs into action. Hearing only the sound of his beating heart and seeing only the mist of his breath in the cool morning air, the runner continues his quest.

8. There are two forms of friends. Your true friends and your associates. The ones you depend on and the ones you don't. A true friend is most likely to be a person you've known for years. A person who knows many things about you.

9. Exercise is a way of getting into shape. Or staying in condition. It keeps your heart strong and healthy. Bettering your chances of living a longer life.

10. I believe that running is the best type of exercise. Especially long-distance running. While I'm running, I think about school, friends, music, or cars. Anything that keeps my mind off the running. That way before I know it, my long run is over.

EXERCISE 18.11

Read the following paragraphs and underline the fragments. Correct the fragments by altering the punctuation or revising the wording.

It was the first couple of months of my new driving experience. My father had just purchased a brand-new Ford F-150 pickup truck. I was taking a music class at night. While en route to my instructor's home. I was headed westbound on West Road, crossing Allen Road. Out of nowhere, I got broadsided by another car. He took out the whole side of the truck. From the front bumper to the tailgate. Try to explain this to your dad right after he told you to be extra careful with the car. Something that he had worked so hard for. It was the worst feeling of my life. I had destroyed his car in a matter of minutes. There was no escaping his wrath. I had no control of the situation.

Math can be very difficult. Maybe it is all the numbers, the formulas, and the boring work. Nowadays there are hundred-dollar calculators that pretty much do the work for you. Some people are opposed to using calculators in class. I can see

EXERCISE 18.11 continued

using them in grade school, when you are just learning the basics. For example, addition and subtraction and then your multiplication and division tables. Kids should know that stuff right away and not need help from calculators to do things like that. They should not be allowed to use a calculator. Until around the sixth grade. At this time calculators should be brought into play. Because most kids will have a good understanding of basic math. In addition, they will have to become familiar with calculators for the coming years. For example, the high school classes that require a calculator. In high school, calculators become essential for math and other subjects.

Looking at myself and my two best friends just proves how much the times have changed. Each of us lives a very different life. Yet one thing separates us from our mothers. We had options. I am a typical college student. At school full-time and working only part-time as a waitress. My friend Lynn chose to get a job straight out of high school. She is a full-blown workaholic. Finally, there is Marisa. Who had a child right out of high school. She manages a full-time job and a child all on her own. Now which one of these women works the hardest? The answer is that they all work equally hard. They have chosen their own path. While remaining the best of friends and thriving off each other.

Intentional Fragments

Intentional fragments are short, emphatic statements with expressive power a longer sentence cannot achieve.

What did I learn after three weeks of summer camp? <u>Not much.</u>
                                                  intentional fragment

Some responsible leaders today argue it would be a good idea to legalize drugs. <u>Wrong.</u>
intentional fragment

Use intentional fragments sparingly in your writing.

EXERCISE 18.12

Place an *F* next to the fragments in the following list. If you think a fragment works effectively as an intentional fragment, write *Int. F.*

1. My mother named me Melissa because of the song by the Allman Brothers, "Sweet Melissa."
2. Which I don't think I've ever heard all the way through.
3. In 1975, when I received my name, she hadn't heard of many girls with that name.
4. She thought she was being unique.
5. This type of thing happens a lot.
6. People find a name, and about a year later, every new baby has the same name.
7. My middle name, however, comes directly from hers.
8. I am Melissa Lane.

EXERCISE 18.12 continued

9. I have never met anyone else with that middle name.

10. If I had been a boy, I would have been named Ian.

11. Again my mother's doing.

12. I think everyone wants a unique name.

13. I always wanted an ethnic name, something different and fun to say.

14. Something that rolls off your tongue.

15. I resemble my mom's side of the family.

16. My dad is Mexican, but by looking at me, you can't tell.

17. To look at all of my cousins, you can see their Mexican background.

18. They have plain names, like Amy, Teresa, Jesse, and Justine, but they look the part.

19. If I'd had a Mexican name, that part of my family background would have been expressed.

20. Fine with me.

COMMA SPLICES

The sentence fragment occurs when a period is used instead of a comma. The comma splice is the reverse. A comma splice occurs when a comma is used instead of a period:

comma splice

My first job ever was a paper route, it was easy, all I had to do was get up early on Sundays and get home early from school on Wednesdays to deliver the paper to seventy-five homes.

There are three complete sentences (or independent clauses) in this example. Each sentence expresses a complete idea and can be written as a separate sentence:

1. My first job ever was a paper route.

2. It was easy.

3. All I had to do was get up early on Sundays and get home early from school on Wednesdays to deliver the paper to seventy-five homes.

To identify a comma splice, you need to be able to identify independent clauses that express complete ideas.

EXERCISE 18.13

Read the following sentences and circle the commas. Identify the independent clauses and write them in enumerated form, as shown above.

1. I believe everyone is intelligent in at least one field, take my brother John, for instance. He's a businessman.

Copyright © 2007, The McGraw-Hill Companies, Inc. All rights reserved.

2. Year after year he would save up his money for his big break, finally it happened. He opened up a restaurant with his friend. A couple of years passed, he was constantly fighting with his friend because they both wanted to do different things.

3. I never lie to my parents about anything major. I'd rather have them know what I'm doing, they were kids once too.

4. My mother does a good job keeping the house together. Even though she's a single parent, she takes care of her responsibilities and makes sure everyone is taken care of, I have to give her a lot of credit.

5. The customer came in for his car. The boss said, "You don't owe us anything, it's on us." The customer just stood there. I will never forget the look on his face. He was extremely happy.

6. Honesty is not an inherited characteristic, it's learned, practiced, and applied in one's life.

EXERCISE 18.13 continued

7. People often think only certain individuals succeed. That's not true, everyone can succeed. They just have to try hard enough to get what they want.

8. I have a best friend who means a lot to me, her name is Jackie. We've been friends for as long as I can remember.

9. I am a little forgetful, to me having a good memory is not everything. As long as I can remember the important things, like the material for tests, birthdays, and anniversaries, I get along just fine.

10. My present employer really likes me and has high hopes for me. It's only because of one thing, I'm a hard worker.

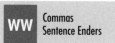

Commas
Sentence Enders

Comma Splices and End Punctuation

Inattentive writers often string together one complete sentence after another, joining them with commas:

> A few weeks ago, my brother and I went to Burger King for dinner, it was terrible, the service was so slow that it felt like we were in there for forty-five minutes.

The sentences are related, but the fact that they are related is no reason to link them with a comma. Each sentence expresses a complete idea and can be written as a separate sentence. One way to correct a comma splice is to change the comma to a period:

> A few weeks ago, my brother and I went to a Burger King for dinner. It was terrible. The service was so slow that it felt like we were in there for forty-five minutes.

Copyright © 2007, The McGraw-Hill Companies, Inc. All rights reserved.

EXERCISE 18.14

In the following exercise, identify the comma splices and correct them by replacing the commas with periods. Some may be correct as written.

1. Kathy has a part-time job, she doesn't have to work, she chooses to.

2. She had eyes that were a prettier blue than the sky itself. I cannot forget her smile and laugh, we always had a great time together.

3. So here's what we did all summer. We made s'mores at the beach, we even developed our own technique. Somehow we didn't gain any weight.

4. My opinion is that the United States is doing the right thing in foreign policy. It is not all our problem, we are just there to help out.

5. When something started to bother me, it took only a few months for me to figure out what it was. I would do some problem solving, a trick I learned from my mother.

6. The crew started using some new software on the job last week. After a while, I thought to myself: this is too easy, it's like a game.

7. The store manager called my parents, he told them that he had caught what my friend and I had done on tape, which meant we were in real trouble.

8. My friend and I played hockey every day for months. One day I was shooting a rock around with my hockey stick when I lifted it into the air, I hit and broke the light bulb that hangs outside the school.

9. I remember one particular day during school, I believe I was ten years old, my friend skipped school to take his little sister home when lunch began, I went with him.

10. The principal called our parents. My mother wasn't home at the time, she was at work.

EXERCISE 18.15

Build on what you practiced in Exercise 18.14. Identify the comma splices and correct them by replacing the commas with periods. Some may be correct as written.

1. One afternoon, in order to pass the time, my brother and I started watching wrestling, we practiced the moves on each other.

2. I was in the fifth grade, I was ten years old. That's when my parents decided to get a divorce.

EXERCISE 18.15 continued

3. The City Beautiful project taught me to keep our city clean. Our city looks beautiful to tourists from outside the city and state who come to visit, they say, "This is a pretty clean city, it would be nice to live here."

4. An old lady came out and yelled, "Go somewhere else and play, this is my home."

5. This year has been my best year, the business has really grown. Although I can't be sure, I hope next year is just as good.

6. Work requires my attention. I have to serve the customer well, I have to do my job right and be on time. I like having this responsibility.

7. One time I went to my friend Dave's house, he had a couple of people over. After a while I started drinking. I drank a lot. I was really messed up.

8. At this time, I feel that my responsibilities are preparing me for great feats in life, I feel having these responsibilities will make me stronger and help me handle life better.

9. This man faced very difficult circumstances, he had to put up with poor working conditions, antagonistic family members, and an all-around living situation that had few if any comforts. It was not easy.

10. When I met up with Mike, he said, "So you ran away, what are you going to do now?"

Comma Splices and Connecting Words

In addition to replacing commas with periods, you have other options when correcting a comma splice.

Option 1: Where the comma splice occurs, add an appropriate conjunction after the comma.

Option 2: Where the comma splice occurs, substitute a semicolon for the comma and, if it makes sense, add a conjunctive adverb followed by a comma.

Conjunction	Conjunctive Adverb
and	therefore
or	consequently
for	indeed
nor	however
but	in fact
yet	on the other hand
so	moreover
	nevertheless
	for example

Copyright © 2007, The McGraw-Hill Companies, Inc. All rights reserved.

Conjunctions and conjunctive adverbs express the relationship of one sentence to another. They add to the coherence of your writing. Here's a comma splice:

I've been going to school for 13 years, I'm beginning to realize how important it is.

The comma splice can be corrected with the comma + conjunction option:

I've been going to school for 13 years, **and** I'm beginning to realize how important it is.

Now another comma splice:

College is simply a lot harder than high school was, I have a lot more homework to do every day.

This comma splice can be corrected with the semicolon + conjunctive adverb + comma option:

College is simply a lot harder than high school was; **moreover,** I have a lot more homework to do every day.

When you exercise these options, you need to keep in mind one rule of thumb: Can you substitute a period for the comma and make two separate, complete sentences? The examples above can also be written as stand-alone sentences.

I've been going to school for 13 years. I'm beginning to realize how important it is.

College is simply a lot harder than high school was. I have a lot more homework to do every day.

Use the comma + conjunction and semicolon + conjunctive-adverb options when they make sense and sound right.

EXERCISE 18.16

Underline the comma splice in each of the following items. Then correct them, using one of the three options: period at the end of the sentence, comma + conjunction, or semicolon + conjunctive adverb + comma.

EXAMPLES:

The band director was <u>great, he</u> always pushed you to do your best.
The band director was great. He always pushed you to do your best.

We took names from the A-team as our code <u>names, my</u> younger brother was Hannibal, my older brother was Face. I was Murdock.

We took names from the A-team as our code names; for example, my younger brother was Hannibal, and my older brother was Face. I was Murdock.

1. The first time I ever saw a real celebrity I was ten years old. A TV personality named Arnold Stang walked out of a restaurant, he looked just like he did on TV, only smaller.

2. When I was a kid, I was very curious about guns. I never touched a real handgun, I saw and heard one once.

3. The doctor said everything he tested for was positive. I couldn't believe it, I was allergic to eighty-two things.

EXERCISE 18.16 continued

4. I'm glad I got the tests over with. Now my doctor and mom won't bug me about it, that will be a great relief.

5. Ah, the last days of summer. It was a cool night, the sun had just gone down.

6. When I was a kid, I thought I would always love dogs. I had one of my own, her name was Lady. She was a big brown retriever.

7. It was a hot June morning, I was coming back from McDonald's when I saw one of my neighbors, Mark, playing with a neighbor's dog.

8. This dog was horrible, it would not stop barking, it kept on slobbering on my new shoes, and it would not listen to anything you said.

9. This thing was crazy, it tried attacking me every time I cut the grass or cleaned my swimming pool.

10. One afternoon I got mad at our cat when she was hissing at me, I started yelling back at her, from that time on she has been a lot nicer to me.

EXERCISE 18.17

Build on what you practiced in Exercise 18.16. Underline the comma splices. Then correct them, using one of the three options: period at the end of the sentence, comma + conjunction, or semicolon + conjunctive adverb + comma.

1. When we have company over, I don't have to worry about putting the cat in a different room, she won't come out from her hiding spot.

2. Our cat is also an indoor cat, so she never wants to go outside, I am happy about that.

3. The math teacher started solving a problem on the board, I was watching every step, so she asked me to do the same problem on the board. I did the problem, and I got it right. I was so happy. From that day I started liking math, that was six years ago.

4. When I was in the seventh grade, I was at a school dance, a boy approached me and asked me to dance, but I turned him down.

5. Then came freshman year, I entered high school. It was a brand new experience.

6. Every time I see people smoking, I have the urge to ask them if I can have one, I just turn my head away instead.

Copyright © 2007, The McGraw-Hill Companies, Inc. All rights reserved.

EXERCISE 18.17 continued

7. Most teenagers want to smoke because they think it makes them look cool. Some smoke because their mom and dad tell them not to, they are rebellious and do it just to disobey.

8. Because of too much homework, kids are losing out on fun after school, but parents can help, they can monitor their kids' homework, they can meet with principals and discuss the amount of homework that kids receive.

9. My mother is a calm person, she loves to chat and laugh with her children, occasionally she gets a little excited. You want to watch out then.

10. Joe and I went to the same school, we went everywhere together, we often spent the night at each other's houses on the weekend.

EXERCISE 18.18

Find and correct the comma splices in the following paragraphs.

Violence has become the answer to many teenagers' frustrations in life. The introduction to violence starts when they are very small. Television dramas show everything from guns to blood and death, media glamorizes the violent behavior. Teens relate to these dramas and feel violence is the way to end their depression. Another important cause of violence is a lack of family structure. Those teens lacking love and family structure often are in trouble, they all too often take out their troubles through violent actions. Finally, violence may be seen as a cry for help or a way to get attention for some adolescents. Teens see that the only time they are noticed is when they become violent, hurt others, or cause trouble, sometimes they are scared or confused and do not know how to properly express or release those emotions, then violence, like so many other times, becomes the vent with which they release steam.

The women's movement as it stands today is still a very effective tool. This is true to the point that we are destroying generations of young men. It bothers me that I can't get our young women to understand this fact, it's not that I don't want women to be on the same plane as men. I just don't want them to use their gender as a leg up to get ahead in the world. I still like to open the door for a woman, pay for dinner, and even tell her she looks nice, I do so with the hope that she won't consider it sexual harassment. The ability of a man to be a man is on its way out the door. Just take a look at our young men out there, they carry purses, wear earrings, and grow their hair way too long. I don't know about you, but that sounds more like a girl than a boy. It's not a question of whether we are both equal; it's a matter of mutual respect. We need to understand that no matter what anybody thinks, we are genetically different. And that's okay, I like it that way.

EXERCISE 18.18 continued

Reality hit home soon after I walked into the club. The place was packed with people. I love hip-hop music, but the noise totally killed it. All the cute guys had their girlfriends with them, the few single guys had attitude problems. The only time I had fun was when I was on the dance floor dancing with my friends. Even that was short-lived, some guy came over and started dancing with me. I enjoyed myself for a while, it was actually fun until he put his hands on my waist and tried to pull me close. I love to dance, but I hate the slightest physical contact with strangers. As the evening went on, the place got more packed, one could hardly breathe.

I think clubs are for people who like being in closed places. Teenagers find clubs an ideal place to act silly and stupid, being stupid is actually encouraged among teenagers in clubs, the stupider they act, the more popular they get. Teenagers also get a kick out of loud noises and flashy lights. The reason I think adults go to clubs is because they have a hard time meeting people in a normal setting, they don't go for all the flashy lights. I would rather sit home and read a good book or watch a nice movie, that's my idea of a good time.

RUN-ONS

Like the comma splice, the run-on is an error involving two complete sentences. Whereas the comma splice occurs when two complete sentences are joined by a comma, the run-on has no intervening punctuation. The sentences simply run together.

> I remember the day we <u>met I</u> was swimming to the raft in the lake.
> run-on

There are two complete sentences in this example:

1. I remember the day we met.
2. I was swimming to the raft in the lake.

Run-ons and End Punctuation

The most effective way to correct a run-on is to put a period at the end of the first sentence and capitalize the first word of the second sentence:

> My brother loves to tease <u>me he</u> doesn't know when to stop.
> My brother loves to tease me. **H**e doesn't know when to stop.

EXERCISE 18.19

Identify the run-on sentences in the following exercise. Underline the final word of the first sentence and the first word of the second sentence in the run-on. Correct the error by putting a period at the end of the first complete sentence and capitalizing the first word of the second complete sentence.

1. Don't get me wrong I enjoyed where I worked and what I was doing, but it was not enough. I wanted more.

Copyright © 2007, The McGraw-Hill Companies, Inc. All rights reserved.

EXERCISE 18.19 continued

2. I decided I do not want to be a secretary for the rest of my life I want to be a registered nurse.

3. I tried skipping class while in the eighth grade my friends didn't. That is when my trouble with school began.

4. I think I watched too much TV when I was a kid it must have had some effect on me. I didn't spend enough time on schoolwork even now I watch too much TV, and it affects my grades.

5. I guess it wasn't the type of work that was important to me it was the place of work that led me to a change of attitude. That was my value system then that's my value system now.

6. I remember one particular day during school. I believe I was ten years old my friend and I skipped school to take his little sister home when lunch began.

7. The project taught me to keep our city clean that way our city looks beautiful when tourists from out of town come to visit.

8. They will say, "This is a pretty clean city it would be nice to live here."

9. We met at the park for a game. There were about fifteen kids we all had a good time playing.

10. Jake and I waited until night to make our move. We went over the fence then I snatched the ball.

EXERCISE 18.20

Build on what you practiced in Exercise 18.19. Identify the run-on sentences. Underline the final word of the first sentence and the first word of the second sentence in the run-on. Correct the error by putting a period at the end of the first complete sentence and capitalizing the first word of the second complete sentence. Some sentences may be correct as written.

1. Things were great we now had a ball, and Joe hadn't said anything about missing any of his stuff.

2. I learned a lot from working at U.P.S. It was hell my job was to load trucks with boxes. Inside the trucks, big heavy boxes would go from a belt to a roller inside the truck.

3. It wasn't one box at a time it was a heavy flow, almost more than one person could possibly handle. Nevertheless, I managed.

4. A large percentage of the employees would quit after the first month. Others would stay because they thought they couldn't get another job. Most of them had no diploma.

EXERCISE 18.20 continued

5. I told my mom not to let my sister go the weather was really bad out there. She told me not to worry she said she wouldn't let her go.

6. The birthday party was wonderful we had junk food, pizza, and everything you would wish for at a party.

7. When we came out of the theater, it was about eleven o'clock it was getting late.

8. This man loved all guns, including rifles, shotguns, and even BB guns. He did not care what kind of gun it was. They were all equal to him.

9. I decided to be more responsible at work. Here's what happened in just two months, I got a promotion.

10. I am responsible when it comes to my schoolwork I can be lazy, but when my teacher gives me something to do, I do it.

Run-ons and Connecting Words

Connecting words like conjunctions and conjunctive adverbs express the relationship of two consecutive sentences.

Conjunctions		Conjunctive Adverbs	
and	but	however	consequently
or	yet	moreover	indeed
for	so	nevertheless	in fact
nor		furthermore	

Use these connectors with appropriate punctuation to correct run-on sentences:

Comma + Conjunction

My son tries hard in <u>school it</u> takes him a little longer to get good grades.
My son tries hard in school, **but** it takes him a little longer to get good grades.

Sometimes you can't tell if a teacher is <u>good you</u> just hope for the best.
Sometimes you can't tell if a teacher is good, **so** you just hope for the best.

Semicolon + Conjunctive Adverb + Comma

I had five hard classes last <u>semester my</u> hardest class was economics.
I had five hard classes last semester; **however,** my hardest class was economics.

The coach said I was a good <u>player he</u> said I should go pro.
The coach said I was a good player; **moreover,** he said I should go pro.

EXERCISE 18.21

Identify the following run-ons by underlining the final word of the first sentence and the first word of the second sentence in each run-on. Correct the error with one of three options: period at the end of the sentence, comma + conjunction, or semicolon + conjunctive adverb + comma.

Copyright © 2007, The McGraw-Hill Companies, Inc. All rights reserved.

EXERCISE 18.21 continued

1. Usually the drive down to Florida would take about nine hours if my mom was driving, it would take twelve.

2. He purposely mixed his languages together to make me confused it took years for me to catch on to this.

3. My aunt is a very important person in my life she's my great aunt, my grandmother's baby sister. She's my mother's favorite aunt, so that's why we're so close.

4. Uncle Pete enjoys playing golf two or three times a week during golf season in the off-season he bowls.

5. My favorite knickknack is a jade elephant it was given to me as a gift.

6. One of my ceramic eggs has green and gold designs all over it and around the rim of the egg itself. This egg opens up it has a working clock inside.

7. She is a friend to everyone, but she is more than a friend to me she is my best friend. She is the person I confide in the most.

8. It's hard enough just being in high school, but my friend turned high school into a roller coaster of love-hate situations. Our freshman year was great we would spend the weekend at each other's houses and study together we even had a duet in our choir spring festival. Then things changed.

9. I thought about the decision quite a while and decided, What the hell. She had her turn now I get mine.

10. I'm using basketball as a tool to reach my goal of becoming an engineer it is not just a game to me. It's my life.

EXERCISE 18.22

Build on what you practiced in Exercise 18.21. Identify the following run-ons by underlining the final word of the first sentence and the first word of the second sentence in each run-on. Correct the error with one of three options: period at the end of the sentence, comma + conjunction, or semicolon + conjunctive adverb + comma.

1. You do not want to be one of the people who says, "I don't like seatbelts they're worthless." The only thing they can do is save your life.

2. The time and place were set now all I had to do was complete the task.

3. As I turned to see what my cousin and his friends thought, I realized they were gone. Seconds later I realized why the trash can had caught on fire.

Copyright © 2007, The McGraw-Hill Companies, Inc. All rights reserved.

EXERCISE 18.22 continued

4. I had to use a lot of heavy machinery it was hard work, but somehow I managed and actually began to like the work.

5. When I was little I was not much of a collector all I collected was dolls. My friends would ask me all the time if they could hold one of my dolls I just said no.

6. My uncles are twins they are the bosses of their catering company. They prepare food for everything. They cater parties. They cater wedding receptions with hundreds of people. It looks like a cool job.

7. I realize everyone has problems some people just have more than others, and that's the way it is.

8. My brother Jim and his friend Joe made my father stop at the fireworks store. They spent a couple hundred dollars each. I went inside and decided to buy some I only had about twenty dollars to spend.

9. All of a sudden Emily wanted to leave. We started walking out the alarm went off. The manager came out and asked us if we had stolen anything. Stolen anything? Me? Never in my life had I stolen anything. Emily, I'm sad to say, was another story.

10. After I misbehaved, the teacher told me to get out and go home I was excluded from the play. I figured I would go back the next day and apologize. Maybe she'd let me back in the play. Wrong that did not work she told me she already had someone else to play my part.

EXERCISE 18.23

Read the following sentences. Mark those that are comma splices *CS* and those that are run-ons *RO*. Correct the error with one of three options: period at the end of the sentence, comma + conjunction, or semicolon + conjunctive adverb + comma.

1. My first job was Franklin Wright Settlements. I started that job the summer of 1994, I was fourteen years old. I was really excited the whole summer about that job. So I did my best.

2. Even strangers teach me things. Sometimes it doesn't matter who it is if it means something to me or relates to me, somehow I never forget it.

3. It's not his fault he was born with AIDS what can he do about that?

4. I operate a forklift, it's hard to drive, but at the end of the day I feel like I did something. The thing I hate about my job is my boss, she always tries to do things too fast and always wants to be right.

EXERCISE 18.23 continued

5. I try to drink orange juice it prevents me from catching a cold, I also really like the taste of it.

6. I think that when you're sixteen or seventeen, you don't think about the value of your job you just want to work so you can earn money to go shopping with friends and blow your money on senseless items.

7. When I was trying to quit smoking, I never wore the patch it's not that I didn't want to put one on it's just that I always forgot.

8. It was very interesting to meet the travelers who had no knowledge of Michigan to them it was just another meeting.

9. Then one day I started doing time cards, making beds, and working overtime while still getting paid only $8.00 an hour, I tried to talk to my boss it wasn't any help, so I finally said goodbye to that job. I really did enjoy that job it was fun and diverse every day.

10. How I got my name is very simple, I was born, my parents looked in the phone book and selected the first name they liked.

EXERCISE 18.24

Build on what you practiced in Exercise 18.23. Mark sentences that are comma splices with *CS* and those that are run-ons *RO*. Correct the error with one of three options: period at the end of the sentence, comma + conjunction, or semicolon + conjunctive adverb + comma.

1. When I was nine years old, we used to collect chestnuts, a lot of them, we used to have buckets full of chestnuts all over the backyard, my mother used to get mad because of all the mess we made that wasn't the bad part, we used to stand on the corner of our block and throw them at cars driving by so that they would chase us I think it was pretty exciting getting chased, because even though we got caught all those times, we kept on doing it.

2. I am usually the person my friends and family members call on for advice. I really don't think it's the advice they are necessarily looking for, I feel it is my well-tuned listening skills and overall my ability to make a bad situation seem not so terrible.

3. My father is a people person he also has an excellent sense of humor and is great at problem solving. Because he raised me since I was four years old, I attribute my ability to him, we are so similar that we can sit in a room and talk about our personal problems for hours and reach a realistic, positive solution most of the time.

4. My friend Andy and I worked for a builder for about six months. If we didn't have certain parts of the house done, we didn't get paid, I was making about nine dollars an hour. Then when I was seventeen I started working for a

EXERCISE 18.24 continued

roofing company. That was okay, even though we were only making seven dollars an hour, my friend got me that job.

5. When I was thirteen years old, most of the girls in school wore lipstick I was forbidden to. My friends talked me into wearing lipstick during school hours, with the understanding that I would wipe it off before I got home. One day I forgot to take the lipstick off and walked into my house, unfortunately for me, my mother was standing right in the doorway. I was caught!

6. Parents need to use punishment that works, whether it is grounding, reprimanding, spanking, or taking away possessions. For some children time-out works, for others it may not. Punishment needs to be effective, or it is really not punishment and will not correct bad behavior.

7. Young people look forward to drinking, why?

8. We danced anywhere from two to four nights a week, we were always on the go. I was in two recitals a year. The first one was usually in January, I danced with the Onyx Ballet Company to music performed by the college symphony. The second one was a spring concert I looked forward to it most of all.

9. The following year, fourth grade, was great. My teacher was Mrs. Kress, she was new to the area. Mrs. Kress was full of life and very creative. We made donuts in class once, they were edible. I learned all of my times tables that year. We even had a contest all of the kids that learned their times tables 1–12 got to go to Showbiz Pizza. I was one of the winners.

10. On the first hole I hit the ball into the water, after that it took me ten shots to get to the green. On the second hole I hit the ball right into the sand bunker, that took about four shots to get out of. The next few holes were not so bad. Coming up to the last hole I was doing well, but I couldn't help wondering why people like to play this game so much. To me it was a nice walk that's about all.

PARALLEL STRUCTURE

Words and Phrases

Problems with parallel structure occur when two or more items in a series don't fit together. These items can be individual words or phrases. For the items to be parallel, they need to have to same form: all nouns or noun phrases, all verbs or verb phrases, or all adjectives or adjective phrases.

EXAMPLES:

My boss was <u>a cool guy</u> and <u>cooperative</u>. (noun, adjective = nonparallel)

My boss was a cool, cooperative guy. (adjective, adjective = parallel)

Copyright © 2007, The McGraw-Hill Companies, Inc. All rights reserved.

After work, we often <u>went</u> to have something to eat together, <u>hung</u> out with each other's friend, and generally <u>have</u> a good time. (past tense, past tense, present tense = nonparallel)

After work, we often went to have something to eat together, hung out with each other's friend, and generally had a good time. (past tense, past tense, past tense = parallel)

To correct errors in parallel structure, identify the items in the series and revise them so that each has the same form.

EXERCISE 18.25

Look for nonparallel items in the sentences below and revise them as needed. Circle the conjunction and underline the items that need to be made parallel. Indicate whether the problem area is a noun, verb, or adjective series.

1. I thought I had everything needed to bowl: balance, good aim, a bowling ball, and I could keep my arm straight.

2. As you approach the pins you must keep your eye on the pins, be aware of your body stance, and must walk straight toward the pins.

3. We didn't have many neighbors like Elmer. He knew everybody, talked to anybody, and would always be much louder than anyone else.

4. Parents of today should step back, re-evaluate their morals, and have taken control of what their children are watching.

5. It was so amazing to walk into the house, see everything almost exactly the same, and to smell the familiar food my father cooked.

6. That day at the cottage felt like when I was younger, sitting in front of the fireplace when everyone else was asleep, playing games with my boyfriend, and we would just reminisce about all the cool things that had happened to us.

7. My brother, clad only in cut-off coveralls, reached the top of the hill first. He was courageous and a spunky boy.

EXERCISE 18.25 continued

8. Some men these days look for partners who are powerful, well compensated, and career women.

9. Many magazines, books, movies, and TV shows are glamorizing sexual indulgences and give improper information about sex.

10. If I hadn't gone to the lake, I would have never learned to fish or how to drive or enjoy the experiences of small town life.

Parallelism in Clauses and Consecutive Sentences

Experienced writers learn to repeat forms and structures in successive clauses. Doing so makes their writing more connected and more forceful. Clauses are made parallel with the repetition of relative pronouns (who, that, which) and adverbs (such as how and what). Consecutive sentences are made parallel with similar noun and verb forms.

Parallel Clauses

My mother is a model of <u>who I want to be</u> and <u>teach my children</u>.

My mother is a model of <u>who I want to</u> be and <u>how I want to</u> teach my children.

She has taught me <u>to be very strong and independent</u> and <u>that I do not need someone else</u> to take care of me.

She has taught me <u>that I can be</u> strong and independent and <u>that I do not need</u> someone to take care of me.

Consecutive Sentences

I'm not saying women <u>cannot have both family and work</u>. I'm just saying <u>it will take sacrifices</u>.

<u>I'm not saying that women cannot have</u> both family and work. <u>I'm saying that having both</u> takes sacrifices.

<u>Family worries can create conflicts at work</u>. <u>Nearer to home, work stress can also cause conflicts</u>.

<u>Family worries can create conflicts at work</u>. At the same time, <u>work stress can cause conflicts at home</u>.

EXERCISE 18.26

Underline the items that seem to be connected. Circle the item that is not parallel. Revise the sentences by creating parallel clauses.

EXAMPLE:

When a movie with a popular actress is released, the media <u>constantly discuss it</u>. People at school are <u>anxiously (waiting) for it</u>. Everyone you know <u>talks about it</u>.

When a movie with a popular actress is released, the media constantly discuss it. People at school anxiously wait for it. Everyone you know talks about it.

Copyright © 2007, The McGraw-Hill Companies, Inc. All rights reserved.

EXERCISE 18.26 continued

1. My female cousins played dolls and Barbies with me and would play hide and seek. They even went horseback riding with me.

2. The trick is to figure out how to release your ball and throwing straight.

3. My favorite TV show in the 80s was "Battlestar Galactica." It was a science fiction show in which good was at war with evil. They had combat pilots battling to find their way home to earth.

4. As I watched my aunt get older, I was thankful that I had the opportunity to get to know her and could spend some quality time with her.

5. I never really fell for the boyfriends who were gentlemen and who sent flowers for my birthday and they treated me well.

EXERCISE 18.27

Underline the items that seem to be connected. Circle the item that is not parallel. Revise the sentences by creating consecutive, parallel sentences or by creating combined sentences with parallel clauses.

EXAMPLE

The waves tossed our boat like a toy in a bathtub. I thought that it would break in half. It seemed as if the motor would fall off.

1. For pastimes, my parents encouraged us to choose activities that were appropriate to our gender rather than what we were interested in. The boys played sports like baseball and hockey, and the girls dance lessons or gymnastics.

2. My father loves to travel. He gave me this New Year's trip as a gift because I performed well in school last year. Also, I have not given my mom a hard time.

Copyright © 2007, The McGraw-Hill Companies, Inc. All rights reserved.

EXERCISE 18.27 continued

3. How can women ever be viewed as equal partners in the workplace? Unfortunately the workplace is a man's world: it's run by men and men make the decisions.

4. If you don't succeed the first time, you get one more try. Knocking down the pins with one ball is called a strike. If you knock them all down with two tries, it's called a spare.

5. I can't get the hang of packing for trips. I bring some of the things I might need and also pack all kinds of junk I don't need, but I always forget essential items.

DANGLING MODIFIERS

Modifiers are generally found very near to the term they modify. For example, adjectives and nouns are often seen side by side: a <u>red</u> car, an <u>impenetrable</u> mystery. Adjective phrases also need to be near the terms they modify.

<u>Opening the newspaper this morning</u>, I learned of the boating accident.

<u>Looking out the window</u>, the man noticed the lawn needs cutting.

In these sentences, there is no question who opens the newspaper and who looks out the window. Who opened it? "I" did. Who looked out the window? "The man" did. In the thinking-writing process, however, sometimes a writer forms sentences with dangling modifiers. The writer understands a sentence, but to a reader, the meaning is confusing and often funny.

At night, <u>walking around</u>, her eyes reflected the storefront lights.
<u>Having chosen to pursue an academic career</u>, my mother will be there every minute to support me.
<u>Running to catch the mailman</u>, the door slammed shut behind Renata.

In these sentences, the reader might well wonder: Who is walking around? Her eyes? Who chose the academic career? Can doors really run? These are dangling modifiers. To correct the error, the writer needs to put a person ("she," "I," and "Renata," respectively) either in the sentence, or closer to the modifier, in order to clarify meaning.

At night, <u>while</u> she <u>was walking around</u>, her eyes reflected the storefront lights.

Now <u>that</u> I <u>have chosen to pursue an academic career</u>, my mother will be there every minute to support me.

<u>Running to catch the mailman</u>, Renata <u>felt the door slam shut behind her</u>.

Correcting this error almost always involves rewriting to clarify meaning. Rewriting involves three steps:

1. Identify the modifier.
2. Identify the word it modifies.
3. Rewrite the sentence so the modifier and the word it modifies are close together.

EXERCISE 18.28

Read the sentences below and underline dangling modifiers. Then rewrite the sentence in the space provided to correct the error and clarify meaning.

1. Now, as a mother and full-time college student, family meals are a hit and miss affair.

2. Almost immediately after gaining independence, a revolution commenced.

3. By reviewing mistakes of the past, a better understanding of the present can be gained by people.

4. The largest polluter in the world is the United States. Aptly named the "ten-ton gorilla," major changes and commitments must be made by the U.S. president.

5. The goal was to reduce gases to 1990 levels by 2000. Looking back, this goal would have been impossible.

6. My brother and I loved to play tricks on Sarah. We told her that if she spun around really fast five times, she would become invisible. With some hesitation, my brother and I talked her into doing it.

7. As a child, there was not much to do to pass the time.

8. In the delivery room for the second time, the fears of the challenges to come were overwhelming.

EXERCISE 18.28 continued

9. A German shepherd came running down the street toward me. When close enough to bite me, the owner grabbed the dog and pulled him back.

10. I went to wake my father up. Entering the room, he was still sleeping.

EXERCISE 18.29

Read the sentences below and underline the dangling modifiers. Then rewrite the sentence in the space provided to correct the error and clarify meaning.

1. Growing up, there were several Lindas in my neighborhood.

2. Not knowing if he was a good driver or not, he offered to take me for a ride.

3. While hiking, a canteen for water comes in handy.

4. We went to the house of an elderly couple. Telling them of our trouble, they let us use their phone.

5. For the first two years of high school, he was always the best at what he did. Going into his junior year his father died.

6. I was told to step out of the car and stand on the curb. Once on the curb, they began to search me.

7. Growing up, most of the men in my family worked for General Motors.

8. We hid in the basement. Almost finished with our devilish plan, the floorboards above began to rumble.

9. Living in a duplex home, our landlord did not allow pets. As most children are, I was fascinated with all animals.

10. Hungrily licking his chops, the zookeeper looked nervously at the Siberian tiger.

Copyright © 2007, The McGraw-Hill Companies, Inc. All rights reserved.

19 *Agreement and Consistency*

Use the following grid to help you keep track of agreement and consistency errors in your writing. When your instructor makes marginal note of these errors in your papers, keep a tally on this grid. For example, in your fourth writing assignment, your instructor might point out two verb agreement errors and a problem with pronoun case. You would then enter those numbers in the appropriate spaces below. As you proceed from one writing assignment to the next, use the grid to monitor your progress. Complete the exercises in this chapter to help you identify and understand agreement and consistency errors. Then become a focused proofreader: search out and correct these errors when you edit final drafts of your work.

	Writing Assignment									
Errors	1	2	3	4	5	6	7	8	9	10
Verb Agreement										
Verb Tense Consistency										
Pronoun Agreement										
Pronoun Case										
Pronoun Consistency										

IN THIS CHAPTER: A PREVIEW

Verb Agreement

- Pairing Subjects and Verbs

Inconsistent Verb Tense

Pronoun Agreement

- Identifying Pronouns and Their Antecedents
- Detecting Errors in Pronoun Agreement
- Indefinite Pronouns and Agreement

Pronoun Case

- Subjective and Objective Pronouns
- Compound and Comparative Forms

Pronoun Consistency

WW Subject-Verb
Agreement,
Verbs in Depth

VERB AGREEMENT

Verb agreement occurs when the verb agrees in number with the subject of a sentence. Singular subjects take singular verbs; plural subjects take plural verbs. In most cases, your ear will tell you if the subject and verb agree. Wrong verbs just don't sound right.

> **Not in agreement:** When I first arrive at school in the morning, there **is** people on either side of me puffing on cigarettes.
>
> **In agreement:** When I first arrive at school in the morning, there **are** people on either side of me puffing on cigarettes.
>
> **Not in agreement:** It's funny how life experiences **influences** a person's attitude.
>
> **In agreement:** It's funny how life experiences **influence** a person's attitude.

Changing the verb, as the preceding examples show, improves the sound of these sentences. This improvement can be made also by changing the subject of the sentence.

> When I first arrive at school in the morning, there is a **person** on either side of me puffing on cigarettes.
>
> It's funny how life **experience** influences a person's attitude.

In both examples, the plural subject of the original sentence was changed to a singular subject: "people" became "person" and "experiences" became "experience."

EXERCISE 19.1

Read the following sentences and underline the subjects. Then circle the verb that agrees with the subject of the sentence.

EXAMPLES:

> Your ear will tell you if the <u>subject and verb</u> (agree)/agrees.
>
> <u>Groups</u> like the National Organization for Women was/(were) formed in response to women's complaints of discrimination.

1. Before the Kyoto Summit, there **was/were** many fingers pointed at assumed guilty parties.
2. Gifford Pinchot's belief was that "the use of natural resources **was/were** for the benefit of humans."
3. We came outside and the police **was/were** sitting right there in front of us.
4. The examples of my uncle and cousin **show/shows** that there are different ways of being intelligent.
5. Then one afternoon my husband and I **was/were** watching TV, and we heard the motorcycle start up.

Copyright © 2007, The McGraw-Hill Companies, Inc. All rights reserved.

EXERCISE 19.1 continued

6. We had lunch at the Olive Garden. The food and service **was/were** excellent.

7. Over time, the capabilities of graphing calculators **has/have** increased significantly.

8. Now which one of these women **work/works** the hardest?

9. My second reason for favoring the war on drugs **is/are** the effects drugs have on newborn babies.

10. Nearly every company, institution, and person **has/have** benefited from the development of the Internet.

EXERCISE 19.2

Build on what you practiced in Exercise 19.1. Underline subjects. Then circle the verb that agrees with the subject of the sentence.

1. Having this kind of technology **make/makes** things easier on everyone.

2. Educational shows also **keep/keeps** the child interested.

3. Music **express/expresses** the way people feel.

4. There **is/are** a lot of changes going on in the workplace.

5. People's jobs **define/defines** who they are.

6. If future proposals to get more people involved in education **doesn't/don't** work, then what is going to be the ultimate goal?

7. Working in a pharmacy wasn't a good job for me because there **wasn't/weren't** good hours and working conditions.

8. In large group settings, I find that my interest and the interests of others **is/are** completely different.

9. I usually got As and Bs. But class participation and classwork **was/were** not all that was needed to pass the class. Completing homework assignments was also included.

10. The number of healthy people **has/have** been increasing over the past ten years.

Pairing Subjects and Verbs

Verb agreement errors occur in sentences in which the writer does not clearly recognize the simple subject. When you think you hear a problem, analyze the sentence, identify the simple subject, and then put the subject and verb together as a pair.

The <u>number</u> of healthy people **has** been increasing over the past ten years.

    subject   verb

<u>*number*</u> *has*

Educational <u>shows</u> also **keep** the child interested.

         subject   verb

<u>*shows*</u> *keep*

The simple subject is often one word. However, be on the lookout for compound subjects. Watch for two subjects joined by a conjunction:

<u>Cars and motorcycles</u> **are** popular forms of transportation

       subject   verb

<u>*cars and motorcycles*</u> *are*

Usually subjects come before verbs in English. In sentences beginning with the word *there,* however, the subject comes after the verb:

There **weren't** <u>good hours and working conditions.</u>
     verb   subject
*<u>good hours and working conditions</u> **weren't***

There **have been** many <u>fingers</u> **pointed** at assumed guilty parties.
     verb   subject
*<u>fingers</u> **have been pointed***

In complex sentences, relative pronouns "repeat" the subject and are either singular or plural:

The <u>peaches</u> <u>that</u> **fall** to the ground rot quickly.
  subject   verb
     relative
     pronoun

*<u>peaches that</u> **fall***

The <u>fruit</u> <u>that</u> **falls** to the ground rots quickly.
  subject   verb
    relative
    pronoun

*<u>fruit that</u> **falls***

Analyze and listen. When you know the simple subject of the sentence, your ear will tell you if the verb agrees with it.

EXERCISE 19.3

Read the following sentences and correct errors in subject-verb agreement.

1. There is things a person can do to get better grades and improve himself as a student.

2. There has been many situations in which people recognized me from the competitions I entered.

3. The areas I worked on was attending classes, keeping up with material, and paying attention in class.

4. So there you have a few areas that has worked for me and is bound to work for you to make you a successful student.

Copyright © 2007, The McGraw-Hill Companies, Inc. All rights reserved.

EXERCISE 19.3 continued

5. Some people have to work at their talents, and some people just has them naturally.

6. His strong family values makes this person stand out above the rest.

7. I know there is many distractions while you're driving

8. So that's my suggestions on how to become a more alert and safe driver.

9. These injuries include pulled muscles, which is usually a result of not stretching at all or not enough before exercising.

10. You can imagine the looks that was on their faces when they saw me.

EXERCISE 19.4

Build on what you practiced in Exercise 19.3. Correct the errors in subject-verb agreement in the following sentences.

1. I didn't know anyone who worked in the store, but when I started, there was a couple good looking girls.

2. This experience taught me that there is many great people out in the world.

3. I rode my bike around town, trying to find someone who would be generous enough to keep a few little kittens. I didn't get home until late. There was no kittens left in my backpack.

4. My favorite game show is *Jeopardy,* which air every night during the week at 7:30 p.m. and is hosted by Mr. Alex Trebek.

5. My skills working with animals gets better all the time.

6. I did not like working at the optical company. The people who worked there was older than I was and not very friendly.

7. Every person I have met with my name were elderly women.

8. There has been times growing up when I would have enjoyed having a different name.

9. Upkeep and maintenance of bicycles is relatively inexpensive.

10. There is all kinds of different exercises a person can do to improve muscle mass.

WW   Verbs In-Depth
Verb Tense

INCONSISTENT VERB TENSE

Verb tense refers to how you represent time in your speaking and writing. Events occur in the past, present, and future. There are ongoing events, events that are concluded, and events that are merely possible. These subtle differences in time and possibility are represented in the verbs you use. The agreement of one verb tense with another is called consistency.

> **Inconsistent:** It **was** a beautiful summer day. My brother and I **had found** ourselves sitting on our rusty swing set with nothing to do.

When possible, use simple verb tenses. Usually one-word verbs are preferable to more complex forms.

> **Consistent:** It **was** a beautiful summer day. My brother and I **found** ourselves sitting on our rusty swing set with nothing to do.

Watch out for auxillary verbs such as *can/could, will/would,* and *may/might,* and keep them consistent with the tense you establish.

> **Inconsistent:** This time we **agreed** that we **will** study together.
> **Consistent:** This time we **agreed** that we **would** study together.

More often than not, consistency errors occur because of inattention. Be alert when you check your writing for these (and other) common errors.

> Jake and I loved to play, watch, or just talk about football. The worst part of it ~~is~~ **was,** we didn't have a football.

> Early on, my mother learned to cook, clean, and take care of the rest of the family. Back then little girls were taught to do these things. They didn't have to worry about creating a career or security. A husband ~~takes~~ **took** care of those things for them.

EXERCISE 19.5

Read the following sentences and underline the verbs. Correct any errors in verb-tense consistency in the space provided.

1. I believe that if people are dependable, it helps a great deal. They could make a positive contribution to the world.

2. I would always be the cop, which means catching and arresting my friend. When I catch him, he would always cry, stomp his feet, and say I was cheating.

3. My stepfather came to me first and asks who drove his truck without permission.

4. My parents always used to brag about how I am the perfect child.

5. A few times my father tried to make dinner, but he could not make it taste the way my mother does.

Copyright © 2007, The McGraw-Hill Companies, Inc. All rights reserved.

6. As soon as this happened, we all take off running.

7. One morning my sister and I were walking to school, and we meet up with some of our friends.

8. A lot of people play their music loud just to get attention. For example, my friend Moe had a system in his car, and he always turns up the sound.

9. One time when I was eight or nine years old, I asked my mother if I can go outside and play with friends.

10. When I was a kid, most of the kids pass their time collecting football cards, basketball cards, and baseball cards.

EXERCISE 19.6

Build on what you practiced in Exercise 19.5. Underline the verbs. Correct any errors in verb-tense consistency in the space provided.

1. After I bought my first pack of baseball cards, I want more.

2. When she became "invisible," we taunted her by saying she will never be seen again.

3. I didn't like math. Math was the worst subject I've ever had. It makes my head hurt.

4. Things were great. We now had a ball, and Joe hasn't said anything about his ball being missing.

5. I don't think Joe even noticed his ball was missing, until he rode his bike by and saw me and Jake playing with it. Needless to say, I've lost a friend that day.

6. School was out. The track team runs on the track. There were long-distance runners, short-distance runners, and shot-putters. I was a shot-putter.

7. A friend saw me walking back to the locker room, so he pulled up and ask if I want a ride home.

8. That same morning on our way to school, we saw my cousin in his car. My brother stop at the light, and my cousin kept going.

9. The ambulance came, and cops were everywhere. I was standing there, hoping that my cousin is okay.

Copyright © 2007, The McGraw-Hill Companies, Inc. All rights reserved.

EXERCISE 19.6 continued

10. A few friends and I were practicing for an upcoming race. The track is all sand and loose mud.

EXERCISE 19.7

Build on what you practiced in Exercises 19.5 and 19.6. Underline the verbs. Correct any errors in verb-tense consistency in the space provided.

1. When I was a little kid, I played with my friends at my backyard. We watch a lot of programs on TV. We took names of characters, went to my backyard, and started playing games.

2. If someday I had a wife and she said that I won't have to work anymore, that she will take care of all the money stuff with this wonderful career that she had, I would be one happy man.

3. Then Tim started to sing. All of us just stop what we were doing and listen to him.

4. So before I knew it, my friend pull out his wallet and hand me some money. It was a five and two ones.

5. All of us were amazed. We start playing cops and robbers. When someone got shot, I pretend that she was dead, with blood coming out of her body, arms, and legs.

6. We made sure he took the car home and tell his parents he borrowed it.

7. To expand on his passion, my friend joined the NRA and attend all the meetings.

8. I needed the testing done so my doctor can help me with my allergies.

9. Her family was from Piqua, Ohio. They drove nine hours to go on a vacation. To an eight-year-old, that seems like an eternity.

10. I knew in advance that we would have to cross the Mackinac Bridge, but I figure I would just sleep while we go over it.

PRONOUN AGREEMENT

Identifying Pronouns and Their Antecedents

You use pronouns automatically when you form sentences. Pronouns are words that take the place of nouns. They eliminate repetition and enable you to manage more information when you speak and write.

WW | Pronouns in Depth

Last night I ate pizza with goat cheese and spinach. The pizza was delicious. My friend Phil paid for the pizza. Phil likes pizza too, but Phil prefers pizza with tomato and walnuts.

Notice the repetition of "pizza" and "Phil." In the following sentence, this repetition is eliminated by the use of pronouns.

Last night I ate pizza with goat cheese and spinach. <u>It</u> was delicious. My friend Phil paid for <u>it</u>. <u>He</u> likes pizza too, but <u>he</u> prefers <u>it</u> with tomato and walnuts.

Following is a list of commonly used pronouns. There are others, but for the time being, these are the ones we need most to talk about.

COMMON PRONOUNS			
subjective	objective	possessive	Reflexive
I	me	my	myself
you	you	your	yourself
it	it	its	itself
he	him	his	himself
she	her	her	herself
we	us	our	ourselves
they	them	their	themselves

Agreement occurs when the pronoun agrees in number with the noun it refers to (also known as its antecedent.) Plural antecedents take plural pronouns. Singular antecedents take singular pronouns.

The **cars** were backed up for miles. There was no counting <u>them</u>.

In this sentence, "them" is the pronoun and its antecedent is "cars." "Them" is a plural pronoun; "cars" is its plural antecedent. Because both the pronoun and antecdent are plural, they agree in number.

Smoking stinks. <u>It</u> also poses terrible health risks. I just don't understand why **people** would want to pollute the air and risk <u>their</u> health at the same time.

In these sentences, "it" is a singular pronoun that refers to "smoking," a singular antecedent. "Their" is a plural pronoun that refers to "people," a plural antecedent. In both cases, the pronouns and antecedents agree in number.

My **sister** was very athletic when <u>she</u> was a kid. <u>She</u> could do just about anything. <u>Her</u> favorite sport was **gymnastics**. <u>It</u> appealed to <u>her</u> because <u>it</u> was a performance, almost like dance.

The antecedent "sister" is followed by a number of singular pronouns: "she," "she," "her," and "her." The singular pronoun "it" refers to the singular antecedent "gymnastics." (Note that some nouns in English are singular in meaning even though they end in *s. Economics, ethics,* and *mathematics* are other examples.)

EXERCISE 19.8

Underline the pronouns and circle the antecedents in the following sentences. Indicate whether they are singular (*S*) or plural (*PL*).

1. Some parents today neglect teaching their children the importance of saving money.
2. Drugs can be a huge problem. They can even destroy a person's life.
3. One time, I was watching Oprah, and she asked members of the audience to raise their hands to show if they would have preferred being raised at a day care center rather than at home.
4. A teacher definitely affects learning. Her voice, attitude, personality, and even her penmanship create this unique feeling of character you can't get staring at a computer screen.
5. I knew a boy who was so full of life. He was also full of surprises.
6. So this neighbor called my parents. He told them that he had caught every- thing my friend and I did on tape. We got in a lot of trouble.
7. It was a beautiful summer day, yet my brother and I found ourselves sitting on our rusty swing set with nothing to do.
8. I bought a new sound system for my car. It was so loud that people ran for cover every time they heard it.
9. It's amazing how many people are working out of their houses these days.
10. A father who can't manage time properly can lose the most important thing in his life, and that's the love of his family.

Detecting Errors in Pronoun Agreement

One of the most common errors in spoken English involves pronoun agreement. In fact, this grammatical misstep is so common that even radio and television profes- sionals frequently make statements like this:

> If an older **person** applies for a job, <u>they</u> will probably be overlooked.

"They" is a plural pronoun that refers to a singular antecedent, "person." The pro- noun and antecedent do not agree in number. In formal English, it would be prefer- able to say and write one of the following:

> If older **people** apply for a job, <u>they</u> will probably be overlooked.
> (*Solution:* make the antecedent plural to agree with the plural pronoun.)
>
> If an older **person** applies for a job, <u>he</u> or <u>she</u> will probably be overlooked.
> (*Solution:* make the pronoun singular to agree with the singular antecedent.)
>
> An older **person** who applies for a job will probably be overlooked.
> (*Solution:* revise the sentence to eliminate the pronoun in question.)

Because of the gap between what you hear in spoken English and what is required in college writing, agreement errors can be difficult to detect and correct. It is good practice to examine plural pronouns every time they occur.

> Every **person** has talents and special abilities. <u>Their</u> talents and abilities make <u>them</u> who <u>they</u> are and determine the impression <u>they</u> make on other people.

Copyright © 2007, The McGraw-Hill Companies, Inc. All rights reserved.

The pronouns here are plural: "their," "them," "they," and "they." The antecedent is singular: "person." (Think *every single person*.) The pronouns in this sentence, then, are not in agreement with their antecedent. Because there are four pronouns for one antecedent, it makes sense to make the antecedent plural. However, there are two other options as well:

> **People** have talents and special abilities. <u>Their</u> talents and abilities make <u>them</u> who <u>they</u> are and determine the impression <u>they</u> make on other people.
> (*Solution:* make the antecedent plural to agree with the plural pronouns.)
>
> **Every person** has talents and special abilities. <u>His</u> or <u>her</u> talents and abilities make that person who <u>he</u> or <u>she</u> is and determine the impression <u>he</u> or <u>she</u> makes on other people.
> (*Solution:* make the pronouns singular to agree with the singular antecedent.)
>
> **Every person** has unique talents and abilities that make an impression on other people.
> (*Solution:* revise the sentence to eliminate the pronouns in question.)

Your goal when correcting these errors is to produce a sentence that both *sounds* good and retains the meaning of the original sentence. In the preceding examples, the first revision sounds the best and expresses the same idea as the original sentence.

EXERCISE 19.9

Circle the antecedents and underline the pronouns in the following sentences. Then determine whether the antecedents and the pronouns agree. Use one of three solutions to correct the errors and write the corrected sentence in the space provided.

- Make the antecedent plural to agree with the plural pronoun.
- Make the pronoun singular to agree with the singular antecedent.
- Revise the sentence and eliminate the pronoun in question.

1. I have noticed that when a person is under the influence of a drug, they are less inhibited and do things that they normally wouldn't do.

2. There are many ways a person can protect themselves from people on the road. One is defensive driving. The person driving next to you might not realize they are crossing into your lane.

3. Not every driver is as good as they should be, but that doesn't mean we are all doomed.

4. This person has gone through many hardships in their life.

Copyright © 2007, The McGraw-Hill Companies, Inc. All rights reserved.

EXERCISE 19.9 continued

5. The strengths of this course would be that the student can work at their own pace and set their work schedule around the rest of their life.

6. A good waitress should have made it her duty to satisfy the customer, regardless of their ethnic or financial background.

7. A child has a vivid imagination, the ability to create things that do not exist, all before the cruel adult world gets a hold of them.

8. Whether it is a nine-to-five office job or a stay-at-home mom's job, every woman has something that they are committed to every day.

9. If I happen to have a teacher who pronounces my name right after the first try, I give them nothing but respect.

10. When I meet a guy for the first time, they always ask my name.

Indefinite Pronouns and Agreement

The following box lists some common indefinite pronouns.

one	nobody
anyone	anybody
everyone	everybody
someone	somebody

In spoken English, speakers frequently use plural pronouns to go with indefinite pronouns. Although these terms sound plural, they are clearly singular in meaning: some*one*, every*one*. In spoken English, people frequently use plural pronouns to go with these terms:

Someone always parks <u>their</u> car too close to mine.

Everyone brought <u>their</u> own lunch on the trip to the museum.

There are three solutions (the same ones discussed earlier) to correct agreement errors involving these indefinite pronoun: make the antecedent plural, make the pronoun singular, or revise the sentence to eliminate the pronoun in question:

People always park <u>their</u> cars too close to mine.

Someone always parks <u>his</u> or <u>her</u> car too close to mine.

Someone always parks too close to my car.

> **All the visitors** brought <u>their</u> own lunches on the trip to the museum.
>
> **Everyone** brought <u>his</u> or <u>her</u> own lunch on the trip to the museum.
>
> **Everyone** brought a lunch on the trip to the museum.

As always, your goal is to choose the revision that sounds the best and retains the meaning of the original sentence.

EXERCISE 19.10

Circle the antecedents and underline the pronouns in the following sentences. Use the space provided to rewrite the sentences so that pronouns and antecedents agree. Use one of the three approaches to revise the sentences.

1. When somebody is addicted, they will want to try stronger and more dangerous drugs.

2. Happiness is something everyone needs in their life.

3. When someone has a good attitude, they bring everyone else's spirit up.

4. No matter what occupation one has or how large their income is, if they're happy with their lives, that's the best fortune they could ask for.

5. Sometimes one's ignorance can get the best of their principles.

6. Anybody can succeed. They just have to try hard enough to get what they want.

7. I need someone who will not turn their back on me.

8. I feel my mother does a good job of keeping the house together. Even though she's a single parent, she makes sure everyone is taken care of and their needs are met.

EXERCISE 19.10 continued

9. Each person is smart in their own way.

10. I hope everyone has someone in their lives that they can truly respect as much as I do my neighbor.

EXERCISE 19.11

Build on what you practiced in Exercise 19.10. Circle the antecedents and underline the pronouns. Use the space provided to rewrite the sentences, so that pronouns and antecedents agree. Use one of the three approaches to revise the sentences.

1. I hate a sonic sound system because they are so loud.

2. Women want to be men, men want to be women, and nobody is happy just being what they are!

3. When an employee doesn't care about their job, it hurts everyone else.

4. If the student feels that they need to talk to the professor, he or she can meet him or her at their office or send a message online.

5. In the final analysis, the student needs to do what works best for them.

6. Each person chooses their own path.

7. Many times smoking can be attributed to low self-esteem. The individual feels they must conform to be accepted into a group.

8. Dry skin, wrinkles, and a leathery appearance—why would anyone do that to themself?

9. This study proves that a child learns math best when it affects them personally or when it is taught in a real-life setting.

10. When a person goes to Las Vegas, they expect to be entertained.

Copyright © 2007, The McGraw-Hill Companies, Inc. All rights reserved.

EXERCISE 19.12

Build on what you practiced in Exercises 19.10 and 19.11. Circle the antecedents and underline the pronouns. Use the space provided to rewrite the sentences so that pronouns and antecedents agree. Use one of the three approaches to revise the sentences.

1. Balding men enjoy a hearty jog before going to work and sitting in a cubicle all day. If they can't have hair, they can at least have a strong, fit-looking body to attract women who normally wouldn't give him a second glance.

2. If this person is unable to meet their own difficult requirements, they become discouraged and gradually forget about their plan.

3. If someone is going to get their tongue pierced, he or she needs to research what they are getting into.

4. An associate is someone you rarely talk to. You probably haven't known them for long. You may only know them from school or work. They would blow you off in your time of need, saying, "Call someone else. I'm busy."

5. If a family member like your mother or father passed away, your best friend would be there. Even if she or he had plans with their boyfriend or girlfriend, they would drop those plans to help you.

6. Motorcycles don't have the same traction as a car, due to the fact that it only has two wheels.

7. My best friend and I are a lot alike. Neither likes to draw attention to ourselves or stand out in a crowd.

EXERCISE 19.12 continued

8. If a person is constantly sneezing and looks deprived of their rest, that is a sign they are getting sick. Another symptom is a runny nose. If that person continues to blow their nose and starts to cough, it is very likely they are coming down with a cold.

9. Nursing is a profession in which a person must be committed to their job.

10. Music is the universal language that everyone, regardless of their background, can understand.

PRONOUN CASE

Subjective and Objective Pronouns

Speakers commonly confuse the subjective and objective pronouns. For this reason, it is also a common mistake for writers to make.

Subjective Pronouns	Objective Pronouns
I	me
you	you
it	it
he	him
she	her
we	us
they	them

The subjective pronouns are used as the subject of a sentence.

<u>We</u> foreign language students **are** a competitive bunch.
<u>She</u> **called** home on her new cell phone and **said** hello to her sister.
After waking up late, <u>he</u> **skipped** breakfast and **went** directly to work.

Objective pronouns are used as the objects of verbs and prepositions.

The principal **called** <u>us</u> down to the office.
My father **gave** <u>me</u> some good advice.
Robert went **with** <u>me</u> to Florida last Spring.

Because pronoun errors are so common in spoken English, they are difficult to detect in written English. With practice and analysis, however, you can begin to hear the difference between correct and incorrect usage.

Copyright © 2007, The McGraw-Hill Companies, Inc. All rights reserved.

EXERCISE 19.13

Circle the pronouns in the following sentences and indicate whether they are subjective (*S*) or objective (*O*) pronouns. Underline the verbs and/or prepositions they belong to. Some sentences will have both subjective and objective pronouns.

1. This kid I met on vacation is the same age as I am.
2. When my parents got home, they found me sitting in the kitchen reading the newspaper.
3. After a while, he opened up a business. It was rough in the beginning, but now the business is doing extremely well.
4. Every day after school, I used to play baseball with my friends.
5. Everyone except me went to Daytona on Spring break.
6. For the past three years I have made it to the finals, but I haven't been able to win.
7. He attended the same school I did.
8. He was younger than she was, but he was also the boss.
9. Her brothers all have their own car, whereas she still takes the bus.
10. I followed her to a room, where she did the paperwork and called the cops. She left as I waited for what seemed a half an hour. Then she came back with the security guard, who began to interrogate me.

EXERCISE 19.14

Build on what you practiced in Exercise 19.13. Circle the pronouns in the following sentences and indicate whether they are subjective (*S*) or objective (*O*) pronouns. Underline the verbs and/or prepositions they belong to. Some sentences will have both subjective and objective pronouns.

1. I found out that my classmate John is majoring in the same thing I am.
2. I remember one particular day during school. I believe I was ten years old. I skipped school with my friend. He and I took his little sister home.
3. The principal talked to my friend and me. He definitely approved of what we were doing.
4. If it were up to me, I would make everyone play basketball every day.
5. Online classes have given women like me the ability to return to school to finish our degrees, without disturbing our work and family life.
6. It made me look bad.
7. It was a beautiful summer day, yet I found myself sitting on our rusty swing set with nothing to do, just wishing something exciting would happen to me.
8. I think it would be great to know I started a trend.
9. I loved to play, watch, or just talk about football. The worst part of it was, I didn't even have a football.
10. Jason picked me up in his new car.

Compound and Comparative Forms

Subjective and objective pronoun errors occur most frequently in sentences with compound and comparative forms. **Compound forms** put two pronouns together with the conjunction *and*.

Copyright © 2007, The McGraw-Hill Companies, Inc. All rights reserved.

Incorrect: **Me** <u>and</u> **Bill** got scholarships
Incorrect: The boss gave **Bill** <u>and</u> **I** a bonus.

As noted, the preceding sentences contain pronoun errors. The best way to detect incorrect pronoun usage is to make two separate sentences of the compound form.

Me got a scholarship. Bill got a scholarship.
I got a scholarship. Bill got a scholarship.
Correct: Bill and I got a scholarship.

The boss gave Bill a bonus. The boss gave I a bonus.
The boss gave Bill a bonus. The boss gave me a bonus.
Correct: The boss gave Bill and me a bonus.

Comparative forms use *as* and *than*.

Incorrect: **She** grew so much faster <u>than</u> me.
Incorrect: **He** played tennis too, only not <u>as</u> well <u>as</u> me.

To detect pronoun errors in comparative forms, complete the sentences with the implied verb:

She grew so much faster than me (*grew*).
Correct: She grew so much faster than I (*grew*).

He played tennis too, only not as well as me (*played*).
Correct: He played tennis too, only not as well as I (*played*).

EXERCISE 19.15

Read the following sentences and underline the subjective and objective pronouns. Correct errors by substituting the correct pronoun. Some sentences may be correct as written.

1. Most of the people I met on vacation were older than me.
2. When they got home, they found Rachel and I in the kitchen reading the newspaper.
3. After a while, my sister and him opened up a business. It was rough in the beginning, but now the business is doing extremely well.
4. Every day after school, me, Dan, and Ron used to play baseball with some friends.
5. Everyone except Rhonda and me is going for an orientation meeting at the college.
6. For the past three years, Cheryl and me have made it to the dance contest finals, but we haven't been able to win.
7. He attended the same school as me.
8. She was as young as him, but she was also his boss.
9. Her brothers all have their own car, whereas her and her sisters still take the bus.
10. I followed her to a room, where she did the paperwork and called the cops. She left as I waited for what seemed a half an hour. Then she and the security guard came back to get me and all the paperwork.

EXERCISE 19.16

Build on what you practiced in Exercise 19.15. Underline the subjective and objective pronouns. Correct errors by substituting the correct pronoun. Some sentences may be correct as written.

1. I found out that my classmate John is majoring in the same thing as I.

2. I remember one particular day during school. I believe I was ten years old. Me and my friend Terry skipped school to take his little sister home.

3. I thought a lot about what him and his friends were doing.

4. If it were up to the coach and I, we would make everyone play basketball every day.

5. The chemistry classes we took gave Cheryl and I a run for our money. I did a little better than her, but we both still passed.

6. When my brother got in all that trouble, it made my family and me look bad.

7. It was a beautiful summer day, yet me and my brother found ourselves sitting on our rusty swing set with nothing to do.

8. It would be great to know it was I who started this trend.

9. Jake and I loved to play, watch, or just talk about football. The worst part of it was that me and Jake didn't have a football.

10. Jason picked up my brother and I in his new car.

EXERCISE 19.17

Build on what you practiced in Exercises 19.15 and 19.16. Underline the subjective and objective pronouns. Correct errors by substituting the correct pronoun. Some sentences may be correct as written.

1. My parents taught my siblings and me manners.
2. My sister told my parents that her and her friends were going out to eat, when really they were going to a club.
3. One day at work, I spoke with a customer. Her and I had the same name. Her voice gave me the impression she was an older woman.
4. I enjoy the time we spend together, just her and I.
5. On senior pride day at my high school, the students were very happy. They had to dress up and look nice. That night, my brother and me picked up our friends with the car, and we all went dancing and singing.
6. Sarah would never talk to anybody, while me and my best friend Nicki were always the center of the parties.

EXERCISE 19.17 continued

7. The principal called my parents. He told them that he had caught everything me and my friend did on tape.

8. So me, my sister, and the rest of my family went out to eat in Chinatown.

9. When I look at the dartboard that hangs in our computer room, it reminds me of all the late nights me and James would stay up competing together for the highest scores.

10. Some relationships are different. Me and my grandmother were always close.

EXERCISE 19.18

Build on what you practiced in Exercises 19.15, 19.16, and 19.17. Underline the subjective and objective pronouns. Correct errors by substituting the correct pronoun. Some sentences may be correct as written.

1. The cop shined his light on us. Callie and Steve ran, leaving Derrick and I to be the ones to get in trouble.

2. The last time I saw my teacher, she invited my cousin and me to Pizza Hut. We had lunch. I went to Lebanon for a visit after that. While I was gone, she moved away.

3. The next day me and my friend would go to another store. We would do the same thing all over again.

4. There are quite a few areas where me and my parents don't agree.

5. There stood a girl a year younger than me with shoulder length hair and freckles.

6. There is only one difference between Nadia and I.

7. Throughout school, she was always the tiniest bit better than me.

8. Two days later, me and my parents were eating lunch.

9. We wanted to go to the great slide for the afternoon. My mother couldn't take my brother and I, so my aunt took us.

10. When I asked my parents how I received the name, mom told me that her and dad could not agree on anything, so finally she said "Melanie or Michelle."

PRONOUN CONSISTENCY

Depending on your subject matter, one pronoun will be more appropriate than another. If you write about yourself, you will probably use the first person *I/me/my*. If you write about a social issue or problem, you may choose *it* to refer to the problem—racism, for example—and *they* to refer to people affected by the problem. It's difficult to avoid some shifting from one pronoun to another, but be aware of these shifts and try to avoid inconsistency.

Copyright © 2007, The McGraw-Hill Companies, Inc. All rights reserved.

Inconsistent: I had a great experience in high school band class. **I** learned to play an instrument and went to competitions with the band. **I** had a great time at these competitions. The director was great. He always pushed **you** to do **your** best.

"I" is first person. The shift to second person—"you" and "your"— is conversational but inconsistent. For formal writing, try to minimize the use of "you" altogether.

Consistent: I had a great experience in high school band class. I learned to play an instrument and went to competitions with the band. I had a great time at these competitions. The director was great. He always pushed **me** and my fellow band players to do **our** best.

The use of "me" and "our" is more consistent than "you" and "your." Here's another example:

Inconsistent: Our class took part in a "city beautiful" program. **We** were assigned to groups and took responsibility for keeping a section of the city clean. This is a good program. It taught **you** to take pride in where **you** live. Once **you** finished, **you** sort of wanted to show off **your** city.

The shift from "we" to "you" is inconsistent pronoun use.

Consistent: Our class took part in a "city beautiful" program. We were assigned to groups and took responsibility for keeping a section of the city clean. This is a good program. It taught **us** to take pride in where **we** live. Once **we** finished, **we** sort of wanted to show off **our** city.

EXERCISE 19.19

Read the following sentences and underline the pronouns. Revise the sentences to make the pronoun use consistent.

1. We have a tendency to pick up something quick on our way home for dinner, instead of going home and taking time to cook dinner. The most important reason to stay home is it is much more healthy for you and your family.

2. A person doesn't always have to be happy all the time. There are many different emotions we go through. You simply have to expect that.

3. The number one important thing an employer looks for is trust. You don't want an employee to cheat you when the employer turns his or her back.

Copyright © 2007, The McGraw-Hill Companies, Inc. All rights reserved.

EXERCISE 19.19 continued

4. I took the test and waited nervously for the results. The level of your score will give you the opportunity to go further.

5. Collecting rocks was easier than collecting seashells because you could find them everywhere. I made use of the rocks I found. I painted them, decorated them, or decorated with them. But mostly I collected them and kept them in my room.

6. I also learned that by helping people in need you can really make a difference.

7. With a cat, you set out her food and she's happy. I don't have to walk them every day or let them outside to use the bathroom.

8. Having a cold is dreadful to me because you feel horrible and just wish it would go away.

9. The cellular phone has had a big impact on my life. You can reach anyone, anywhere, at any time.

10. I tried to drive and use my cell phone a couple of times. I was so distracted it was horrifying. I became unaware of my surroundings to such a great degree. It was like driving in a dream, and nothing around you was real.

EXERCISE 19.20

Build on what you practiced in Exercise 19.19. Underline the pronouns. Revise the sentences to make the pronoun use consistent.

EXERCISE 19.20 continued

1. A person has no role in deciding what his name will be. You just take it for granted and get used to it.

2. What is the big deal about curling? It's a sport where a person slides a rock down the ice toward a target. As it is going toward the target, two people from the team sweep the ice in front of it to make it go farther. The goal is to get it as close to the target as you can and also try to knock your opponents away from the target.

3. Kids coming into high school are pressured by their friends and sometimes family to do things they don't want to. Drinking is a big thing to do when you get into high school.

4. Most teenagers drink to get drunk, not knowing their own limit. When you vomit, you know you have had too much, and sometimes kids won't stop until they get to that point.

5. I hate going to bed hearing the noise in my head over and over again while you're trying to sleep.

6. I hate TV because of my father. Whenever you saw him he had the remote in his hand. He was like a zombie. He hardly ever set it down. If he did, you never picked it up. Otherwise, there would be a fight.

7. A person uses math on an everyday basis. When people cook, they use math to measure ingredients; when they shop, they use it to figure a certain percent off

EXERCISE 19.20 continued

the ticket price. A person doesn't realize how much math you use on any given day.

8. My father plays golf a lot, and he really enjoys it. He says that sometimes he gets frustrated, but you just have to relax and slow yourself down.

9. What people do for a job might become a career. Choose something that one will enjoy and can take great pride in. If one doesn't enjoy what he or she does, then their lives are just wasted, and what pride is there in that?

10. What is the big deal about turning twenty-one? How many times can a person go to a bar? You are fully an adult. I have to pay my own bills. You can't believe how high car insurance is when you have to put it under your own name. I don't mind living on my own, but that means having to make my own food and clean my own house.

Copyright © 2007, The McGraw-Hill Companies, Inc. All rights reserved.

20 *Punctuation*

Use the following grid to help you keep track of punctuation errors in your writing. When your instructor makes marginal note of these errors in your papers, keep a tally on this grid. For example, in your first writing assignment, your instructor might point out five comma errors and one semicolon error. You would then enter those numbers in the appropriate spaces below. As you proceed from one writing assignment to the next, use the grid to monitor your progress. Complete the exercises in this chapter to help you identify and understand common punctuation errors. Then become a focused proofreader: search out and correct these errors when you edit final drafts of your work.

Error	Writing Assignment									
	1	2	3	4	5	6	7	8	9	10
Comma										
Semicolon and Colon										
Quotations										
Apostrophe										

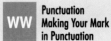

Punctuation
Making Your Mark
in Punctuation

IN THIS CHAPTER: A PREVIEW

Comma

- Commas and Conjunctions
- Commas and Introductory Modifiers
- Commas with Interrupters/Parenthetical Modifiers
- Commas in a Series

Semicolon and Colon

- Semicolon
- Colon

Quotation Marks
- Complete Sentences
- Partial Quotes
- Indirect Quotes

Apostrophe
- Contractions
- Possessive Form

WW Commas

COMMA

Most student writers use too many commas. They think, "I'm pausing in this sentence, so I must need a comma." While it is true that the comma signals a pause, correct usage relies on understanding the role of the comma: it joins related parts of a sentence to one another.

Commas and Conjunctions

One of the most common punctuation errors is placing a comma before a conjunction when it is not needed. The conjunctions *and, but,* and *or* often link pairs of terms that do not require commas.

> **No comma required:** My mother, and my sisters explained to me that lying will get me nowhere in life.

> **No comma required:** My father loves to chat, and laugh with his children.

Note, however, that a comma *is* required before a conjunction that joins two complete sentences (or independent clauses):

> **Comma required:** I agree that discipline is needed, but I don't think corporal punishment is the answer.

> **Comma required:** I wasn't making very much money, and my social life was beginning to suffer.

Whenever you want to use a comma with a conjunction, ask yourself, Could I put a period here instead? Is what comes after the conjunction a complete sentence? If the answer is yes, the comma is probably needed.

EXERCISE 20.1

Circle all conjunctions in the following sentences and add commas as needed.

1. I got into trouble often and for the dumbest reasons and a lot of the time it was at the dinner table.

2. I tried not to make trouble but I was human.

3. It was morning and I was alone with some matches and my curiosity.

4. At first, it was a small fire but it increased quickly because it was summer and very dry.

Copyright © 2007, The McGraw-Hill Companies, Inc. All rights reserved.

5. I tried to put out the fire with some water but it was futile and the flames rose higher and higher.

6. He often uses the lecture method of punishment but sometimes he uses other ways, depending on the offense and the child.

7. I shouted at my little sister so he hit me. It didn't hurt but it was the first time he hit me and I was shocked.

8. My mom was screaming and crying and dad was red with anger.

9. The pain was intense but having to see the look on my mother's face and in her eyes was more devastating.

10. I wasn't a particularly evil or disobedient child but I had my moments like all kids do.

EXERCISE 20.2

Build on what you practiced in Exercise 20.1. Circle all conjunctions in the following sentences and add commas as needed.

1. The drill was always the same each time my sister or I were punished. We were asked what we did wrong. My parents knew the answer but wanted us to admit our transgressions openly.

2. Dad counted out the spanks and between each spank he talked to us about what we did wrong and asked if we had learned our lessons. We always said yes.

3. Drinking was permitted only if we were with our parents and only on special occasions and even then only sips were allowed.

4. Dad asked me if I had been drinking and I said yes but I admitted to drinking only one glass.

5. The next morning I was ready for the same old punishment routine but it never came.

6. In the essay "Making a Case for Corporal Punishment," Walter Williams talks about giving spankings to disobedient and disrespectful children and he argues that such forms of punishment ultimately deter bad behavior.

7. When children are younger, they do not have the mental capacity to know right from wrong and they don't realize that each of their actions will have consequences. Spanking is a good way to get through to them and help them learn not only about right and wrong but also about consequences.

8. Teenagers have a better understanding of right and wrong but they need to realize that their actions have consequences, like losing a drivers license or not being allowed to go to the "most important concert of the year."

EXERCISE 20.2 continued

9. At the age of six I picked up a basketball and started applying myself.

10. She went through a divorce and after that she decided to have her tongue pierced and get a few tattoos. It made her feel unique. It was a statement to her. She was aware of the risks involved and decided to do it anyway.

Commas and Introductory Modifiers

WW Modifiers

Sentences that begin with introductory words, phrases, and clauses take a comma. There is a natural pause in such sentences. The pause occurs where intonation falls.

As I sat alone at the picnic table, Joanna and her boyfriend began to dance.

| introductory word, phrase, or clause | comma comes where intonation falls | main part of the sentence |

Watch for the following words as signals of introductory modifiers:

Subordinators		Conjunctive Adverbs
after	since	consequently
although	when	furthermore
as	whenever	indeed
because	whereas	in fact
if	while	moreover
not only		nevertheless

EXERCISE 20.3

Look for introductory words, phrases, and clauses in the following sentences. Read the sentences out loud. Listen for the natural pause, where your intonation falls. Add commas as needed.

1. When I have worries on my mind my grandmother is always there to let me know that everything will be just fine.
2. Money also causes great debate between both groups. Indeed it is a primary cause of conflict.
3. Once I got in high school I had chores to do in my house.
4. She was the nicest girl in the whole world, and she loved me a lot. But although we were best friends we were very different, and we would fight a lot. She was such a perfectionist.
5. When I was in the sixth grade a French teacher told me my name was French, and when I was in seventh grade a Spanish teacher told me my name was Spanish.
6. When I was in elementary school some of my friends and I used our "soap opera" names. A soap opera name was your middle name and the name of the street you lived on. My name was Dawn Michigan.
7. After a short time the officer let us go, and when we went into the house Derrick's dad started to yell at us.
8. In five minutes or so my dad would come out just as mad as my mom, and she would say, "I already spanked him."

Copyright © 2007, The McGraw-Hill Companies, Inc. All rights reserved.

EXERCISE 20.3 continued

9. If you were not good you knew what would happen to you, and the punishment would not be a time-out.

10. In most cases an adult tone of voice gave the impression of authority, and you knew they were in charge.

EXERCISE 20.4

Build on what you practiced in Exercise 20.3. Look for introductory words, phrases, and clauses in the following sentences. Read the sentences out loud. Listen for the natural pause, where your intonation falls. Add commas as needed.

1. I remember a friend who received a spanking for stealing a candy bar from the store. When that happened to her she said she would never steal again.

2. As she was looking around she noticed that the bedroom windows were open.

3. When my father is deeply angered he sits me down and thinks about what he can take away to teach me a lesson.

4. Although sometimes I wished I had received another form of punishment I am proud of the way my parents raised me.

5. When he saw I still wasn't in bed my dad called the theater and asked when the movie had ended.

6. When we both got home just seeing the look on our mothers' faces was enough to tell us we were in deep trouble.

7. For individuals who feel the desire to perform their daily activities in the street there are two significant things to be aware of: motor vehicles and human nature.

8. If people want to unwind or relieve stress they should go for a jog.

9. Every time there was a math test we made sure we were sitting next to someone who was smart.

10. A few people at work are really good at math and other subjects. If you throw any number problem at them they respond pretty quickly.

Commas with Interrupters/Parenthetical Modifiers

Use a pair of commas to insert a parenthetical word, phrase, or clause into the middle of a sentence. Parenthetical modifiers, as they're sometimes called, interrupt the natural flow of the sentence. The commas act like parentheses, and thus are used in pairs.

> The teacher would say our first and last names when he called on one of us. His name was Mr. Cowell

> The teacher, **Mr. Cowell,** would say our first and last names when he called on one of us.

Eric was the first name my parents chose for me. It means a powerful leader or king.

Eric, **which means a powerful leader or king,** was the first name my parents chose for me.

My sister is always picky about where she eats. She is picky for a variety of reasons.

My sister, **for a variety of reasons,** is always picky about where she eats.

When these modifiers come at the end of a sentence, the parentheses are formed by a comma and a period:

I was in the eighth grade. That made me fourteen years old.

I was in the eighth grade, **which made me fourteen years old.**

It was starting to get late in the evening. It might have been around midnight.

It was starting to get late in the evening, **maybe around midnight.**

EXERCISE 20.5

Read the following sentences and identify the parenthetical modifiers. Those coming in the middle of a sentence will need two commas; those coming at the end will need one comma. Punctuate accordingly.

1. My friend with his chiseled good looks and quick wit couldn't master the task of inserting an IV in a patient in the back of a speeding ambulance.

2. Japan host of the environmental conference proposes to reduce global warming despite the country's weakened domestic economy.

3. Failure to take action to reverse this cycle however would mean a world in peril.

4. My friend always went to the mall with her friends. Every time she went, her mother gave her a time to be back which was 10:00 p.m.

5. I choose to be honest even if the truth hurts someone.

6. A couple weeks later after days and nights of terrible arguments he filed for divorce.

7. In the summer of 1996 the year my father passed away my brothers and I all received social security checks.

8. The rule is that you receive the checks until you're nineteen or graduate from high school whichever comes first.

Copyright © 2007, The McGraw-Hill Companies, Inc. All rights reserved.

9. We had a long talk which consisted mostly of her telling me what she'd been up to for the last ten years. Through the whole conversation, I kept pondering what her name might be.

10. The only downside to memory enhancement for humans is that they will remember everything such as an annoying song on the radio.

EXERCISE 20.6

Build on what you practiced in Exercise 20.5. Read the following sentences and identify the parenthetical modifiers. Those coming in the middle of the sentence will need two commas; those coming at the end will need one comma. Punctuate accordingly.

1. Having a good memory is not everything. As long as you can remember the important things like birthdays and anniversaries you will be just fine.

2. Many young people today without realizing that everything they do has very real consequences end up with major financial responsibilities on their hands.

3. I stood in my closet for about two hours looking through all my clothes trying to decide what outfit to wear.

4. Ten years before, my sister who is eight years my senior experienced her first real abuse.

5. I have gotten a lead part in two plays which I never thought I'd get to do. I even have a shot at going professional which is my dream.

6. Auto mechanics also have a few health risks such as inhaling brake dust and carburetor cleaner fumes.

7. Music is the universal language that everyone regardless of his or her background can understand.

8. Computer Information Systems the most interesting class I'm in right now is also the first online class I have taken.

9. We expect people especially adults to be kind to us and to give us what is ours without struggle.

10. I had always wanted to go to Florida as most kids do.

Commas in a Series

Use commas in a list of three or more items. Lists can consist of nouns, verbs, adjectives, phrases, or clauses.

At the shop, I pushed the cart while he picked up the items we needed, such as **wet and dry towels, wheel cleaner, car wash detergent, car wax, buffer, and tire gloss.**

Once you lose control of a child, he will end up doing **what he wants, what his friends want, but definitely not what you want him to do.**

Todd was a cool name. It sounded **tough, mean, and just plain cool.**

When I came back outside, the ball wasn't on the porch. It had **rolled off the porch, hit the hood of my dad's car, and put a huge dent in it.**

In college writing, readers expect you to use a comma before the conjunction and the last item in a series:

I read the newspaper, a few magazines, **and** an occasional novel.

Identify and punctuate items in a series in the following sentences. Add commas as necessary to set off introductory and parenthetical modifiers and before conjunctions introducing independent clauses.

1. After I finish school I go home do my homework and then go out to have fun.

2. Responsibility is important. When you want to go away to college get a job or move away from home mom and dad won't have second thoughts.

3. The other night my friend came over to my house drunk got sick and then passed out.

4. When it comes to art history I can remember the artist's daily routine his or her relatives and in most cases what drugs he or she took but I forget his or her most famous piece of art.

5. Jake and I loved to play watch and just talk about football. Unfortunately not all the other kids we played football with shared our enthusiasm. If it had been up to me and Jake we would have made everyone play every day.

6. Our bad guy would be thrown in our makeshift jail and moments later he or she would break out repeating the same cycle of running hopping fences and getting into trouble.

7. Where I work sometimes a car is parted out which means the parts are sold the proceeds go to charity and someone's life is made a little easier.

Copyright © 2007, The McGraw-Hill Companies, Inc. All rights reserved.

8. The principal wanted to send me home because of my tank top short skirt and slingback sandals. Honestly I was very angry and didn't agree with his decision. As a matter of fact I had a big argument with him.

9. I still like to open the door for a woman pay for dinner and even tell her she looks nice. When I do this I hope she doesn't consider it sexual harassment.

10. After an hour of lecturing my kids about the television their future and the importance of education I am back again in my wonderful kitchen.

EXERCISE 20.8

Build on what you practiced in Exercise 20.7. Identify and punctuate items in a series in the following sentences. Add commas as necessary to set off introductory and parenthetical modifiers and before conjunctions introducing independent clauses.

1. My friends live for clubs. They go to clubs every weekend stay up all night and sleep all day.

2. There's no need to run around with your feathers all up your chest sticking out and a nasty look on your face. Nobody is impressed and probably most people think you're out of your mind.

3. You don't need to dress like a man cut your hair like a man and act like a jerk to let people know you're equal to a man.

4. People do goofy things when they use drugs. These usually include saying inappropriate things getting crazy and committing crimes.

5. Every day computers become more outdated complex and confusing. System conflicts and programming errors hinder the access to the Internet causing delays and downtime.

6. I was waiting for my nephew to come around the corner with his hair sticking up from his nap. I thought we'd get into his secret cupboard and have a snack.

EXERCISE 20.8 continued

He never came. I walked over to the cupboard opened it and had some crackers and that's how I said good-bye.

7. One task I despise is cleaning up the basement. It takes up too much time and I don't like getting dust in my hair. My kids have a different point of view. They enjoy cleaning the basement because they get to run around like maniacs listen to music and drive me crazy at the same time. Besides all that I wonder if they enjoy the cobwebs dust and bugs.

8. She's a young intelligent beautiful classy lady and at the same time she's also bright and sexy.

9. We had a black BMW 740ii Series with black-tinted windows large 18-inch chrome wheels and a bad-boy aura. We nicknamed it the Baron.

10. My nephew is eight years old. His poor bicycle which sits in the garage is covered with dust. You can hardly tell what color it is. Jim would rather spend hours on the couch watching TV eating chips and playing his video games especially that NBA basketball game.

WW Semicolons Colons

SEMICOLON AND COLON

The semicolon and colon are strong marks of punctuation, almost a strong as the period. Used correctly, they express the relationship of ideas within sentences.

Semicolon

Use a semicolon between two complete sentences that express contrasting ideas.

> These nicknames didn't say anything meaningful about my personality; they just made fun of my name.
>
> Charity isn't doing something you have to do; it's doing something that you want to do.

Use a semicolon with a conjunctive adverb to link two related sentences.

> Big cars have a lot of room; consequently, people who carry around a lot stuff are likely to buy them.
>
> My grandfather is in a nursing home; however, he is in control of all his faculties.

Copyright © 2007, The McGraw-Hill Companies, Inc. All rights reserved.

Use a semicolon for items in a series that need internal punctuation.

> When I was a kid I mowed lawns, a job I kind of liked; weeded the flower beds, which I liked less than mowing; and washed windows, a job I totally hated.

Colon

Use a colon to connect a list to a complete sentence. The list can come either before or after the complete sentence.

> So that was our idea of fun: running, hopping fences, and screaming like maniacs.
>
> Building hot rods, fixing a leaking water pump, or fixing a flat tire: it's all fun to me.

Use a colon between two complete sentences when the second sentence explains the first or when one is general and the other is specific.

> My mother was sad: she was mourning the loss of her mother.

EXERCISE 20.9

Insert semicolons and colons in the following sentences as needed. In the space provided, briefly explain your reason for using the mark of punctuation you choose.

EXAMPLE

> The food there was amazing, duck, steak, roast, they had everything, and it was delicious.
>
> *The food there was amazing. Duck, steak, roast: they had everything, and it was delicious.*
>
> *Use a colon to connect a list to a complete sentence.*

1. The police academy allowed us to handle two types of guns. Machine guns and hand pistols.

2. Although we had the same name, we were different in every other way. She was the oldest child in her family. I was the middle. She was chubby. I was thin. She had two brothers. I had three.

3. First I had doubts about police work. Then the recruiter started telling me about the benefits. Pay for college tuition, self-discipline, or even better a motorcycle.

EXERCISE 20.9 continued

4. For kids who play in the street, there are two significant things to be aware of. Motor vehicles and human nature.

5. He has to walk his dog every day or let it outside to use the bathroom. I simply set out food for my cat and keep her litter box clean.

6. I hoped I would never see this customer again. I didn't get mad because she didn't tip me. I was mad at the fact that she was so rude.

7. I learned a lot from this experience. Don't be greedy and take what you're given.

8. I learned that whipping a child does not indicate parental failure. It is a necessary measure that teaches kids right from wrong. Parents should use corporal punishment.

9. I say teach real math first. Allow kids to use a calculator once they have the basics in place.

10. I will name my son one of three names. It could be Richard because that is the name of my deceased father. It could be Mick for a friend of mine. Then again, it could be Nicholas for Nicholas Cage, my favorite actor.

EXERCISE 20.10

Build on what you practiced in Exercise 20.9. Insert semicolons and colons in the following sentences as needed. In the space provided, briefly explain your reason for using the mark of punctuation you choose.

Copyright © 2007, The McGraw-Hill Companies, Inc. All rights reserved.

1. Most of my family just calls me Alex for short. My grandfather on my mother's side likes to call me Big Al.

2. My boyfriend and I have a fundamental disagreement. He's a dog person. I'm a cat person.

3. My father and I disagree on the subject of small cars. He thinks they're inexpensive to operate. I think they're noisy and uncomfortable.

4. One of the cars was a piece of junk. The other cost more than it was worth.

5. One ticket was for noise pollution. The other was for underage possession of tobacco.

6. Our cat is also an indoor cat. She never wants to go outside. I'm happy about that.

7. The officer did the usual. He asked for my licence and registration and then asked me how old I was.

8. The one officer came back with my tickets. Only he didn't bring one. He brought two.

EXERCISE 20.10 continued

9. There was a student in my bio class named Michelle. I am quiet and polite. This girl was annoying to everyone around her.

10. This semester I signed up for a logic class. The more I get involved in the class, the more I begin to like it. It really makes me think.

WW Quotation Marks

QUOTATION MARKS

A quotation is language you borrow from someone else. Place quotation marks around exact words that are clearly not your own. These words might be speech you write in the form of dialogue, or they might be a phrase, sentence, or multi-sentence passage you borrow from the newspaper, a magazine, or a book. When you write quotations, observe punctuation conventions both before and after the quote.

Complete Sentences

A complete-sentence quote is preceded by a comma and begins with a capital letter. It ends with a period, question mark, or exclamation mark, which goes inside the closing quotation mark.

My father looked up from his work. He said, "Hand me that end wrench."

Every so often, the thoughtful citizen should look up from her personal pursuits and ask, "Where is this country going?"

Partial Quotes

A quote less than a complete sentence, such as a word or phrase, is not preceded by a comma and does not begin with a capital letter (unless the word is a proper noun). Periods always go inside quotation marks.

My name means "dark-skinned" in Arabic.

It says right on the side of the cigarette pack that smoking can cause "fetal injury, premature birth, and low birth weight."

EXERCISE 20.11

Correct the punctuation and capitalization as necessary in the following quotations.

1. I learned very little in the sixth grade. Consequently, I was held back. Teachers said I had a very difficult time "Concentrating and absorbing the information" that was needed in order to pass that grade.

Copyright © 2007, The McGraw-Hill Companies, Inc. All rights reserved.

EXERCISE 20.11 continued

2. I ran home screaming "It's alive"!

3. One thing I recall from my younger days is when we played "spy".

4. I was afraid for my sister that night. I told my mom "Please don't let her go, because the weather is really bad out there".

5. The next day I woke up to the phone ringing, and I heard my aunt talking to somebody. I heard her say Oh my God, what happened? And right there and then I started crying because I knew something had happened to my sister.

6. When we finally got to the hospital, we had to wait in the emergency entrance. I was sitting with my head down when my uncle said there's your dad.

7. Come on, man. Try it. It won't hurt. It makes you feel good. These are just some of the temptations teens have to deal with these days. Words such as these can affect a teen's life greatly.

8. Every time I introduce myself to someone and I tell them my name is Val, they always respond by saying "what, short for Valerie?" Sometimes they say "let me guess. You were born on Valentine's Day!"

9. The doctor looked up at the mother and said she was going to have "A little princess"

10. Steve said "here" and handed me the keys to the Chevelle.

Indirect Quotes

Indirect quotes paraphrase what someone said. They do not require quotation marks. Indirect and direct quotes differ in their use of pronouns and verb tense:

Direct: My father looked up from his work and **said, "Hand me** an end wrench."

Indirect: My father looked up from his work and **told me to hand him** an end wrench.

Direct: A friend saw me walking back to the locker room, so he pulled up and **asked, "Do you want** a ride home?"

Indirect: A friend saw me walking back to the locker room, so he pulled up and **asked me if I wanted** a ride home.

EXERCISE 20.12

Rewrite the following quotations as indirect quotes.

1. When I asked the teacher if I could make up the assignment, she said, "I don't think so."

2. My son is always telling me, "I hope my comic book collection is worth something some day."

3. When I stepped in the house, my mother asked me, "What's wrong?"

4. I asked my uncle, "Do you know anything about constellations, and if you do, can you help me?"

5. Our neighbor's son grew up saying, "I will never do drugs."

6. I stopped and got out of my car and asked him, "What is going on?"

7. Being in a hurry I thought to myself, "I won't forget."

8. I asked her if she gets bored reading all these books. She said, "No, I love reading them."

9. With this suspicious look on their faces, they politely asked us, "Where did you get the money?"

10. When he asked about the spelling of my name, I said, "My parents couldn't spell."

APOSTROPHE

Contractions

An apostrophe can be used to replace a missing letter in contractions:

cannot	can't
have not	haven't
it is	it's

Note: The words *its* is the possessive form of the pronoun *it*. Writers often accidentally interchange *it's* (it is) and *its* (belonging to it). Be on the lookout for this common mistake when proofreading your work.

Another frequent error is the addition of apostrophes in simple plurals, as illustrated in the following example:

I didn't like dog's when I was a kid.

"Dogs" is a simple plural. The apostrophe is not needed. Be aware of this common pitfall when proofreading your writing.

Copyright © 2007, The McGraw-Hill Companies, Inc. All rights reserved.

EXERCISE 20.13

Edit the following sentences. Delete unnecessary apostrophes and add apostrophes where they are missing from contractions. In the space provided, rewrite contractions in their full form (it's/it is, don't/do not).

1. Television has made many advances since it's debut.
2. The news let's you know whats happening around your city, state, and country right away.
3. There were five of us: one sister, three brother's, and myself.
4. Its Christmas, always a good time for us to catch up on the latest news in the family.
5. As I look back on it now, I really dont think the dog was going to hurt me. It didnt bite my dad or even really bark.
6. It makes sense to society that mother's carry a child for nine months, care for it when it is born, listen and meet it's needs, feed it when it is hungry, and reassure it that it is going to be safe and happy all it's life.
7. Lets say things have improved somewhat. We are in the 21st century, and women are playing role's that were once dreamt about but have now become reality.
8. Every morning the cat will sit with me as Im having my coffee. At night, I know when its time for bed because thats when she comes out of her hiding spot.
9. I dont want to take the chance of having too many friend's that might hurt me one day. Its hard to trust anyone.
10. The age of electronic education is here, and like everything it has it's advantages and it's disadvantages.

Possessive Form

Use the apostrophe in possessive forms. In the case of singular nouns, including those ending in *s* and plural nouns not ending in *s*, add *'s* to indicate possession (*the store manager's attention, Chris's book, the children's toys*). In the case of plural nouns ending in *s*, simply add the apostrophe (*so many mammals' habitats*).

EXERCISE 20.14

Complete the following table below, filling in the possessive forms.

EXAMPLES

my brother	Ford Mustang	*my brother's Ford Mustang*
the class	assignment	*the class's assignment*
most women	career plans	*most women's career plans*
the delegates	conference	*the delegates' conference*
a kid	first role model	
kids	first role models	
the book	last chapter	
most books	last chapters	

EXERCISE 20.14 continued

the child	good fortune
children	good fortune
the airlines	responsibility
my job	biggest drawback
the boss	pet peeve
that man	bad attitude
most movies	earnings
the idea	power
modern music	audience
a woman	time to act
my neighbor	French poodle

EXERCISE 20.15

Read the following sentences to determine whether the correct possessive form is being used. Correct any errors you find. If you find no errors, write *correct* in the space provided.

1. Every kid's idea of fun is different.
2. My mother read every novel by Charles Dickens. She says the book's portraits of miserable children interested her.
3. I used to work in the childrens' department.
4. The airline's pilots refused to cross the picket lines that day.
5. My job's benefit package includes dental insurance.
6. His cousins' real trouble began when their stepfather lost his job.
7. I read in this mornings' paper about a mans' journey around the globe in a hot air balloon.
8. Some movies' content is too violent for little kids to see.
9. He was obsessed with time travel. The idea's appeal was both complete freedom and the chance to meet historical people.

EXERCISE 20.16

Correct apostrophe errors in the following sentences.

1. We went to this kids house after school. It was at his house that the wiffle ball game began.
2. Although many of todays songs have pro's and con's, I believe that music is the language of the heart and soul.
3. Physical education examines a persons strengths and weaknesses.
4. Some student's find that doing the lab work is too difficult or too boring.
5. The object of the game is to knock your opponents stone away from the bullseye.
6. Work was occupying so much of the parent's time that they barely saw their family.

Copyright © 2007, The McGraw-Hill Companies, Inc. All rights reserved.

7. I knew a boy who got bitten in the face by a dog. He was only four years old and over at a friends house.

8. The boy's mother rushed over. When she got there, the whole side of her sons face was torn off and bleeding steadily.

9. My dads name is James.

10. My names' origin is from the Islamic religion.

EXERCISE 20.17

Build on what you practiced in Exercise 20.16. Correct apostrophe errors in the following sentences.

1. With sophisticated computer model's, scientists can predict that through thermal expansions in the oceans, water levels will rise and the polar ice will melt.

2. We decided to order pizza, which meant we had to go in her parents room and mess with their money cup.

3. I recently learned the importance of a good nights rest.

4. It's funny how life's experience drives a persons attitude.

5. Unfortunately I find being at home a great distraction. Between my boyfriends fidgeting, his brother's loud music, and his mother's TV, I get no peace and quiet when I'm working on my papers'.

6. Every Halloween, before eating it, the kids take their pound's of candy to their parent's to be checked.

7. "Damn," I thought to myself. "My cars busted again. How will I fix it?"

8. Corporal punishment would only make todays' youth more angry. I believe that violence breed's violence.

9. I don't think word's can explain how I feel about my girlfriend.

10. The writer makes the point that childrens interest's are as important as academic learning.

PART FIVE

Reading and Thinking Critically: Texts and Visuals

21 *Developing Critical Reading, Thinking, and Writing Skills*

What is my approach to reading? If you do not have an answer to this question, then you need to develop an approach. Critical reading is one of the most important skills you develop as a college student. It is a skill that is not limited to written texts: it extends to visual images as well, as we will discuss later in this chapter. Whether you are reading, thinking, or writing critically, your understanding will be improved if you apply four basic strategies:

- Make personal connections.
- Determine important information and ideas.
- Ask questions to focus and clarify.
- Draw inferences.

As a strategic reader, you will be in control as you approach any reading, even assigned reading. You will go to work like a miner, prepared to excavate the rich ore of content each reading holds.

Copyright © 2007, The McGraw-Hill Companies, Inc. All rights reserved.

WW Reading Master Class

CRITICAL READING AND THINKING BEFORE, WHILE, AND AFTER READING

This section contains several readings to help develop your critical reading and thinking skills. There are three exercises to complete before, while, and after reading each selection, as well as a follow-up exercise to write about your personal connection to the reading.

Before reading, **preview** a text. Previewing allows you to become familiar with a text, and enables you to establish a plan for reading. Ask these questions before each reading:

- What kind of text am I about to read?
- How is the text organized?
- How difficult is the reading?

While reading, combine the following interactive strategies to **determine how a text works** and how to gather information from it. Read with a pen, using four strategies to understand and evaluate the information and the author's purpose:

- Make personal connections to understand the purpose of a text.
- Determine the most important ideas and themes in a text.
- Ask questions of yourself, the author, and the text as you read to focus and clarify the reading.
- Draw conclusions by connecting the parts of a text.

As an interactive reader, monitor your understanding and adjust your reading strategies to ensure an effective reading experience.

After reading, **examine the focus and design** of a text by analyzing its content, structure, and purpose.

Make Personal Connections

Making personal connections while reading will increase your understanding. A narrative, like the reading below, will prompt memories, and remembering your life as you read will make the reading enjoyable as well as increase your understanding of it. Think about the following questions as you read:

- Have I ever had an experience similar to this?
- What do I know about the subject?
- What else have I read on this subject?

Before Reading: Preview the Text

EXERCISE 21.1

Answer the following questions by previewing the reading "Bottle Caps." Be sure you only preview the text before moving on to Exercise 21.2.

1. What kind of text am I about to read?
   - Is the text a story, an essay, or an excerpt from a book?
2. How is the text organized?
   - Are there any parts of the reading that will give me additional information or help with the reading?
   - Does it have subtitles, sections, or illustrations that might help me make sense of it?

EXERCISE 21.1 continued

3. How difficult is the reading? Does it contain technical or difficult vocabulary?

   • Will I need a dictionary?

   • Do I know something about this subject? Can I use my prior experience to understand this reading?

READING: "Bottle Caps," by Stuart Dybek

Each day I'd collect caps from beer bottles. I'd go early in the morning through the alleys with a shopping bag, the way I'd seen old women and bums, picking through trash in a cloud of flies. Collectors of all kinds thrived in the alleys: scrap collectors, deposit-bottle collectors, other-people's-hubcap collectors. I made my rounds, stopping behind taverns where bottle caps spilled from splitting, soggy bags—clinking, shiny heaps, still sudded with beer, clotted with cigarette ashes from the night before.

I'd hose them down and store them in coffee cans. At the end of the week, I'd line up my bottle caps for contests between the brands. It was basically a three-way race between Pabst, with its blue-ribboned cap, Bud, and Miller. Blatz and Schlitz weren't far behind.

That got boring fast. It was rare and exotic bottle caps that kept me collecting—Edelweiss; Yusay Pilsner; Carling's Black Label, with its matching black cap; Monarch, from the brewery down the street, its gold caps like pieces of eight; and Meister Brau Bock, my favorite, each cap a ram's-head medallion.

By July, I had too many to count. The coffee cans stashed in the basement began to smell—a metallic, fermenting malt. I worried my mother would find out. It would look to her as if I were brewing polio. Still, the longer I collected, the more I hoarded my bottle caps. They had come to seem almost beautiful. It fascinated me how some were lined with plastic, some with foil. I noticed how only the foreign caps were lined with cork. I tapped the dents from those badly mangled by openers. When friends asked for bottle caps to decorate the spokes of their bikes, I refused.

One afternoon I caught my younger brother in the basement, stuffing my bottle caps into his pocket.

"What do you think you're doing?" I demanded.

At first he wouldn't talk, but I had him by the T-shirt, which I worked up around his throat, slowly twisting it to a knot at his windpipe.

He led me into the backyard, to a sunless patch behind the oil shed, and pointed. Everywhere I looked I could see my bottle caps half buried, their jagged edges sticking up among clothespin crosses and pieces of colored glass.

"I've been using them as tombstones," he said, "in my insect graveyard."

While Reading: Make Personal Connections

EXERCISE 21.2

Now that you have previewed "Bottle Caps," read it closely. Identify at least two spots in the narrative where you make personal connections. Summarize each connection with a word or phrase in the margin.

After Reading: Respond to a Reading through Questions

EXERCISE 21.3

Reflecting on what you read will enable you to deepen your understanding. Answer the following questions independently or discuss them with a reader response group composed of one or two classmates.

About Content

1. Who is the speaker and what do you know about him or her?

2. Which event in the narrative is most important?

3. Why is this event important to the speaker and how does he or she react to it?

About Structure

1. How many paragraphs are in this narrative?

2. If you were to divide this narrative into three parts, where would the divisions occur?

3. How are shifts in time, subject, or attitude signaled to the reader?

About Purpose

1. What is the main purpose of the narrative?

2. Why is this idea or attitude significant?

3. What personal experiences connect to the purpose of this narrative?

Respond to a Reading by Writing

EXERCISE 21.4

"Bottle Caps" explores how Dybek may have passed his time as a kid. He talks about doing something that was normal for a boy. But perhaps collecting bottle caps in alleys was something his mother did not particularly want him to do. Respond to the reading by freewriting about a similar experience you had as a kid.

Copyright © 2007, The McGraw-Hill Companies, Inc. All rights reserved.

EXERCISE 21.4 continued

- How did you pass your time?
- If possible, talk about a pastime that could have been regarded as "mischief."
- Write two or three paragraphs with a beginning, middle, and end.

Determine Important Information and Ideas

An essay constructed with examples, like the next reading, provides specific details to entertain a reader and to clarify the purpose of the essay. However, you must sift down to the key examples that clarify and support the writer's purpose. With this reading, focus on separating essential examples from interesting examples.

Before Reading: Preview the Text

EXERCISE 21.5

Answer the following questions by previewing the reading "Night Walker." Be sure you only preview the text before moving on to Exercise 21.6.

1. What kind of text am I about to read?
   - Is the text a story, an essay, or an excerpt from a book?
2. How is the text organized?
   - Are there any parts of the reading that will give me additional information or help with the reading?
   - Does it have subtitles, sections, or illustrations that might help me make sense of it?
3. How difficult is the reading? Does it contain technical or difficult vocabulary?
   - Will I need a dictionary?
   - Do I know something about this subject? Can I use my prior experience to understand this reading?

READING: "Night Walker," by Brent Staples

My first victim was a woman—white, well dressed, probably in her early 20s. I came upon her late one evening on a deserted street in Hyde Park, a relatively affluent neighborhood in an otherwise mean, improverished section of Chicago. As I swung onto the avenue behind her, there seemed to be a discreet, uninflammatory distance between us. Not so. She cast back a worried glance. To her, the youngish black man—a broad six feet two inches with a beard and billowing hair, both hands shoved into the pockets of a bulky military jacket—seemed menacingly close. She picked up her pace and was soon running in earnest. Within seconds she disappeared into a cross street.

That was more than a decade ago. I was 22 years old, a graduate student newly arrived at the University of Chicago. It was in the echo of that terrible woman's footfalls that I first began to know the unwieldy inheritance I'd come into—the ability to alter public space in ugly ways. It was clear that she thought herself the quarry of a mugger, a rapist, or worse. Suffering a bout of insomnia, however, I was stalking sleep, not defenseless wayfarers. As a softy who is scarcely able to take a knife to a raw chicken—let alone hold one to a person's throat—I was surprised, embarrassed, and dismayed all at once. Her flight made me feel like an

EXERCISE 21.5 continued

accomplice in tyranny. It also made it clear that I was indistinguishable from the muggers who occasionally seeped into the area from the surrounding ghetto. I soon gathered that being perceived as dangerous is a hazard in itself: Where fear and weapons meet—and they often do in urban America—there is always the possibility of death.

In that first year, my first away from my hometown, I was to become thoroughly familiar with the language of fear. At dark, shadowy intersections, I could cross in front of a car stopped at a traffic light and elicit the thunk, thunk, thunk, thunk of the driver—black, white, male, female—hammering down the door locks. On less traveled streets after dark, I grew accustomed to but never comfortable with people crossing to the other side of the street rather than pass me. Then there were the standard unpleasantries with policemen, doormen, bouncers, cabdrivers, and others whose business it is to screen out troublesome individuals before there is any nastiness.

I moved to New York nearly two years ago and I have remained an avid night walker. In central Manhattan, the near-constant crowd covers the tense one-on-one street encounters. Elsewhere, things can get very taut indeed.

After dark, on the warrenlike streets of Brooklyn where I live, I often see women who fear the worst from me. They seem to have set their faces on neutral, and with their purse straps strung across their chests bandolier-style, they forge ahead as though bracing themselves against being tackled. I understand, of course, that the danger they perceive is not a hallucination. Women are particularly vulnerable to street violence, and young black males are drastically overrepresented among the perpetrators of that violence. Yet these truths are no solace against the alienation that comes of being ever the suspect, an entity with whom pedestrians avoid making eye contact.

It is not altogether clear to me how I reached the ripe old age of 22 without being conscious of the lethality nighttime pedestrians attributed to me. Perhaps it was because in Chester, Pennsylvania, the small, angry industrial town where I came of age in the 1960s, I was scarcely noticeable against a backdrop of gang warfare, street knifings, and murders. I grew up one of the good boys, had perhaps a half-dozen fistfights. In retrospect, my shyness of combat has clear sources. As a boy, I saw countless tough guys locked away; I have since buried several, too. They were babies, really—a teenage cousin, a brother of 22, a childhood friend in his mid-20s—all gone down in episodes of bravado played out in the streets. I chose, perhaps unconsciously, to remain a shadow—timid, but a survivor.

The fearsomeness mistakenly attributed to me in public places often has a perilous flavor. The most frightening of these confusions occurred in the late 1970s and early 1980s, when I worked as a journalist in Chicago. One day, rushing into the office of a magazine I was writing for with a deadline story in hand, I was mistaken for a burglar. The office manager called security and, with an ad hoc posse, pursued me through the labyrinthine halls, nearly to my editor's door. I had no way of proving who I was. I could only move briskly toward the company of someone who knew me.

Copyright © 2007, The McGraw-Hill Companies, Inc. All rights reserved.

EXERCISE 21.5 continued

Relatively speaking, however, I never fared as badly as another black male journalist. He went to nearby Waukegan, Illinois, a couple of summers ago to work on a story about a murderer who was born there. Mistaking the reporter for the killer, police officers hauled him from his car at gunpoint and but for his press credentials would probably have tried to book him. Such episodes are not uncommon. Black men trade tales like this all the time.

Over the years, I learned to smother the rage I felt at so often being mistaken for a criminal. Not to do so would surely have led to madness. I now take precautions to make myself less threatening. I move about with care, particularly late in the evening. I give a wide berth to nervous people on subway platforms during the wee hours. If I happen to be entering a building behind some people who appear skittish, I may walk by, letting them clear the lobby before I return, so as not to seem to be following them. I have been calm and extremely congenial on those rare occasions when I've been pulled over by the police.

And on late-evening constitutionals I employ what has proved to be an excellent tension-reducing measure: I whistle melodies from Beethoven and Vivaldi and more popular classical composers. Even steely New Yorkers hunching toward nighttime destinations seem to relax, and occasionally they even join in the tune. Virtually everybody seems to sense that a mugger wouldn't be warbling bright, sunny selections from Vivaldi's "Four Seasons." It is my equivalent of the cowbell that hikers wear when they are in bear country.

While Reading: Determine Important Information and Ideas

EXERCISE 21.6

Now that you have previewed "Night Walker," read it closely. Identify the spots where you make personal connections. Look for sentences that you like and find interesting. Comment on your personal connections in the margins. However, go beyond making personal connections. Read this essay twice, completing the following analytical tasks to help you determine the important information.

- Underline the details that describe other people's fear.
- Circle the details that exemplify the impact of this fear on Staples.
- Place asterisks in the margin to identify sentences that express the point of the essay. Place a question mark in the margin to indicate any part of the essay you do not understand.
- Put a check mark next to a line that suggests why other people's fear was dangerous for Staples.

After Reading: Respond to a Reading through Questions

EXERCISE 21.7

Reflecting on what you read will enable you to deepen your understanding. Answer the following questions independently or discuss them with a reader response group composed of one or two classmates.

Copyright © 2007, The McGraw-Hill Companies, Inc. All rights reserved.

EXERCISE 21.7 continued

About Content

1. Who is the speaker and what do you know about him or her?

2. Which event in the essay is most important?

3. Why is this event important to the speaker and how does he or she react to it?

About Structure

1. How many paragraphs are in this essay?

2. If you were to divide this essay into three parts, where would the divisions occur?

3. How are shifts in time, subject, or attitude signaled to the reader?

About Purpose

1. What is the main purpose of the essay?

2. Why is this idea or attitude significant?

3. What personal experiences connect to the purpose of this essay?

Respond to a Reading by Writing

EXERCISE 21.8

Staples shares his anger and his personal viewpoint on a problem he cannot solve. An innocent nightwalker, he became the victim of other people's fear. In his short essay, he provides a detailed look at the language of fear. Respond to this reading by writing a short paper in which you look at fear in your life.

- As you write, keep this question in mind: What seemingly innocent actions instill fear?

EXERCISE 21.8 continued

- If possible, cite some examples of how fear can restrict a person's actions. Explain each example.
- Write two or three paragraphs with a beginning, middle, and end.

Ask Questions to Focus and Clarify

Critical readers monitor their understanding as they read. They stop when they're confused and ask questions. The next reading captures the attitude and actions of a single person. The author presents her subject so readers can understand how that person sees the world. The viewpoint may not be easy to grasp, especially if it disagrees with your own. Ask questions to help you identify confusions and contradictions between the subject's viewpoint and your own. To answer your questions, summarize the text or read while looking for the answers. This work will help you focus and clarify the author's point.

Before Reading: Preview the Text

EXERCISE 21.9

Answer the following questions by previewing the reading "In the Current." Be sure you only preview the text before moving on to Exercise 21.10.

1. What kind of text am I about to read?
   - Is the text a story, an essay, or an excerpt from a book?
2. How is the text organized?
   - Are there any parts of the reading that will give me additional information or help with the reading?
   - Does it have subtitles, sections, or illustrations that might help me make sense of it?
3. How difficult is the reading? Does it contain technical or difficult vocabulary?
   - Will I need a dictionary?
   - Do I know something about this subject? Can I use my prior experience to understand this reading?

READING: "In the Current," by Jo Ann Beard

The family vacation. Heat, flies, sand, and dirt. My mother sweeps and complains, my father forever baits hooks and untangles lines. My younger brother has brought along his imaginary friend, Charcoal, and my older sister has brought along a real-life majorette by the name of Nan. My brother continually practices all-star wrestling moves on poor Charcoal. "I got him in a figure-four leg lock!" he will call from the ground, propped up on one elbow, his legs twisted together. My sister and Nan wear leg makeup, white lipstick, and say things about me in French. A river runs in front of our cabin, the color of bourbon, foamy at the banks, full of water moccasins and doomed fish. I am ten. The only thing to do is sit on the dock and read, drink watered-down Pepsi, and squint. No swimming allowed.

One afternoon three teenagers get caught in the current while I watch. They come sweeping downstream, hollering and gurgling while I stand on the bank, forbidden to step into the water, and stare at them. They are waving their arms.

Copyright © 2007, The McGraw-Hill Companies, Inc. All rights reserved.

EXERCISE 21.9 continued

I am embarrassed because teenagers are yelling at me. Within five seconds men are throwing off their shoes and diving from the dock; my dad gets hold of one girl and swims her back in. Black hair plastered to her neck, she throws up on the mud about eight times before they carry her back to wherever she came from. One teenager is unconscious when they drag him out and a guy pushes on his chest until a low fountain of water springs up out of his mouth and nose. That kid eventually walks away on his own, but he's crying. The third teenager lands a ways down the bank and comes walking by fifteen minutes later, a grown-up on either side of him and a towel around his waist. His skin looks like Silly Putty.

"Oh man," he says when he sees me. "I saw her go by about ninety miles an hour!" He stops and points at me. I just stand there, embarrassed to be noticed by a teenager. I hope my shorts aren't bagging out again. I put one hand in my pocket and slouch sideways a little. "Man, I thought she was gonna be the last thing I ever seen!" he says, shaking his head.

The girl teenager had had on a swimming suit top with a built-in bra. I cross my arms nonchalantly across my chest and smile at the teenage boy. He keeps walking and talking, the grown-ups supporting him and giving each other looks over the top of his head. His legs are shaking like crazy. "I thought, Man oh man, that skinny little chick is gonna be the last thing ever," he exclaims.

I look down. My shorts are bagging out.

While Reading: Ask Questions to Focus and Clarify

EXERCISE 21.10

Now that you have previewed "In the Current," read it closely. Beard uses a failed vacation to tell the story of something sad, frightening, humorous, and extremely honest. She packs her narrative with detail, creating a complex emotional response for her readers. However, it may be difficult to understand her viewpoint about pre-teen girls. Ask yourself:

- How does this experience affect the narrator?
- What does this mix of emotions reveal about the narrator?
- What does Beard want a reader to understand about young girls?

Observe how Beard packs the narrative with a range of emotional detail. As you read, indicate your emotional response in the margin. Ask questions when the essay seems confusing. If you find answer to your questions later in the text, draw arrows to the sentences that clarify your questions.

After Reading: Respond to a Reading through Questions

EXERCISE 21.11

Reflecting on what you read will enable you to deepen your understanding. Answer the following questions independently or discuss them with a reader response group composed of one or two classmates.

About Content

1. Who is the speaker and what do you know about him or her?

EXERCISE 21.11 continued

2. Which event in the narrative is most important?

3. Why is this event important to the speaker and how does he or she react to it?

About Structure

1. How many paragraphs are in this narrative?

2. If you were to divide this narrative into three parts, where would the divisions occur?

3. How are shifts in time, subject, or attitude signaled to the reader?

About Purpose

1. What is the main purpose of the narrative?

2. Why is this idea or attitude significant?

3. What personal experiences connect to the purpose of this narrative?

Respond to a Reading by Writing

EXERCISE 21.12

Beard's short narrative explores her emotional reaction to an event. She sets the scene, telling the reader about her family vacation. Then she explains a single event that occurred. However, Beard uses the event to focus on what she was like as a young girl. She describes her self-consciousness. Respond to the reading by freewriting about an event that describes you as a child. Pack your freewrite with details.

- How did you view yourself?
- If possible, talk about your emotional reaction to an event from your childhood and the people involved in it.
- Write two or three paragraphs with a beginning, middle, and end.

Draw Inferences

As a reader, you continuously draw inferences while reading. It may be so automatic that you are not conscious of it. Developing an awareness of how often you draw inferences will help improve your skill at making connections in your reading. Monitor your habits as you read by using the following strategies to help you understand an author's purpose:

- Use personal connections.
- Apply personal knowledge gained from other readings or experiences.
- Determine important details, examples, or facts.
- Analyze an author's techniques or structure.

In the reading below, focus on drawing conclusions to connect the parts of the essay.

Before Reading: Preview the Text

EXERCISE 21.13

Answer the following questions by previewing the excerpt from *The Corrosion of Character.* Be sure you only preview the text before moving on to Exercise 21.14.

1. What kind of text am I about to read?
   - Is the text a story, an essay, or an excerpt from a book?
2. How is the text organized?
   - Are there any parts of the reading that will give me additional information or help with the reading?
   - Does it have subtitles, sections, or illustrations that might help me make sense of it?
3. How difficult is the reading? Does it contain technical or difficult vocabulary?
   - Will I need a dictionary?
   - Do I know something about this subject? Can I use my prior experience to understand this reading?

READING: from *The Corrosion of Character,* by Richard Sennett

A year or so ago, I went back to the Boston bakery where twenty-five years ago, in researching *The Hidden Injuries of Class,* I had interviewed a group of bakers. Back then, the bakers worried about upward social mobility among themselves; they feared the children would lose their Greek roots in becoming more American. And the bakers were certain Boston's white Anglo-Saxon Protestants looked down on immigrant Americans like themselves—perhaps a realistic assessment.

Work in the bakery bound the workers self-consciously together. The bakery was filled with noise; the smell of yeast mingled with human sweat in the hot rooms; the bakers' hands were constantly plunged into flour and water; the men used their noses as well as their eyes to judge when the bread was done. Craft pride was strong, but the men said they didn't enjoy their work, and I believed them. The ovens often burned them; the primitive dough beater pulled human muscles; and it was night work, which meant these men, so family-centered, seldom saw their families during the week.

Copyright © 2007, The McGraw-Hill Companies, Inc. All rights reserved.

EXERCISE 21.13 continued

But it seemed to me, watching them struggle, that the ethnic solidarity of being Greek made possible their solidarity in this difficult labor—good worker meant good Greek. The equation of good work and good Greek made sense in the concrete, rather than the abstract. The bakers needed to cooperate intimately in order to coordinate the varied tasks of the bakery. When two of the bakers, brothers who were both alcoholic, showed up plastered on the job, others would berate them by referring to the mess they were making of their families and the loss of prestige of their families in the community where all the Greeks lived. Not being a good Greek was a potent tool of shame, and thus of work discipline.

When I returned to the bakery years later, I was amazed at how much had changed.

A giant food conglomerate now owns the business, but this is no mass production operation. It works according to principles of flexible specialization, using sophisticated, reconfigurable machines. One day the bakers might make a thousand loaves of French bread, the next a thousand bagels, depending on immediate market demand in Boston. The bakery no longer smells of sweat and is startlingly cool, whereas workers used to frequently throw up from the heat. Under the soothing fluorescent lights, all is now strangely silent.

Socially, this is no longer a Greek shop. All the men I'd known have retired; some young Italians now work here as bakers, along with two Vietnamese, an aging and incompetent WASP hippie, and several individuals without discernible ethnic identities. Moreover, the shop is no longer composed only of men; one of the Italians was a girl barely out of her teens, another woman has two grown children. Workers come and go throughout the day; the bakery is a tangled web of part-time schedules for the women and even a few of the men, the old night shift replaced by a much more flexible labor time. The power of the bakers' union has eroded in the shop; as a result, the younger people are not covered by union contracts, and they work on a contingent basis as well as on flexible schedules. Most strikingly, given the prejudices which ruled the old bakery, the shop-floor foreman is black.

From the vantage of the past, all these changes should be confusing. This mixture of ethnicity, gender, and race certainly makes it hard to read up and down in the old way. But the peculiarly American disposition to translate class into the more personal terms of status still prevails. What is truly new is that, in the bakery, I caught sight of a terrible paradox. In this high-tech, flexible work place where everything is user-friendly, the workers felt personally demeaned by the way they work. In this bakers' paradise, that reaction to their work is something they do not themselves understand. Operationally, everything is so clear; emotionally, so illegible.

Computerized baking has profoundly changed the physical activities of the shop floor. Now the bakers make no physical contact with the materials or the loaves of bread, monitoring the entire process via on-screen icons which depict, for instance, images of bread color derived from data about the temperature and baking time of the ovens; few bakers actually see the loaves of bread they make.

Copyright © 2007, The McGraw-Hill Companies, Inc. All rights reserved.

EXERCISE 21.13 continued

Their working screens are organized in the familiar Windows way; in one, icons for many more different kinds of bread appear than had been prepared in the past—Russian, Italian, French loaves all possible by touching the screen. Bread had become a screen representation.

As a result of working in this way, the bakers now no longer actually know how to bake bread. Automated bread is no marvel of technological perfection; the machines frequently tell the wrong story about the loaves rising within, for instance, failing to gauge accurately the strength of the rising yeast, or the actual color of the loaf. The workers can fool with the screen to correct somewhat for these defects; what they can't do is fix the machines, or more important, actually bake bread by manual control when the machines all too often go down. Program-dependent laborers, they can have no hands-on knowledge. The work is no longer legible to them, in the sense of understanding what they are doing.

The flexible time schedules in the bakery compound the difficulties of working this way. People often go home just as disaster is coming out of the oven. I don't mean the workers are irresponsible; rather, they have other demands on their time, children to tend, or other jobs where they must arrive on time. To deal with the computerized batches which misfire, it's easier now to chuck out the spoiled loaves, reprogram the computer, and start all over. In the old days, I saw very few waste scraps in the shop; now each day the huge plastic trash cans of the bakery are filled with mounds of blackened loaves. The trash cans seem apt symbols of what has happened to the art of baking. There's no necessary reason to romanticize this loss of human craft, though; as an avid amateur cook, I found the quality of the bread which survives the production process to be excellent, an opinion evidently shared by many Bostonians, since the bakery is popular and profitable.

In order to be hired now, the people on the shop floor have to prove they are computer-literate. However, they won't use much of this knowledge on the job, where they are simply pushing buttons in a Windows program designed by others. "Baking, shoemaking, printing, you name it, I've got the skills," said one of the women on the shop floor with a laugh as we stared at the trash cans. The bakers are vividly aware of the fact that they are performing simple, mindless tasks, doing less than they know how to do. One of the Italians said to me, "I go home, I really bake bread, I'm a baker. Here, I punch the buttons." When I asked him why he hadn't attended the foreman's baking seminar, he replied, "it doesn't matter; I won't do this the rest of my life." Again and again, people said the same thing in different words: I'm not really a baker.

While Reading: Draw Inferences

EXERCISE 21.14

Sennett organizes his essay through comparison and contrast. His two visits to a bakery, spaced twenty-five years apart, illustrate the dramatic changes in baking bread. However, the essay also speaks to the dramatic changes in many other things. Readers must draw inferences as they read the essay to understand these changes, which were highlighted by Sennett's second visit to the bakery.

EXERCISE 21.14 continued

- Underline sentences that state Sennett's view of the bakery and bakers on his first visit. Look for key phrases that label his point. Summarize each example you find in the margin.
- Underline sentences that illustrate the changes he noticed on his second visit. Be selective. Look for key phrases in the essay that label his observations. Summarize each example you find in the margin.

After Reading: Respond to a Reading through Questions

EXERCISE 21.15

Reflecting on what you read will enable you to deepen your understanding. Answer the following questions independently or discuss them with a reader response group composed of one or two classmates.

About Content

1. Who is the speaker and what do you know about him or her?

2. Which event in the narrative is most important?

3. Why is this event important to the speaker and how does he or she react to it?

About Structure

1. How many paragraphs are in this narrative?

2. If you were to divide this narrative into three parts, where would the divisions occur?

3. How are shifts in time, subject, or attitude signaled to the reader?

About Purpose

1. What is the main purpose of the narrative?

Destinations: A Voyage into Critical Reading

The Critical Citizen

All of us are bombarded these days with information—online, on television, in print, in the classroom, and on the street. To be able to function effectively, it is necessary to hone your critical thinking skills. In other words, you need to learn to efficiently separate the wheat from the chaff—to reject what is false or inaccurate and to accept what is trustworthy and reliable. You indoubtedly do this already, to some extent. After all, do you really trust a tabloid newspaper as much as *The New York Times* or CNN? But practice is necessary for finer distinctions: Which op-ed piece makes more sense on the issues of the upcoming election? Which candidate should you vote for, and why? Consider the ways in which this sort of thinking occurs in other aspects of your life, and ask yourself: How you could become a more "Critical Citizen"?

Reading Visuals

It would be hard to overstate the importance of critical thinking in the academic world. A key component of academic thought in every discipline, from the sciences to the humanities, is the critical analysis of data, information, and ideas. However, one facet of critical thinking is often overlooked: the critical reading of visuals. You will come across many types of visuals—maps, graphs, charts, photographs, advertisements, and Web sites, to name a few—over the course of your studies. Consider why each author chooses to present the information as a visual. What information does the visual convey? Does it go beyond merely informing? Does it express, analyze, or argue something? Is it misleading? Would the same materials suggest a different conclusion if they were presented as text? As you read or study, pay attention to visuals and "read" them as carefully as you would the written word.

The Critical Worker

All the critical skills covered in this chapter can be applied directly to the working world. Critical thinking does not end when you leave school. Your employer will expect you to be able to analyze business records or memos and draw conclusions, understand the business of which your company is a part, and take action based on that understanding. The more skilled you become in school at approaching situations critically, the more valuable you will be as a decision-maker on the job.

EXERCISE 21.15 continued

2. Why is this idea or attitude significant?

3. What personal experiences connect to the purpose of this narrative?

Respond to a Reading by Writing

EXERCISE 21.16

Sennett compares two visits to a bakery. His description portrays the changes in the bakery and the people. Respond to this reading by writing a short paper in which you compare your view to the view of another person.

- Select an individual or group of individuals who are different from you in how they dress, work, raise children, take care of their car, do homework, save or spend money. Keep this question in the back of your mind: Why is my view so important to me?
- Include examples that illustrate how you are different from this other individual or group.
- If possible, cite some examples of how you came to believe this is the "best" way to be. Provide as much detail as possible for each example.
- Write two or three paragraphs with a beginning, middle, and end.

Copyright © 2007, The McGraw-Hill Companies, Inc. All rights reserved.

BUILD ON WHAT YOU HAVE LEARNED: ADDITIONAL READINGS

READING: "You've Got *Hate* Mail," by Lydie Raschka

Hate mail confirms a vague, nagging feeling that you've done something wrong. It's a firm tap on the shoulder that says, "The jig is up." So when the first letter came, it was expected. The second, however, was a shock. By the third I was a wreck. How did he know it would take exactly and only three?

I started writing a few years ago, after I had a baby. I haven't completely figured out what led me to writing, but it was probably tied up with my son's birth and the attendant emotions that needed sorting.

I like the solitary work life. I write at a table in the bedroom. I send my ideas out into the void. The bedroom seems a safe enough place. I have been told that I am an introvert. What on earth makes me want to communicate with strangers in this perilous way—standing naked in a field?

"You have to expect these things when you are a writer," my father says about the hate mail. "When you're in the public eye, anyone can read what you write."

The letters are effective and unsettling, to say the least. I have an unusual name, so he thinks I'm foreign. He calls me "Eurotrash." It's a relief because it means he doesn't really know me—although he makes some pretty accurate guesses. He doesn't know that my parents simply like unusual names.

He spells my name correctly. I can only hope he's mispronouncing it. He uses it in ways I've never seen it used before—paired with obscenities and crooked thoughts.

It bothers me that he has written my name and my address three different times on three different envelopes. My name is next to the buzzer outside my building so that people will have easier access to me. I am two doors and one buzzer away from danger. But the mail slips through, into the letter box, into my psyche.

I call the postal inspector but she never calls me back. One day I leave a message on her machine and I am in tears. Finally she calls. She tells me that letters like these don't usually lead to violence. She says there's nothing we can do; we have to wait until he makes a mistake.

My fingers shake when I open the mailbox. I pick through the stack. When a letter arrives I open it quickly. You read your mail. You do.

I spend most of a morning sitting in an old school chair at the police station, the kind with a desk attached. The police are standing around. They joke with one another. They drink coffee and ask me what I need in a skeptical way, as though there is nothing I can offer that will surprise them.

"I am getting anonymous hate mail," I say.

"Is it threatening?" they ask.

"Not specifically," I answer. "But the first one had feces in it." Sending feces is threatening, in my mind. At the very least it's a health hazard. The policewoman writes down what I say and photocopies the letters. She makes a file.

I am vulnerable to people's opinions of me. I partly believe what he says. When I tell my friends and family, I imagine that they partly believe what he says, too. They ask me what I wrote, what he wrote. "What does it matter what I wrote!?" I say. "Do you think I did something to deserve this?!" I can't yell at him, so I yell at them. I want unconditional support from everyone I know. I want protection. I have revealed too much about who I am.

I cling to his most obvious mistakes—Eurotrash—in the hope that he has gotten other things wrong, too. He is sarcastic and angry and a good speller. A person can be a good speller and be crazy, right? But still, it's hard that he's a good speller.

I try to have rational conversations with him in my mind, but it's hopeless. We get nowhere.

He owns a dog. It's his dog's feces he has sent. I always thought animal lovers were especially sensitive human beings. In my vulnerable state—in spite of this blatant example of insensitivity—dog ownership gives him stature.

He has decided I'm rich because I live in a certain neighborhood. He has decided I've stolen someone's job because I'm foreign. He attacks my writing and everything he can eke out about me from what I have written. But he reveals who he is in his writing, too. He has an aunt and a disabled sister. He doesn't know how much we have in common. He doesn't know that I have a sister and a disabled aunt.

I think about changing my byline. I will remove my address from the phone book. I will use only a first initial. I will give up writing.

But then he wins, says my editor.

I am unable to write for a month, two months. My editor calls. I say I'm not ready. He hires someone else to write on a topic I wanted to write about. I don't trust my motivations. Perhaps there's truth in what he says. I have been flippant. I have been patronizing. I have been biased.

At home I put the letters in a brown envelope and write "Anonymous Mail" in the top right-hand corner, avoiding the word "hate." I make a mental note to throw them away before my son can reach the shelf where I have put them. I don't want him to read these letters that have my name written all over them, with their inaccuracies and assumptions and possible wayward truths.

The feces were wrapped in a piece of foil; they came in a small padded envelope. I threw the feces away, then fished them out again and put them in a baggie. I washed my hands with soap, and rubbed them red. I am afraid of contamination or disease. I am afraid I will pass on germs to my son.

"Here's a little present from my best friend," he writes. The way he uses language is absurd: little present, best friend. He writes in sentences, with periods and commas and capital letters. He ignores the typical friendly greeting—he does not say "Dear."

I imagine him in a room, at a desk or a table. I imagine the light in the room, and the clothes tossed on the bed. He has paper and a pen. He pulls up a chair. Something compels him to write. He doesn't know how much we have in common.

READING: "The Body of the Beholder," by Michele Ingrassia

When you're a teenage girl, there's no place to hide. Certainly not in gym class, where the shorts are short, the T-shirts revealing and the adolescent critics eager to dissect every flaw. Yet out on the hardwood gym floors at Moran Park High,

Copyright © 2007, The McGraw-Hill Companies, Inc. All rights reserved.

a largely African-American school on Chicago's Southwest Side, the girls aren't talking about how bad their bodies are, but how good. Sure, all of them compete to see how many sit-ups they can do—Janet Jackson's washboard stomach is their model. But ask Diane Howard about weight, and the African-American senior, who carries 133 pounds on her 5-foot 7½ inch frame, says she'd happily add 15 pounds— if she could ensure they'd land on her hips. Or La'Taria Stokes, a stoutly built junior who takes it as high praise when boys remark, "Your hips are screaming for twins!" "I know I'm fat," La'Taria says. "I don't care."

In a society that worships at the altar of supermodels like Claudia, Christy and Kate, white teenagers are obsessed with staying thin. But there's growing evidence that black and white girls view their bodies in dramatically different ways. The latest findings come in a study to be published in the journal *Human Organization* this spring by a team of black and white researchers at the University of Arizona. While 90 percent of the white junior-high and high-school girls studied voiced dissatisfaction with their weight, 70 percent of African-American teens were satisfied with their bodies.

In fact, even significantly overweight black teens described themselves as happy. That confidence may not carry over to other areas of black teens' lives, but the study suggests that, at least here, it's a lifelong source of pride. Asked to describe women as they age, two thirds of the black teens said they get more beautiful, and many cited their mothers as examples. White girls responded that their mothers may have been beautiful—back in their youth. Says anthropologist Mimi Nichter, one of the study's coauthors, "In white culture, the window of beauty is so small."

What is beauty? White teens defined perfection as 5 feet 7 and 100 to 110 pounds—superwaif Kate Moss's vital stats. African-American girls described the perfect size in more attainable terms—full hips, thin thighs, the sort of proportions about which Hammer ("Pumps and a Bump") and Sir Mix-A lot ("Baby Got Back") rap poetic. But they said that true beauty—"looking good"—is about more than size. Almost two thirds of the black teens defined beauty as "the right attitude."

The disparity in body images isn't just in kids' heads. It's reflected in fashion magazines, in ads, and it's out there, on TV, every Thursday night. On NBC, the sitcom "Friends" stars Courteney Cox, Jennifer Aniston and Lisa Kudrow—all of them white and twentysomething, classically beautiful and reed thin. Meanwhile, Fox Television's "Living Single," aimed at an African-American audience, projects a less Hollywood ideal—its stars are four twentysomething black women whose bodies are, well, *real*. Especially the big-boned, bronze-haired rapper Queen Latifah, whose size only adds to her magnetism. During a break at the Lite Nites program at the Harlem YMCA, over the squeal of sneakers on the basketball court, Brandy Wood, 14, describes Queen Latifah's appeal: "What I like about her is the way she wears her hair and the color in it and the clothes she wears."

Underlying the beauty gap are 200 years of cultural difference. "In white, middle-class America, part of the great American Dream of making it is to be able to make yourself over," says Nichter. "In the black community, there is the reality that you might not move up the ladder as easily. As one girl put it, you have to be realistic—if you think negatively about yourself, you won't get anywhere." It's no accident that Barbie has long embodied a white-adolescent ideal—in the early days, she came with her own scale (set at 110) and her own diet guide ("How to Lose Weight: Don't Eat"). Even in this postfeminist era, Barbie's tight-is-right message is stronger than ever. Before kindergarten, researchers say, white girls know that Daddy eats and Mommy diets. By high school, many have split the world into physical haves and have-nots, rivals across the beauty line. "It's not that you hate them [perfect girls]," says Sarah Immel, a junior at Evanston Township High School north of Chicago. "It's that you're kind of jealous that they have it so easy, that they're so perfect-looking."

In the black community, size isn't debated, it's taken for granted—a sign, some say, that after decades of preaching black-is-beautiful, black parents and educators have gotten across the message of self-respect. Indeed, black teens grow up equating a full figure with health and fertility. Black women's magazines tend to tout NOT TRYING TO BE SIZE 8, not TEN TIPS FOR THIN THIGHS. And even girls who fit the white ideal aren't necessarily comfortable there. Super model Tyra Banks recalls how, in high school in Los Angeles, she was the envy of her white girlfriends. "They would tell me, 'Oh, Tyra, you look so good,' " says Banks. "But I was like, 'I want a booty and thighs like my black girlfriends.' "

Men send some of the strongest signals. What's fat? "You got to be *real* fat for me to notice," says Muhammad Latif, a Harlem 15-year-old. White girls follow what they *think* guys want, whether guys want it or not. Sprawled across the well-worn sofas and hard-back chairs of the student lounge, boys at Evanston High scoff at the girls' idealization of Kate Moss. "Sickly," they say, "gross." Sixteen-year-old Trevis Milton, a blond swimmer, has no interest in dating Kate wanna-bes. "I don't want to feel like I'm going to break them." Here, perfection is a hardbody, like Linda Hamilton in "Terminator II." "It's not so much about eating broccoli and water as running," says senior Kevin Mack.

And if hardbodies are hot, girls often need to diet to achieve them, too. According to the Arizona study, which was funded by the National Institute of Child Health and Human Development, 62 percent of the white girls reported dieting at least once in the past year. Even those who say they'd rather be fit than thin get caught up. Sarah Martin, 16, a junior at Evanston, confesses she's tried forcing herself to throw up but couldn't. She's still frustrated: ". . . have a big appetite, and I feel so guilty when I eat."

Black teens don't usually go to such extremes. Anorexia and bulimia are relatively minor problems among African-American girls. And though 51 percent of the black teens in the study said that they'd dieted in the last year, follow-up interviews showed that far fewer were on sustained weight-and-exercise programs. Indeed, 64 percent of the black girls thought it was better to be "a little" overweight than underweight. And while they agreed that "very overweight" girls should diet, they defined that as someone who "takes up two seats on the bus."

The black image of beauty may seem saner, but it's not necessarily healthy. Black women don't obsess on size, but they do worry about other white cultural ideals that black men value. "We look at Heather Locklear and see the long hair and the fair, pure skin," says *Essence* magazine senior editor Pamela Johnson. More troubling, the

Copyright © 2007, The McGraw-Hill Companies, Inc. All rights reserved.

acceptance of fat means many girls ignore the real dangers of obesity. Dieting costs money—even if it's not a fancy commercial program; fruits, vegetables and lean meats are pricier than high-fat foods. Exercise? Only one state—Illinois—requires daily physical education for every kid. Anyway, as black teenagers complain, exercise can ruin your hair—and, if you're plunking down $35 a week at the hairdresser, you don't want to sweat out your 'do in the gym. "I don't think we should obsess about weight and fitness, but there is a middle ground," says the well-toned black actress Jada Pinkett. Maybe that's where Queen Latifah meets Kate Moss.

READING: "Smart Pills," by William Speed Weed

"The world will little note, nor long remember, what we say here, but it can never forget what they did here." Without reading that sentence from Lincoln's Gettysburg Address again, you can probably recite most of the words because they're stored in your short-term memory, that bustling depot of the brain where fleeting ideas come and go but never stay.

Long-term memory is another thing. Most people would have to read the sentence out loud, write it down, and test themselves repeatedly to get it permanently down pat. Repetition is the mother of all learning because our brains must undergo a physical change in order to form a long-term memory: Neurons have to grow new connections to one another to create a structural basis for whatever it is we'll remember, be it a fresh idea, a telephone number or a famous speech. As anyone who's ever been a student knows, memory construction takes work.

But what if you could swallow a little pill that gave you a photographic memory, the ability to form long-term memories instantly? With such a pill, the world as a whole would long remember, for the first time in history, anything it wanted to.

Clinical trials for a memory-enhancing drug are just two to five years away, say Jerry Yin and Tim Tully of Cold Spring Harbor Laboratory on Long Island, New York. At the center of their work is a protein that helps nerve cells in the brain store memories. A sudden increase in the activity levels of the protein sends the memory-making process into overdrive and allows neurons to make long-lasting storage structures immediately, without the slow work of repetition.

Yin and Tully first discovered the importance of this memory protein (a form of CREB, for Cyclic AMP Response Element Binding protein) while working with fruit flies. They created two new, genetically altered strains of fruit fly: one with extremely high levels of memory protein and one with almost none of it. Then they conditioned the flies by placing them in tubes and blowing in scented air currents. One scent "smelled like my tennis shoes in July," says Tully. The other smelled like licorice and was accompanied by a small electric shock. A fly that is zapped every time it smells licorice should eventually build a set of neural connections that says, "Avoid licorice!" The question is: How much repetition does it take for that long-term memory to form?

Yin and Tully tested the flies by placing them in the middle of a double-ended tube and blowing tennis-shoe scent in one end and licorice scent in the other. Flies with normal levels of the memory protein needed to be zapped 10 times before they stopped moving toward the licorice scent. In other words, they could build the neural connections needed for an "Avoid licorice!" memory, but it required spaced repetition—just as normal humans must say a sentence over and over again to memorize it. Yin and Tully then tested a strain with low levels of memory protein and found that those poor flies never made the structural changes necessary for lasting memory. No matter how many shocks they received, they went for the licorice scent as often as they went for the tennis-shoe scent.

The flies with an overabundance of memory protein formed long-term memory instantly. After only one trial, they knew to avoid licorice the rest of their lives. Tully points out that these flies haven't gotten smarter—they'll never solve quadratic equations. Extra memory protein simply accelerates the pace of memorization by eliminating the need for repetition. Yin and Tully suspect that the memory protein is a sort of construction crew foreman in the brain that turns on the genes neurons need to grow new connections, a process that normally occurs bit by bit with repetition. When a brain is awash in memory protein, the building process occurs all at once. "You require less training to initiate memory," Tully says. "That's a dramatic switch." The finding could ultimately have dramatic implications for all of us because it so overwhelmingly likely that memory protein has essentially the same role in human brains as it does in fly brains.

The pharmaceutical challenge Yin and Tully must solve—and they say they're close—is to find a compact chemical that can infiltrate neurons, stimulate an over-production of the protein, and thereby give the human brain a hurry-up, neural-connection construction crew. This pop-a-pill enhancement is expected to last only a few hours before memory protein levels return to normal, but while levels are up, we'll be like the one-zap flies, with super-charged memory-making.

What great news! Wash down a pill, read one of Shakespeare's plays, and you'll know it by heart! Learn a new language in a month—without flash cards! Get a law degree in one semester! The possibilities are endless—which is itself a problem. Perhaps the reason evolution made repetition the mother of learning is that repetition ensures that you remember only what you try to remember. On memory pills, you take the chance of memorizing the ingredients on your cereal box, the disclaimer at the end of the movies, and every word of that annoying conversation you heard on the bus. The minutiae that once flitted lightly through your short-term memory will lodge in your brain forever, like it or not. "We're not sure society is ready for this," Yin admits. It might be best, he says, to administer the pill only to people with certain types of mental retardation that compromise memory. "But," he adds, "if we really have something that's the neuronal equivalent of Viagra, it's going to get out."

 READING: "SARS: A Rehearsal?" by Frank Clancy

In the end, severe acute respiratory syndrome didn't turn out to be the viral Big One that epidemiologists had been warning about—a pandemic causing the deaths of millions. But SARS did prove that the worriers have a point: Emergent diseases can spread with great speed; the public health response is inadequate; and the economic impact can be huge.

Copyright © 2007, The McGraw-Hill Companies, Inc. All rights reserved.

SARS seems to have originated in the exotic meat markets of southern China in November 2002, then festered while the Chinese government tried to suppress and conceal the problem. The disease traveled to Hong Kong in February 2003, then followed airline routes to Vietnam, Singapore and Toronto. By August, cases had been reported in more than two dozen countries in North and South America, Europe and Asia. More than 8,000 people fell ill; 774 died. The U.S. was mostly spared, with just 29 reported cases, none fatal.

At the height of the fears, Taipei subway riders were required to wear medical masks. Police guarded Toronto hospitals to ensure everyone who entered was screened for symptoms. Jittery San Franciscans and New Yorkers avoided local Chinatowns. Several airlines suspended most flights to Asia, suffering major financial losses. Perhaps the most terrifying aspect of SARS was the ease with which it spread. A Chinese doctor who stayed a single night at a Hong Kong hotel may have infected up to 16 people—many of them, experts theorized, when he sneezed while waiting for an elevator.

SARS was nowhere near the most deadly disease of 2003: Far more people died from the flu. But public health officials warn we should expect more such outbreaks, and worse ones: Continued incursions into the environment give microorganisms the opportunity to jump from wild animals to human hosts, and air travel practically ensures that diseases go global. And as bad as SARS was, it's easy to envision something worse—more contagious, more deadly. "I look at SARS as a dress rehearsal for something bigger," says Stuart Cohen, an epidemiologist at the University of California, Davis. "There will always be emerging diseases. How our public health system responds will be critical."

In a heroic effort, a network of 13 labs in 10 countries identified the SARS coronavirus barely two months after China first notified the World Health Organization of an odd pneumonia outbreak in Guangdong Province. Researchers soon sequenced the virus's entire genome, but that knowledge didn't lead to a vaccine, much less a cure; it only provided a slowpoke way to confirm suspected cases.

What ultimately brought SARS under control were old-fashioned methods: isolating people with symptoms (high fever, aches and a dry cough) and tracking down those they'd come in contact with. The global response was swift, experts say; still, an outbreak that infected a tiny percentage of the world's population taxed public health systems to their limits. "Our bench science and high tech were beautiful, but when it came to control, it was a real struggle," says Cohen. The number of health care workers infected—in some countries they accounted for more than half of those who fell ill—exposed weaknesses in the system. Hospitals must ensure that employees take basic precautions such as washing hands and properly disposing of contaminated items. They also need negative-air-pressure rooms in which to isolate patients. Barry Bloom, dean of the Harvard School of Public Health, wrote in *Science* that the U.S. should be training epidemiologists and strengthening lab capabilities around the world: "This investment would protect our country and every other against global epidemics [and] save millions of lives."

READING: "Nature or Nurture?" by Robert Sapolsky

As a scientist doing scads of important research, I am busy, very busy. What with all those midnight experiments in the lab, all that eureka-ing, I hardly have any time to read professional journals. Thus, I only lately got the chance to peruse *People* magazine's most recent compilation of "The 50 Most Beautiful People in the World." It was fabulous. In addition to offering helpful grooming tips, the issue grapples with one of the central conundrums of our time: Which is ultimately more influential, nature or nurture? "About beauty," opine the editors, "the arguments can be endless." No such shilly-shallying for the Chosen Ones themselves: The 50 Most Beautiful and their inner circles appear to harbor militant ideologues in the debate.

Consider first the extreme nurturists, who eschew the notion that anything is biologically fixed. There's Ben Affleck, who in service to stardom has slimmed down, pumped up, and had his teeth capped. Affleck is clearly a disciple of John Watson, famous for the nurture credo: "Give me a child and let me control the total environment in which he is raised, and I will turn him into whatever I wish." It's hardly surprising that Affleck's celebrated affair with Gwyneth Paltrow, clearly of the genetic determinist school (read on), was so short-lived.

A nurture viewpoint is also advanced by TV star Jenna Elfman, who attributes her beauty to drinking 100 ounces of water a day, eating a diet based on her blood type, and using a moisturizer that costs $1,000 a pound. Jaclyn Smith, the erstwhile Charlie's Angel, maintains her beauty has been preserved by not smoking, not drinking, and not doing drugs. However, even a neophyte student of human developmental biology might easily note that no degree of expensive moisturizers or virtuous living would get, say, me on *People*'s pulchritudinous list.

Naturally, similarly strong opinions emanate from the opposing, nature faction—the genetic determinists among the Most Beautiful. Perhaps the brashest of this school is Josh Brolin, an actor whose statement could readily serve as a manifesto for his cadre: "I was given my dad's good genes." Similar sentiments emerge from the grandfather of the aforementioned Paltrow, who avows that she was "beautiful from the beginning."

The very epitome of the natalist program, in which genetics forms an imperative trajectory impervious to environmental manipulation, is TV host Meredith Vieira. *People*'s editors cite various disasters that have befallen her—shoddy application of makeup, an impetuous and unfortunate peroxide job on her hair—and yet, it doesn't matter. She is still beautiful because of her "phenomenal genes."

One searches the pages for a middle ground, for the interdisciplinary synthesist who perceives the contributions of both nature and nurture. At last, we espy Monica. The single-name singer, we are told, has an absolutely wondrous skill for applying makeup. This, at first, seems like just more nurture agitprop. But where does she get this cosmetic aptitude?

Her mother supplies the answer. With Monica, Mom says, "It's something that's inborn." One gasps at the insight: There is a genetic influence on how one interacts with the environment. Too bad a few more people can't think this way when figuring out what genes have to do with, say, intelligence, substance abuse, or violence.

Copyright © 2007, The McGraw-Hill Companies, Inc. All rights reserved.

READING: "Keeping Hands on Wheel, and on Bow, and Strings," by Dan Barry

It being Wednesday, Hugh McDonald parked on the West Side and reached for the large black case that contains his obsession. He tugged on the bill of his baseball cap and started walking east, toward Carnegie Hall.

You might guess his profession just by looking at his clothes: gray pants, blue sweater, white shirt bearing the company name, and blue tie with the pattern of small buses. Mr. McDonald is a bus driver, at least by day.

He is 54, unassuming and agreeable, the kind of man who says, "Yes, uh-huh" a lot. But once he makes a decision, he can be as rigid as a bus schedule. He now eats salad every day for lunch, because no way is Hugh McDonald going to be another overweight bus driver.

He and his wife, Beverly, live with their four dogs in Berlin, N.J., near Philadelphia. She runs a pet grooming business out of the house, and he steers a 45-foot, 57-passenger commuter bus for Academy bus lines.

At 5:30 every weekday morning, he drives 30 miles to the bus depot in Westhampton, climbs aboard his assigned bus and drives 25 miles to East Windsor, then Monroe, then Jamesburg, and finally to the park-and-ride lot at Exit 8-A of the New Jersey Turnpike. Next stop, Manhattan. He lingers a few hours, collects his passengers and returns to deep New Jersey, though he does not reach his own home until 8 or 9 at night. His long bus drives have no music to help pass the time, only a two-way radio offering dispatcher chatter.

One afternoon about three years ago, while killing time until rush hour, Mr. McDonald came upon a man playing Bach on a cello in the Times Square subway station. The sweet song of this cello, the first one he had ever heard, soared above the train rattle and jangle.

"The sound, the feeling, the intensity, the emotion of it," he recalled. "It was like a wave that came over me. I had never felt that before."

Suddenly, he wanted to play the cello.

When he was a child in a Bronx housing project, he had wanted to learn a musical instrument. But the bleats of a trumpeter-in-training would have been too disruptive for the neighbors, his parents had said, so that was that. Later, as a young man, he often listened to classical music on a transistor radio in his bedroom, recognizing some of the pieces as ones that he had heard in church.

But this cello music.

For nearly a year that subway cellist's music lingered in Mr. McDonald's mind—as he drove, as he ate his salad, as he drove some more. Finally, his passion to learn overcame his fears of being too old. Between one day's rush hours, he went to the New York Public Library and picked a school at random out of the telephone book: The French-American Conservatory of Music at Carnegie Hall.

"They said, 'We'll teach you cello,'" he recalled. "I said, 'I can't play a note, can't read a note.' They told me, 'No problem.'"

Cellos cost several thousand dollars, so Mr. McDonald began renting one for $49 a month, which was on top of the $45 he paid for his weekly hour of instruction. But cost did not matter, he said. "I wanted to play the notes the way I heard them coming off that train."

He spent nearly four months trying to get the sound of bow upon string to evoke sounds that were pleasing to the ear. And when that moment came, when the stroke of his bow summoned sweetness, he thought, wow, this is Hugh McDonald making that sound.

"It was like, 'Oh, I've reached it,'" he recalled. "At least I can make it sound good."

Now, some 18 months later, he can coax recognizable music from the cello, thanks to his commitment to practice. On most days, during his break between rush hours, he parks in a Hoboken bus lot and heads with that black case to the back of his empty bus. He has discovered that if he sets the cello in the aisle, lays out his music on a seat and lifts a couple of arm rests, he has just enough room to play.

On Wednesdays, though, he does not drive to Hoboken. He parks instead on West 54th Street in Midtown and carries his obsession to Carnegie Hall for his weekly session with Biana Cvetkovic, cello instructor.

Ms. Cvetkovic, imbued with the patience of a natural teacher, continues to drill the basics into Mr. McDonald. Keep the back nice and tall, the legs spread apart, the feet flat. Keep the thumbs soft and the fingers nice and round. Relax the right elbow. Keep the bow stroking the cello's powerful place—the highway. Now listen to the tempo. Tap, tap, tap.

Last Wednesday, Mr. McDonald took his seat in Ms. Cvetkovic's studio and began to summon music from his rented cello. He played haltingly. But the afternoon rush was hours away, and he had the time.

USING PHOTOGRAPHS TO THINK AND WRITE WITH A CRITICAL VOICE

You have something to say about your life, your ideas, and the subjects you study. Developing critical thinking through observation will build your critical writer's voice. Use five strategies to develop your critical voice:

- Get close-up.
- Look for the story.
- Observe the details.
- Define an object.
- State an opinion.

Get Close-up

EXERCISE 21.17

You will write twice about the photograph below, each time with a different emphasis. Assume that your reader cannot see the photograph.

1. First writing: practice making connections.
   - What is your emotional reaction to the photograph?
   - What personal connection do you make as you look at it?
   - What activity or experience comes to mind as you view it?

Copyright © 2007, The McGraw-Hill Companies, Inc. All rights reserved.

EXERCISE 21.17 continued

2. Second writing: practice description. Write a description of what you see. Be as thorough as possible. Consider what you write to be a "verbal sketch" that enables your reader to see the photograph.

EXERCISE 21.18

Why would a photographer or a writer withhold information? In the photograph above, the photographer uses a close-up, but the close-up makes it difficult to know everything about the person peeling the potatoes.

- Is the person a man or a woman?
- How old is the person?
- Is the person experienced? Is peeling potatoes a job or a chore?

The photographer does not provide you the answers to these questions. Use the concept of a close-up to brainstorm writing ideas:

- List of five to ten activities about which you might write.
- Next to each activity, list of three or four objects you associate with that activity.
- Begin your writing with a close-up description of the activity.
- Then freewrite about the activity, trying to create an emotional response for a reader.

Look for the Story

EXERCISE 21.19

You will write twice about the photograph below, each time with a different emphasis. Assume that your reader cannot see the photograph.

1. First writing: practice making connections.
- What is your emotional reaction to the photograph?
- What personal connection do you make as you look at it?
- What activity or experience comes to mind as you view it?

Copyright © 2007, The McGraw-Hill Companies, Inc. All rights reserved.

EXERCISE 21.19 continued

2. Second writing: practice description. Write a description of what you see. Be as thorough as possible. Consider what you write to be a "verbal sketch" that enables your reader to see the photograph.

EXERCISE 21.20

The photographer tells a story with the details of the picture above. The story is easy to construct because of the details. Use the detailed photograph here to brainstorm writing ideas:

- List of five to ten memories about which you might write.
- Next to each memory, list of three or four details you associate with that memory. Focus on the key details for each memory.
- Begin your writing with a description of the setting. Where did this memory occur?
- Then freewrite about the memory, trying to create an emotional response for your reader.

Observe the Details

EXERCISE 21.21

You will write twice about the photograph below, each time with a different emphasis. Assume that your reader cannot see the photograph.

1. First writing: practice drawing conclusions. Explain what the woman in the photograph is doing by speculating on the circumstances of the event.
   - Where is the woman?
   - How does her environment influence her actions?
   - What details enable you to draw these conclusions?
2. Second writing: practice description. Write a description of what you see. Be as thorough as possible. Consider what you write to be a "verbal sketch" that enables your reader to see the photograph.

EXERCISE 21.21 continued

EXERCISE 21.22

Details are the key to good writing and good photographs. The above picture captures a common scene—a woman at the computer. However, the photographer does not provide details of the exact setting. The focus of the photograph is on the woman, not the situation. What do the details tell us about the woman? How do we define ourselves? Consider this photograph as you brainstorm writing ideas:

- List of three to five possible scenarios that you feel define you.
- Next to each scenario, list of three or four objects or details that would further define the scene. Be selective, focusing on the objects and details that make a statement about you.
- Begin describing yourself.
- Then freewrite about your self-defining scenario, trying to create an emotional response for your reader.

Define an Object

EXERCISE 21.23

You will write twice about the photograph below, each time with a different emphasis. Assume that your reader cannot see the photograph.

1. First writing: practice making connections.
   - What is your emotional reaction to the photograph?
   - What personal connection do you make as you look at it?
   - What activity or experience comes to mind as you view it?

2. Second writing: practice description. Write a description of what you see. Be as thorough as possible. Consider what you write to be a "verbal sketch" that enables your reader to see the photograph.

EXERCISE 21.23 continued

Copyright © 2007, The McGraw-Hill Companies, Inc. All rights reserved.

EXERCISE 21.24

Did the photographer happen upon this woman? Or did the photographer create a situation to define something larger than the woman and her dog? What possession defines you? What possession defines a person you know? Use this photograph to brainstorm writing ideas:

- List of five to ten objects about which you might write. Select something that defines a person, job, or activity.
- Next to each object, list of three or four details that help define it. Imagine that you are creating a still life like the photograph of the boots.
- Begin your writing with a description of the object. You may want to work close-up like this photographer did, or you may want to describe the complete object.
- Then freewrite about the object, trying to create an emotional response for your reader.

State an Opinion

EXERCISE 21.25

You will write twice about the photograph below, each time with a different emphasis. Assume that your reader cannot see the photograph.

EXERCISE 21.25 continued

1. First writing: practice making connections.
   - What is your emotional reaction to the photograph?
   - What personal connection do you make as you look at it?
   - What activity or experience comes to mind as you view it?

2. Second writing: practice description. Write a description of what you see. Be as thorough as possible. Consider what you write to be a "verbal sketch" that enables your reader to see the photograph.

EXERCISE 21.26

Photographs can create a variety of emotional reactions and interpretations. Compare your verbal sketch with the verbal sketches of other writers in your class. Did you see the photograph in the same way? Now look back at the photograph. What details led you to your reaction and interpretation? Consider this photograph as you brainstorm writing ideas:

- List of five to ten topics about which you might write. Select something about which you feel strongly.
- Next to each topic, list of three or four people, events, or objects that will grab your reader and establish a similar emotional reaction.
- Begin your writing with a description of the person, event, or object. You may want to work close-up like the photographer did, or you may want to describe the complete picture.
- Then freewrite about the person, event, or object, trying to create an emotional response for your reader.

22 *Group Work: Collaboration and Public Speaking*

*Y*ou'll be working together in groups on this project. The final project will be presented orally. During your time in college, you'll hear variations of these two instructions over and over again. You'll be asked to work collaboratively in a variety of situations and to make oral presentations of many different kinds. Ultimately, of course, most of you are making journeys toward specific professions, and in work, collaborating with others and making effective oral presentations are essential skills. (For examples of classroom collaborations related to writing projects, see the "Talk" sections on pages 14, 63, 135, and 264.)

IN THIS CHAPTER: A PREVIEW

Study and Work Collaboratively

- Understanding the Collaborative Task
- Understanding Approaches to Collaborative Study and Work
- Recognizing the Advantages and Challenges in Collaborative Study and Work

Follow a Group of Students as They Work Collaboratively

- Reflecting: Build Confidence

Speak in Public with Confidence

- Understanding the Speaking Task
- Evaluating Your Audience and Creating Your "Speaker Self"
- Preparing to Speak
- Giving the Speech
- Reflecting: Build Confidence

STUDY AND WORK COLLABORATIVELY

In the following exercises, you will explore the structures and purposes of groups. You will also examine the ways you have collaborated with others at school, home, and work. You will also examine teamwork in formal and informal settings.

Copyright © 2007, The McGraw-Hill Companies, Inc. All rights reserved.

EXERCISE 22.1

Think of your own collaborative experiences and circle the purpose that best relates to each one. Indicate the reason for the collaboration and the structure of the group with which you worked. Some collaborative work may have more than one purpose. The first row has been filled in as a model.

Purposes for Collaboration

A. Brainstorming for ideas

B. Creating a finished product or project

C. Achieving a victory

D. Gaining a financial reward

Purpose	Reason	Structure
Ⓐ B C D	Deciding on possibilities for family vacation	My mother, father, two sisters, myself, and travel agent
A B C D		
A B C D		
A B C D		
A B C D		
A B C D		

EXERCISE 22.2

You may have not yet worked collaboratively in college classes or in the professional world. However, you can become familiar with academic and professional collaboration by evaluating the following situations. For each collaborative task listed, circle the purpose. Some tasks may have more than one purpose. In addition, note whether the task might relate to academic work, professional work, or both. The first row has been filled in as a model.

Purposes for Collaboration

A. Brainstorming for ideas

B. Creating a finished product or project

C. Achieving a victory

D. Gaining a financial reward

Purpose	Collaborative Task	Academic or Professional?
Ⓐ B C Ⓓ	Planning a sales campaign	Professional
A B C D		
A B C D		
A B C D		
A B C D		
A B C D		

Destinations: Making the Journey with Others

Working on a Team

Collaborative work is often described as "working on a team," and a student or a professional may be praised for being a strong "team player." The concept of a sports team is useful for explaining some aspects of collaboration. On a sports team, players may have different strengths. They may face different individual challenges. Yet they must all learn ways of working together to achieve common goals. Sometimes the goals relate to preparation and practice. But the ultimate goal is to build a group of individuals who work together to win. While academic and professional teams are not exactly the same as sports teams, we can learn a great deal about productive collaborative work by considering our own experiences with team sports, both as participants and as observers.

Informal and Formal Collaboration

Most of us have done a great deal of informal collaboration. For example, when members of a family get together to plan a birthday party or a wedding, they are collaborating. That is, they are working together to exchange ideas, to evaluate those ideas, and to take action to make the family celebration a success. Usually, an informal collaboration takes place fairly casually, through e-mails, phone calls, and some face-to-face meetings. There is no set structure for the group, and often individuals will join the group or leave the group, depending on their time constraints or their personal commitment to the final goal.

In a formal collaboration, for example in academic or professional situations, the structure is usually much more prescribed. In the classroom, for instance, a professor may choose the members of a group to work on a specific project and set a series of deadlines for their work. In addition, the professor may outline aspects of the process, as well as the final goal of the collaboration.

Collaboration at Work

Collaboration in professional situations is often formal. For instance, a supervisor may appoint a task force or committee to address a particular concern, to plan a sales campaign, or to explore options for recruiting new employees. In situations like these, the supervisor may leave the process of the collaboration up to the committee members, but he or she typically sets the date for an expected outcome. Because all team members are usually held responsible for the outcome, it is very important for them to understand how to work together effectively.

EXERCISE 22.3

Review your responses in Exercises 22.1 and 22.2 and write short answers to the following questions. Explain your thinking.

- Have your collaborative experiences within your family or community been mainly positive or mainly negative? Focus on one or two examples in your response. Use details to explain your answer.

- What similarities and differences do you see between personal collaborative experiences and collaborative work you have done (or anticipate doing) in college classes?

- In what ways do you think academic collaboration and professional collaboration are similar and different?

Copyright © 2007, The McGraw-Hill Companies, Inc. All rights reserved.

Understanding the Collaborative Task

When working in collaboration, the first step should be to discuss the task. Your group work will go more smoothly and be accomplished more quickly if everyone understands clearly what needs to be done. (For an example, see "Creating Powerful Response Groups" on page 24, which relates to the academic collaborative task of peer response.)

Five Strategies for Understanding Collaborative Tasks

1. Listen to (or read) the assignment carefully.
2. Identify any terms or phrases that you do not understand and ask for clarification
3. List each step of the assignment so that nothing gets left out.
4. Note the deadlines (or time frame) for each step of the assignment.
5. Identify the goal and/or the expected outcomes for each step of the assignment, as well as the final outcome of the assignment.

EXERCISE 22.4

Use the previous list of strategies to analyze the following collaborative tasks. Do the analysis first on your own, then (if possible) discuss and compare your responses with those of several classmates. Use the following example as a sample for your response.

EXAMPLE:

> Memo to: *Committee for Ourtown Environmental Improvement Fund-Raising*
> From: *Katherine Green, Director, Ourtown Office of Environmental Impact*
>
> *Thank you for volunteering to work on this important committee. As you know, your primary task is to develop innovative ways to raise at least $100,000 by July 1 of this year. At the first meeting of the committee, you chose Dawn Kirschbaum as your chair. I am asking Dawn to set a schedule for committee meetings, at least one per month, by January 14. Dawn, please submit that schedule to me as well as to all the committee members. As you develop ways to finance Ourtown's environmental improvements, consider soliciting grants from public and private sources. In addition, develop at least one fund-raiser event, organize the event, and see that it is carried out effectively. I expect progress reports in writing from the committee chair each month. A final report should be submitted by August 1. Thank you again for your willingness to serve on this committee.*

Analysis

> Clarification: *Have Katherine Green clarify what she means by "grants from public and private sources." Does she have suggestions for organizations or individuals we might approach?*

Steps to Follow	Outcomes Expected	Deadlines
Dawn sets schedule	*Committee meets at least once a month*	*Schedule to Katherine and committee members by January 14*
Consider soliciting grants	*Raising money*	*Need to set deadlines*

EXERCISE 22.4 continued

Steps to Follow	Outcomes Expected	Deadlines
Generate ideas for fund-raiser event	*Discovering many possibilities*	*Need to set deadline*
Decide on fund-raiser	*Choosing one fund-raiser*	*Need to schedule date for event*
Carry out event	*Raising money*	*Need to set deadline*
Provide progress reports	*Communicating with Katherine*	*Dawn does once a month*
Meet goal of raising $100,000	*Raising money*	*Complete by July 1; Dawn sends final report to Katherine by August 1*

Using the structure of the previous example, analyze the following collaborative tasks:

Collaborative Task 1:

Memo to: Shipping Department Administrators

From: W. A. Sharpone, President, F & G Widgets

An increasing number of employee absences have been noted in your department. These absences interfere with the efficiency and collegial aspect of the department. Please form a task force to investigate this problem. Choose a chairperson for the task force and submit her or his name to me. Each task force member should submit to the chair a report that shows the number of absences for each employee within his or her section. The chair should consolidate these reports and send them to me by May 5. The task force should then meet to discuss ways to address this problem and then send a list of proposed solutions to me by July 15.

Collaborative Task 2:

Assignment for PS325 Current Issues—Term Research Project:

On September 21, you will receive a handout listing the groups for this project. Your first group meeting will be in class on September 23. All students must be present at this class. When you arrive in class on September 23, you will discuss within your group of five or six individuals the following term research project: "Identify a controversial issue related to legislative or judiciary process." Submit a brief summary of this issue on October 5. During the semester, you will research various points of view on this issue. On October 25, you will submit an outline of your research, indicating which aspects of the issue are being researched by each group member. During the weeks of November 23 and December 6, each group will present an oral panel discussion, explaining the various points of view they have discovered. On December 14, each group member will submit a ten-page, individually written paper describing his or her own research on the topic. This paper should be properly documented in APA format and should include a "References" page.

Understanding Approaches to Collaborative Study and Work

When you are working on a collaborative task in an academic or professional setting, it is important to consider various qualities of the collaborative team. Understanding these qualities, as well as considering the nature of the task (see page 000), will help you determine the most effective working process. (For one way of evaluating a collaborative task, see Exercise 2.14 and "Creating Powerful Response Groups" on page 24.)

Copyright © 2007, The McGraw-Hill Companies, Inc. All rights reserved.

Five Strategies for Developing Approaches to Collaborative Tasks

1. Understand the composition of the group: the number of members, the reason members were chosen to be in the group, and the individual strengths of each group member.

2. Organize the group. For example, note whether the task requires that one person act as chair or reporter for the group. If so, identify who that person will be.

3. Identify what responsibilities each person will have for the project.

4. Consider dividing large tasks into small tasks and assigning these to specific subgroups or individuals.

5. Identify the best locations for working together. Will you meet in person for each working session? Or will some of your work be done via telephone or online? If you are working online, will someone set up a listserv to facilitate communication?

EXERCISE 22.5

Consider the previous list of strategies as you evaluate specific aspects of Collaborative Tasks 1 and 2 in Exercise 22.4. Do the evaluation first on your own, then (if possible) discuss and compare your responses with those of several classmates. Before answering the questions below, review the following example, which refers to the example collaborative task in Exercise 22.4.

EXAMPLE:

1. From the details in the memo, what can you tell about the composition of this group?

   The members of this group are all volunteers. Since they have volunteered for this work, they probably all have an interest in environmental issues in their town.

2. From the details of the memo, what organizational task has already been accomplished? State one other organizational task that you think needs to take place.

   The group has already elected a chair, Dawn Kirschbaum. The next step might be for Dawn to contact the members of the committee to find out their schedules so she can make a calendar listing their meeting dates for the next few months.

3. What is the group's primary goal? What tasks that lead to that goal might be accomplished by smaller subgroups?

   The group's primary task is to develop innovative ways to raise at least $100,000 by July 1 of this year. This task might be divided into four subgroups: one to investigate government grants, another to investigate donations from companies and corporations, a third to seek donations from individuals, and a fourth to plan the fund-raising event.

4. What are two tasks that the committee might do through e-mail?

   Coordinating schedules might be done through e-mail. Subcommittees might send their findings to others on the larger committee through e-mail.

Copyright © 2007, The McGraw-Hill Companies, Inc. All rights reserved.

EXERCISE 22.5 continued

Respond to each of the following questions for Collaborative Task 1 in Exercise 22.4:

1. From the details in the memo, what can you tell about the composition of this group?

2. From the details of the memo, what organizational task has already been accomplished? State one other organizational task that you think needs to take place.

3. What is the group's primary goal? What tasks that lead to that goal might be accomplished by smaller subgroups?

4. What are two tasks that the group might do through e-mail?

Respond to each of the following questions for Collaborative Task 2 in Exercise 22.4:

1. From the details of the assignment, what can you tell about the composition of this group?

2. From the details of the assignment, what organizational task has already been accomplished? State one other organizational task that you think needs to take place.

3. What is the group's primary goal? What tasks that lead to that goal might be accomplished by smaller subgroups?

4. What are two tasks that the group might do through e-mail?

Recognizing the Advantages and Challenges in Collaborative Study and Work

Working together with others offers many advantages. A large and potentially difficult task can be shared by several individuals. A group working together can often accomplish a task more quickly than one person working alone. More important, a collaborative approach encourages consideration of many different points of view. The strengths of many different individuals come together to solve a problem, to address an issue, or to work toward a common goal.

Working in groups, however, also presents challenges. Most of these challenges relate to individual differences.

Five Challenges of Collaboration Related to Individual Differences

1. *Meeting deadlines:* Some group members may view deadlines as suggestions, while others may view them as absolute and nonnegotiable.
2. *Contributing effort:* Groups members may disagree about the amount of time that each person should contribute to a particular task.
3. *Communicating effectively (speaking):* Some group members may have great difficulty expressing their own viewpoint, while others may try forcefully to impose their views on others.
4. *Communicating effectively (listening):* Some group members may be inexperienced in strategies of active listening. They may fail to pay attention when others are speaking, or they may misunderstand or fail to remember what is said.
5. *Seeking help:* Some group members may rush to seek help from others (such as the professor or a work supervisor) as soon as the slightest problem arises; other members may resist seeking help, no matter what difficulties are facing the group.

WW People Skills

WRITER'S WORKOUT ALERT

To evaluate your own approaches to working with others and to develop your skills, read the information and do the exercises in the "People Skills" section of "Writer's Workout."

FOLLOW A GROUP OF STUDENTS AS THEY WORK COLLABORATIVELY

STUDENT MODEL

The Collaborative Task Assignment

For this writing project, you will be working together in groups of four. Each member of the group will be pursuing the same major course of study. Together, you will develop a project addressing a communication problem you consider to be important in your field of study. Please choose a reporter at the first session. The reporter will provide brief memos on the group's progress to me on October 12 and November 15, in writing. During the weeks of December 5 and 12, groups will report their findings to the class through a panel presentation. In addition, on December 16, each group member will submit a five-page report explaining and evaluating her or his contributions to the project.

Transcript of the First Group Meeting

Kate: *So, we're all nursing majors here.*

Pieter: *And we're supposed to work on a communication issue related to nursing?*

Kate: *Or maybe to some part of the medical field?*

Tamaryn: *Should we maybe check to see if it has to be just about nursing?*

Kate: *Ok. Can you do that?*

Tamaryn: *Mmhmm.*

Pieter: *Should we elect a reporter first?*

Tamaryn: *How about Kate? She's already worked in a hospital, so she's got experience in the field.*

Pieter and Terry: *Yes. Kate's good.*

Kate: *Ok. But can we all get each other's e-mail addresses and maybe cell numbers so we can all be in touch a lot? Because I don't want responsibility for deadlines unless everyone agrees to be in touch and get everything done on time. I worked with a group last year, and that was a problem—getting in touch and people meeting deadlines. [Kate passes a sheet of paper to everyone to get their e-mail addresses and cell phone numbers.]*

Pieter: *Ok. I'm sure we agree. How about the project? What's a communication problem we might see in the field of nursing?*

Terry: *Well, I . . .*

Kate: *At the hospital, I see patients totally confused with all the paperwork at the admitting office.*

Tamaryn: *Oh, yeah—all those forms. And people are already so stressed.*

Terry: *I remember when . . .*

Pieter: *So that would be written communication, right? Is that what we're supposed to be looking at?*

Terry: *Well, I think . . .*

Kate: *I'll check on that. So class time is almost over. I'll e-mail everybody to find a time for our next meeting.*

Students' Evaluation of the Transcript of the First Group Meeting

Kate's evaluation: *We stayed on task and got some important organizing done. Also, we identified some questions we need to ask the professor. I think the idea of the way hospitals communicate with patients is a good one, but I don't know if we should focus just on admitting forms. Maybe this is too narrow. I noticed that I tended to interrupt Terry, but I'm trying to make sure everything gets done on time. Especially since I am the reporter for the group.*

Pieter's evaluation: *I thought it was good that the transcript showed that a lot of us asked questions instead of just making statements. It was easy to choose a recorder because Kate has the experience, and she is willing to do it. When I read the transcript, I saw that Kate and I talked way more that Tamaryn and Terry. So that would be something to think about for the next meeting.*

Copyright © 2007, The McGraw-Hill Companies, Inc. All rights reserved.

Terry's evaluation: *When I read the transcript, I was not surprised. I just have a hard time speaking in groups. I don't know why. I can see that I need to maybe speak louder or something. I need to work on this. The topic about patients and medical forms is interesting, and I actually know about this because of work I did in an admitting office last summer.*

Tamaryn's evaluation: *From the transcript, I think we did a good job in the short time we had. We picked a reporter, and we got some ideas about a communication problem in the nursing field. I think it's a good idea for the group to communicate more by e-mail. I need more time to think sometimes. I don't just jump into a group discussion that easily. So if we do some e-mailing, I think it would help me and Terry, especially, to get our ideas out there.*

EXERCISE 22.6

1. Write a paragraph describing a collaborative experience (at school, at work, in your community, or in connection with a hobby). Explain the goal of the collaboration. In addition, briefly describe the members of the group.

2. Keeping in mind the five challenges of collaboration listed on page 496, explain any challenges your group encountered.

3. Briefly describe how your group faced each of these challenges.

4. Briefly evaluate how successful your group was in reaching their goal.

Reflecting: Build Confidence

How have I changed as a participant in collaborative work? Working together with others (whether in academic, professional, or personal life) opens new paths, yet it also offers challenges. Reflecting on your own work as a member of a group, team, or committee can help you see how you have grown in your own skills and in your outlook toward others. The process of reflection can lead you to be more confident as you face future collaborative experiences.

Identify Successes

Remember what you do well and what you enjoy, and focus on those experiences that have contributed to your personal growth. Becoming a strong collaborative participant involves recognizing and using your strengths.

Copyright © 2007, The McGraw-Hill Companies, Inc. All rights reserved.

EXERCISE 22.7

Take a few minutes to reflect on your successes. Write one or two sentences that explain two things you have learned from this chapter. In addition, explain how you might apply what you have learned to future collaborative work.

Set Goals

As you consider future collaborative work, set realistic goals. Use your successes to identify positive achievement. Be aware of insights you have gained into the collaborative process and stay alert to new insights, both in structured and informal group situations.

EXERCISE 22.8

Now that you have examined your successes, determine what challenges you face. Rate yourself on the following scale—5 indicates a task that you consider a challenge most of the time, and 1 indicates a skill that you identify as a strength.

Collaborative Skill or Task	5	4	3	2	1
Meeting group deadlines	—	—	—	—	—
Initiating ideas and possibilities	—	—	—	—	—
Listening thoughtfully to others	—	—	—	—	—
Expressing ideas to others	—	—	—	—	—
Attending all group meetings	—	—	—	—	—
Responding promptly to e-mails and phone calls related to the task	—	—	—	—	—
Putting full effort into the task rather than depending on others	—	—	—	—	—
Asking for help or clarification when necessary	—	—	—	—	—

EXERCISE 22.9

Finish the following sentences in order to explore your learning experience and to set goals:

1. My attitude toward collaborative work is

2. I still need to work on

SPEAK IN PUBLIC WITH CONFIDENCE

Both at school and in the work world, you'll almost certainly be asked to speak to an audience. While relatively few people speak to large audiences with hundreds of listeners, nearly all of us must speak to smaller groups. For example, you may be asked to research a question and provide an oral response to a committee on which you are serving. You may participate in a conference as a member of a panel discussion. Or you may be assigned to give an oral report in a course you are taking.

As you think about your journey toward becoming a confident speaker, it is important to reflect on how you respond to a request (or required assignment) to speak to others. Keep in mind the acronym MAPS (*m*ental state, *a*ctions, *p*hysical feelings, and *s*peech patterns). Create "maps" of your past public-speaking experiences and determine what you want your "maps" of the future to be.

In the following exercises, you will explore public speaking as an audience member and as a speaker—both in the past and the future. In addition, you will evaluate your response to the experience of or anticipation of speaking in public

EXERCISE 22.10

Circle the letter that best describes your experience with various public speaking situations.

A. You have experienced this public speaking situation as an audience member.

B. You have experienced this public speaking situation as the speaker.

C. You have experienced this public speaking situation both as an audience member and as a speaker.

Your Experience	Public Speaking Situation
A B C	Presenting information to a committee
A B C	Speaking to a group of peers (people of similar age and circumstances)
A B C	Speaking in front of a teacher and classmates
A B C	Speaking to a community group
A B C	Speaking at a professional conference (audience of less than 50 people)
A B C	Speaking at a professional conference (audience of more than 50 people)
A B C	Speaking as a member of a panel

EXERCISE 22.11

Refer to your responses in Exercise 22:10. Choose two of the speaking situations for which you circled B. For those two speaking situations, you will write a brief "MAPS" evaluation. Refer to the example below before responding to the MAPS questions that follow it.

EXAMPLE:

Speaking situation: *Speaking as a member of a panel.*

My specific speaking situation: *Presentation for high school history class.*

My mental state: *When I first was given this assignment I was very nervous, but by the time of the presentation, I felt quite confident.*

My actions: *I did a lot of research on my part of the project. When it was time to present, we were allowed to stay sitting down, which I think really helped. I would have been more nervous if I had had to stand up. Also, I tend to fidget with my pen, so I had to remember not to do that.*

My physical feelings: *Some other people on the panel said they had "butter-flies," but I didn't feel like that. I did notice that I was breathing faster when it was almost my turn to present.*

My speech patterns: *I tend to talk really fast, and it was hard to remember to slow down. The teacher stopped me once to ask me to slow down.*

Destinations: Building Confidence in Public Speaking

Speaking in Public: Facing Anxiety

Most people dread speaking in front of others. In fact, many surveys show that the anticipation of public speaking is one of the highest anxiety producers in our society today. Knowing that public speaking is a common fear is the first step in moving past this obstacle. The next step is discovering ways to address the anxiety. One strategy that works for many people is learning to focus outward (on the audience) rather than inward (on yourself). If you are working to make a talk interesting and lively for your listeners, you begin to think about your effect on them rather than their effect on you.

Speaking in Public: Formal and Informal Situations

Another way to develop a higher comfort level with speaking to a group is to recognize the differences as well as the similarities between formal and informal speaking situations. Most of the speaking situations people fear are formal: for instance, standing in front of a class giving a presentation or serving on a panel at a conference. On the other hand, most of us are at ease speaking to groups of people in informal settings, such as stating an opinion at a committee meeting or in a class discussion. In addition, many people have served as coaches or leaders of commu-

nity groups. If you have worked with children, for instance, in a club or team situation, you have almost certainly spoken to them as a group. Recognizing and evaluating your successful informal speaking situations can help you develop confidence and skills for formal speaking situations.

Speaking in Public: On the Job

In the professional world, you will often be called on to speak informally. For example, you may serve on committees or task forces where you will need to explain your point of view to others. In addition, within a business or organization, you will probably take part in department or division meetings where expressing your views clearly and confidently will be essential. Your work may also require you to participate in various formal speaking situations. For example, to progress in your chosen profession, you may be expected not only to attend conferences but also to make presentations or serve as a speaker on a panel at those conferences.

EXERCISE 22.11 continued

Speaking Situation 1:
Speaking situation:

My specific speaking situation:

My mental state:

My actions:

My physical feelings:

My speech patterns:

Speaking Situation 2:
Speaking situation:

My specific speaking situation:

My mental state:

My actions:

My physical feelings:

My speech patterns:

Copyright © 2007, The McGraw-Hill Companies, Inc. All rights reserved.

Understanding the Speaking Task

When you are asked to speak to others, your first step is to understand the task accurately. Your work will go more smoothly and be accomplished more quickly if you understand clearly what you are being asked to do.

Six Strategies for Understanding Speaking Tasks

1. Listen to (or read) the assignment (the request or requirement to speak) carefully.
2. Identify any terms or phrases that you do not understand and ask for clarification.
3. Identify your audience. If you are not sure who your audience will be, ask for clarification.
4. Note the deadlines (or time frame) for each step related to the oral presentation.
5. Understand the format of the speaking task. For example, will you be a panel member or a solo speaker? Will you stand on a platform or be seated behind a table?
6. Identify the purpose for the oral presentation. For example, are you being asked to present information in an objective way? Or are you being asked to argue for or against a particular position on a controversial issue?

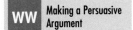

WW Making a Persuasive Argument

WRITER'S WORKOUT ALERT

If the speaking task asks you to make an argument, you can develop your persuasive speaking skills by going to the "Best Practices" parent section and then clicking the "Making a Persuasive Argument" link.

EXERCISE 22.12

Use the previous list of strategies to analyze the two speaking tasks below. Do the analysis first on your own, then (if possible) discuss and compare your responses with those of several classmates. Use the following example as a model for your responses.

EXAMPLE:

> Memo to: *Rene Runner*
> From: *Carl Charger, Director of Outreach Programs*
> Subject: *Request to speak to Girls' Club of Ourtown*
>
> *We are requesting that you speak to our staff professionals and to a group of our members (ranging in age from 10 to 14) about your experiences related to college athletic scholarships. It is my belief that both our members and our staff professionals need a realistic understanding of the challenges involved in applying for and receiving an athletic scholarship. The Girls' Club members in this group all come from families that will need substantial financial help when it comes time for their children to attend college. This presentation would be given on October 12. If you are willing to accept this request, please let me know in writing (letter or e-mail) by September 15.*

Analysis:

> Clarification: *What does Carl Charger mean by my "experiences related to college athletic scholarships"? Does he mean just my own scholarship or what I know about other situations with athletic scholarships?*

Copyright © 2007, The McGraw-Hill Companies, Inc. All rights reserved.

EXERCISE 22.12 continued

Audience: *Club members (girls ages 10–14) and staff professionals. Also, I think Mr. Charger will be there, too. Need to find out how many people will be in this audience.*

Deadlines: *I need to notify Mr. Charger by September 15 (in writing—need to check his e-mail address). Speech to be given on October 12.*

Format: *Sounds like a formal presentation. I need to check what the room setup will be like. Could I use PowerPoint? Will there be a mic?*

Purpose: *Sound like he wants more than just information and a description of my own experience. He wants me to convince the staff and club members that getting an athletic scholarship can be difficult and complicated.*

Using the structure of the preceding example, analyze the following speaking tasks:

Speaking Task 1:
Assignment for PSY 212, Psychology of Adolescents, Panel Presentations (Team 2): Team 2 will present to the class their findings on adolescents and body adornment (tattoos, piercing, etc.) in the contemporary United States. Keep in mind that students in this class are majoring in many different subjects; for example, education, business, nursing, English, and art. In addition, the class has students ranging in age from 18 to 45. Each of you should decide on some aspect of this issue and research the pros and cons. By September 30, the panel should have decided the specific topic each member will research. By October 15, each of you should submit a preliminary proposal noting your specific topic and listing sources you have consulted so far. During the week of December 5, the panel will make a presentation to the class. Please let me know what visuals (if any) you will be using for your presentation so that I can make the necessary arrangements.

Speaking Task 2:
E-mail to: David_Teche@Algoode.com
From: Isabel.Comtee@Knotso.com

This is to confirm our conversation on Monday about the need for our Information Technology staff to develop clearer communication skills. This concern applies both to the older, more experienced members of the IT staff, as well as to the younger members (the interns from the Cross City C. C. program). Thank you for agreeing to speak to our interns, staff members, and the administrators of that department. Since this need is urgent, I'm asking you to speak as soon as possible, preferably on March 30, although April 7 is also a possibility. Can you get the title of your talk, along with a brief summary, to me by March 15? I know our organization will benefit from hearing about the changes you made at Algoode and any suggestions you would have for similar changes here at Knotso. As we discussed, your speaker's honorarium will be $1,500, to be paid at the conclusion of your presentation. Thanks for your willingness to do this.

Evaluating Your Audience and Creating Your "Speaker Self"

Evaluate Your Audience

To determine what aspects of yourself you want to convey to your listeners, it is important to evaluate your audience.

At this point, it would be helpful to review the sections titled "Consider Your Audience," which appear in earlier chapters of this book (see pages 19, 66, 90, 117, 137, 165, 193, and 301). Once you understand the composition of your audience clearly, you can decide how you want to approach your topic and which personal aspects (your ideas, beliefs, and values) you want to make apparent as you speak to that audience.

Six Questions to Ask as You Evaluate Your Audience

1. How old are my listeners: Are they approximately the same age, or do their ages vary?
2. What is the gender makeup of my audience: mostly male, mostly female, or mixed?
3. What is the socioeconomic background of my audience?
4. What are the beliefs and values of my audience?
5. What can I expect my audience to know about my topic?
6. What preformed opinions might my audience have about my topic?

EXERCISE 22.13

Use the previous list of strategies to analyze the audience for Speaking Tasks 1 and 2 in Exercise 22.12. Do the analysis first on your own, then (if possible) discuss and compare your responses with those of several classmates. Use the following example, which refers to the example speaking task in Exercise 22.12 as a model for your responses.

EXAMPLE:

Age: *Club members will be 10–14 years old. Staff members? Could range in age from 20s to retirement age.*

Gender: *Club members will all be female. Staff members probably male and female.*

Socioeconomic background: *Club members will all need substantial financial aid to attend college. Staff works with club members and thus will be concerned with these needs.*

Beliefs and values: *Club members who attend this presentation will probably value higher education (staff also). Both staff and club members also probably believe that being an outstanding athlete means that a student can easily get an athletic scholarship.*

Knowledge of topic: *Staff will probably know more than club members about the process of college admission and applying for scholarships. Club members probably will need details on the process of scholarship application as it relates to athletic scholarships.*

Preformed opinions about topic: *From what Carl says, it sounds like both club members and staff professionals may be placing too much hope on the possibility of athletic scholarships.*

Analyze Speaking Task 1 in Exercise 22.12:

Age:

Gender:

Socioeconomic background:

Copyright © 2007, The McGraw-Hill Companies, Inc. All rights reserved.

EXERCISE 22.13 continued

Beliefs and values:

Knowledge of topic:

Preformed opinions about topic:

Analyze Speaking Task 2 in Exercise 22.12:
Age:

Gender:

Socioeconomic background:

Beliefs and values:

Knowledge of topic:

Preformed opinions about topic:

READING: from 1854 Speech by Chief Seattle

Born around 1786, Seattle was chief of the Suquamish and leader of other tribes in current-day Washington State. This speech is Seattle's reply to an offer made by the governor of Washington Territories in 1854 to buy two million acres of land from the tribes that lived there. Seattle was the leader of and spokesman for these tribes.

Yonder sky that has wept tears of compassion upon my people for centuries untold, and which to us appears changeless and eternal, may change. Today is fair. Tomorrow it may be overcast with clouds. My words are like the stars that never change. Whatever Seattle says, the great chief at Washington can rely upon with as much certainty as he can upon the return of the sun or the seasons. The White Chief says that Big Chief at Washington sends us greetings of friendship and goodwill. This is kind of him for we know he has little need of our friendship in return. His people are many. They are like the grass that covers vast prairies. My people are few. They resemble the scattering trees of a storm-swept plain. The great, and—I presume—good, White Chief sends us word that he wishes to buy our land but is willing to allow us enough to live comfortably. This indeed appears just, even generous, for the Red Man no longer has rights that he need respect, and the offer may be wise, also, as we are no longer in need of an extensive country.

There was a time when our people covered the land as the waves of a wind-ruffled sea cover its shell-paved floor, but that time long since passed away with the greatness of tribes that are now but a mournful memory. I will not dwell on, nor mourn over, our untimely decay, nor reproach my paleface brothers with hastening it, as we too may have been somewhat to blame.

Youth is impulsive. When our young men grow angry at some real or imaginary wrong, and disfigure their faces with black paint, it denotes that their hearts are black, and that they are often cruel and relentless, and our old men and old women are unable to restrain them. Thus it has ever been. Thus it was when the white man began to push our forefathers ever westward. But let us hope that the hostilities between us may never return. We would have everything to lose and nothing to gain. Revenge by young men is considered gain, even at the cost of their own lives, but old men who stay at home in times of war, and mothers who have sons to lose, know better.

DISCUSSION QUESTIONS

1. What can you tell about the audience to whom Seattle aimed this speech?
2. What are the qualities of character and personality that Seattle displayed in the "speaker self" he chose to address his audience?
3. Give specific examples of ways that Seattle tried to establish connection with his audience.
4. What direct hopes did Seattle express?
5. How did he criticize his listeners yet still appear to be praising them?

Preparing to Speak

Once you understand your speaking task clearly and have evaluated your audience, you must begin the challenging tasks of writing the speech, developing visuals and other materials related to the speaking event, and rehearsing the speech.

Writing the Speech

Even though, in most cases, you will speak from note cards or from memory when you give your final presentation, it is very helpful to write out the speech, just as if it were a paper you were preparing for a class or for a professional journal. Therefore, you can put to use all that you have learned from earlier chapters in this book, following these basic steps:

- Prewrite (for example, by brainstorming, researching, mapping)
- Organize the materials you have gathered through the prewriting process (for example, by listing or outlining)
- Write a draft
- Revise the draft (as often as needed)

EXERCISE 22.14

Imagine that you are preparing a speech on one of the following topics: safety issues on campus, financial aid concerns of today's students, parking problems on campus, time-planning strategies for new college students. Do whatever research is needed and then write a one-page speech on your topic. Then, using the information in the written speech, prepare no more than two note cards that you could use to speak (rather than read) your speech to an audience.

Preparing Visuals and Rehearsing the Speech

In addition to preparing a written draft of the speech, there are at least two other important steps to the preparation process. One step is to create or gather those visuals or other props you will be using to support and illustrate your talk. The second, and final, preparatory step is to rehearse your talk.

Preparing visuals and other props

Visuals and props could include (but are not limited to) the following:

- PowerPoint presentations
- Overhead-projector presentations
- Note cards to remind you (the speaker) of key points
- Posters (when speaking to small groups)
- Handouts (with information you want your audience to have during the speech and to take with them when the speech is over)

EXERCISE 22.15

Assume that you are giving a speech on one of the following topics: safety issues on campus, financial aid concerns of today's students, parking problems on campus, time-planning strategies for new college students. Suggest two visuals related to the topic you choose. Then briefly explain how each visual would help you present your thoughts and ideas more clearly to your audience

Topic chosen:

First visual to accompany speech:

Explanation:

Second visual to accompany speech:

Explanation:

Copyright © 2007, The McGraw-Hill Companies, Inc. All rights reserved.

Rehearsing the speech

Four Key Reasons for Rehearsing a Speech

1. To become very familiar with the information in the speech.
2. To become comfortable and adept with the visuals and props that accompany the speech.
3. To make sure to keep the speech within the prescribed time limits.
4. To work on tone and level of voice, as well as gestures and body movements.

Four Ways to Rehearse a Speech

1. Give the speech to yourself while looking in a mirror.
2. Give the speech and make a tape-recording or (even better) ask a friend to videotape the rehearsal.
3. Give the speech to one or more friends, relatives, or colleagues. Try to pick people who will take what you are doing seriously and will give you honest feedback.
4. To evaluate and improve your speech, keep in mind what you have learned from reading this chapter, using the Writer's Workout (see the "Writer's Workout Alert" on page 000), and considering previous speaking experiences.

Giving the Speech

On the day of your speech, you will need to evaluate and set up the speaking site. Most important, of course, will be the speech itself. When you have finished speaking, you may conduct a question-and-answer session. And, finally, you will evaluate your accomplishments.

Evaluating and Setting Up the Site

- Arrive early.
- Familiarize yourself with the speaking site. Determine, for example, the location of the podium.
- Be sure any electronic equipment is in good working order (computer for a PowerPoint presentation, for example).
- Arrange any props (charts, for example) so that the audience can easily see them and they are convenient for you.

Giving the Speech

As you present your speech, your primary concern is to communicate clearly and accurately with your audience. One of the best ways to develop the skills needed to connect with your audience is to read the information and complete the exercises offered through the "Writer's Workout."

WW Presenting
Best Practices

WRITER'S WORKOUT ALERT

- Parent Link: Presenting (Includes the following: Organizing the Presentation, Establishing Rapport with the Audience, Greeting Your Audience, Setting the Frame for the Presentation, Platform Skills, Eye Contact, Pronunciation, Handling Questions from the Audience)
- Parent Link: Best Practices (Provides suggestions for Putting More Power into Presentations)

Reflecting: Build Confidence

How have I changed as a public speaker? Learning to speak effectively to groups of people (whether in academic, professional, or personal life) creates new options, but it also requires addressing challenges. Reflecting on your public speaking experiences can help you evaluate the skills you have developed and determine goals for further improvement. The process of reflection can enhance your confidence as you face future speaking experiences.

Identify Successes

Remember what you do well and what gives you pride, and focus on those experiences that have contributed to your personal growth. Becoming a strong public speaker involves recognizing and using your strengths.

EXERCISE 22.16

Take a few minutes to reflect on your successes. Write one or two sentences that explain two things you have learned from this chapter. In addition, explain how you might apply what you have learned to future speaking tasks.

Set Goals

As you consider future speaking tasks, set realistic goals. Use your successes to identify positive achievement. Be aware of insights you have gained into public speaking and stay alert to new insights. Consider the way you speak to groups, both in formal and informal situations.

EXERCISE 22.17

Now that you have examined your successes, determine what challenges you face. Rate yourself on the following scale—5 indicates a task that you consider a challenge most of the time, and 1 indicates a skill that you identify as a strength.

Speaking Skill or Task	5	4	3	2	1
Speaking to groups informally	__	__	__	__	__
Speaking to groups formally	__	__	__	__	__
Planning a speech	__	__	__	__	__
Researching material for a speech	__	__	__	__	__
Writing a speech	__	__	__	__	__
Evaluating your audience	__	__	__	__	__
Making a connection with your audience	__	__	__	__	__
Speaking clearly	__	__	__	__	__
Speaking slowly	__	__	__	__	__
Speaking loudly enough	__	__	__	__	__
Using gestures and body language effectively	__	__	__	__	__
Using visuals effectively	__	__	__	__	__
Asking for help or clarification when necessary	__	__	__	__	__

Copyright © 2007, The McGraw-Hill Companies, Inc. All rights reserved.

EXERCISE 22.18

Finish the following sentences in order to explore your learning experience and to set goals:

1. My attitude toward public speaking is

2. I still need to work on

READING: from "Ain't I a Woman," by Sojourner Truth

Sojourner Truth (1797–1883) was born into slavery in New York State and named Isabella by the family that owned her. In 1843, she took the new name Sojourner Truth because she believed she had been called by God to deliver the truth: all people deserved their freedom and dignity. She was particularly concerned with the rights of women, and she delivered the following speech in 1851 to the Women's Rights Convention in Akron, Ohio

Well, children, where there is so much racket there must be something out of kilter. I think that 'twixt the negroes of the South and the women at the North, all talking about rights, the white men will be in a fix pretty soon. But what's all this here talking about?

That man over there says that women need to be helped into carriages, and lifted over ditches, and to have the best place everywhere. Nobody ever helps me into carriages, or over mud-puddles, or gives me any best place! And ain't I a woman? Look at me! Look at my arm! I have ploughed and planted, and gathered into barns, and no man could head me! And ain't I a woman? I could work as much and eat as much as a man—when I could get it—and bear the lash as well! And ain't I a woman? I have borne thirteen children, and seen most all sold off to slavery, and when I cried out with my mother's grief, none but Jesus heard me! And ain't I a woman?

Then they talk about this thing in the head; what's this they call it? [member of audience whispers, "intellect"] That's it, honey. What's that got to do with women's rights or negroes' rights? If my cup won't hold but a pint, and yours holds a quart, wouldn't you be mean not to let me have my little half measure full?

Then that little man in black there, he says women can't have as much rights as men, 'cause Christ wasn't a woman! Where did your Christ come from? From God and a woman! Man had nothing to do with Him.

If the first woman God ever made was strong enough to turn the world upside down all alone, these women together ought to be able to turn it back, and get it right side up again! And now they is asking to do it, the men better let them.

Obliged to you for hearing me, and now old Sojourner ain't got nothing more to say.

DISCUSSION QUESTIONS

1. From reading this speech, what assumptions do you think Sojourner made about her audience?

2. What aspects of her "speaker self" did Sojourner choose to show to her audience?

3. What gestures do you imagine she made? Do you think these gestures would have been effective? Explain.

4. Give one example of the way Sojourner anticipated a criticism of her point of view. Explain how she addressed that criticism.

5. If Sojourner were giving this talk today, what visuals might she use to support her argument?

Copyright © 2007, The McGraw-Hill Companies, Inc. All rights reserved.

Credits

Text Credits

"American Heart Association Declares War on Fad Diets," from www.americanheart.org. Reproduced with permission. © 2004 American Heart Association.

Barbara Lazear Ascher, "On Compassion," from *The Habit of Loving* by Barbara Ascher. Copyright © 1986, 1987, 1989 by Barbara Lazear Ascher. Used by permission of Random House, Inc.

Dan Barry, "Keeping Hands on Wheel, and on Bow, and Strings," *New York Times*, April 28, 2004. Copyright © 2004 New York Times Company, Inc. Used with permission.

Jo Ann Beard, "In the Current," pp. 3–4 from *The Boys of My Youth* by Jo Ann Beard. Copyright © 1998 by Jo Ann Beard. By permission of Little, Brown and Company, Inc.

Samantha Bennett, "Oh #$@%*! The Rise of Public Profanity," *Pittsburgh Post-Gazette*, 12/15/99. Copyright © 1999 Pittsburgh Post-Gazette. All rights reserved. Reprinted with permission.

Ira Berkow, "A Deadly Toll is Haunting Football," *New York Times*, 7/28/01. Copyright © 2001 New York Times Company, Inc. Used with permission.

Douglas J. Breithaupt, "Making Your Own Map—Success at a Two-Year College." Copyright © Douglas J. Breithaupt and College Planning Network. Used with permission.

Kenneth Chang, "Tree Rings Show a Period of Widespread Warming in Medieval Age," *New York Times*, 3/26/02. Copyright © 2002 New York Times Company, Inc. Used with permission.

Frank Clancy, "SARS: A Rehearsal?" *Popular Science*, January, 2004. Copyright © 2004. All rights reserved.

Mark Clayton, "Calculators in Class; Freedom from Scratch Paper or 'Crutch'?" This article first appeared in *The Christian Science Monitor* on May 23, 200 and is reproduced with permission. Copyright © 2000 The Christian Science Monitor (www.csmonitor.com). All rights reserved.

Suzanne Daley, "Paris Journal: A Green Light for Sinful Drivers: It's Election Time," *New York Times*, 3/26/02. Copyright © 2002 New York Times Company, Inc. Used with permission.

Mary Duenwald, "Two Portraits of Children of Divorce: Rosy and Dark," *New York Times*, 3/26/02. Copyright © 2002 New York Times Company, Inc. Used with permission.

Stuart Dybek, "Bottle Caps," pp. 40–41 from *The Coast of Chicago*. Copyright © 1990 Stuart Dybek. Reprinted by permission of International Creative Management, Inc.

Education Development Center, Inc. "Service-Learning Satisfies Young People's Desire for Public Service," February 2002. Copyright © 2002 Education Development Center, Inc. All rights reserved. Used with permission.

P. M. Fabian, "Keep Your Hormones Outside the Classroom!" *New University*. Copyright © 2001 New University Newspaper. Reprinted with permission.

Ted Fishman, "A Simple Glass of Water," *New York Times*, 8/23/01. Copyright © 2001 New York Times Co., Inc. Used with permission.

Ellen Goodman, "The Tapestry of Friendships," from *Close to Home* by Ellen Goodman (pp. 140–41). Copyright © 1979 by The Washington Post company. Reprinted with permission of Simon & Schuster Adult Publishing Group. All rights reserved.

Lisa Guernsey, "Toy Story: Looking for Lessons," *New York Times*, 1/3/02. Copyright © 2002 New York Times Company, Inc. Used with permission.

"Housework Still Women's Work," © 2000 United Press International. Reprinted with permission.

Michele Ingrassia, "The Body of the Beholder," *Newsweek*, 4/24/95. Copyright © 1995 Newsweek, Inc. All rights reserved. Reprinted by permission.

Martin Luther King, Jr., from "I Have a Dream." Copyright © 1963 Martin Luther King, Jr. Copyright renewed 1991 Coretta Scott King. Reprinted by arrangement with the Estate of Martin Luther King, Jr., c/o Writers House as agent for the proprietor, New York, NY.

Janet Kornblum, "Effects of TV on Kids Becoming Less Remote," *USA Today*, 11/10/03. USA TODAY, Copyright © November 11, 2003. Reprinted with permission.

Linda Kulman, "What'd You Say?" *U.S. News & World Report*, 4/26/99. Copyright © 1999 U.S. News & World Report, L.P. Reprinted with permission.

Dawn MacKeen, "Just Say No to DARE," Salon.com, 2/16/01. Copyright © 2001. All rights reserved.

Thomas Moore, "Care of the Soul," pp. 3–4 from *Care of the Soul*. Copyright © 1992 by Thomas Moore. Reprinted by permission of HarperCollins Publishers, Inc.

National Association of Chewing Gum Manufacturers, "The Story of Gum," http://www.nacgm.org/consumer/storyof.html. Reprinted with permission.

Brenda Peterson, "Growing Up Game," excerpted from *Living by Water: True Stories of Nature and Spirit* by Brenda Peterson. Copyright © Brenda Peterson. Used with permission.

James Popkin & Katia Hetter, "America's Gambling Craze," originally appeared in *U.S. News and World Report*, 8/25/97. Copyright © 1997 U.S. News & World Report, L.P. Reprinted with permission.

Lydie Raschka, "You've Got Hate Mail," Salon.com, 2/16/01. Copyright © 2001. All rights reserved.

Rutgers University, "Study Finds 20-something Dating Culture Focused More on Seeking 'Low-commitment' Relationships Than Finding Marriage Partners," 6/7/00. Copyright © 2003 Rutgers, The State University of New Jersey. All rights reserved.

Robert Sapolsky, "Nature or Nurture? The 50 Most Beautiful People in the World Assess the Source of Good Looks," *Discover*, February 2000. Copyright © 2000 Robert Sapolsky. Used by permission.

Kathy Seal, "Too Much Homework, Too Little Play," *New York Times*, 9/3/01 Copyright © 2004 The Birmingham News. Reprinted with permission of The Birmingham News.

Richard Sennett, pp. 64–75 from *The Corrosion of Character: The Personal Consequences of Work*. Copyright © 1998 by Richard Sennett. Used by permission of W. W. Norton, Inc.

Sherice Shields, "Piercing Opens Body to Potential Health Risk," *USA Today*, August 8, 2000. Copyright © USA Today, August 8, 2000. Reprinted with permission.

John Simpson, "Tiananmen Square," *Granta* 28: Birthday Special.

Kathy Slobogin, "New Phys Ed Favors Fitness over Sports," cnn.com, 5/17/01. Copyright © 2001 CNN, Inc. All rights reserved.

Brent Staples, "Night Walker," from *Parallel Time: Growing Up in Black and White*. Copyright © Brent Staples. Used with permission from the author.

Lori Hall Steele, "Golf Course's Closure Meant to Save Land," *The Detroit Free Press*, 4/24/00. Copyright © 2000. All rights reserved.

Laurence Steinberg, "Bound to Bicker," *Psychology Today*, December 1989. Reprinted with permission from Psychology Today magazine. Copyright © 1989 Sussex Publishers, Inc.

Amy Tan, "Mother Tongue." Copyright © 1990 by Amy Tan. First appeared in *The Threepenny Review*. Reprinted by permission of the author and the Sandra Dijkstra Literary Agency.

The American Heritage Dictionary of the English Language, Fourth Edition, Definition of "soul." Copyright © 2000 by Houghton Mifflin Company. Reproduced by permission.

Christina Waters, "Screaming Me Me's," *Metro Santa Cruz*, January 9–16, 2002. Copyright © 2002. All rights reserved.

Webster's New World Dictionary and Thesaurus, Second Edition, Definitions of "quest," "flaw," "sensitive," "psyche," "culture," "explain," and "explorer." Copyright © 2001 Wiley Publishing Inc., a subsidiary of John Wiley & Sons, Inc. Used with permission.

Webster's New World Thesaurus, Definitions of "conspicuous," "cradled," "limping," "river," "flow," "bland," "haranguing," "lecturing" and "crushing." Copyright © 1971 Wiley Publishing, Inc., a subsidiary of John Wiley & Sons, Inc. Used with permission.

William Speed Weed, "Smart Pills," *Discover*, June 2000. Copyright © 2000 William Speed Weed. All rights reserved.

Charles Wheelan, "Lives Changed in a Split Second," *New York Times*, 1/10/01. Copyright © 2001 New York Times Co. Used with permission.

Photo Credits

Compass and map, © Comstock Images; Palm trees, Tomi/PhotoLink/Getty Images; p. 15, Karl Weatherly/Getty Images; p. 16, © Sage Sohier; p. 85, © Marke D. Gilbert; p. 332, © Marke D. Gilbert; p. 367, Philadelphia Museum of Art: Purchased with funds contributed by Lynn and Harold Honickman with the Lynne and Harold Honickman Fund for Photography. Photo by Graydon Wood, 1998. Acc. #1998-69-13; p. 369, John Vachon, photographer, Look Magazine Photograph Collection, Library of Congress, Prints & Photographs Division, LC-USF34- 065792-D; p. 378, Man Ray. *Black and White (Noire et Blanche)*. 1926. Gelatin-silver print, 6 3/4 × 8 7/8". Gift of James Thrall Soby. (132.1941). Digital Image © The Museum of Modern Art/Licensed by Scala/Art Resource, NY. © Man Ray Trust/Artists Rights Society (ARS), NY/ADAGP, Paris. p. 484, Courtesy George Eastman House. Bequest of Edward Steichen by Direction of Joanna T. Steichen. Reprinted with permission of Joanna T. Steichen; p. 485, Courtesy Walter P. Reuther Library, Wayne State University; p. 486, © Chuck Savage/Corbis; p. 487, © Michele Jin; p. 488, © William Klein/Courtesy Howard Greenberg Gallery.

Index

Copyright © 2007, The McGraw-Hill Companies, Inc. All rights reserved.

Copyright © 2007, The McGraw-Hill Companies, Inc. All rights reserved.

Copyright © 2007, The McGraw-Hill Companies, Inc. All rights reserved.